Patterned Ground

Patterned Ground

Entanglements of Nature and Culture

Edited by Stephan Harrison, Steve Pile and Nigel Thrift

REAKTION BOOKS

Published by
REAKTION BOOKS LTD
79 Farringdon Road
London EC1M 3JU, UK

www.reaktionbooks.co.uk

First published 2004

Printed and bound by
Cromwell Press, Trowbridge, Wiltshire

British Library Cataloguing in Publication Data

Patterned ground: entanglements of nature and culture
    1. Landscape assessment
    2. Landscape - Symbolic aspects
    3. Geographical perception
    I. Harrison, Stephan II. Pile, Steve 1961– III. Thrift,
    Nigel, 1949–
    304.2'2

ISBN 1 86189 181 4

Contents

Preface 7
Introduction 13
Guide for Readers 43

section one: *Flow*

Introduction 48
Pipes 50
Cities 52
Ecosystems 55
Rivers 57
Ridges 60
Cliffs 62
Scree 64
Drifts 66
Virtual Space 68
Post Offices 70
Drumlins 72
Glaciers 75
Climate 76
Lakes 78
Rivers 80
Meanders 82
Railways 84
Freeways 86
Fields 88
Trade 91
Colonies 93
Continents 94
Battlefields 96
Dust 98
Pollution 100
Climate 103
Lakes 105
Fire 107
God 110
Water 111
Oceans 113
Ice Sheets 115
Sun 117
Water 119
Pollutants 122
Trade 124
Airports 126

section two: *Site*

Introduction 130
Mountains 132
Fields 134
Fieldwork 136
Hospitals 137
Wilderness 139
Parks 142
Farms 144
Bogs 146
Humans 148
Islands 149
Beaches 151
Deserts 153
Floods 156
Dams 157
Churches 160
Villages 161
Home 164
Shelter 166
Tors 167
Caves 170
Zoos 172
Police Stations 174
Boundaries 175
Natural Resources 177
Central Places 179
States 181
Refuges 184
Enterprise Zones 185
Town Halls 187
Slums 190
Garden Cities 192
Towns 194
Ghost Towns 196
Cities 199
Suburbs 200
Farms 203
Floodplains 205
Hills 208

section three: *Matter*

Introduction 212
Bees 214
Pubs 216
Pigs 218
Humans 220
Moon 222
Nonhumans 224
Viruses 228
Lichens 230
Trees 232
Jungle 234
Slums 235
Buildings 238
Archives 240
Streets 242
Subways 244
Cities 246
Organics 248
Food 250
Livestock 252
Horses 253
Wildlife 255
Animals 258
Shadows 260
Mammals 262
Fish 264
Waves 266
Radio 269
Island Nations 270
Regions 272
Territory 274
Mountains 276
Moraines 278
Ice 279

References 282
Contributors 294
Photo Acknowledgements 302
Index 303

Preface

Patterned Ground is an attempt to meet head-on the entangled relationships between nature and culture. Take a quick flick through the pages
of this volume and you will find that it is comprised of short pieces
that focus on various 'objects' in the landscape – from archives to zoos,
from beaches to waves, from cities to wilderness. Each piece explores
the way in which we understand that 'object' and its relationship to the
world around it. Each 'object' is invested with the preoccupations and
passions of the author, from their point of view. This book is neither
encyclopaedia nor dictionary, but a knowledgeable and impassioned
engagement with the world. It sits, therefore, somewhere in that curious
space between wonder and thought. In this sense, this book resonates
with earlier experiments in understanding the earth and its landscapes,
whether these endeavours have been conducted within the sciences, the
social sciences or the arts. In many ways, it is an attempt to backtrack
from familiar and obvious ways of seeing patterns in the world, and
to attempt to discover the world anew. In some ways, it is deliberately
anachronistic, put together as if it was a catalogue of curios or a cosmology that hasn't yet figured out the cosmos. More than this, there is
no single Disciplinary (in an academic sense) voice. In this way, we hope
to open up new possibilities for thinking about patterns, and thinking
about the ground on which we build pictures of the world.

There are many ways to know the world and many forms of
expertise have developed to describe aspects of the world. To backtrack from this world is not to abandon the expertise that has
developed in investigating and exploring it. Instead, it is to go back to
the world with eyes full of wonder, and to ask questions about the
patterns we see. There are some old tactics of creating wonder: one
relies on introducing strange elements without properly preparing
the 'audience'; another creates strange combinations of elements.
These tactics can be seen in certain ways of painting, writing poetry
and music. By design, we have crowded different elements together,
and hope that through this arrangement we might wonder again

about *patterned ground* (for further guidance on this, see the 'Guide for Readers').

We believe Klee's 1926 painting *'Florentinisches' Villen Viertel* (*'Florentine' Residential District*) offers a fine illustration for this book. What intrigues us about this painting is the way Klee seeks to depict the landscape using a new form of 'spatial calculation'. Klee sees in the landscape not only an arrangement of patches of colour but also a rhythm that ebbs and flows through it. In this painting, he models his depiction of the landscape using an analogy to the written (down) form of music. Standing before the landscape, then, we would argue that Klee backtracks and explores another way of seeing patterns in the world. His solution, music, is worth dwelling on, but the stance of *Patterned Ground* is to suggest there may be other ways to go; as yet unimagined ways.

In many ways, Klee's landscape paintings ask questions similar to those posed in this book: for example, are patterns in the landscape natural or cultural? In fact, the title *'Florentine' Residential District* hints at Klee's ambivalence. In this work, seeing patterns involves on the one hand, an attendance to the movement, arrangement and substance of the landscape, its times and spaces; and on the other, a purity of intellectual abstraction in the identification of categorical features of the landscape. To achieve this in the painting, Klee transposed landscape elements into a notation resembling those in musical scores.

Musical scores comprise staves and notes, along with indicators of duration, intensity and timing, that determine phrasing, tempo, weighting, scale and the like. This is a highly abstract and formal representation of the sound (of music). Rhythm, however, is more than this. In this abstract experience of music, it can involve repetition, division, regular and irregular elements, alterations in structure, overlapping phrasing and so on. Klee used many of these 'timings' in his graphic representation of the rhythm of the landscape. In one sense, the eye is invited to move along the horizontal lines. In doing so, the eye catches the characters on the lines, their colour, tone, repetition, regular and irregular alterations in form. This horizontal pacing is interrupted by vertical lines. These vertical lines suggest other rhythmic forms that work vertically and, further, diagonally. This picture, then, is comprised of timings and spacings of the landscape: the pattern of the landscape emerges from both its times and spaces, simultaneously. The 'thinking eye' now shuttles across the painting, producing the landscape anew, as the formal elements are juxtaposed in new ways.

In Klee's 'rhythmic' paintings, complex patterns emerged from a fairly simple visual structure, based on the grid. Onto this grid pattern, Klee would layer the results he derived from a form of analysis he called 'spatial calculation'. Klee broke down the landscape into 'squares' that have a particular colour and tone. These were then mapped onto the grid to produce a formal, abstract representation of the landscape. So, the patches of colour that underlie *'Florentine' Residential District* echo earlier attempts to map light and tone. Yet, in this painting, the patches of colour are not so clearly demarcated and explicit; the edges blur, the colours bleed. For us, this suggests that the puzzle of whether patterns in the landscape are natural or cultural remains. More than this, it also begs questions about how we identify, delineate and categorize patches of ground, landforms and landscape features. Such patterns, moreover, are never static, fixed only temporarily, and silent only where we cannot hear the rhythm: there's movement and noise, even in the stillest and quietest of places.

Patterned Ground, then, explores the ways in which we understand the patterns in the world around us. Its premise is that 'landscapes' are not self-evident and that common-sense ways of thinking about land-scape patterns (or 'patterns on the ground') need to be unsettled. Of course, there are an almost unlimited number of possible tactics through which to unsettle prevalent understandings of the relationship between nature and culture. *Patterned Ground* is an experiment in one such tactic.

We invited authors to write short essays that discussed one element in the landscape that they are particularly passionate about. We hoped to mirror some recent developments in the ways in which the landscape is being reconceptualised, as well as responding to certain political demands that the 'social contract' between humans and nonhumans (organic and inorganic) is being renegotiated, and hardly ever on terms more favourable to nonhumans. New ways of thinking about 'nature' and 'culture' (always implicitly in scare quotes) have undoubt-edly become one of the most important and exciting sites of interest in the social sciences and humanities because they bear the traces of three different debates: on the history and sociology of science; on nature and the environment; and, on the rapprochement between art and science. But they have also become an important part of thinking about the natural sciences as a result of, for example, new ways of thinking about evolution, awareness, self-consciousness, emergence, information and, indeed, what science is.

Patterned Ground reaches out to these various innovations in thinking about nature and culture: innovations which are specifically located in the blurred terrain where nature and culture are not so easily (as if they ever were) distinguished and dichotomized. In this vein, the title of the book draws on the terminology of physical geog-raphy, and simultaneously resonates with an intuitive understanding that the landscapes in which we live have distinct patterns. In some ways, this is because we are arguing that there is a 'new geography', because it is important to appreciate that the world is now patterned by both nonhuman and human processes. It is to these entanglements – that comprise what we know as landscape – that this book is oriented.

As part of this project, we have had to engage landscape features – landforms – as they currently map into our topological imaginations. Thus, landforms have traditionally been seen as discrete entities (as things in themselves). Geomorphological maps employ solid black lines around landforms, yet in the field the boundaries between (and within) landforms are often very far from clear. The identification of geographical landforms, therefore, involves a set of clear assumptions not only about the nature of the landform, but also about its history (both as a landform and as an intellectual category, since these are intertwined). In many ways, the 'objects' that comprise the landscape – such as glaciers, dunes, hills, mountains – have had to be invented and stabilised as discrete features of the landscape, separable not only from other landforms, but also from (their) humanity. In this book, we wish to unsettle these ontological and epistemological assumptions about the processes producing the landscape as we know it – which, of course, is also to question the 'we' who knows and produces that landscape. In part, this is achieved by writing about the 'objects' of analysis – including cities, mountains, towns, oceans, villages, bogs and the like. In part, we have also used the organisational structure of the book to place human and nonhuman worlds side by side in a deliberate attempt to cross and blur the conceptual and practical boundaries between them (and us).

In this book, authors take seriously the entanglements – the invisible hyphens – between nature and culture, human and nonhuman. There are many ways in which it would be possible to tease out, and explore, these tangled relations. More than this, there are already long histories of people's attempts to understand these relationships. In this volume, as a starting point, we begin with the 'object': that is, with some 'thing' in the world. But these objects are not taken at face value. Nor, indeed, do authors see themselves as somehow uninvolved in their own ways of seeing the object. Authors take seriously those accounts of 'objects' that have written them into earth (precisely geo-, -graphia). This is not to say that the pieces gathered in *Patterned Ground* are histories of the science of the 'object'. Instead, essays chart, variously, the changing cultural meanings (in both a scientific and a lay sense) which have added different layers of understanding to landforms and landscapes as well as some of the different attempts at explanation of phenomena which have occurred through time. More than this, we wished to open up a creative space in which new forms of communicating, imaging and writing about the earth can be tried out and set side by side.

Finally, we would like to thank Michael Leaman and Joe Kerr at Reaktion. This book contains a wide range of images – and, indeed, a key aim of this project was to use 'visual' images (whether photographs or cartoons, paintings or sketches) to parallel text-based arguments about the patterning of the landscape – so we'd like to thank all those who gave permission to use their images. Acknowledgements and credits for specific images are provided at the back of the book. We have been able to provide such a richly illustrated text only through the generous support of the Geography Department at the Open University. In particular, we'd like to thank the Head of Department, John Allen, for his understanding that this project would be impoverished without its non-text elements. The Geography Department also provided substantial secretarial support: Michèle Marsh speedily typed up and smoothed the distribution of various drafts amongst the editors, Susie Hooley helped organize meetings of the editors and Jan Smith managed the permissions for the images, the most frustrating task of all. Without all of this 'hidden' support, *Patterned Ground* really would be so much less.

We hope that the sequencing and progressions in the essays in *Patterned Ground* help to tap out different rhythms, and that the cadences in the voices – whether concordant or dissonant – enable different patterns to emerge and breathe. Most of all, we hope that the book will enable further experiments to take place, for we have only just begun to explore and map the world about us.

Stephan Harrison, Steve Pile, Nigel Thrift

introduction

Grounding Patterns:

Deciphering (Dis)Order in the Entanglements of Nature and Culture

Stephan Harrison, Steve Pile, Nigel Thrift

1. The Curious, the Exalted,
the Occult, the Passion

There is a widespread curiosity about whether there are patterns in the world around us. For example, observers of the night sky have long seen shapes and forms, regularities and signs in the stars. Even in the most vague and random of scenes, people can make out patterns. In many ways, this book is an attempt to look upon the world with eyes that are curious and attentive, but eyes that are not yet able to decipher the precise nature of the pattern before them. This is neither an inexperienced nor an inexpert way of approaching the world, but it is one that is prepared to imagine the world before its patterns became obvious – in whatever way they became obvious – and were parcelled up into domains investigated and policed by academic disciplines. *Patterned Ground* looks at elements in the world around us, and seeks to (re)arrange them in unusual ways. In this, it follows a wider 'geographical impulse' to see patterns in the world. But it seeks to do so in ways that enable other, perhaps less visible, patterns to emerge.

Often, this geographical impulse is profoundly 'popular': ordinary, everyday. Popular geographies are fascinated by the earth and people's engagement with it. On television, we can watch programmes on the National Geographic channel, when we're not leafing through the glossy pages of the magazine. No week goes by without a travel programme of some kind on TV. Travelogues are another popular form, with people writing about the strange encounters they had on their visits to there and elsewhere, or across this or that stretch of the earth. Almost invariably, people discover both themselves as well as the planet around them. People's curiosity about the planet leads to observations about those curiosities – theirs and others. Popular geographies celebrate the immense diversity of the world, but more than this they attempt to see designs in the world that might have remained hidden. The world, as strange and bizarre, is put together, made up, through these observations – whether on television, in books, or even in song or poetry. However, these strange and bizarre patterns are not to everyone's taste. Sometimes the laughter of recognition is strained.

Classifying Things

There are many ways of describing patterns in the cosmos. Other people's categorizations can often seem strange, bizarre. Indeed, the process of identifying and classifying things can itself seem to be a funny thing to do. Indeed, for years, the philosopher Michel Foucault's hollow laughter echoed around the halls of the academy – a dreadful laugh that called into question the very foundations on which the humanities, sciences and social sciences were kept apart. For Foucault's laughter stemmed from an anxiety when confronted by a way of knowing that saw the world very differently from him.[1] The ways in which other people classify the objects they see in the world might seem strange to others. According to Dr Franz Kuhn's (apocryphal?) description concerning, 'a certain Chinese encyclopaedia', they might look like this:

> In its distant pages it is written that animals are divided into (a) those that belong to the emperor; (b) embalmed ones; (c) those that are trained; (d) suckling pigs; (e) mermaids; (f) fabulous ones; (g) stray dogs; (h) those that are included in this classification; (i) those that tremble as if they were mad; (j) innumerable ones; (k) those drawn with a very fine camel's-hair brush; (l) *etcetera*; (m) those that have just broken the flower vase; (n) those that at a distance resemble flies.[2]

Later, we will turn to Borges' essay in which this classification appears. For now, let us listen to Foucault's observations on this taxonomy, for it will tell us something about how the world is observed. In the first instance, Foucault says that he is drawn to the unfamiliarity of the taxonomy. He says that it 'shattered . . . all the familiar landmarks of [his] thought – our thought', significantly adding that 'the exotic charm of another system of thought' had the effect of raising the possibility of the impossibility of systems of thought that attempt to order 'things'. It is this question of the impossibility of producing order out of the wild profusion of things that detains Foucault. For us, this question is important too. For it strikes at the heart of the agenda of this book – how can we delimit patterns on the ground? What are the consequences of seeing certain orderings and not others? What wonders do 'we' behold and what powers of awe do 'things' hold over us? Foucault's laughter is hollow. He is 'shattered'. While he enjoys the bizarre juxtapositions in the taxonomy – say, the placing side by side of 'fabulous ones' and 'stray dogs' – he begins to worry about the proximity of such extremes: are fabulous ones and stray dogs interconnected, or not? Is there more to this pattern than meets the eye? The taxonomy is a chaotic heap of things, connected in the taxonomy, but apparently unconnected. Foucault's laughter strains even more. Suddenly the taxonomy bears no relation to 'things', but simply floats in the unthinkable space of thought. In this space, no one can hear you laugh. Borges even eliminates this space. According to Foucault, Borges

> adds no figure to the atlas of the impossible; nowhere does he strike the spark of poetic confrontation; he simply dispenses with the least obvious, the most compelling, of necessities; he does away with the site, the mute ground upon which it is possible for entities to be juxtaposed.[3]

For our purposes, the nature of the 'site' or 'ground' on which these orderings might be juxtaposed is precisely what is at issue. Where Foucault's laugh breaks off in a certain uneasiness that he finds hard to shake off, we begin to look on with wonder . . . and ask how these patterns emerge to our eyes, how they call our attention? Of course, it is Foucault's purpose to challenge those knowledges that think they know what 'things' exist and in what order they are to be put. His laughter is deliberately uneasy – with the intention of unsettling those sciences (social or otherwise) that purport to have certain and steadfast categories through which to identify and classify things. With Foucault, then, we are seeking to unsettle these knowledges. However, knowledges are not quite where they were when Foucault was writing. Perhaps now we are keener to see the bizarre translations involved; a certain Chinese encyclopaedia read by Franz Kuhn read by Jorge Borges read by Michel Foucault read by us, written for you. But we do not want to lose sight of the taxonomy, whether Franz made it up or not. For what we have in this taxonomy is more than the seemingly bizarre and wonderful juxtaposition of apparently incompatible and unlike elements. Here, we have a code, a definite design – one that we might even see on the ground . . . even if it does resemble a fly at a distance. Let us go to Borges' essay.

The spur for Borges was that the fourteenth edition of the *Encyclopaedia Britannica* had dropped its entry on John Wilkins. Borges admits that this is probably of little consequence, since the original entry was hardly informative: born 1614, died 1672, rector of an Oxford college and not much else. For Borges, however, Wilkins was an intriguing character of

> happy curiosity: interested in theology, cryptography, music, the manufacture of transplanted beehives, the course of an invisible planet, the possibility of a trip to the moon, the possibility and principles of a world language.[4]

Let us be clear about the difference in attitude between Foucault and Borges. Borges is driven to celebrate a life led in curiosity, while Foucault laughs nervously about classificatory systems that are both bizarre and binding. In *Patterned Ground* we wish to hold these ideas about, on the one hand, the strangeness and, on the other, the necessity of classificatory systems together, and allow the tension between them to play itself out. However, we must be clear about another lesson that Wilkins teaches us: there was a time before Discipline. His curiosity ranged over the ground, and the heavens. If we are to pursue this endeavour of thinking about how we discern patterns in the landscape, then we must open up our ways of looking at the world – whether we look down at our feet or up at the stars. This is not, despite Foucault's increasingly hysterical laughter, an argument for abandoning classificatory systems.

Borges uses Wilkins to suggest that classificatory systems of some kind are both necessary and useful, no matter how bizarre they seem. For Borges,

> The words of John Wilkins' analytical language are not dumb and arbitrary symbols; every letter is meaningful, as those of the Holy Scriptures were for the Kabbalists. Mauthner observes that children could learn this language without knowing that it was artificial; later, in school, they would discover that it was also a universal key and a secret encyclopaedia.[5]

Borges refers to Wilkins's attempt to create a general language for analytical thought, in which some 40 classes of words are invented, each of which is subdivided into 'differences', then 'species' (along 'natural' lines perhaps). For example, a category of stones is subdivided into those that are common, moderate, precious, transparent and insoluble. Such a classification is reminiscent of those found in other places, such as *Roget's Thesaurus* (which is based on six classes, subdivided further into sections and then numbered heads: for stones, see under the 'Head' 344 Land). It is less the system of classification that detains Borges, though, than the idea of a 'universal key' or 'secret encyclopaedia'. The idea that every letter is meaningful is significant here, especially when correlated with another analytical language, namely mathematics.

This leads us to wonder about mathematical models for interpreting the world (so, we'll return to this issue on p. 27). Here, we would include the Kabbalists, who attempted to understand the underlying principles of creation by converting God's Word into numbers using the Hebrew Bible. After all, as the Hebrew Bible states, in the Beginning was the Word. This biblical clue to the origins of the universe led some to believe that the key to understanding the structure of creation was to be found in the underlying structure of Hebrew. For the Kabbalists, the laws of grammar in Hebrew were not just the stuff of language, they were the stuff of the creation.[6] So, through the substitution of numerical values for the letters of the Hebrew alphabet, and the various arithmetical operations that could now be performed on words, they expected to reveal the divine patterning of the cosmos.[7]

For now, let us simply note that not all patterns are visible. This Kabbalistic mathematical model of the structure of the universe has modern-day equivalents. For example, we can think of the more quantitative interpretations of human and physical systems that, like the Kabbalists, seek to reveal the underlying structure of the cosmos through mathematics. In this light, the most 'science-identified' approaches to physical and human systems rely on a presumption that the universe works according to mathematical laws: laws that, we now might reason, are the work of God. In science, arguably, there is a natural philosophy that implies the existence – and creativity – of God. It is well worth bearing this paradox in mind while you read the various essays in *Patterned Ground*, for here you will find the work of scientists; scientists who would disagree on exactly this matter.

Let us remember Foucault's hysteria, though. These ways of seeing patterns in the world, in the cosmos, are also ways of placing people in that world, in that cosmology. There is an uncomfortable sense that the way we see patterns is also the way they see us. In other words, systems of thought create thinkers who cannot think outside those systems of thought: people are unable to move beyond the horizons of their meaningful world. But is this really so? There is a strange paradox at the core of Foucault's work. It often seems that he is worried by the ways in which humans produce knowledges that can constrain, and even dominate, human life. Yet, it is also hard to see, sometimes, exactly who is producing, and imposing, these knowledges. Indeed, sometimes it is easy to get the impression that no one is actually responsible since everyone is somehow within the horizon of understanding, whatever form this understanding takes. But what if these horizons are blurred, variable, constantly in contact with other forms of thought, and indeed other worlds?

We will pursue this question using the 'life and times' of Dr John Dee. Dr Dee is, of course, a significant figure in his own right (see below), but for us his story is important for three reasons. First, we would like to show that knowledges, from all corners of the earth, were in a constant state of flux in the mid- to late sixteenth century. Of course, this suggests that knowledges have never been 'pure'; that they have always been interfered with by knowledges that have come, as it were, from somewhere else. This leads to our next point. Systems of knowledge involve very different ways of thinking about the underlying principles governing life, the universe and everything – whether grounded in the divine or physical laws or something else. Third, as we will see, Dr Dee was a rigorous, even scientific, thinker. His science was grounded in a very different cosmology: that is, in a specific way of seeing the hidden, divine connections that underlie the cosmos. Although we are concerned with the specifics of Dr Dee's thought, what amazes us is the way these ideas can be found in the foundations of contemporary science (as we will show, pp. 23–5). Dr Dee, we would argue, has a lot to tell us about *Patterned Ground*.

Divining Hidden Relationships

John Wilkins was not alone in attempting to make, or discover, 'God's secret dictionary', as Borges puts it.[8] Indeed, there had been many earlier attempts. These were not founded entirely on a holy search for The Truth. More human motivations were involved, for it was reasoned that deciphering God's 'code' of creation would enable that creation to be changed, at will. In Elizabethan times, when the fate of European nations seemed in the balance, such knowledge was a matter of State. It was mainly for this reason that Elizabeth 1 of England was prepared to give a certain Dr John Dee (1527–1608/9) so much of her attention and, indeed, majesty. For us, what is of interest in Dr Dee's activities and ideas is that he stands between knowledges – of magic, of the divine, of mathematics, of cartography and navigation – yet also set in a heady context of the politics of State and Church. For this reason, we would prefer to hear Foucault's increasingly anxious laughter as less to do with the arbitrary and bizarre nature of all understandings of the world than with their imaginative and geopolitical consequences.

John Dee began his studies at Trinity College, Cambridge University, where he studied the quadrivium: geometry, arithmetic, harmonics and astronomy.[9] His main passion was for mathematics, despite the fact that the subject was viewed with great suspicion at the time. For most, mathematics was directly linked to the 'black arts' of magic because calculating (calculing) was understood to be synonymous with conjuration. Indeed, one of the foundational figures of the quadrivium, Pythagoras, was widely believed to be a magician. It was assumed that numbers had inherent powers. For example, the first four integers, 1, 2, 3 and 4, were believed to have more than simply generative powers, since they also described the basic elements of geometry: a point (1), a line (2), a triangle (3) and a solid (4).[10] In numbers were not just the abstract relationships of mathematics, but also the divine design underlying the true nature of things. (It is worth remembering the Kabbalists, both old and new, at this point.)

Dee, however, was not only interested in mathematics, so in 1548 he left for the Low Countries to discover the very latest in European scientific thinking. At that time, the Low Countries stood at the crossroads in a variety of flows of ideas, from Spain, Italy, Portugal, Germany, north Africa and beyond.[11] Dee enrolled in the finest university in the region, Louvain. There, he studied under Gemma Frisius, who pioneered one of the most widely practised ways of determining 'patterns on the ground', triangulation (used in land surveying).[12] Dee was also to meet, and become fast friends with, the most famous cartographer of the time, Mercator.[13] Science, in this period, was actively creating ways to measure the earth – or more precisely to create a world that was grounded in the measurement of space: location, distance, direction, orientation, area. This way of cutting space up into measurable and patternable elements remains at the core of modern mapping techniques. And, of course, mapping is one of the most common and intuitive ways of representing patterns in the world.[14] But mapping was (and is) more than simply about the measurement of distance or about drawing the shape of the world onto a map or globe. It was a whole system for philosophizing the world, of calling it into being. The centre of the map not only described where one was, it was also about showing where the centre of the universe was. Often, for this reason, medieval maps would be centred on Jerusalem. The map was – and, we would argue, still is – an entire cosmological system.

Dr Dee's cosmology – based in mathematics and calculating, in astronomy and astrology – was grounded in a critical science: meticulous, curious and suspicious, it was designed to uncover the foundational patterns of nature.[15] To do this, he charted the path of celestial bodies and attempted to show their influence on events on earth. Dee theorized that there were hidden forces that bound the universe together and enabled mutual influence to occur, like the magnetism in ore. This single force emanated from, and confirmed, the unity of the cosmos: a cosmos created by God. Dee experimented with a range of instruments – such as a crystal ball, lenses and mirrors (some of which are now on display in the British Museum) – designed to reveal these forces. Unfortunately, these were not enough to enable Dr Dee to decipher God's code for creation, so he tried another – perhaps more direct – method: he tried to communicate with angels. But, although they promised to, the angels never gave him what he needed.

Through careful analysis and strict arithmetic reasoning, Dee nonetheless hoped that he would uncover God's code of the universe. More than simply being an earthbound visible form, landscape is understood in relation to the heavens and the divine. The landscape is not just an object of contemplation, it is something to be in awe of, to wonder at, since it is designed by God. More than this, through the Word of God, he hoped to be able to influence affairs: both through communicating with angels and also by using the Word to engineer new things and to influence the course of history. For us, the important point is this: not only are hidden connections and forces in nature being theorized, but they are also being researched and verified (or falsified) – and acted on.

Today, it may seem that science is very far from being entangled with assumptions about codes of creation or the divine. Yet it would be a mistake to assume that the patterns that contemporary scientists observe and delineate on the ground or in the heavens owe nothing to assumptions about hidden forces, nor to an interest in an all-too-human intention to influence the world. At the very time that contemporary sciences – such as geology, biology – were beginning to take shape, many thinkers were working with ways of seeing patterns in the world that owed as much to Dr Dee as to detached observation and new classificatory systems. In order to get a sense of this, we will turn to a central figure in the development of modern physical – and, indeed, human – geography, Alexander von Humboldt.[16] His, however, was not a physical geography devoted only to the study of the earth's surface, but a total physical geography that looked into the world below the surface and up into the heavens and all things in-between.

In the next section, we will take a look at Alexander von Humboldt's classic work, *Cosmos*. This work is arguably his greatest achievement, but we are interested in it because of the way he seeks to synthesize the knowledges from different scientific disciplines; at a time before these had mutated into contemporary scientific disciplines. As a result, *Cosmos* tells something about how universal patterns are derived from quite disparate forms of scientific learning, in this case also involving passionate observation and a particular sense of divine purpose.

Seeing Patterns in a World of Wonders

Alexander von Humboldt is a central figure in Enlightenment science. He was widely travelled and, from his diverse experiences, sought to discern the universal principles ordering the various patterns and peculiarities in the world. For us, in von Humboldt's work, there is an entanglement of nature and culture that produces a wonderful way of seeing patterns in the world: that is, a way of seeing that is full of wonder. He described his form of science in this way:

Science is a labor of mind applied to nature, but the external world has no real existence for us beyond the image reflected within ourselves through the medium of the sense.[17]

On the one hand, taking a familiar and commonplace stance within the scientific community, von Humboldt counter-poses and separates the internal world (of mind and body) from the external world. The human mind-and-body is the centre of knowledge, with the body drawing in sense impressions of the external world and the mind labouring to make sense of those sensations. It is, first and foremost, an empirical science – a science of first-hand observation. In this, and perhaps surprisingly, it has sympathies with Dr Dee's careful observation and painstaking measurement of earthly and heavenly phenomena. Von Humboldt probably spent little time scrying – that is, attempting to divine the cosmos through a crystal ball – but he did observe the cosmos using extraordinary devices. The crystal ball might have been replaced by one of modernity's magical scientific instruments, the telescope, but both are devices for improving both sight and insight. For Dee and von Humboldt alike, patterns were to be grounded in the observation of nature and in discerning the hidden principles that governed the properties of life.

For von Humboldt, observed nature was highly 'heterogeneous'.[18] Nonetheless, he argued, the 'immense diversity of phenomena' of the cosmos was founded on a principle of unity.[19] The universal principles underlying the observable heterogeneity and diversity of the cosmos had to be approached (though not necessarily ever apprehended) through the production of rational empirical knowledge. Nevertheless, he averred,

Experimental sciences, based on the observation of the external world, can not aspire to completeness; the nature of things, and the imperfection of our organs, are alike opposed to it.[20]

Von Humboldt was more (or less) than a modest witness[21] to the cosmos, he was a self-avowed *flawed* witness,[22] for he knew he could not even aspire to understanding God's work – a thought that does not seem to have crossed Dr Dee's mind. While there may be a perfect universal unity in which the observable patterns in the cosmos were grounded, the flawed scientist could never understand it in its totality. He could, however, wonder at its heterogeneity and diversity. Through open-minded investigation, it would be possible to discern certain mysteries and to suggest principles of the development of land and life. For this reason, von Humboldt deliberately schooled himself in various, seemingly separate, sciences of the day: 'descriptive botany, geognosy, chemistry, astronomical determinations of position, and terrestrial magnetism'.[23] To today's minds, the juxtaposition of these 'sciences' may seem almost as fantastic as those through which Dr Dee laboured to understand the cosmos. Like Dee, von Humboldt attempted to synthesize these diverse sciences in

> the earnest endeavour to comprehend the phenomena of physical objects in their general connection, and to represent nature as one great whole, moved and animated by internal forces.[24]

Von Humboldt's integrative science was holistic and motivated by an assumption that there were internal connections between 'things' and hidden and mysterious – 'occult'[25] – forces that gave 'things' life and form. Such intentions and assumptions are entirely consistent with those of Dr Dee, and less than a stone's throw from much empirical and experimental science today. There is more to it than this, according to von Humboldt.

> The contemplation of the individual characteristics of the landscape, and of the conformation of the land in any definite region of the earth, gives rise to a different source of enjoyment, awakening impressions that are more vivid, better defined, and more congenial to certain phases of the mind.[26]

Thus, in speaking about the vault of the heavens, von Humboldt describes his feelings of the infinite. He continues:

> The solemn and imposing impressions excited by this sentiment are owing to . . . the enjoyment and emotions awakened in us, whether we float on the surface of the great deep, stand on some lonely mountain summit enveloped in the half-transparent vapory vail of the atmosphere, or by the aid of powerful optical instruments scan the regions of space, and see the remote nebulous mass resolve itself into worlds of stars.[27]

The science of observation was a passionate one. It was an aesthetic and poetic experience.[28] Contemplation, in this view, is far from the quiet, internal contemplation enforced in contemporary libraries, museums and art galleries. It was a heightened awareness of the cosmos in which enjoyment, awe, wonder were fundamental. It would be impossible to understand the cosmos unless one first experienced enjoyment and wonder in encountering any phenomenon.[29] Von Humboldt honed this passionate observation during his scientific travels. Indeed, these travels to 'other lands', such as the 'wild and gigantic' landscapes of South America,[30] were formative of his scientific and spiritual understanding of the world. This science was not simply a science through detached eyes, but a fully embodied knowledge. It was felt at the same time that it was thought – no separation of mind, body, nor spirit.

For us, this passionate, flawed, embodied, self-aware understanding of science remains of vital importance. That is, our approach to the landscape is one in which we attend to the senses, the labour of the mind, the limits of our knowing and a passionate attitude to the things we observe. More than this, we should be in awe and wonder of the immense diversity of the cosmos. We should hold off our presumptions of hierarchies and boundaries between (scientific) knowledges long enough to question how the cosmos has been split up into discrete elements, each with its own place in the great scheme of things. Whether we are dealing with a Chinese encyclopaedia or an attempt to discern the mathematical principles governing the movement of the stars, whether we stand as flawed witnesses to God's scheme or laugh at the bizarre ways that systems of thought seek patterns in the world, the uncertainty of principle or observation might be enough to suggest a book such as *Patterned Ground*. More than this, with its close and passionate scrutiny of elements in the world around us and the way it produces an almost pre-disciplinary outcome, *Patterned Ground* offers much promise in the future.[31]

So far, we have thought about certain assumptions about how the world is patterned (as in the Chinese encyclopaedia) or the underlying principles of the universe (as in God's Word or a divine purpose). We have seen, as a result, both continuities and differences in the cosmologies of Dr Dee and Alexander von Humboldt. We have dealt, however, with the internal logic of their systems of thought. It is, though, also the case that the limits to their knowledge – be it the difficulty of gaining access to God's code for the universe or the presumed impossibility of understanding God's plan – are constitutive of Dee's and von Humboldt's understandings of the world. The limits to science do not simply determine what cannot be known, they tell us about the relationship between what can be known and what cannot. So, it is to the consequences of thinking that science might not have a full grasp of the real, and/or of cosmological designs, that we turn in the next section.

2. Science and the Landscape

The landscape that we travel through and research is patterned. Some of these patterns are immediately apparent, or quickly come into view (indeed some can be seen from the air and from space); others are less obvious and emerge only after detailed scrutiny. While it can be argued that the identification of symmetries, repetitions and regularities may be fundamental to the survival and well-being of humans (it seems instinctual and their recognition presumably bestows evolutionary advantages on us), these patterns open up a number of questions and, here, we attempt to discuss how these patterns we see in the landscape are *scientifically* meaningful; that is, how they convey a message that we may or may not be able to decipher using scientific knowledges. In this section, we want to highlight the types of messages available and the various ways in which our scientific theories and our instruments of knowledge cope with them.

We should also ask: is scientific knowledge a knowledge of reality?[32] If so, patterns on the ground really exist and convey deep meaning. We can therefore explore them by exploring their geometries and their statistical regularities and the various correlations between and within them. Yet we are always aware that much of nature is non-linear and the landscape is a palimpsest, and deep in its structures may be where true understanding resides. Alternatively, other views might argue that such patterns are a red herring and lead us, at best, to partial understandings. Both suggest that science may attain a knowledge, but may never obtain complete understanding.

Science and its Grasp of the World

Science provides us with a set of devices and procedures with which we may explore the landscape. Popper said that theories were nets designed by us to catch the world. Despite this, scientific knowledge may not be a faithful representation of reality. More than this, reality might not in fact be decipherable. As Mead argues:

> in the world of immediate experience, the world of things is there. Trees grow, day follows night, and death supervenes on life. One may not say that relations here are external or internal. They are not relations at all. They are lost in the indiscernibility of things and events, which are what they are. The world which is the test of all observations and all hypothetical reconstructions has in itself no system that can be isolated as a structure of laws or uniformities, though all laws and formulations of uniformities must be brought to its court for its imprimatur.[33]

What Mead is saying is that the order that we place upon the world may not be the way in which the world is, in fact, ordered. Plato's famous metaphor of the cave illustrates this idea. Here, Plato argues that the 'reality' that we experience may be similar to the shadows cast upon a cave wall from the light of the outside world. Anyone who had spent their lives living in the cave would assume that the patterns and messages borne by the shadows *were* reality; their experience could not allow them to think of a reality outside the cave.

Mead also stresses the *entanglement* between things. Modern constructions of science around systems theory would have us believe, however, that we can isolate sets of phenomena from one another; that complex phenomena can be dividable. However, non-linearity, computational intractability and the complexity of natural systems may illustrate several things. One is to call into question the reductionist mathematical modelling, which has assumed the mantle of the ruling paradigm in subjects such as geomorphology and forms the *modus operandi* of the 'new Kabbalists'. There is a shared assumption that there is a 'machine code' to the universe – in this case, concerning process/form relationships – reminiscent of the Kabbalists of old. What is important, then, is less the principle that mathematical knowledge describes the workings of the cosmos, but rather it is the assumption that reductionist model-building is the best way to apprehend its forms and functions. It is not that complex systems, always inherently (or logically), can never be reducible to simpler principles. If this were so, then we would be forced to concede that complex phenomena and structures of matter were made up of something other than their elementary building blocks;[34] a sort of supernatural emergence. It is more that practical limits to knowledge create a barrier to understanding patterns in the landscape.

Accordingly, the complexities of patterned ground may also hide from us forever the deepest workings of the landscape. We can see that not only do we live in a world where uncertainty (in the form of irreducible unknowability) is an inherent attribute of all reality, but that all systems interact with all other systems and any distinction between them must be artificial; a sort of macroscopic decoherence. We should not be disheartened by this, nor should we be fooled into thinking that this unknowability is merely a consequence of the inadequacy of our computer models or our measurements. Instead we should be liberated by the suggestion that science, the landscape and the patterns we see around us cannot be reduced to a few equations on a page.[35]

As a consequence, we should incorporate unknowability and the limits to knowledge. These limits may be technical (based upon the nature of computing power, data retrieval and analysis); social or economic (where limits are set by the ability and willingness of society to pay the cost of data inputting and analysis); neurological (based upon limitations imposed by the nature of the human brain); practical (where the complexity of the problem increases faster than any possible increase in computational power); or logical (where limits are imposed by the nature of physics or mathematics). In certain ways, then, a new understanding of the patterns on the ground would embrace this uncertainty by combining forms of narrative and qualitative discourse about landscape with some of the new understandings of the limits of science and of the boundary conditions within which such landscapes and patterns must develop. Recent ideas on the role, nature and rapidity of climate change, the influence of tectonics and improved dating schemes would set the limits on these new models.

Deciphering Patterns in the Landscape

For some, patterns in the landscape are 'out-of-context messages' that require deciphering. Such a view shows us that patterns in the landscape are not readable in isolation from the scientific, cultural and *behavioural* context within which we exist. What is at stake in this section, therefore, is the multi-layered structure of reality. To illustrate this, Hofstadter identifies three aspects to reality, which he calls 'messages': frame, outer and inner.[36] The frame message is that which draws attention to the need for a decoding device and is conveyed by the structure of the information-bearer. Once the nature of the frame message has been recognized then the outer message is level two. This forms information by carrying symbols, structures and patterns, which tell us how we can decode the inner message. This outer message is composed of a set of triggers; there can be no instructions telling us how to decode the outer message since these would form the inner message. Thus, it is argued that the entire structure of the world and its context forms the frame message. As humans, it is suggested, we necessarily attempt to decipher its messages. Within it, the landscape and its patterns form the outer message; the patterning and symmetries of the world call to us to decipher their meanings. Whether we have read these correctly and consequently whether we are able to decode them correctly or not, the inner message may never be knowable.

While we assume that it takes intelligence to decipher patterns on the ground, since we impute significance to these 'out-of-context messages', it may be that the supposed indifference to (certain) patterns displayed by other phenomena (trees? birds?) is not a sign of 'non-intelligence' but merely a response to other meanings embedded in the landscape of which we are unaware. Here, the central problem involves the role of a specifically human intelligence (as opposed to, or independent from, the intelligences of trees and birds, for example) in the deciphering of patterns in the world. Jauch raises this issue through an imaginary dialogue between Salviati and Sagredo, who are discussing the hidden meanings that emerge from the chaos of nature:[37]

> Salviati: Nature presents us with a host of phenomena which appear mostly as chaotic randomness until we select some significant events, and abstract from their particular, irrelevant circumstances so that they become idealized. Only then can they exhibit their true structure in full splendour.
>
> Sagredo: This is a marvellous idea! It suggests that when we try to understand nature, we should look at the phenomena as if they were messages to be understood. Except that each message appears to be random until we establish a code to read it. This code takes the form of an abstraction, that is, we choose to ignore certain things as irrelevant and we thus partially select the content of the message by a free choice. These irrelevant signals form the 'background noise,' which will limit the accuracy of our message.
>
> But since the code is not absolute there may be several messages in the same raw material of the data, so changing the code will result in a message of equally deep significance in something that was merely noise before, and conversely: In a new code a former message may be devoid of meaning. Thus a code presupposes a free choice among different, complementary aspects, each of which has equal claim to reality.

Jauch therefore makes the point that we may not discover things as much as actually create things according to our own predilections.

This is to say more than that the patterned world is also composed of 'background noises' that we ignore, but to take seriously the 'full splendour' of things. To convey a message, patterns in the ground must have embedded in them more information than is contained by the external, manifest pattern itself: that is, they must have a hinterland. A Digital Video Disc (DVD), for instance, is a patterned structure. Its form is geometric and displays symmetry. These are all clues that betray the presence of information residing deep within the DVD itself. Only with a decoding device (a DVD player) does the richness of the message make itself known.

Therefore, aperiodic patterns and geometric regularities appear to have meaning imbedded within them in ways in which random and chaotic patterns appear not to have. Some positions suggest that meaning comes from the brain. From this, no message in the landscape can have inherent meaning since this message has to be input via a device that can comprehend it. As Hofstadter cautions, we can easily fall into the trap of thinking that we require a pre-existing message that enables us to understand any message;[38] an infinite hierarchy of messages. We don't, he argues, for the simple reason that human brains are pre-coded to recognize certain messages and for their decoding. The interesting implication, here, is that one brain responds in similar ways to the next to the same stimulus (which is why there are societies and why geomorphology and other sciences can exist), which means that *meaning* in a message must reside in the message itself since human brains seem to possess a universal decoder. This argument about the limits to the deciphering of patterns has implications for thinking about how we explain the existence of the patterns *in* the world, since in important ways these patterns are abstractions *from* the world.

Explaining Patterns

Many assume that once patterns on the ground have been identified it is a short step to explanation. However, it is not clear that all patterns are explainable or computable. The first problem, in getting from pattern to explanation, is thinking about the relationship 'scale' at which the pattern exists and the 'scale' where the assumed causes of those patterns are believed to lie. For instance, convection cells develop in liquids once they are differentially heated. Such convection cells can be explained only at the level at which they can be discerned. No analysis explaining convection cells by reducing them to general principles in fluid dynamics – which would involve the solving of Navier-Stokes equations[39] for turbulent fluids – can be fully achievable. Structures like convection cells can be seen to emerge from the non-equilibrium conditions that allow the system to obtain energy from the environment and to form ordered, dissipative structures. As a result, the system displays symmetry breaking and macroscopic probabilistic behaviour in what quite recently was assumed to be contained within a deterministic framework.

It can be argued that probabilistic explanations, which were formerly restricted to applications of quantum theory at the microscopic scale, are also valid and necessary at the macroscopic scale while describing the operations of complex systems.[40] Here, therefore, is complexity manifesting itself through self-organization.[41] Consequently, it has been argued that explanation is scale-dependent and the reductionist, empiricist and critical rationalist route shows itself to be a dead end when we engage in the practice of trying to understand complex systems like the landscape.[42]

Other problems lie in the assumptions governing what constitutes a pattern and its inherent characteristics and in how these are to be explained. A common view is that for patterns on the ground to exist, they must possess geometrical regularities. Such patterns are, logically, amenable to statistical and mathematical treatments. But certain patterns and structures lie outside the limits of such formalism (i.e., formal mathematical logic). How can these be categorized? A number of attempts have been made to categorize the types of phenomena that might lie beyond the possibility of formalism. Borrowing from Gödel and Turing, Myhill argued that the aspects of reality that are most measurable and accessible (including patterns in the landscape?) are those that are computable.[43] This appears to be the domain within which landscape modelling operates.

Outside this computability, and less amenable to quantification, are those properties that Myhill suggests are listable. It would be possible to construct a procedure that could list all the cases that exhibit the required characteristic, although this list might be infinitely long. Barrow distinguishes between computable and listable attributes by using the example of a page of a book:

> The problem of deciding whether [the] page possesses the attribute of grammatically correct English is a computable one. But the page could still be meaningless to a non-English reader. With time, the reader could learn more and more English, so that bits of the page became intelligible, but there is no way of predicting where the meaningful parts will be located on the page. The attribute of meaningfulness is thus listable but not computable.[44]

There are also characteristics that are neither computable nor listable. These are called 'prospective' and can neither be generated nor recognized deductively in a finite number of steps. An example of this is the property of being a true statement of arithmetic. As a result, Barrow argues that these 'show that there is a place for ingenuity and novelty'[45] in our exploration of the world, and quotes Myhill, who says that 'No non-poetic account of reality can be complete'.[46] This can be compared to the role of wonder and passion in the work of Alexander von Humboldt.

In conclusion, we can see that patterns emerge from complexity and that regularities contain greater meaning than randomness. It is these basic ideas, which seem both simple and obscure, that underpin this book. In producing a book that is full of things, we are not suggesting some inherently fragmented world, with loose and loosening connections between those things. Exactly the opposite. Our understandings of the nature of mathematics, physics and computer theory show that simple patterns may be produced from the operations of complex systems. Conversely, simple systems such as cellular automata obeying simple rules can produce complexity. As a starting point to explore the landscape, these binary positions deliver both opportunities and restrictions. Or, alternatively, that when we trace the impact of the 'models' through which patterns in the world have been identified then we can begin to discern the surprising and splendid complexity of the world.

3. Developing Patterns: Ethologies and the Intense Entanglements of Process

Patterns of Ground

> The disunity of science is not merely an unfortunate consequence of our limited computational or other cognitive capacities, but rather reflects the underlying ontological complexity of the world, the disorder of things.[47]

Right at the start of any enquiry, there is the question of how the world turns up, passes, exists. But describing that 'ground' is not easy. Usually, it will be described as a series of linked entities that exhibit some kind of organization, community even. That might mean a series of geometrical laws that order the universe as coldly and beautifully as an orrery. It might mean a set of affects expressing a kind of forceful synthesis. It might mean a set of more or less prosaic practices that in their humdrum but still effective way bring all kinds of things into alignment. It could be a sublime or wonderful moment that briefly welds things together as a revelatory whole. And so on. In each case, the means of holding things together – of grounding them – is not just a physical device. It will have all kinds of moral resonances, explicit or implied, which are part and parcel of that understanding of how the world is made up.

In this final section, we want to explore the entanglements between the patterns through which the world turns up. In particular, we will do so by examining how one specific notion of the ground turned up, and its assumptions about the linkages between 'things'. This is the idea of the world as being like an organism in which very different parts can nevertheless organize themselves and come to function as a whole community, complete with its own cognitive styles and affective intensities. This notion has become more and more influential in the social sciences and humanities – not least in thinking on ecology, the environment and other areas of study that foreground 'nature',[48] while, ironically, it has continued to struggle to make much headway in the sciences.

Obviously, it is possible to approach this topic in very many ways and forms, from fundamental philosophical debates about monism (as, for example, in Spinoza's idea of one substance called God or Nature or Goethe's idea of 'God–Life–Nature'); through more recent, but at root similar, ideas of cognition and life as being inseparably connected (such that mental activity is immanent in matter at all levels of life); through more focused debates about the spontaneous generation of life from various combinations of 'inert' matter;[49] through to the often intense feelings of environmental protesters that a natural order has somehow been violated. However, we want to trace out some of the problems and possibilities through an examination of 'ethological' models of animal behaviour, which see animals as continually redefining the relationship between the animate and inanimate through their behaviour. These models first developed in the early twentieth century and are gradually becoming extraordinarily influential in the social sciences and humanities. In some ways, this influence is a puzzle. After all, some have billed the present day as the triumph of a reductionist molecular account, leaving little room for the whole organism and even less for interactions between the worlds of different organisms.

What we want to do is to trace out how a particular ethological notion of the space we live in, born out of a particular apprehension of natural science, has come to take hold of the imagination of the social sciences and humanities – flowing into its very perception of how the world turns up. It is a notion that challenges a mechanistic way of thinking that reduces the life world to a special case of chemistry, physics and thermodynamics – and to a transient coalition of genes, bound together in a project to promote the genetic interests of its members. It stresses the sheer beingness of the organism but, at the same time, also questions what is meant by the organism: instead of being thought of as a thing, the boundary of an organism is thought of as a process that continually redefines what is considered as living and non-living.

> If an organism modifies its environment for adaptive purposes, is it fair to say that in doing so it confers a degree of livingness to its apparently inanimate surroundings? If we agree, just for the sake of argument, that it does, then the boundary between organism and non-organism, the boundary that seems so tangible – so obvious – to our senses of vision and of touch, dissipates into an indistinct blur, much as a turbulent eddy merges imperceptibly into the water surrounding it.[50]

We will trace the spread of this ethological notion through the works of three representative figures from the worlds of biology, art and philosophy, attempting to show how they each added something as they passed the notion on.

Inside/Outside Nature

Let us start back in the world of turn-of-the-nineteenth-century German biology with Jacob von Uexküll's Umwelt theory. Von Uexküll (1864–1944) came out of that rich intellectual soup of nineteenth- and early twentieth-century German anthropology, biology, physiology and psychology that is currently being rediscovered, not least because it provides a powerful critique of current forms of Darwinian reductionism while retaining its anti-humanism.[51] For von Uexküll, a biologist who was, like von Helmholtz and others before him, obsessed with reflexes and depicting them,[52] the point was to produce a scientific knowledge of life that could also move beyond linear-causal thinking.[53] What became clear to von Uexküll was that each animal lived in a different functional world from every other as the active creator of its own reality, which differed according to the capacities that an animal had available to it (e.g., different kinds of sense organs).[54] Instead of a machinic view of the world favoured by many German biologists,[55] von Uexküll argued for a kind of scientific phenomenology in which the claims of science interacted empirically with 'a reality whose deeper purposes and meaningfulness could only be known through immediate experience, intuition and the felt imperative of moral commandment'.[56] Why? Because of 'the basic, but much too infrequently heeded fact; namely, that every living being, the moment its sensory organs begin to function and its body establishes a relation to the outside world, finds itself in an Umwelt that is its own, constructed for its own needs'.[57]

The classic example of this Kantian a priori that von Uexküll used was the tick, because here was an animal with a stripped-down series of sensory relations to the world in which all mammals constituted the same sort of perceptual thing: a target. The tick operated according to three cues to mammals' presence and reacted with three responses only. The cues were light (response: climb to the top of a branch), smell (of sweat, response: fall on to the mammal that passes beneath the branch) and touch (of heat, seek the area without fur – the warmest spot – and begin to suck blood – which the tick neither tastes nor sees). Of course, many organisms exhibit more complex Umwelts than the tick, as von Uexküll illustrated via a set of charming and rightly famous pictures of the world as perceived by various kinds of organism, to the point where in humans we are not exactly sure what means of affecting or being affected a human body is capable of, not least because humans can extend their Umwelts through the use of various continually evolving technical means.

For von Uexküll, organisms were more than machines, both because they possessed extra-mechanistic properties of potentiality and self-creativity and because, as a result, they had no definite boundaries but lived in constant interaction with the world, producing extensions to it (from nests to skyscrapers), which present-day biologists such as Turner have argued should be thought of as external organs.[58] All kinds of writers have attacked von Uexküll's work for its palpable longing for order as manifested in its metaphysical elements[59] and its unwise forays into political thinking. Yet, at the same time, we can see how this old-style aristocrat also sets free, perhaps for the first time, a certain notion of the space of nature as essentially *propulsive* that has become formative. He allowed the world being discovered by science to sing by discovering a 'dappled world, a world rich in different things, with different natures, behaving in different ways'.[60]

If today, fields as diverse as philosophy, physiology, medicine, ethology, semiotics, cybernetics and systems theory all claim von Uexküll as a predecessor, it is in part because he brought a new way of thinking space into the world, one that has periodically taken hold since his death – in the rise of systems theory in the 1950s and '60s, in the more recent reformulation of systems theory to be found in complexity theory, in the extraordinary contemporary hold of the work of 'biological' philosophers such as Deleuze and Varela, and so on. This propulsive notion of space, which understands space as a constantly changing set of eddies, is inevitably difficult to represent, but what is interesting, we think, are the attempts to do just that. In the Preface, we saw how Paul Klee (1879–1940) attempted to portray the ebbs and flows of the landscape in his paintings. And so we return to Klee, that most philosophical of painters, this time to trace out how new practices of space are able to be born.

Uncomposed in Space

Once space is seen as constantly shifting, then we can see in Klee a persistent search for a way to represent motion. His propulsive technique of painting is often understood as a journeying in search of nascent formations that, in turn, allowed him to produce the plasmatic shapes for which he is so well known. But as many writers have pointed out, this spatially active opening-up was more than the Surrealist idea of an automatism dictated by the unconscious. Rather it was an attempt to tap an intermediary realm. Thus:

He never referred to the 'unconscious', so dear to Breton's understanding of automatism as a 'dictation of the unconscious'. For Klee it was the unintentional approach that was crucial to his drawing, and for this he orientated himself to the grammar of ancient Greek, with which he was familiar through his classical education. There is a middle voice between the active and passive in ancient Greek, which is used for all those actions that are neither actively directed nor passively endured, such as 'appearing', 'speaking', 'dancing'.[61] Drawing as the movement of a point that 'sets itself in motion' can be seen as such a middle voice. There are many references to the analogy between drawing and speaking in Klee's work quite apart from the poetic fabrication of his titles.[62]

Such an intuition flowed into Klee's later work and especially its heightened preoccupation with rhythm. Klee was, of course, a highly trained musician, so that this rhythmic sensibility had been imbued from an early age, but he was also following a more general cultural interest in rhythm, as found in, for example, the work of writers such as Bergson, Bachelard and others.[63] Many of his paintings are perhaps best thought of as rhythmic scripts that blend the cultural and the natural together through simple repetition, regular alternations, various syncopations built up out of overlaps and irregularities, delicate filigrees, sudden, even brutal, shifts and pointed, even barbed, poundings. Such scripts continue to grow and evolve, being therefore both latent and propulsive. They therefore gain a curious kind of weight (or perhaps weightlessness) which Kudielka likens to the work of gardening and to a consequent model of the careful extension of organism,[64] thereby pointing to the kinds of practices of creation that – because they continue to spread, often using new materials in that process of process – have 'almost all their life before them':[65]

Perhaps one has to pick up the other end of the analogies provided by Klee in his rhythmic compositions: 'Il faut cultiver le jardin'. There is a way of dealing with the creative impulses which is clearly reminiscent of the work of a gardener who cultivates and tills, plants and prunes, cuts and grafts. For instance, the comparison between *Flower Garden* and *Horticulture* shows a certain species of recurrent signs and marks, which have obviously been developed, transplanted and regrouped. The mature Klee seems to come close to artists such as Brancusi and Matisse who introduced the ethos of the gardener into the world of plastic autonomy.[66]

Another model of this type of growth might just as well be music. It is no surprise, then, that Klee often turned to music for a model, referring frequently to musical notation, rhythm and improvisation and to a 'keyboard of colours'.[67] In Klee's work, painting is clearly like the sounds of music,[68] in that it plays with the structures of space and time, attempting to produce consecutive motion and flux[69] that will continue to echo and modulate long after it is first played. This commitment to a musical sense of space and time is taken up much later in the twentieth century by that equally polyphonic philosopher Gilles Deleuze, when he writes about the active texture of the fold, and it is with the new refrains and territories that Deleuze tried to produce out of the work of writers like von Uexküll and painters like Klee that we want to end.

The Passage of Nature

According to Stivale, Deleuze did not like animals much but, nevertheless, he managed to do an awful lot of thinking about them, especially revolving around the notion of territory.[70] In his neo-baroque conception of the spaces of the world, in which turbulent motion and uncertainty hold sway,[71] two things fascinated him about animals. One, drawn from von Uexküll, is their world-making power, often based upon just a very few stimuli, which allows us to think outside our own worlds and into other worlds with their own sensory clatter and hum. These are different lookouts, if you like. The second, drawn partly from Klee's rhythmic appropriations of the world, is their ability to construct territories. For Deleuze, constructing a territory out of the repetition of certain behaviours is fundamental to life – and art. 'In making a territory, it is not merely a matter of defecatory and urinary markings, but also a series of postures (standing/sitting for an animal), a series of colours (that an animal takes on), a song (or chant). These are the three determinants of art: lines, colours, song', says Deleuze, 'art in its pure state'.[72] Animals' territories are marked out by an endless emission of signs which can be thought of as a kind of refrain, gradually building a territory and, at the same time, signifying what is not in that territory, what is out-landish.

Thus we come to the nub of the matter, for in taking on these various sensory territorializations of land and life, Deleuze is able to find the problem that he wanted to answer.

Modern art and modern philosophy converged on a similar problem: both renounced the domain of representation and instead took the conditions of representation as their object. Paul Klee's famous phrase echoes through Deleuze's writings on the arts like a kind of motif: 'not to render the visible, but to render visible'. Twentieth century painting aimed not at the reproduction of visible forms but the presentation of the non-visible forces that act behind or beneath these forms. It attempted to extract from these intensive forces a 'block of sensations', to produce a material capable of 'capturing' these forces in a sensation'.[73]

The block of sensation is itself, of course, a composition of forces, an intensive synthesis of differential relations. But what Deleuze is attempting to get at is a new way of patterning ground that forges a community of intensity out of all manner of refrains, from simple repetitions through complex syncopations to extreme kinds of propulsions. What he particularly wants to give up is the old form–matter relation in favour of a material–force relation that recognizes that,

> Matter is never a simple or homogeneous substance capable of receiving forms, but is made up of intensive and energetic traits that not only make (an) operation possible but continuously alter it (clay is more or less porous, wood is more or less resistant); and forms are never fixed moulds, but are determined by the singularities of the material that impose implicit processes of deformation and transformation (iron melts at high temperatures, marble or wood splits along their veins or fibres). This is the importance of Deleuze's notion of intensity: beyond prepared matter lies an energetic materiality in continuous variation, and beyond fixed form lie qualitative processes of deformation and transformation in continuous development. What becomes essential in modern art, in other words, is no longer the matter–form relation, but the material–force relation. The artist takes a given energetic material composed of intensive traits and singularities, and synthesizes its disparate elements in such a way that it can harness or capture these intensities, what Paul Klee called 'the force of the cosmos'.[74]

The simultaneously calculated and headstrong nature of intensity to be found in both Klee's and Deleuze's notions of propulsive space is where we want to end for now, for it is here that so much exciting work is currently taking place, in the productive paradoxes that arise from experiments in producing a 'discourse' whose aim is exactly to make room for the 'non-discursive':

> The concepts of nature and culture need serious reworking, in a way that expresses the irreducible alterity of the nonhuman in

and through its active connection to the human, and vice versa. It is time that cultural theorists let matter be matter, brains be brains, jellyfish be jellyfish, and culture be nature in irreducible alterity and infinite connection.[75]

Conclusions

All kinds of things can come together in the world and, in that process of encounter and settling down into at least a short-term equilibrium, they can creatively produce new kinds of organization that are greater than the sum of their parts.[76] This is hardly an original observation on the nature of materiality, but its implications are perhaps more far-reaching than is often realized. In this Introduction, we have tried to show the way that people have tried to re-describe materiality as a constantly emergent process, and the way that their work runs on into each other's as a result of a tradition of unusual thinkings, or perhaps flows from thinkings that have yet to separate into disciplines.[77] In particular, we have sought to show the way that (to name but a few) biological, geological, spiritual, magical, cosmological, artistic, poetic and philosophical ideas do not become mixed up but are already producing and nurturing each other in creative and sometimes counter-intuitive ways. In some ways, the unimaginable complexity of interrelationships between ideas, let alone their capacity to mutate and transform in unexpected ways, may leave us bewildered and confounded. Nevertheless, there are several important points to draw from this.

One is that, right at their heart, none of these ideas holds to a clear-cut divide between nature and culture, with one being natural and the other being artificial, and quite rightly too.

> Nature does not make any distinction at all between things that might be called natural and things that might be called artificial. Artifice is fully a part of Nature, since each thing, on the immanent plane of Nature, is defined by the arrangements of motions and affects into which it enters, whether these arrangements are artificial or natural.[78]

Nor, for that matter, does God! Instead, we might be more concerned with the mysterious ways that nature and culture cease to be adequate to the description of 'things'. This is not to obliterate the distinction (or to put 'nature' and 'culture' forever in scare quotes), but to ask about the intense entanglements of human (nature) and nonhuman (culture) that go into making the natural and artificial worlds sensible (without, of course, leaving the body as some artificial arbiter of what is natural, and what is not). It follows that we should see nature as being capable of 'doing' things. Thus, nature is creative: it produces new materials, spiralling out of what seem to be commonplaces.[79] This connects to arguments that take the 'background noise' of nature seriously. There is, simply, more going on in the world than are dreamt of in our models (as Hamlet might have said). In this sense, we are arguing that our analytical intelligences have to be combined with a sense of wonder and awe, as well as with passionate forms of observation. Not because these somehow add to our models of the world, but because in essence they are already implicit in models of the world. This is, very directly, to argue for two sides of a coin: first, that all knowledges are partial and localizable; and, second, that this impels us to make more links between 'things', and not less.

To recognize, and understand, that we are flawed witnesses does not remove the obligation to think about the things that we see. Nor to judge them. We should just be careful when we assume we're right. The third is, to end where we began, with the underlying ontological (and, as we can also see, epistemological) complexity of the world. We may not be able to predict the course of many complex systems, not because we don't know enough but because the world is fundamentally uncertain. The implications of this are profound (whether we're thinking about non-linearity and cause/effect or how to write a science of splendour), but we'd just like to end on this thought. What we need are arts and sciences that can work with rather than against that insight, patterning ground in new ways that are capacious enough to hold to it.

Guide for Readers

In the Preface, we have stated that one aim of this book is to investigate the boundary between nature and culture. One aspect of this engagement with the entangled relationships between nature and culture has involved a questioning of the form in which such findings might be presented (see also our Introduction). A secondary – but no less important – aim, then, is to contribute to fashioning new forms of engagement between the human and the nonhuman worlds. In part, this has been achieved by gathering a variety of writings together, and then, in these different pieces, by demonstrating the (practical, intellectual) consequences of drawing boundaries between nature and culture in different ways. Some contributors have settled on the idea of 'patterns on the ground' to make their point, while others have explored the presumptions built into how we imagine the human and physical aspects of landscapes; yet others have seen the nature in culture and the culture in nature.

We have invited contributors to write as accessibly as possible, for a non-specialist audience. Not all forms of engagement with these issues are accessible, however, and we have allowed some authors to write pieces that exemplify specialist knowledges. We see the value in all the pieces, and even those that you might initially find hard to follow will reap rewards in the end – perhaps especially those pieces that start in unusual places, or trace out arguments that are not always immediately clear. We know, for sure, that readers are not a homogenous group, so certainly there will be no consensus over whether any one piece is accessible or obscure, imaginative or just plain difficult. But this is also true of landscapes!

Taken together, we believe that this book gives readers new resources to conceptualize a world in which the division between nature and culture, between the human and nonhuman, is neither clear-cut nor stable. One way to get a sense of this is to look at different understandings of these nature / culture relationships. So, in the introductory essay, 'Grounding Patterns', we explore some markedly different conceptions of what is natural and cultural, and of what patterns can be discerned, in the world. By approaching this issue through different lenses – indeed, different sciences – we seek to open up new ways to put the world into different grounded patterns. In some ways, we think it might be best to read 'Grounding Patterns' after you have explored a few of the essays. This is mainly because you'll have a better sense of the project overall. There is one more thing we'd like to say about the book as a project, before getting to how you might want to read it. We envision this book as both an intervention and a cultural – a scientific! – tool: that is to say, as something that will be of *use* in thinking about the entanglements of nature and culture.

Below, we offer some ideas about how to use this book. Since this volume is made up of many short essays, in particular we suggest tactics of reading that will enable you to make connections between the various pieces collected together: that is, to make your own patterns out of the ground work conducted here.

1. Of course, the most obvious method is to read the book from beginning to end! In line with our suggestion (in the Preface) that the landscape is understood through forms of 'spatial calculation', we have made an initial distribution and / or division of the essays into three sections. These are Flow, Site and Matter. Each of these sections has its own introduction, which describes its core content. Our sequence of flow, site and matter is deliberate. As a reading strategy, however, we believe that it is possible to work through the sections in any order you want. Within each section we have tried to place elements side by side using two opposing principles. On the one hand, we have juxtaposed essays because we can see some continuity between them, either in terms of content or in terms of argument. On the other, we have sometimes placed essays side by side in order to highlight the contrast between them. In this way, we hope to provoke some surprising thoughts, simply out of the entanglements between essays.

2. Another tactic is simply to flick through and read essays that interest you. Alternative patterns will necessarily emerge as you jump about from essay to essay. As we envisage it, this is entirely within the spirit of the book. As we debated and eventually decided to place one essay alongside another, we were fully aware of a kind of arbitrariness in our choices. In many ways, we believe, this echoes a certain arbitrariness in commonplace divisions and groupings of elements of the landscape: why are cities human? why are mountains natural? More than this, a covert aim of the book is to suggest that there are occluded connections between nature and culture – and we would wish a certain flexibility and openness in bringing these out. There will be connections we have

missed, and patterns we have overlooked. We therefore hope that an 'arbitrary' or 'abstract' approach to the contents of the book might cast new light on *Patterned Ground*.

3. We have provided an index to this book that enables other mappings of the contents, whether based on the titles, contributors or subject matter of the essays. This approach to the book is not to be under-estimated, for it is another way to make connections between essays that may not be apparent at first.

4. We would like to suggest one further tactic – and that is to look only at the images. Many contributors wished to provide illustrations with their pieces. As we negotiated their selections (we were often presented with choices), we began to see that there were certain connections between the images – either in terms of their form or content. We would argue that it is possible to 'read' the book by charting a path based on the images alone. Indeed, we can speculate that the images might be making an argument about the landscape that is somehow only partially connected to the words. This tactic, in some ways, highlights the role of the visual in making patterns out of the ground. We would argue, however, that there is more to the visual than the obvious 'what is seen'. We believe that the images evoke a variety of embodied experiences of the world, and of ways of putting the world together. For these reasons, we point you to the illustrations in the book, for there is design there too.

In this book, we are asking questions both about the patterns we see on the ground and also about the ground on which we choose to see those patterns. We are asking if it is possible to draw on alternative 'spatial calculations' to discern alternative patterns. Of course, this book sits among a wide range of possibilities for putting the world together. There are maps, of course. And travel writing. Stories, lyrical poetry, scientific texts, popular sciences and geographies. Even bio-graphy implies patterns on the ground. Given all these resources, we might not expect the world to add up to a coherent and integrated pattern. And this is one conclusion we might draw from all this. Nevertheless, patterns emerge – like music – out of noise. There might be some abstract justification after all. Even so, you will find that *Patterned Ground* contains impassioned essays. Ways of making sense of the world may be abstract, but they are rarely cold-blooded. By making up the world in this way, we hope that it is clear that it can be made up in other ways – and that at least suggests we can intervene to make the world differently . . . and perhaps even better.

Flow

In the Preface, we suggested that patterns in the landscape could be understood using an analogy with music. The observer would focus his or her attention on the rhythms of the world. These would be made up of the repetition of elements in the landscape, and their pacing in both time and space. The idea that the landscape has rhythm highlights elements that recur, that suggest some kind of uniformity, tempo and periodicity, as well as a certain symmetry – ebb and flow. It also suggests that there is a kind of beauty that arises from this regularity of timing and spacing. It is not an objection to this sensitivity to rhythms to argue that landscapes are also arrhythmic. They can contain unique, irregular, asymmetrical – and ugly – elements that do not seem to add up to a rhythm, or pattern. In this tension between the rhythmic and arrhythmic in patterns in the world there is something that they have in common: motion in time and space. In this section, we have sought to highlight the different ways in which 'things' move through the world, or indeed move the world, however mysteriously.

In fact, motion is absolutely normal: all things move. The things that seem settled in the world only are so because they move slowly. This is as true of continents and mountains as it is of cities and skyscrapers. So, in gathering the pieces in this section under the heading 'Flow', we are really asking questions about what we mean by 'Flow'. The sheer variety of answers to this question is in itself instructive. We start with a conduit, the pipe. Pipes, of course, imply some kind of continuous flow, whether of oil, steam, blood or lava. And we end with airports, as sites that exist only to move people around the world, much like (but quite different from) a port or highway service station. Whether we see flows as continuous or discontinuous depends, to a degree, on the timescale over which the flow is measured. So we include ice sheets in this section. Ice sheets, of course, can move very rapidly, and they also expand and contract with the seasons of the year. Far from being static, ice is constantly on the move.

There are, then, different kinds of 'flow': regular and irregular, continuous and discontinuous, fast and slow. And there are different things 'on the move': history, people, information, ideas, goods, energies, elements and 'things' (very small and very big). And these flows leave different traces on the landscape. It is these traces, or tracks, that provide the focus for all of the pieces gathered here. Of course, some of these traces might not immediately appear to be flows at all, so we hope that there are some surprises in this section. However, there is an argument that we are making as well. It is not so much that 'things' move in time and space, as if time and space were somehow a fixed template within which the world simply is. It is more that these flows – be they walkers on ridges or droplets in a water cycle – produce different forms of time and space: for example, cycles, channels, reversals, folds, scapes, interferences, inversions, convergences, divergences, expanses, details. And patterns.

Pipes

Stephen J. Collier

A visitor to cities in post-Soviet Russia cannot but be struck by the obtrusive presence of pipes. Thick silver heating pipes up to a metre in diameter emerge suddenly from the ground, in the midst of a park or walkway, often two in parallel. Heating pipes and slim yellow gas pipes may run discreetly along fences or buildings, but then leap over driveways and roads, the heating pipes often draped with shreds of insulation or metal wrapping. Hot water (or steam) flows from massive centralized boilers through these pipes, which pass indoors through bathrooms and kitchens on their way to upper storeys and wind through radiators that lack control mechanisms. Residents can adjust indoor temperature only by casting windows open or huddling in the kitchen with the stove-top and oven turned on.

The impositions of indoor temperature and the omnipresence of pipes in the urban landscape can stand for the broader intransigence of pipes amid post-Soviet reform in Russia. Whether through urban services such as heat or through national gas production and distribution systems, pipes materially link geology, geography, industrial activity, human settlements, valuable resources and incredibly expensive but vital services to the Russian population in a network of common fate. Thus, if one wants to understand the human, political, economic and natural geography of Russia today – or, for that matter, the political economy of post-socialist reform – pipes are not a bad place to start.

The system of pipes in Russia was produced by the distinctive Soviet projects of economic coordination and social regulation. Soviet planners sought to organize rational adjust-ments among industrial firms, workers and the distribution of resources required to satisfy daily needs. The integration of national space through infrastructure and utility networks was an essential part of this project.

While there was some integration of national space (through railways and electricity) during the late Tsarist and early Soviet periods, daily life remained little touched. In the first Soviet decades, urban infrastructure was virtually absent in new industrial sites. Significant gains in balanced urbanization came only in the post-Second World War period. Universal social services (health and education) and protections (pensions) were instituted. Ramshackle houses and barracks were replaced by concrete apartment blocks, which were plugged universally and uniformly into national utility infrastructures. No system illustrates more vividly the new spatial and material relationships among infrastructure, human populations and natural resources than that of heat.

Soviet heating systems incorporated two great networks of pipes, both built largely in the last three decades of the Soviet period. First, a national network of gas pipes linked virtually all elements of industry and most urban heating systems with newly exploited Siberian gas deposits, as gas became the most important primary energy source in Russia and provided a critical source of hard currency from exports. Second, heat pipes plugged the apartment blocks that housed most Soviet citizens into massive centralized boiler complexes. The largest of these, the co-generating heat / electric complexes, each serve millions of residents in big cities, while entire small cities are served by single heat-only complexes.

The heating 'apparatus' – not just the material structure, but the entire biological, geological, technical and administrative ensemble – served to 'hard wire' spatial and

3 Heating pipes in Moscow.

institutional relationships between the natural and human worlds, linking a planned distribution of human settlements, climatic conditions (cold), natural resources (gas in remote deposits) and facilities for the production of a basic service (heat). The exigencies of climate and the disposition of natural resources were calibrated in human terms through technical norms that defined the heat requirements – and thus resource requirements – of human beings in given climatic conditions. Further, as the heating apparatus incorporated more and more of the Soviet population, humanism and heat were ever more tightly linked in the moral project of the Soviet state. To indulge an anthropological conceit: in Soviet Russia *anthropos*, as a subject of need, an object of regulation and a bearer of dignity, was a warm body in a cold country.

At one level, these developments were typical both inside and outside the socialist world. Networks of pipes, wires, cables and roads fixed interactions among human settle-

ments, climate, natural resources and physical geography in many twentieth-century projects of national social and economic regulation.[1] But the Russian case was distinct. Nowhere else (not even in the rest of the former socialist bloc) was such a large percentage of a national population linked to a service as vital and as centralized as heat in Russia. Nowhere else did utility networks inscribe a distribution of population and production characterized by such a remark-able preponderance of small and geograph-ically dispersed industrial cities. And nowhere else were these networks so rigidly fixed by an inflexible infrastructure that contained no mechanism for differentiated delivery or user control.

The fixities of the heating apparatus followed logically from the unbending certainties of Soviet social and economic regulation. For post-socialist reformers, however, these certainties and fixities appear as problematic sources of allocative ineffi-ciency. In neo-liberal times, questions are raised that were foreign to Soviet admin-istration. Can the State still treat heat as a social *sine qua non* – delivered without refer-ence to cost – in what is now a quite poor country? Are there not better ways to manage Russia's unique gas resources (the domestic price of which remains a fraction of European prices) than to provide effective cross-subsidies to what have become non-viable cites and non-viable industries? Should inhabitants of such cities move somewhere richer . . . or warmer? Reformers insist, in any case, that the reassuring regularities of a system oriented to normatively defined 'need' must be balanced with the imperatives of allocative efficiency and fiscal balance.

Consequently, reform of the heating apparatus emerged as a crucial element in programmes for 'structural adjustment' in post-Soviet Russia.[2] Reformers propose the creation of a real price mechanism by deregulating tariffs and permitting choice, calculative action and competition at every level in the system: the production and delivery of gas, the production and delivery of heat, and the consumption of heat by end-users. They propose, in short, that the heating apparatus be transformed by automatic adjustments resulting from the formally free action of producers, users and administrators. Normatively defined 'need' would be replaced by 'effective demand' as a central allocative mechanism.

These programmes for reform seem splendid in early summer, or during an economic boom, when cost recovery can rise with personal income and the burden of delivering heat seems less overwhelming. But the material characteristics of the heating apparatus itself, and its intimate entanglement with human needs, mean that in late autumn – or when terms of trade shift – reforms suddenly seem problematic. Because the system is technologically collective – it is impossible to regulate individual use or shut off individual households – the 'pain' of payment discipline is felt collectively, and is thus politically impossible to impose. And the stakes are very high. A shut-off can result (and has indeed resulted) in the destruction of much of a city heating system in 24 hours on a cold winter day. Because heating systems require massive commitments of resources, a transfer of the cost burden to 'users' – in the name of rationalization, fiscal prudence, individual discipline – might undermine the viability of entire cities, particularly the ubiquitous small, dispersed, mono-industrial cities in which 30 million Russians live. Because Russia is *really* cold, the policy on heat is a matter of life and death. As one observer put it, in other countries turning off heat 'might be unpleasant. But in Russia it could be [and has been] fatal'.[3] Finally, because the State can tap domestic energy supplies, it is extraordinarily difficult to forego the material possibility of providing heat. And indeed, despite the poverty of the population and despite the endemic failure of local governments to pay heat producers, shut-offs have been a rare exception.

The continued embeddedness of human need fulfilment in the concrete, inflexible materiality of pipes, boilers and apartment blocks helps us to understand the stuckness of resources and human beings in post-Soviet Russia around the heating apparatus. Thus far, in any case, there has been no great outflow of population from poorer areas, and a large proportion of national resources remains tied up with the spatial pattern of Soviet modernity. Structural adjustment has been forestalled, for now at least, by intransigent infrastructure.

Cities

Eric Sheppard and William S. Lynn

When we think of cosmopolitan cities, we think of places like London or Toronto. Contemporary globalization has opened up cities of all sizes to new and rapidly changing influences from the world at large, including a profound diversification of city populations. Urban landscapes are being transformed by their diversifying populations, whether temporarily, as when London's Caribbean population celebrates their distinct heritage in Notting Hill during Carnival week, or more permanently, as diverse groups of residents in cities such as Toronto seek to express and reinforce their presence by creating distinctive urban neighbourhoods. And then there is Harmony, whose planners are making it animal- and pet-friendly by incorporating, among other things, dog parks, wildlife corridors and pet therapy. Might this new urbanist community in Florida be more cosmopolitan than London?

To answer this question, we need to consider what cosmopolitan might mean. The idea of a cosmopolitan city has received much attention in recent years. It is envisioned as a place where residents are open to and accepting of the world. It draws on the notion that a cosmopolitan person is a 'world citizen', aware and engaged with the well-being of the world lying both within and without his or her place of birth. Cosmopolitanism is an antidote to the xenophobic reactions that too often accompany the diversification of urban populations, and a justification for respecting diversity and pluralism in urban society. In this view, multicultural cities such as London and Toronto provide a vision for a more cosmopolitan future.

But where does the nonhuman world figure in this? Ancient Greek thinkers conceived of the *cosmopolis* as a way of thinking about how humans and the natural world coexist. They made a distinction between *cosmos* and *polis*, what today we might translate as nature and culture, but also believed that universal reason pervaded all natural and human phenomena, pulling the *cosmos* and *polis* into a common orbit of ethical meaning. This was the basis for an ethics that 'followed nature', as well as a 'natural law' binding on all human communities. Together, nature and culture constituted a cosmopolis. Today, some scholars use this idea as an interpretive frame for understanding the ethics of being human in a predominantly nonhuman world, and

4 'Puppy' by Sue Coe.

challenging the privileged placement of any one group or species in ethical-political thought and practice. In this view, the cosmopolis is a prerequisite for exploring what it would mean to have justice and well-being for all members of the mixed human and nonhuman community. It serves as a meta-theory to guide human understanding of our place in the natural world, and as a signifier of particular instances of such understandings.

This latter understanding of the cosmopolis is not widely applied to cities. The neglect of the nonhuman world in discussions of the cosmopolitan city is symptomatic of how cities have long been conceived as in opposition to nature. This opposition between 'civilization' and 'wilderness' is reproduced within the city when we make rigid distinctions between the built form of urban spaces (e.g., buildings, streets) and the parks, gardens and other green spaces that seem more natural. The first is termed 'artificial' and the latter 'natural', and taken together they are believed to be in a state of uneasy coexistence. A dichotomy of this kind neglects the fact that urban open space, no matter how green and full of life, is structured by and predominantly for people. There is, in fact, a continuity between artificial and natural in urban areas. Thus, modern strategies for urban sustainability envisage a rearrangement of the city so that urban and natural landscapes interpenetrate via corridors that promote the health of native plants and wildlife, domestic pets and people. This is the vision held forth in Harmony, Florida.

Coexistence and continuum do not, however, describe fully the relations among people, animals and the rest of nature in urban settings. In some ways, cities and the nonhuman world are inseparable in thought and practice. Take the example of the domestic animals most familiar to urban dwellers, cats and dogs (illus. 4). The house, neighbourhood and city are, for them, the natural environment from which they obtain food and sustenance, and where they deposit their waste. Urban landscapes contain a surprising diversity of wildlife, including songbirds, raptors, ducks, geese, mice, rats, squirrels, rabbits, weasels, minks, racoons, deer and fox. An increasing number of North American metropolitan areas are learning to live with large predators: alligators, coyotes, pumas and bears. Some, like domestic animals, are dependent on the landscapes of cities; others simply treat cities as another ecological niche. Thus cities serve the same function for animals as agricultural and other landscapes do for humans: our urban culture is their nature. Habitats range from backyards to graveyards, isolated rooftop gardens to networks of public and private lands, and resource-poor urban cores to resource-rich wetlands. At smaller scales, even those corners of the urban landscape most transformed by human action may contain vibrant ecologies: spider webs in dark corners, fungi in damp spaces and bacteria everywhere (Stephen J.

Gould's candidate for the most evolutionary successful beings).[1] These are reminders that many successful natural landscapes look nothing like the green spaces that we associate with 'nature' in cities. Some vibrant nonhuman landscapes, such as glaciers, deserts, volcanoes and oceans, are not green at all. From this point of view, both humans and cities are a part of nature, and should be conceived as an important and active component of the ecosystems that we help to generate and live within. In short, our separation of humans, and cities, from the nonhuman world does not hold up to scrutiny.

This does not mean that the distinction between humans and the rest of nature can or should be eliminated. For better or worse, humans have come to dominate the nonhuman world. While some anthropocentrism may be unavoidable in our thinking about the place of humans within nature, society has an asymmetric relationship with, and peculiar responsibility towards, animals and the rest of nature. A cosmopolitan sensibility about urban life should therefore make us sensitive to the moral issues that mediate the connection between nature and culture. And a cosmopolitan city resident should value both its cultural and biological diversity. This entails rejecting invidious exclusions and oppressions based on race, class, gender, ethnicity or species. There are no straightforward or universal ethical principles to guide our conduct. Seeking a cosmopolitan city implies a situated moral understanding of the needs and values of human and nonhuman beings in urban landscapes, and how we respond to those needs and values will be an open question. Cosmopolitan thinking about the landscapes of cities welcomes the diversity of nonhuman life into these landscapes, and poses significant challenges to the processes of urban politics, economics and planning that for so long have shaped the city and separated it from nature.

Ecosystems

Laura Cameron

Vienna: March 1922. Fifty-one-year-old Arthur George Tansley FRS begins analysis with Sigmund Freud. Reporting to a colleague in London, Freud describes him as 'a nice type of the English scientist. It might be a gain to win him over to our science at the loss of botany.'

Freud, the founder of psychoanalysis, Tansley, the founder of British ecology – about to undertake several months of psychoanalytic dialogue. Although undoubtedly it was Tansley's dreams and unconscious that they were exploring, Tansley recalled that theirs was a relationship of equals. With such words as 'dynamic' and 'complex' being key terms for each of these new sciences, we might well wonder how Freudian ideas might have overlapped, interlocked with Tansley's ecology. Did early ecology take patients? Would Tansley's creation of the concept of the 'ecosystem' in 1935 have any connection with psychoanalysis? The answers may not be direct or linear, but the questions become more promising as we approach the couch and begin to trace Tansley's life geography.

Somewhere in London during the First World War, Tansley dreamt that he was standing in a clearing, holding a rifle, surrounded by 'savages'. It was, he would later make very clear, one of the major turning points in his life. From the self-interpretation of this dream came his interest in psychoanalysis and the desire to write the *The New Psychology and its Relation to Life*, a bestseller published in 1920 and reprinted ten times in

5 Sigmund Freud's couch in the study at the Freud Museum, London.

four years. Swamped with requests for advice that he felt little authority to give, the dream journey took a radical turn in 1923 when he resigned his post in the University of Cambridge Botany School to undertake further study with Freud in Vienna.

At Cambridge, Tansley had been sparking interest in psychoanalysis among botany students such as E. P. Farrow by mentioning Freud in his lectures. Farrow, whose own dream led to pioneering studies of rabbit attack on Breckland, an area in Norfolk, would correspond with Freud and publish on self-analysis. Harry Godwin was another student who experimented with Freud's ideas. Later he became, like Tansley, a leader in ecological thought, a president of the British Ecological Society and a founder-member of the Nature Conservancy. Tansley's and Godwin's case study at the nearby National Trust reserve, Wicken Fen, perhaps affords us a glimpse of one of professional ecology's first 'abnormal' patients at a time when dream analysis and vegetational analysis might work hand in hand.

At Wicken Fen, Godwin and Tansley were investigating vegetational succession, the idea (developed in part by the American F. E. Clements) that natural vegetation, when left to itself, progresses from 'pioneer communities', such as fen, to 'climax communities', such as oak woods. In this model, mature normal vegetation existed in isolation from humans, but Tansley was not willing to apply this notion to his beloved English countryside, a landscape that was largely, as he termed it, 'anthropogenic' (produced by man). Instead, they identified deflected successions owing to human cutting activity, 'plagioseres', that deviated from the normal course of vegetational succession. The 'plagioclimax' with its characteristic species could re-enter normality when cutting ceased. But at Wicken Fen, and elsewhere in the British Empire, appropriate management for Tansley did not entail ending human intervention: the new ecological experts aimed to locate and control the deflecting factors that produced the vegetational types that they judged to be desirable.

In 1927 Tansley returned to what Godwin referred to as the 'mother subject' of ecology, accepting a chair at Oxford. But he was still preoccupied with psychology. Introducing a paper for the Magdalen Philosophy Club in 1932 with the admission that he didn't know if he was 'regarded primarily as a biologist or as a psychologist by my fellow members of this club', Tansley proceeded to outline his scheme for approaching the gap between psychology and biology. Here Tansley's concept of mind is an 'interwoven plexus of moving material . . . a more or less ordered system, or rather a system of systems . . . acting and reacting',[1] its ontology bearing intriguing resemblances to the concept of 'ecosystem' that he would describe three years later in a paper entitled 'The Use and Abuse of Vegetational Concepts and Terms'. Tansley had argued in 1920 that all life, including mental life, was dominated by the need to discharge energy, aiming towards an equilibrium state. Like the mind, ecosystems aim towards equilibrium: its components, both organic and inorganic, maintain the system through their interaction. In his understand-

ing of 'positions of equilibrium', Tansley was modern (and Freudian) in stressing how rarely, if ever, the stable state was achieved: 'on the contrary they contain many elements of instability and are very vulnerable to apparently small changes in the factor-complex'.[2]

The master factor – for maintenance and disturbance of nature – was man. 'Regarded as an exceptionally powerful biotic factor which increasingly upsets the equilibrium of pre-existing ecosystems and eventually destroys them, at the same time forming new ones of a very different nature, human activity find its proper place in ecology.'[3] Wicken Fen, for instance, contained abnormal successions created by man, but in the study of ecology – as in Freudian analysis – one could study the disturbed to study mechanisms at work in the normal: '. . . anthropogenic ecosystems differ from those developed independently of man. But the essential formative processes of the vegetation are the same, however the factors initiating them are directed.' Fieldwork here entwined with dreamwork. In his obituary for Freud written for the Royal Society, Tansley wrote:

The great importance of Freud's work on dreams lies in the fact that in it he was able to demonstrate for the first time the principles and mechanisms he had discovered in neurotic minds at work also in a perfectly normal activity of the healthy mind. This led the way to psychological constructions of universal validity.

A dynamic relationship existed between formative concepts in ecology and psychoanalysis, extending to the new role of the ecologist as the expert who might work to stabilize vulnerable systems. The countryside was 'unbalanced' and required special care. If the components of life were inside the ecosystem, so were the seeds of its own destruction.

Rivers

Keith Richards

The Chobe River is a south-bank tributary of the Zambezi River just upstream from the Mambova Rapids, at the eastern end and on the southern edge of the Caprivi Strip between Namibia and Botswana (illus. 6). It appears to be the downstream part of a river that can be traced, with varying modern names, as the Cuando-Mashi-Linyandi-Chobe drainage system. The Chobe has impressive meander loops with scroll-bar patterns, of the kind that large dynamic meandering rivers are often seen to possess (illus. 7).

In 1890 an Anglo-German treaty was signed that was designed to establish the spheres of influence in southern Africa of these two colonial powers. As well as dealing with disputes over Helioland and Zanzibar, the treaty established a boundary between German and British influence in southern Africa, to the west and east respectively. It provided access to the Zambezi for German interests by creating the Caprivi Strip, with a southern boundary following the 18th parallel of latitude eastward '. . . till it reaches the River Chobe; and descends the centre of the main channel of that river to its junction with the Zambezi, where it terminates'. What was the basis on which this broad-brush colonial assertion was made, and what is the nature of the river that was sweepingly determined as a boundary and which, today, is an inevitable source of dispute between Botswana and Namibia?

European explorers in the mid-nineteenth century reported conditions that suggest that this region was then relatively wet, compared to the conditions experienced through much of the twentieth century. Nicholson states that 'Moffatt (1842) and Livingstone (1958) both reported periods of heavy rainfall and expanses of surface water in now drier regions',[1]

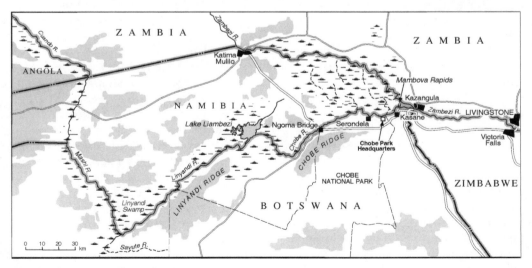

6 The eastern Caprivi, showing the Cuando-Mashi-Linyandi-Chobe drainage system, its junction with the Zambezi above the Mambova Rapids, Lake Liambezi and the Linyandi Swamp.

although she adds that it is unclear whether these conditions were typical. She also writes that 'numerous reports of European explorers in the Lake Ngami region confirm its high stands of the mid-nineteenth century but at the same time suggest it had by then already commenced a long downward trend'.[2] Lake Ngami rose to cover an area of about 800 square kilometres around 1850, and declined progressively from then to cover about 250 square kilometres in 1880, and to dry out completely in the early twentieth century. Of course, Lake Ngami is a long way from the Caprivi Strip. It exists in a similar geological context to the Chobe River, however, and both are equally subject to the vicissitudes of regional climatic variability. These geographical and temporal factors were unknown to the explorers and to the architects of the Anglo-German Treaty, with its assumption of a continuous river.

An understanding of the Cuando-Mashi-Linyandi-Chobe river system is assisted by an examination of three parallel rivers draining to the south-east from the Angolan Highlands: the Okavango, Cuando and Zambezi. Their drainage was disrupted in the Pliocene and early Pleistocene as a result of fault displacements along mainly south-west–north-east alignments, producing north-west facing escarpments across the courses of the three rivers. This rifting is probably a southerly extension of the East African Rift.

The Okavango River has built a low-gradient depositional fan (the Okavango Delta) with its distal end abutting the fault-scrap created by this rifting. As this fan accumulated, the river shifted across its surface, sometimes feeding the Ngami Basin at the south-western corner and at other times the Mababe Basin at the north-eastern corner. The river at the distal end of the fan follows the fault line (the Thamakalane River), draining to both basins, and this can

flow in either direction, depending on the timing of the arrival of seasonal floodwater and on recent tectonic activity. As the Okavango fan accumulated during the Quaternary period, sedimentation at times outstripped movement on the fault, with the result that, especially during wetter periods, the Okavango has formed a lake and spilled over a low col into the Makgadikgadi Basin to the south-east in Botswana, via the Boteti River.

The Cuando is parallel to the Okavango, and also reaches a fault-guided ridge (the Linyandi Ridge), at which point it has created a triangular marshy depositional area, which is fan-shaped like the Okavango Delta. It is, however, much smaller, since the Cuando is a smaller river. The Cuando is diverted by the ridge, into a fan-toe river (the Linyandi). In wet years, Cuando run-off reaches Lake Liambezi to the north-east, but occasionally also overspills the ridge to the south-west.[3] Thus again, flow can occur in both directions at the toe of the Cuando fan. Lake Liambezi was frequently dry during the twentieth century, because the Cuando flow was rarely strong enough to supply evaporation rates in the Linyandi swamps and also maintain flow this far to the north-east.

At the far eastern end of the Caprivi Strip, the larger Zambezi River has been continuously able to maintain its course and its sediment transport through the developing, fault-guided Chobe Ridge at the Mambova Rapids. It has cut through the ridge, resulting in less extensive deposition upstream from the ridge than in the case of the Okavango Delta. However, the Eastern Caprivi also has characteristics echoing those of the Okavango, albeit on a smaller scale. A rough triangle, with vertices at Katima Mulilo, Mambova and Lake Liambezi, defines a low-gradient alluvial fan butting against the fault-guided Chobe Escarpment. There are numerous palaeo-channels on the fan surface to indicate that there have been other alignments of the Zambezi across the fan during the Quaternary. The existence of the Mambova Rapids at the north-eastern corner of the fan precludes the formation of a lake to mirror that in the Mababe Basin on the left-hand corner of the Okavango Delta, but Lake Liambezi in the south-eastern corner mirrors the Okavango's right-hand corner lake, Ngami. The Chobe River drains the toe of the Zambezi fan between Lake Liambezi and the Mambova Rapids, just like the Thamakalane at the foot of the Okavango, and the Linyandi at the foot of the Cuando (Linyandi) fan.

The meander bends of the Chobe River (illus. 7) are much larger than would be expected for the maximum discharges carried by the river today (the Chobe bankfull discharges are of the order of 400–500 m^{3}s^{-1}, while the meander bends are more appropriately scaled to a discharge five or six times larger than this, and closer to that of the Zambezi River). It therefore seems probable that the Chobe occupies a (palaeo) channel that was originally created by the Zambezi in an earlier route across its fan. In fact, the Chobe is more reliant on the Zambezi than simply inheriting its channel. Every year, when the Zambezi floods, the floodwaters overspill the eastern Caprivi fan, and the people of this region of low gradients and marshy conditions migrate to the higher points (usually fossil sand-dunes). When this happens in March, water from the Zambezi flows *up* the Chobe, past Ngoma Bridge, and occasionally reaches Lake Liambezi. Only when the floodwater levels in the Zambezi decrease in May can the water in the Chobe drain back *down* the river. The Chobe, therefore, is a reversible river, because its gradient is very low, and the water surface slopes that drive the flow change direction seasonally.

7 A meander bend on the Chobe River at Serondela; flow is towards the camera, and the Chobe Ridge is to the top of the photograph, with a terrace at its foot at the neck of the bend.

The Chobe River is thus part of an ephemeral drainage system. Its upstream Linyandi reach was dry for many kilometres during long periods of the twentieth century; its hydrology has always been strongly dependent on inputs from the Zambezi; its channel is inherited from the Zambezi; and its floodwater reverses its flow direction seasonally. It is hardly surprising that Namibia and Botswana have had to resort to the International Court of Justice to resolve a dispute about one tiny part (Kasikili Island, near Kasane) of a boundary drawn in such cavalier and imperial fashion along a 'river' that can hardly be said to live up to the normal definition of that term.[4] The case of the Chobe River therefore poses many questions. Is it a river, in the conventional sense of that term? Was it reasonable of the 1890 Treaty to treat it as one? Is it reasonable for a modern interpretation of that treaty to ignore today's scientific understanding of the feature? Answers might help with clarification of the boundary along the rest of the 'river', given that the feature is ephemeral and frequently indistinct, and that Botswana's maps explicitly refer to the boundary as 'undefined'.

Ridges

Yvonne Rydin

Scene: the English Lake District. The car has just struggled up a steep incline to a car park with a terrific view. The car park is situated on a 'raise', the brow of the pass that carries the road between two of the area's hilly 'fells'. To the east and north-west, the land falls away so that the eye can readily pass over vistas of green, grey and orange ranges. In the car park, people are sitting in folding chairs by their cars, enjoying the view and a cup of tea or coffee from a flask. Children are racing around. A coach pulls up and unloads its cargo of some forty overseas tourists. They all dutifully take pictures with their cameras, gasp admiringly and get back into the coach, all within about ten minutes. And alongside other vehicles stand other people – usually on one leg – putting their boots on and preparing for a walk up the fells that rise to the north and south-west of the car park. For this car park offers access onto two of the spectacu-lar higher peaks of the Lake District. Having driven up to a height of some 350 metres, paths made clear by decades of walkers' feet lead up the hillside to peaks of more than 700 metres. And, more enticing for the walker, from these peaks lead paths along ridges. These paths may climb and fall but the adjoining land is never higher than the path. Views are therefore continuously available to left and right (weather permit-ting) and the walker is rarely forced into descents. This follows the advice of Alfred Wainwright – the Cumbrian local authority officer whose hand-written and hand-drawn walking guides have been indispensable to generations of Lake District walkers – always to choose a walk where height, once gained, is never given up.

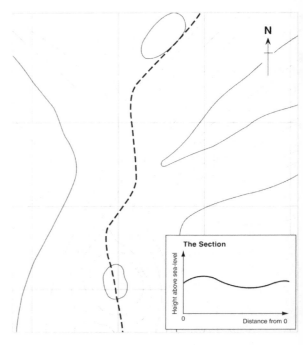

8 The Map and The Section.

The physical features of such a ridge are immediately apparent on any Ordnance Survey map, that other indispensable item for the walker. A mass of contour lines will run parallel to the ridge on both sides for significant lengths, before crossing the line of the ridge to indicate a change of level and then – with luck – turning parallel again. Even where contour lines cross the ridgeline, they will usually do so with gaps between the lines indicating shallow inclines. The pattern of contour lines indicates the massing and lifting of rock strata that form the geological reality of ridges. But they are not that reality, only one way of imposing a perceptual order. In the case of os maps, this is an order defined by the measurement of height by the contour lines and of orthogonal distance by the grid lines (see illus. 8). There are, however, different ways of 'taking a line for a walk' along a ridge. Illustration 8 also provides a single-line definition of the ridge as section. This plots the height of the ridge against the distance from some given point. The purpose of such a section is to give an indication of the effort involved in walking the ridge, something that on an os map can be worked out only by close attention to contour lines. Such sections are commonly found in guides to walking, and they raise the interesting question of the exact purpose of such engagement with the physicality of the ridge.

Why walk along ridges? Why is there a need to know about the exact rise and fall of a ridge path? Insofar as walking is about bodily effort and exercise, isn't the effort of climbing and descending to be welcomed? There are many sides to the pleasure gained from the physical effort of walking and the impact on the body: the aching muscles, the breathlessness, the working up of a sweat. The physical sensations are, within limits, directly pleasurable. But this is supplemented by the moral currency of taking exercise, doing something that is healthy and worthwhile. Perhaps there is the pleasure of punishment involved in such morality. And then there is the sense that, by physically traversing the land, one is making the engagement with nature uniquely one's own. The fell may be there for everyone to walk, but *this* walk, *this* effort is mine alone.

Ridges as a means of traversing the fells *are* about physical effort, as the machismo of any walkers' shop or 'where did you walk?' conversation demonstrates. But that effort is also measured in relation to the other purpose of leisure walking. For this is not the forced traverse of rural residents without horses or cars, as depicted, for example, by Thomas Hardy, when Tess Durbeyfield dons her boots to walk the miles from farm to farm and house to house. Rather, in leisure walking the purpose is the walk itself and not the destination alone. And the signifier of the value of a walk is the view, the 'gaze', the visual engagement with the countryside. This is why ridges are so prized by walkers, since they combine the

effort of physical traverse (but not too much effort) with the assurance of views throughout the walk. The peaks are achieved, so that the walker can confirm that they 'went up' this or that summit and saw the view from the highest and, therefore, 'best' vantage point. But the way itself has a purpose as a high-level climb (and not therefore easily accessible) and one that offers, on a continuous basis, the romantic experience of the vista: fells, mountains and dales layering in to the distance.

The romance of walking is doubly captured in the cover of a fairly typical tourist guide, *Illustrated Walks and Drives in the Lake District: A Pitkin Guide* (1990), reproduced in schematic form in illustration 9. In the foreground a couple set off on a path that leads along a ridgeline to a peak. They are hand in hand and, in the original, have their dog with them. On top of the peak can just be seen four people outlined against the sky. But the couple are distanced from this group, taking the walk together alone. Behind them are the silhouetted layers of receding peaks and ridges. The view, the traverse and the attainment of the peak are all captured in this image. The meaning of the ridge is encapsulated in these combinations

9 The Walk.

of the romantic and the physical, the vista and the experience of walking, the relationship of the couple and the relationship with the ridge. Meanwhile, in the car park, others merely watch.

Cliffs

Kevin Howett

Climbing on cliffs has been variously, through time and all over the world, vital for survival (typified today by the Wadi Rum climbs of the Bedouin Huweitat tribe), a rite of passage (such as those of the Gaelic inhabitants of the Scottish islands of St Kilda), a place of worship (best represented by the Australian Aboriginal peoples' regard for Uluru) and a place of residence. Today climbing is a type of recreation and sport, but it owes more to its ancient roots than do other sports. And with its dance-like quality, it is more of an art form than a sport.

The rock is a canvas painted by the fingers, thumbs and toes of the climber as they brush across the surface, sometimes flowing, sometimes staccato – and even stationary for long periods. Sometimes the climber brushes up and down the same piece of rock, over and over again, in order that the body may learn every intimate detail of the surface and the multitude of body movements needed to grip them, all the while discovering a match between what animate nature has provided and the physical abilities of the organic. This 'learning through mental imprinting' is how climbers transcend the limitations of both mediums.

Sometimes the whole body leans against the rock, the canvas and artist sensuously entwined. At those times, when the body and the rock forget each other, the canvas can scrape away the skin to paint itself red from the very fibre of the brush, changing the relationship from the excitement of infatuation to the agony and pain of rejection.

A climber's nirvana lies in a period of calm, when the mind synchronizes perfectly not only with the body but with that of the unknown canvas stretching above. All three become one as the climber enters 'the zone', a place where doubts do not exist, where movement is subconscious and the paucity of holds becomes immaterial. Such times hide great climbers.

On the other hand, the Holy Grail of climbing lies in a moment of suspended activity. A time when the hairs of the brush may only whisper their turbulence against the rock as they jump beyond the climber's reach. To be able to defy both gravity and an area of rock lacking any reasonable holds, by forcing the body to operate in the vacuous 'dead point' of a vertical leap, would appear to be outside the laws of known physics. But one climber has come very close.

What happens in every second of every climb is dictated by the rock and its environment, its geological past and its present ecosystems; from birth to scouring weather, to colonization by plant or animal. And just as every climber is predisposed to different abilities by inherited genetics, then so too is every 'climb' and every rock type.

Granite, forged by violent force, offers up vertical cracks. To climb such fissures involves the hands, feet and torso aligned in symmetry. Finger strength is redundant as muscles, bones and ligaments are torqued to provide outward force on the sides of the crack, enough to carry the weight of the hanging climber.

Schist appears to the uninitiated as more accommodating, since it is covered in holds, but they invariably slope the wrong way for vertical climbing. Success is found by forcing the body to twist feet high to the side, gecko-like, in order to balance; straining the back muscles and quickly forcing an oxygen debt upon the forearms as in no other medium.

Sandstone feels like a young rock that is still being formed. It has a surface texture that disintegrates in single grains under one's fingertips. But it is a rock designed for vertical ballet. Flowing, instantaneous and often gymnastic movements link small features: flat holds, one-digit pockets, ladders of fingernail-deep fragile flakes, and rounded arêtes that have to be squeezed by fingers and thumb or ridden *à cheval*. Ebb and flow, encapsulated in its very formation, reappear in its climbing.

In contrast, *Lewisian gneiss* can be regarded as a thinking climber's rock. Tiny, partially useless holds are hidden in a sea of silver-grey ripples offering up a vertical puzzle. Movement is made under duress after strenuous positions must be held while the fingers Braille the rock ahead and the brain analyses the pattern. This is an ancient rock that plays a strategic game, with stamina and longevity being vital skills to climb it.

But all rock climbing styles are eclipsed by a loose rock such as *shale*. Heightened balance and increased fear are its legacy. Every hold must be caressed; every movement considered and rehearsed in the mind before being executed. Here, climber and rock can share the same timescale.

The wildlife of the cliff is as important as its geology to the success of a climb. Lichens of all shades of colour, shapes and type cover most rocks. Some are so smooth that they appear to be the rock itself and so offer no obstacle, except when wet. Some form a gravel on the vertical surface that offers the same lack of stability for a climber's rock shoe as scree at the base of a mountain. Others are beards, blanketing the rock in a miniature forest, hiding the climb's secrets,

10 Climbing on the Lewisian gneiss cliffs on the island of Mingulay, Outer Hebrides, Scotland.

its holds and its character. Mosses cling to the softer rocks that accept them. Their 'roots' erode the surface and form tiny dimples – perfect for finger ends once their tenuous grip has been forsaken by pecking bills in search of grubs.

Insect life abounds. Rock shrimps hide in cracks. They spew out across the surface when disturbed, and make the rock come alive in waves. Bats too spend time within rock, like a climber's jammed hand, and bird's nests cling to the undersides of roofs; the wren's ball of moss camouflaged as a solution pocket.

The beauty of these communities are of great importance in the mind of a climber in a heightened state of awareness. Instances are recorded where climbers executing difficult moves, in life-threatening situations, have had to choose between standing on and killing a small insect alighted on a crucial foothold, or fall. Such dilemmas elicit Taoist concern.

Combine all these elements of the cliff, then remove the modern trappings of safety (rope, harness, protection devices), as well as the 'confidant' climbing partner, and a climber will experience the ultimate commitment to the nature of the rock. Climbing solo hibernates time itself, ignores preconceptions and allows the climber to travel over frozen millennia with the ease of a fly on the ceiling. But the higher rewards for success bring greater penalties too. Failure to marry the patterns of both rock and mind rarely allows a second chance.

Scree

Martin Kirkbride

A rockfall may involve the dislodgement and fall of a single rock particle, or it may involve the sudden collapse of a huge mass of rock that breaks on impact into a vast number of smaller pieces which continue to bounce, roll, and slide downslope before friction and decreasing gradient brings them to a halt.[1]

Scree slopes are the signs of a decaying mountain. They are the residue of erosion that accumulates on the flanks of the crumbling rock mass, eventually to bury the mountainsides that provided the rock-fall. Wilderness cliché has it that mountain summits are the timeless, soaring pinnacles of the landscape's resistance to the forces of nature. But really they're just provisional: the temporary survivors, opened up by dilation

and exposed to the onslaught of frost, wind and rain. They're just the bits that haven't fallen down yet.

. . . many authors have recorded a general increase in clast size with distance down-slope from the source rockwall. Such fall sorting has been explained in terms of the generally greater kinetic energy of larger clasts, though Statham . . . interpreted this phenomenon in terms of higher frictional losses for smaller clasts. Once fall sorting has been established, however, it tends to be self-perpetuating, as the talus acts as a kind of sieve with individual clasts tending to settle amongst others of similar calibre.[2]

An active scree is a population, a dynamic and evolving society, a lithopolis if you like. Its citizen clasts organize themselves into groups according to similar characteristics. The population is vertically and cross-stratified. Clasts rolling across the scree rarely settle where the surface clasts are significantly smaller. They move on to arrive at a place where the interstices are large enough to absorb them into the particle network: they settle with like kind. Big clasts with more energy go further. Small ones nestle down among the big ones and are able to move only when their more massive neighbours mobilize. On occasions, whole areas shift and migrate, shuffling and chattering, never moving in the same way but always keeping together. Some groups burst forward then pile up from the base upwards, shearing in thin layers as they slow, dilating en masse then locking into a rigid framework. Yet others speed overhead in large bounces, sending puffs of dust into the air on impact. Gathering momentum, an accelerating clast will roll, wobbling increasingly on its long axis until it sits up in a vertical plane and begins to skip then leap as it spins, sometimes down the fall line, more often arcing off to left or right. Such delights of motion usually terminate explosively among the immovably massive boulders bordering the toe slope. Among the fractured debris one's senses are roused by the glint of cleaved crystal faces and boulder edges razor-like to the touch. The smell of the lithopolis is of moist lichen and dry rock flour, where the pungent cordite of rock-fall impact stings the nostrils and encourages a watchful eye that looks nervously upwards in the hope that there'll be no sharp report, no volley of shots until you're on the corrie floor and well out of range.

Two models of rockfall talus accumulation have been proposed to account for this consistent gradient. The traditional view is that this angle represents the *angle of repose* of coarse talus material, in other words the gradient at which accumulating talus comes to rest after dry avalanching. This interpretation implies that debris is periodically redistributed over the surface of a talus by shallow debris slides.[3]

Long screes possess an almost alarming geometry of form, brought out by the pervasive irregularity and cragginess of their surroundings, and by the absence of smooth things in the mountain landscape. Screes drape the lower slopes in long sweeps and regular aprons, often tapering upwards into gullies seaming the cliff. The roughness of their surface texture, apparent at close acquaintance, at distance gives way to unbroken diagonals and gentle concavities. They are a constant and recognizable form, even a landmark – Wastwater Screes, Great Hell Gate, The Great Stone Shoot and the eerie voices of the quartzite on Foinaven.

Scrambling up fresh scree at the angle of repose isn't really on. A person's weight is just

11 An Stac screes, Isle of Skye, Scotland.

enough to overload the surface layer and set it in motion. At first it seems that just a few clasts have been dislodged. But the slight slippage of a few undermines the support of the others. Before long, the climber is treading water on a clattering slope, resignedly observing the upper edge of the mobilizing layer retreat upslope as boots stumble around for a firm footing, shins collecting bruises and hands grazes. Gutters of coarser bedded-down blocks, where coalescent cones overlap, are routes that avoid the chattering classes and provide as light and delicate an ascent as heart and lungs allow. There is something rather satisfying about climbing unstable scree without setting it in motion: a perverse (and often premature) feeling that one has somehow outwitted nature. In descent, the opposite rules apply. The ankle-twisting coarse debris won't run, but one can dig one's heels into the fine grey streams and balance gracefully down the moving walkway, keeping just enough momentum to stay ahead of the dislodged clasts, and now and then making a smart jump sideways to avoid a jam around a half-buried boulder.

In the warmer climates of the post-glacial period there are parts of the world where the migration of rocks from cliff to scree slopes has almost ceased. The winter cold is no longer of the penetrative intensity needed to disintegrate the rock mass. The scarred patchworks of frost-riven rock faces have dulled to a uniform grey-brown. Inactivity leads to stability. Cutting off the supply to the top of the screes means that the gradient cannot be quite sustained at an angle to generate the downslope migration. The living, shifting surface has settled, consolidated and choked on the accumulated silt washed and blown into the interstices. The raw white scars of impacts have tarnished to softer greys, tans and rusty browns. New colonizers take advantage in the form of lichens and mosses, and later sedge, heather and bilberry. The suffocating soil blanket masks the palimpsest of a former more energetic time.

Drifts

Deborah Parsons

To drift is to move passively, aimlessly or idly. It is also to move without purpose or foreseen direction, paying little attention to the limits of time or to divisions of space. Drifting ignores the ordering and intentionality of space, and instead makes space a fluid entity, interdependent with the flux and flow of the individuals that move through it. Drifting can take place in many states – boredom, idleness, daydream, contemplation, intoxication, depression – and indeed is perhaps facilitated by such, but the drifter *experiences space* physically and sensually, subordinating his or her conscious mind to the un-choreographed movements and sensations of the body.

Within critical thinking on the city, drifting has been appropriated as a specifi-cally metropolitan practice, adapted to the

tempo and conditions of the city and epi-tomized by the idle wandering of that arche-typal urban walker the *flâneur* (in all his or her many guises). Drifting the asphalt is central to a romanticism of the street found in the spleen of Charles Baudelaire, the cultural rag-picking of Walter Benjamin, the modern mythologies of the Surrealists, the rebellious *dérives* of the Situationists, and the exhilaration or fascinating repulsion of the city for innumerable poets, novelists and artists across the nineteenth and twentieth centuries. The *flâneur* fetishizes the practice of drifting, surrendering to the erotics of the urban imaginary. For this tradition of urban thought, it is the experience of drifting that provides access to the desperately desired 'chance encounter', 'heightened moment' or 'profane illumination'.

By contrast, drift is also what has been attacked by the anti-urban idealism of a concurrent history of city planning and classification. The drifting body contradicts the ordered formation of social and geo-graphical space. In the studies of nineteenth-century observers, the urban nomad was the focus of Victorian fears of both the body and the city, threatening a contagion that despite encyclopaedic attempts at categorization and regulation could not be fixed on the social and topographical map. Through the putrid miasma of the poor or the syphilitic disease of the prostitute, the demon 'other' of the urban underworld refused containment and invaded the bourgeois drawing room. The response was urban reform and a call for a sanitized, decongested, rationalized city. When Le Corbusier advocated the killing of the street, it was the chaotic, un-segregated multiplicity of the city, and the directionless, functionless, purposeless nature of drift, that he attacked.[1]

Pleasure and transgression, as Roland Barthes suggests, are the defining qualities of drift.[2] The drifter does not respect the city of the urban planner, revelling instead in the caprice and desire invoked by the rhythms of the street. Yet drifting is also by definition passive, not so much a random act as an instinctive or acquiescent response to stimuli. The drifter gives up will-power to the city, allowing himself (or herself) to move according to its forces of effect and affect. To what degree can we read such unintentional patterns of pedestrian wandering, the poetics of drifting, as a politics of transgression? Moreover, as consumer culture increasingly commodifies leisured urbanity, facilitated by the renaissance of heterotopic public space in civic planning, is drift not being co-opted as an important part of the design? The legitimated drifting encouraged by the squares, arcades and pedestrianized streets of the gentrified city is that of the modern *flâneur*; pleasure separated off from transgression.

A common consensus in urban theory argues that contemporary regeneration, and the security schemes that accompany it, have tamed the streets of the city centre into a blandly homogeneous and anodyne locale for the middle classes, ultimately stifling their role as a democratic public space of freedom and diversity. Based in a nostalgic romanticizing of the street's potential for political expression and struggle, at its most cynical this approach posits the concept of a postmodern 'fortress city' (although Haussmann's Paris is a manifest contradiction of the view that urban control is a contemporary phenomenon), where street life is regulated by various forms of more or less explicit surveillance in the name of public safety.[3] In this apocalyptic vision of a disciplinary urban society, the potential of public space for social and political transgression has been erased, either destroyed or appropriated by totalitarian planning. While it is important to be aware that the restructuring of urban

12 Piccadilly Arcade, New Street, Birmingham.

space increasingly involves systems for the prescription and regulation of behaviour, we should also recognize that cities nevertheless continue to be deeply ambiguous and mutable environments. They may be insignificant examples, but on a hot summer's day the attraction of a fountain for impromptu paddling, of fresh green turf as a lunch-time picnic site, or a flat stone sculpture for a moment of sunbathing, will usually outweigh any scruples occasioned by the 'NO ENTRY', 'DO NOT WALK' OR 'DO NOT TOUCH' signs that invariably accompany them. Groups and individuals within the city constantly manipulate and adapt the urban blueprint, using space in improvised and unpredictable ways. For the city's multitude of heterogeneous users, the street takes on any number of multiple meanings, and the pull or push of emotional ambience, of memories, desires, prejudices, anxieties and whims, may often act as stronger forces than the marketing or surveillance strategies of contemporary commercial culture.

Michel de Certeau argues that the casual wanderings of a myriad urban pedestrians signal a reappropriation of city space.[4] Faced with the contingencies of the street rather than a panorama devised by the urban planner or cartographer, pedestrianism involves making detours, retracing steps, lingering – drifting. Drifting thus becomes part of an everyday contestation of governed, panoptic space, resisting control exactly because it refuses to be located. When we drift, our relationship to the space of the street becomes purposeless, haphazard and indecisive, and we practise a placelessness antithetical to any ordered and prescriptive map. We are attuned to the complex psychodynamics of the city, the personal and local myths and connotations that form alternative spatial patterns from the subjective and vernacular rhythms of the everyday. In the contemporary moment of new homogenizing urban narratives, pervaded by gloomy pronouncements on the globalist commodification, CCTV systems, and social and cultural differentiation of our carefully manufactured simulacra of urbanity, the drifting body eludes regulation. Through drifting we pattern the city landscape according to the traces of its collective daydreams.

Virtual Space

Ken Hillis

Consider Microsoft's slogan 'Where do you want to go today?', a corporate seduction on its way to becoming a proverb. Microsoft invites you to 'enter' networked virtual space via the logic of Microsoft's IE browser. The implicit promise is that space, time and your body dissolve upon entering the virtual space that IE manifests, that you *do* travel the earth, that virtual experiences are equivalent to concrete realities. *You*, the subject of Microsoft's address, are positioned as bodyless. Encouraged to accept non-being as a mode of self-identification, you are asked to believe that there is an *actuality* to the virtual space you enter. Virtual space, therefore,

raises complex questions. What are the implications for bodies 'there'? How do virtual spaces complicate the ways that people perceive and judge their experiences of existence? And how might corporate interests dovetail with the seeming ability of virtual space to reposition relationships among 'the real', 'the virtual' and 'the actual'?

The meanings of 'real', 'virtual' and 'actual' are over-determined: any move towards definitional closure is suspect. Situating the terms, however, is essential. One understanding of virtuality and reality, partly grounded in historical understandings, partly in hype-propelling technologies such as Virtual Reality, *sees* the virtual space that virtual technologies manifest as running parallel to and separate from material reality. This binary metaphysics is asserted in films such as *The Matrix* or *The Thirteenth Floor*, and by academic theorization that virtual space and simulation constitute a wholly different plane from material reality. Other critics, such as Rob Shields, argue, however, that the virtual – neither fully material nor fully abstract – contains aspects of the real *and* the ideal.[1] Shields also suggests that the *actual* – a site equally open to material facts and cultural truths – refers to both the real and the virtual.

Pierre Lévy, whose work redefines the actual to render it more consonant with the *experiences* that virtual technologies make possible, argues that the virtual–real dichotomy is unproductive.[2] Rather, he argues, the actual (or, what is evident and manifest) and the virtual (or, what remains latent and not yet manifest) engage in a mutually productive networked relationship. Theories such as Lévy's arise just as the virtual loses its shiny status of the new – precisely when actuality emerges as a needed concept to suture the virtual to the real. And the remainder of this entry illustrates how a virtual technology, one that manifests the

13 Giant sign at Zion Canyon.

logics of actuality and the commodification of experience, sunders modern understandings that distinguish between 'real' and 'virtual'.

The photograph (illus. 13), taken at the Zion National Park in Utah, promotes a form of virtual space connected to an intense personal experience of quasi-fantastical visual spectacle and proprioceptive disorientation. Here the IMAX technology of experience is advertised: 'You have seen the park, now experience it.' I will now consider the relationships among virtual technologies, actuality, utopian theory and capital's globalizing processes. The sign's message critiques embodied perception; seeing isn't enough – technology's sensorium is better than our own, and only it can 'really' convey the canyon's majesty.

At Zion Canyon consumers are promised something better than their non-mediated perception of the park. Applying Lévy's argument to the Cinemax Theatre's claim, patrons extend themselves 'between' things clearly situated in space *and* between events in time. Visitors, by handing over a sense of themselves to visual representation, imaginatively engage with the disembodied point of view that the technology makes available to sensation – either by interpellating their points of view with footage shot from helicopters, or by identifying with the virtual

space that lets them experience hanging from a 610-metre-high cliff. The promise of a collapse of time is also on offer as the experience promotes 'discovering Zion Canyon with Mormon pioneers'. Privileging mediated experience over embodied perception, IMAX and its hype together undermine the status of embodied perception; they suggest that it is handicapped and, like the embodied present, standing in the way of progress. One of the Theatre's promotional web pages asserts that the giant IMAX screen 'leaves heads and hearts spinning with painfully spectacular views and images of unsurpassed clarity and impact. This ain't no walk in the park!'[3] Here commodification unleashes the virtual's latency, pushing it toward actualization. 'Ain't no walk in the park!' highlights the Theatre's subverting of more embodied forms of existence and the patterns they leave on the ground in favour of commodification of experience; unmediated embodiment is seemingly in the way of machine-dependent corporate versions of actualization or becoming. At the scale of individual reception, then, the giant sign suggests that these immersive technologies of light both can and should replace less commodified and more actively embodied perceptions of the world, because the latter are less vivid than those that virtual technologies such as IMAX and their promoters can now provide. Indeed, this use of virtuality works to promote acceptance that techno logically dependent illusion somehow offers a better life than the material world and the necessarily embodied and supposedly failed politics of this earthly plane. Yet unthinking acceptance of these corporate assertions courts the risk of altering, even reducing, the meaning of humanity. For, recalling the exalted claims of the promoters that 'this ain't no walk in the park', if existence is a standing in place, then so too is walking the earth's places unmediated by technologies such as IMAX.

The Zion Canyon Theatre promotes *viewing* the increasingly distant nonhuman parts of the natural world as inferior to their trademarked and branded simulations. And this example of the dynamic of actuality also reflects a cultural yearning for virtual technologies to address the consequences of a belief that our senses and the codes that structure communication together restrict us from true unmediated perception, and that the promised sensory augmentation of virtual technology, operating as a kind of prosthesis, finally can do away with this long-standing impediment to 'true knowledge'. IMAX claims its virtual experience is more direct, more real, more true. Regrettably for technotopians, however – and with unintended irony – IMAX delivers its product through super-saturating the 'same old' supposedly faulty senses of consumers.

Today, companies deliver epiphanies and transcendence daily, and the commodification of actuality points to the real power of the virtual in global systems. The resurgence of actuality as a concept heralds the power of the virtual more clearly precisely when capital benefits from revealing its own structural underpinnings. The IMAX sign promotes belief that mimesis and the sympathetic magic it connotes together offer viewers greater sensual rewards than the material landscapes that virtual space now upstages. From Microsoft to IMAX – by virtue of actuality – thy will be done.

Post Offices

David Matless

Post offices are not The Post Office. That modern organization of governmental intelligence, postal communication, welfare payment, film production and mail delivery stretches beyond this entry. Literary history has been recast as 'an epoch of the postal system',[1] but that too is not our concern. Post offices are something else, something less and something more, pieces of commercial public space through which letters and money and knowledge pass but which serve purposes beyond their walls. As the public sector retreats from public space, as moves to privatize persist, as the UK Post Office is rebranded as 'Consignia' (and then, realizing its public folly, attempts to rebrand the unbrandable back again), these little pieces of the State linger in every city, town and suburb and many villages, even in hamlets. That these are buildings in a landscape is of note, whether that landscape is of fields and lanes or streets and more streets. Political outcry over moves to close rural post offices indicates a powerful symbolic social economy. The public geography of post offices is an inheritance not to be taken or shaken lightly.

Some post offices occupy buildings of their own; some shelter in small shops, sub-postmasters mixing business to survive. The post office counter offers stamps, envelopes, etc. – the full works for letter writing, with letterboxes inside and out – and the facilities for individual interaction with the state. Screens protect staff, the relationship of citizen and State transparent and secure. Bills may be paid, benefits and pensions drawn, licences obtained.

Between 1934 and 1943 the US Treasury Section of Painting and Sculpture commissioned murals for post offices across America, New Deal art with a democratic geography. Scenes of America appeared in buildings in an institution that stretched from coast to coast, a continental public art in distinctly modern style, giving significance to and drawing significance from its post office setting:

Milestones in American Transportation
(Towson, Maryland)

Cheese Making
(Plymouth, Wisconsin)

Indian Pony Round
(Safford, Arizona)

Men and Wheat
(Seneca, Kansas)

The Return of Annie Oakley
(Nutley, New Jersey)

Early Spanish Caballeros
(Los Banos, California)

First Pulpit in Granville
(Granville, Ohio)

The Fertile Land Remembers
(Worland, Wyoming)

Mural America painted in a common space, with all the ideological and aesthetic tensions that public art may carry.[2]

Public space and the arts of living within it shift. Many people in the UK never visit a post office. There are other ways to pay, draw and validate: by phone, by direct debit, by e-mail, by post. Stamps are sold by shops. The post office, especially the smaller urban post office occupying a building of its own, can become the resort of the elderly and the poor, those with neither facility nor inclination to debit direct. Counter screens are reinforced. Queuing continues in the digital age, mono-

tonous with occasional pleasures. On pension day an elderly queue forms early on the pavement, weekly social meetings before money. Waiting does not involve being put on solitary hold with Bach in a far-off call centre.

Political outcry over closure taps nostalgia for an earlier, seemingly public age; values, depending on one's outlook, of service, state authority, geographic democracy whereby the country is united through a network that does not discriminate and makes everywhere equal at least for the standard price of a stamp. Places fit for murals in one country, royal insignia in another. Royal heads on stamps are matched by initials on post boxes; Victoria still etched in the landscape, the Georges and an Edward too. Postboxes work beyond monarchical life.

Nostalgia accrues to the figure of the rural postman moving beyond boxes and offices and touching all homes. The international popularity of the animated Postman Pat attests to such appeal, for children and adults alike. An earlier human celebrity provides a more cautionary tale. Allan Smethurst (1927–2000), a Norfolk postman, gave up the mail for pop fame. Smethurst's self-penned Norfolk folk songs featured on the BBC from the late 1950s: 'The Singing Postman' was born. Who now recalls 'Oi Can't Git a Noice Loaf a Bread' or the classic lifeboat number 'Hev The Bottum Dropped Owt'? Sleeve notes presented Smethurst as an 'early-rising public benefactor' with a 'homespun' philosophy and 'determined bachelor' status. The man mixed nostalgia, misery, regret, pathos, misogyny, occasional sardonic wit and the faintly bizarre. Limited stardom and a Parlophone contract followed the 1965 hit, 'Hev Yew Gotta Loight, Boy?'. Smethurst reached number seven in the charts:

My days with the post bag were numbered by the news that the Windmill Theatre,

Great Yarmouth, were interested in booking me for the summer season and in 1965 I left the Post Office for good . . . glimpsing the big time. I also travelled around Norfolk and Suffolk, visiting lots of delightful towns and villages. I would never have been able to see them if I had stayed a postman.[3]

One postman gains the big time geographic reach of the Post Office. Subsequent EPS and LPS ('Second Delivery', 'Recorded Delivery', 'Please Mr Postman'), covered with Smethurst on his bike and in uniform, reached an ever more specialist market. Local entrenchment and painful shyness led The Singing Postman to the bottle, a Cleethorpes court appearance in 1976 following a chip-pan incident being a rare public outing. Smethurst died in December 2000 in a Salvation Army hostel in Grimsby. National and local obituaries sang the life of a singular man of letters.

Drumlins

John Menzies

Perhaps no other glacial landform is better known yet least understood than these streamlined terrain markers of glaciation. Everyone knows what a drumlin looks like. Those long ovoid hills of glacial debris, that every schoolchild knows as 'basket of eggs topography' when in groups or swarms. Drumlins populate the glaciated world of the Northern Hemisphere from Finland, Poland and Russia to the valleys of Cumbria in northern England, to the green, lush rolling topography of Ireland to the barren, frozen wastes of the Canadian Shield to the

myriad of drumlins in New York State, Wisconsin and elsewhere. Likewise drumlins are found in southern polar lands, for example, in the once-glaciated regions of Patagonia and New Zealand. It is held as a truism that glaciers have eroded and deposited vast dumps of till and associated glacially ground debris, moulded them in the glacier's transit and left them as tangible symbols of the 'ice age'. Drumlins, however, are not unique to the last ice age and appear in Mauritania, for example, within the windy Saharan desert terrain of exposed remnants of Ordovician age ice sheets. Even in the Parana Basin of Brazil and Uruguay, drumlin vestiges have been discovered.

Typically, drumlins exist as small hills, as the name derived from the Irish Gaelic implies (*druim*). They may range in height from a few metres to tens of metres from a few hundred metres long to occasionally kilometres in length. Drumlins do occasionally dot the glaciated landscapes of the world as single isolated forms but more often occur in vast fields or swarms of more than several thousand. The western New York State drumlins fields, for example, which occur between Syracuse and Rochester, number more than 76,000 drumlins. Drumlins come in all shapes and sizes, but it is intriguing to surmise that human fascination with these glacial hills may also be their simple, yet evocative, shape. Drumlins are half-egg-shaped, a shape that is almost primordial, a shape that returns in many formats where streamlining has or will occur, where the shape almost is indicative of an evolutionary form of growth and 'birth'. That drumlins are an evocation of the birthing process may underline or enter the human appreciation of drumlins in so many different manners. To expand such a view it is intriguing that the 'drumlin form' appears even as a symbol for political and social purposes. For example,

Edith Ebers, a German expert in drumlin studies, published in 1937, at the height of Nazi power in Germany, a long detailed paper on drumlins and their morphology in which a large photograph shows a racing car with the Nazi swastika emblazoned on its side. This juxtaposition of geological and political symbolism is more than curious since the latter is presumably linked to notions of power, speed, efficiency and the mistaken idea that in Nazidom there existed some higher value to be attained by human effort and civilization. That the drumlin form should be so directly linked to such a politically corrupt and sordid regime still, however, suggests this enigmatic link between drumlins in the physical world and human consciousness.

That drumlins exist within the inner recesses of the human consciousness in the northern lands of Europe and North America is commonplace. Cities such as Glasgow, Scotland, and Boston, Massachusetts, have been built upon such drumlin fields. The problems of urban transportation systems, planning and the urban landscape itself in these cities have been and continue to be predicated by the very presence of these drumlin fields. Drumlins have been viewed as unique features, absolute and unequivocal evidence that these same northern lands have been visited by glaciers and ice sheets in the past.

The peoples of these same terrains have used many different terms to describe these unusual hills. Long before Maxwell Close around 1867 used the term 'drumlin', descriptors such as whalebacks, mammilary hills, till tumuli, sowbacks, drums, indian ridges, *schildrücken* and *ispatinow* have appeared both in the common speech of the people of a particular district of a country and in local lore, even mythology, and in the written word. C. S. Lewis, for example, being from Northern Ireland, was well aware of the aesthetic and social component that drumlins played within the landscapes of Ireland. The Cree of eastern Canada used the term *ispatinow* to describe these long low hills that exist in seemingly endless serried ranks across the impenetrable bush of that part of Canada. In New England, the early colonists preferred terms such as sowbacks and mammilary hills, while in Scotland and Ireland the term drumlin was well known and used long before a glacial theory had been accepted.

There is a sense that drumlins are also unique and somehow enigmatic. Even today their origin is still unclear. Every layperson, of course, knows, including every game-show host, that they are formed by glacial erosion and deposition. But to the scientist the deeper question remains simply how, in actual process terms, do these forms develop, evolve or simply appear from beneath an ice sheet or glacier? There are strangely few drumlin appearing today from beneath present-day glaciers. Reports from James Ross Island in Antarctica and eastern Switzerland confirm isolated drumlins, and in front of Myrdals glacier in Iceland drumlins 'carved' from overridden glacial outwash are known, but there are no fields or swarms of drumlins. Perhaps such a dearth of modern drumlins only heightens their uniqueness and puzzling appearance.

The precise origin of drumlins remains obscure to the extent that the specific processes of formation are still, in places, hotly debated. Essentially, drumlins can be formed by erosion of previously existing deposited earth material which in the sculpting process is streamlined by the passage of the ice or formed by deposition either around a pre-existing obstacle in the glacier's path, such as a bedrock knob or higher strength sediment, or by direct deposition from the lower sub-glacial environment. It is this latter means

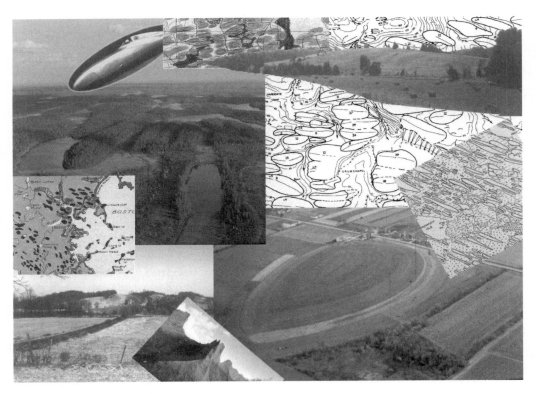

14 Drumlins in the physical world and human consciousness.

of formation that engenders debate. It seems likely that drumlins form in the mobile sediment that moves beneath large ice masses as a heterogeneity or differential variation in sediment strength, which occurs as a function of sediment geotechnical properties, ice dynamics, meltwater and thermal conditions. Of course, other theories on drumlin formation abound, and much needs to be understood yet as to the nature of the ice-bed interface and the dynamics of ice and sediment under stress. In direct contrast to the 'mobile bed theory' has been the appearance of what has become known as the 'flood theory'. In this latter theory it is postulated that vast glacial meltwater outpourings may have occurred that either sculpted cavities beneath the underbelly of the glacier and into which sediment accumulated, or the floodwaters carved pre-existing sediment into drumlin shapes, or a combination of both. This

flood theory has been co-opted to some degree by creationists, believers in Atlantis and by those who perceive drumlins as the telltale 'marks' of the Creator. Such links in no sense should be seen to denigrate or support this theory, but it again highlights the curious relationship that drumlins engender in the human mind and the desire to connect the physical and human worlds.

That drumlins have a place in human history is an accepted fact. The drumlin at Bunker Hill in Boston, where the American colonists fought for their independence; similarly at the Hill of Cumora, near Palmyra, New York State, a huge drumlin capitalized by a tall white plinth capped by a golden winged statue is deemed the place where Joseph Smith discovered the golden tablets of the Mormon Faith, the Book of Mormon or Golden Bible; both are instances where drumlins again enter the human psyche. To paraphrase Mark

Twain, who noted in his *A Tramp Abroad* (1880) that 'a man who keeps company with glaciers comes to feel tolerably insignificant by and by', so in the presence of drumlins, conceivably, there is a sense of human frailty and the ephemeral nature of sentient life.

Glaciers

Nick Spedding

As any devotee of the James Bond films can testify, glaciers are a prominent feature in landscapes of fantasy and romance. Francis Spufford, in his account of the relationship between 'ice and the English imagination', traces these popular geographies of the cryosphere back to men and women's fascination with the sublime. With Edmund Burke as its champion, the sublime became fashionable in the late eighteenth and early nineteenth centuries, at the same time as western Europeans – notably the British – began a systematic exploration of the Alps and the polar regions. Here they found not dragons,[1] but ice in profusion. The public's appetite for details of these ventures ensured that glaciers were soon installed as leading repositories of the sublime. The aesthetic of the sublime transcended beauty to inspire sensations of awe, rapture and menace, transporting the consumer from the familiar spaces of the pastoral to exotic landscapes figuratively and physically on the edge of nature, where he or she was able to contemplate the incomprehensible. Few had the means or the nerve to confront the sublime at first hand, but many were able to experience its pleasures and fears vicariously, by way of travel writings or fre-

quently lurid fiction. The public devoured accounts of (preferably tragic) expeditions, such as those of John Franklin, Edward Whymper and Robert Falcon Scott. Spufford argues that the imaginative association of ice with the sublime was fed by the gothic novel, a genre packed full of 'constant peril', 'breathless escapes', dastardly villains and too-good-to-be-true heroes.[2] The ancestry of 007 is clear. Licensed to chill, the frozen extremes of nature provide the stage on which the extremes of human behaviour are played out, both in fact and fantasy.

Science and the quest for the sublime share the desire to move beyond everyday experience, so it is not surprising that the publications of the pioneer glaciologists mixed observations and theories with chronicles of their physical exploits. Horace Benedict de Saussure made the third ascent of Mont Blanc, and set endurance records for high-altitude living. James David Forbes's accounts of his experimental design began with a description of the long journey from London to Chamonix, and stressed the arduous character of glacier travel. John Tyndall made the first ascent of the Weisshorn, and ran Whymper close for the prize summit of the Matterhorn. The fledgling pursuits of science and alpinism drew on each other for respectability. Science, however, operates a different framework, and the symbiosis did not endure. Science sets out to capture and dissect a reality that the aesthetic of the sublime insists we cannot comprehend. The aesthetic that physicists like to talk of is that of the 'beauty' of nature – and this implies the domestication of the sublime. In fact, Forbes invented an experiment to support his theory of ice flow that was so simple that readers of his work were able to try it out at home: the mysterious essence of the glacier exposed in a simple bucketful of plaster of Paris and glue.

The beauty that physics depicts is a strange, austere kind of beauty. Outsiders are rarely impressed by the physicists' neat tables of data, fail to see the elegance and power of their equations, and scoff at the arrogant claims that physics alone can provide 'true' knowledge of nature. The athletes and amateur poets of the Alpine Club found the prosaic routines of the scientists increasingly tiresome, and sought to purge their creed of such lowly diversions. Romanticism and reductionism cannot sit comfortably at the same dinner table: in 1861 Tyndall clashed with Leslie Stephen (a disciple of John Ruskin's, and editor of the *Alpine Journal*) and resigned from the Alpine Club in disgust.

The rope that ties the glaciologists to the mountaineers and artists, although badly frayed, has yet to be cut right through, as textbook forewords and award acceptance speeches often demonstrate.[3] The university student, entranced by the prospectus pictures of metal-festooned heroes posing against spectacular backdrops of ice, may feel betrayed by the sterile calculus of the contemporary *Journal of Glaciology*, but can still take comfort and inspiration from its glossy cover illustrations. Even W.S.B. Paterson's *The Physics of Glaciers* (1994), the bible of mathematical glaciology, carries on its front a dramatic photograph of Kaskawulsh Glacier, Yukon Territory, and not the equation for Glen's Law.

Those who wish to deny the power of science, and uphold the elusive character of glaciers, can point to their popular definition as 'rivers of ice'. We must invoke the familiar to try to make sense of the unfamiliar. Indignant glaciologists, protective of their authority, can mock the ignorance of the public. Ice is far from still and silent, 'glacial' transformations are often rapid rather than imperceptibly slow, and glaciers do *not* flow like rivers – but to argue like this illustrates a phenomenal diversity that continues to confound science. The success of Forbes's DIY glacier kit in the drawing rooms of Victorian England did not solve the riddle of glacier motion. Forbes's seminal fieldwork involved just himself, a local assistant and a theodolite. We can only wonder at how he would react to the grandiose campaigns of today's 'siege glaciology' (to use a neat term coined by Peter Knight).[4] Pageantry joins forces with technology. The glamorous image of the field glaciologist sets him (it's usually a 'him') up as the earth sciences' answer to James Bond – and he does indeed have at his disposal an array of ingenious gadgets worthy of Q's laboratory. However, the more we probe, the more complex the behaviour of ice seems to become. It gets increasingly difficult to think of glacier flow as a 'natural', given fact. Fans of science studies will readily talk of it as a 'fabrication', arising from an intricate 'dialogue' between the glacier, the rocks and sediments over which it moves, the field-workers, their many instruments and the theoreticians. Or is it just that the reality *is* sublime, and so forever out of our reach?

Climate

David N. Livingstone

In modern parlance, the label 'climate' signifies the relatively long-term atmospheric features of specific segments of earth space. In contrast to 'weather', the climate of a particular locality is taken to be the synthesis of the quotidian values of a range of factors – in the main, precipitation, temperature, humidity, sunshine and wind velocity. These meteorological data are typically produced through the standard operations of natural science. Instrumentally, they are derived from a variety of diagnostic readings using such devices as anemometers, hygroscopes, thermoscopes, barometers and pluviometers. Organizationally, they constitute the aggregate mensural yield of widespread meteorological networks through which affiliated observation stations return standardized records to weather information centres.

Notwithstanding these images of climate as a natural state of atmospheric affairs, and of meteorology as a species of natural science driven by observational data and untouched by cultural circumstances, there has been a remarkable and persistent inclination to read climatic conditions through the lens of political ideology, moral imperative, medical diagnosis and such like. Climate, to put it another way, has been culturally constituted. The nineteenth-century Dublin geologist Samuel Haughton, for example, went so far as to *define* climate in 1875 as the 'complex effect of external relations of heat and moisture upon the life of plants and animals', including the human species.[1] Or again, when the Harvard climatologist Robert DeCourcy Ward published his book on *Climate* in 1908, he appended to it the subtitle 'Considered Especially in Relation to Man'. Even more recently, generations of students learned from Austin Miller's textbook on *Climatology* – a work first published in 1931 and still in print in its ninth edition in 1961 – that 'psychologically each climate tends to have its own mentality, innate in its inhabitants and grafted on its immigrants'.[2]

Such interventions cannot be dismissed as historical aberrations. Weather and climate, in fact, have been deployed as cultural resources so persistently that they can coherently be considered social formations. In the ancient world, for instance, the identification of several climatic bands circling the earth – the *klimata* – was mobilized to portray the 'torrid zone' as an uninhabitable wasteland and to valorize the temperate as most suited to human habitation. Since then climatic ideas have served socio-political needs of various stripes. In sixteenth- and seventeenth-century England, for example, unusual weather was interpreted, in eschatological tones, as presaging the end of Roman Catholicism or Judaism or Mohammedanism or some such. In the aftermath of the 'All Saints Flood' of November 1570 and the St Bartholomew's Day Massacre of Huguenots in France in 1572, Thomas Hill, a mathematical practitioner, produced a treatise disclosing the range of weather phenomena that heralded such ominous political happenings. The Baconian strictures on inductively scrutinizing 'true particulars' served only – for the meantime – to reinforce the importance of recording strange weather and its warning signals.

During the period of the European Enlightenment a range of philosophers, notably Kant, Hume, Montesquieu and Hegel, sought, in one way or another, to root human worth in the particularities of regional climate. Kant may be taken to speak for this 'enlightened' tradition when he noted that the

> inhabitant of the temperate parts of the world, above all the central part, has a more beautiful body, works harder, is more jocular, more controlled in his passions, more intelligent than any other race of people in the world. That is why at all points in time these peoples have educated the others and controlled them with weapons.[3]

And much more recently, the American mammalian palaeontologist William Diller Matthew told the readers of his volume on

Climate and Evolution of 1939 that 'the higher races of man are adapted to a cool-temperate climate' where they reached the 'highest physical, mental and social attainments'.[4] In all these cases, declarations about weather conditions and the imperatives of climate reveal a fundamental merging of the 'natural' and the 'cultural'.

Three further diagnostic moments will serve to identify something of the medical-moral-political complexion of climatic discourse and their continuing deployment in the interests of various cultural projects. The writings of the Victorian meteorologist Ralph Abercromby provides a useful first cut. The author of a number of scientific works on such subjects as the velocity of ocean waves and the use of weather charts in forecasting, it is clear from his more popular writings that Abercromby was profoundly implicated in the elucidation of what might be dubbed medico-moral meteorology. Reporting in 1888 on his travels in search of peculiar weather, he insisted that even a short-term 'residence in a tropical climate' had a 'debilitating effect' on the individual. And tropical degeneracy was not simply a private condition. It was a political predicament. The colonial difficulties that Europeans faced in Africa was 'due to the climatic demoralization of the agents'. Accordingly, Abercromby was convinced that the 'best protector of the African savage from European aggressors is the deadly climate of that dark continent'.[5]

Secondly, what further fortified the power of such prescriptions was the tradition of tropical medicine that, both in its environmentalist and parasitological phases, constructed tropical climate in the language of pathology. Whether it was because tropical climate was considered – in earlier days – a direct determinant of degeneracy and debility, or, later, because the tropical zone was depicted as a site of parasitic fecundity,

tropical medicine as a species of scientific endeavour contributed to the global 'pathologization of space'. Moral circumspection and medical regimentation alike were recommended as necessary to long-term survival under a tropical regime.

Finally, the political imperatives that such exercises in moral climatology demanded come through with particular clarity in the writings of DeCourcy Ward, to whom we have already referred. A vigorous proponent of tough American immigration policies, Ward could see in climate a political tool for mounting assaults on what he considered undesirable immigrant types emanating from those zones where 'a debilitating and enervating climate' had left its indelible mark of inferiority on the social and 'mental characteristics' of their inhabitants.[6] As a leading light in the late nineteenth-century Boston Immigration Restriction League, Ward did much to marshal academic work on what he called 'anthropoclimatology' in the cause of racial politics.

While ordinarily thought of as simply a constituent element of the natural order, climate has persistently surfaced as a cultural category. As such it has routinely been deployed as a hermeneutic resource to advance moral, political and social interests of various kinds.

Lakes

John Dearing

Tuami looked at the line of darkness. It was far away and there was plenty of water in between. He peered forward past the sail to see what lay at the other end of the lake, but it was long, and there was such a flashing from the water that he could not see if the line of darkness had an ending.

William Golding, *The Inheritors* (1955)

Lakes mirror landscapes. Silhouettes of dark, wooded slopes or barren wind-swept moorland. Clouds rushing past snow-capped mountains. Or yellow and grey desert. Patchwork fields. Green, algae-coated houses. Fuzzy patterns in the ripples. Peaceful and restless. See the low boundary between lake and land where water turns into impenetrable swamp forest. Subterranean waters seeping from the ground. A glacier's snout may break off. The sun bakes hard the exposed mud, leaving behind a salty crust. A snake lies coiled up on a deserted beach. Where streams and rivers link the lake to its hinterland, energizing the lake with nutrients and water, or dumping the waste and toxins. A one-way route. A landscape with people who congregate at the lakeside. To wash and to swim, and to build houses on stilts and rocky islets. Boundaries reinforced with jetties and embankments. Where rice paddies step down to the shore to meet the fishermen's nets.

Below the mirror lies the world we rarely glimpse. One of micro-organisms and monsters, algae, larvae and fish, linked within an invisible web. Sometimes existing below ice, but always driven by the sun. Perturbed by fertilizers and acid rain, effects reverberating in space and time. And down further still, to where the water becomes mud. A divide between life and death, between the present and the past. Where, millimetre by millimetre, the lake bottom grows. Destined to become the lake surface. But for now a watery grave, and a depository of flotsam and jetsam coming from the sky or land. Sawmill chippings. Microscopic plankton fossils. Fragments of reed broken off in a gale. Clay particles dislodged by a farmer's plough. Dusts blown from distant deserts or volcanoes. Sand grains swept down the rivers in flood. Soot particles from chimneys. Pollen grains from the surrounding fields and forests. Charcoal from a raging wildfire. Molecules of pesticides. Here seasonal layers record summer blooms; of meadows and algae. Or winter storms and meltwaters that bring sediment-laden floodwater. Palecoloured layers register salts deposited in a heat-shrunken lake. Sometimes there are no layers, but just a continuous accumulation fed by a silent rain of detritus. Truly an end. But also a beginning.

An environmental journey through time, resurrected. Scratch the surface to see the end of the second millennium. Below lies the radioactive fallout from Chernobyl and post-Second World War nuclear tests. Phosphorus marks a reliance on artificial fertilizers, and the ineffectiveness of sewage plants. Eroded soil particles tell about deforested Asian mountains. A pale band is a low lake level and disappearing groundwater. Desertification and pollution. Wealth and poverty. Continue past soot-laden layers from city smogs. To the first recorded acid-loving algae and heavy metals. Industrialization. To flood layers that signal the pioneer farmers of the New World or resonate to the cycle of sunspots. Into layers that mark colder times, when alpine glaciers advanced down their valleys and rivers froze. To the Black Death, passing by largely unannounced. But here are also the Maya, the Roman Empire, Iron Age and Neolithic times. Harmony and disharmony.

And eventually on to Tuami's time, and beyond. The world's experience not lost, but forever reflecting on its future.

Rivers

John Western

In Strasbourg I used to go jogging along the levee of the River Rhine. There was a place on the French side, north of the city, where a long sweeping curve made it possible to look in a straight line of vision across the river to today's Germany, then back across to today's France, to see the spire of the cathedral rising up from beyond the waterlogged floodplain forest – still with its wild boar – and then to see the Vosges mountains defining the western horizon, perhaps 30 kilometres away.

The predicament of Alsace: where is the frontier, in Rhine midstream or further west, on Vosges crestline? For tens of thousands of Alsatians still living, this is no mere geographer's conundrum. On that same straight sightline, between the far edge of the forest and the city-centre spire, lies the suburban village in which I was then living: La Robertsau, formerly Ruprechtsau (Rupert's water meadow, in the Alsatian language). Octogenarians who have lived in the family house all their lives were born German, became French (1918), reverted to German (1940) and changed to French once more (1944) just by staying put and minding their own business. Probably they willed none of this. Probably they were neither unquestioning French patriots nor Nazis. That is not to say that they found Parisian rule the terrible equivalent of Berlin's wartime rule . . . but they might have been agreeable to being left alone by both. Keep your head down.

So, what has been made of the Rhine? The great river has always been the very converse of fixity. However much it has been canalized and dredged and ponded and barraged, this Rhine is always in motion, always flexing. Appreciate its alchemy, continuously transforming ice-shattered rock fragments of Alpine snowfields into North Sea salt-mud-flats. Yet those who collectively maintain the contemporary territorial nation-state system must impose their discipline upon the river: its midstream is to be the line of international demarcation between two supposedly fixed entities, France and Germany. *Here* is one place, *there* is another. Inevitably, they have to abut.

Suppose instead one tried the Vosges watershed as demarcation – at first sight a less fluid possibility than the river's midstream. Up here along the Vosges crest is the long-standing 'Romance' – 'Teutonic' linguistic border. 'The Blue Line of the Vosges', say the Alsatians, beyond which are 'les français de l'interieur': The French of The Interior. The place called France is yonder, to the west. Wheel out those old, descriptive cultural-geographical verities. West beyond the cols the settlements are named Saint-Dié, Gérardmer, Baccarat, Laveline-devant-Bruyères. Down here on the fat plain of Alsace beneath the Vosges – here in The Exterior, one takes it – the northern Strasbourg / Strassburg suburbs rejoice in names like Souffelweyersheim, Niederhausbergen, Mittelhausbergen,

15 The Rhine, with the present German bank to the left, looking upstream to the spire of Strasbourg Cathedral. La Robertsau church at right centre, with the Vosges crestline beyond.

Oberhausbergen. The cultural essentialist proposes that historically here we are in the westernmost lands of *Mitteleuropa* – and who could dispute it? Here we speak Alsatian (well, a number of Alsatian dialects, in fact); and across the river we speak Badisch, which is much the same. Out of these and other tongues emerged today's official German, boosted along the way by the emergence in Strassburg and Mainz of *Schriftdeutsch* – supralocal written German – for here it was that Gutenberg invented printing. This cannot be France. The French were Other, to be at various times feared or admired or both, whether for their strong royal military state, for their culture and style, or for their unwanted Romish religion once Strassburg had become one of the half-dozen great centres of the Reformation.

Once upon a time vast floods of annual snowmelt, snaking and squirming in multiple braided channels, forced Strasbourg back two or three kilometres from the main stream to the Rhine's more tractable tributary, the Ill. The city has only really grown eastward to grasp the Rhine since the late nineteenth century. Nevertheless, in medieval times we could, however gingerly, pick our path out across the marshes and find a more or less sure way over, via one of the earliest bridges on the entire river below Lake Constance. Hence strass-burg: city of roads. East–west routeways converge, to intersect and to cross the greatest north–south artery of western Europe. Imagine the traffic, the ideas and innovation, the verve and commotion, the talk of God, the making of riches, the good deeds and the dirty deals. This is the very converse of a static demarcation. Here the flows continuously converge and collide. This is the Rhine-land.

Louis XIV rode out from France, over the Col de Saverne, and took Strasbourg. The Rhine became the great French kingdom's

boundary. Strasbourg and Alsace were clamped into the post-Treaty of Westphalia template of the nation state. The acquired territories helped to form France into a taken-for-granted hexagonal shape. If you take away Alsace and the adjoining Moselle portion of Lorraine, the French are no longer contained within their agreeably familiar hexagon. *Alors . . . impossible.*[1] The hexagon strives for fixity, and one of its sides is fixed by the Rhine: France's 'natural' eastern boundary.

Are we not, demand the post-1945 Euro-idealists, meant now to be repudiating these worn-out old containers, these static opposed blocs called 'France' and 'Germany'? They are to fade. In their stead – urge Monnet, Schuman, indeed Churchill – shall we soon not have a western European supranational state-in-the-making?

If so, then the new Eurostate would presumably need a capital. Why not Strasbourg? proposed Ernest Bevin, Britain's post-war foreign minister. Its new role would thus symbolize a future of Franco-German comity and of international community. Alsace is finally liberated. Flanders, Wallonia, The Saar, Luxembourg, The Palatinate, Alsace-Lorraine, the Swiss cantons – all those marchlands question-marks for past geopoliticians pondering some buffering 'shatter-belt' between the great blocs of France and Germany – they all breathe more freely now.

And more prosperously. For they're within the proverbial 'banana': the zone of economic vitality curving from London across to the Rhineland and south down to northern Italy. Berlin the Occupier and Paris the Centralizer find themselves marginalized. Those old geopolitical verities are turned inside out by (re)new(ed) geo-economic verities. It's a Frankfurt-focused world: Euro-land. The Rhineland has become The Interior, whereas France becomes The Exterior, off on the far side of the Vosges crests. The Rhine entangles western Europe, unifies it – the converse of its role as the bristling separator for Louis XIV or Maginot, or the line where the sentinel watches in Bismarck's marching song *Wacht am Rhein*. How the world has changed! A hundred years ago Strasbourg was defended by a ring of German forts and had thousands upon thousands of troops as garrison: one of the world's armed camps, waiting for trouble. But today the sleek Eurocrats savour the lovely city's temples of gastronomy, while a continual traffic of Swiss, French, German, Belgian and Dutch barges chugs profitably beneath the Pont de l'Europe.

Meanders

David Pinder

Flying high over the landscapes of South America in late 1929, Le Corbusier was struck by sights 'that one may call cosmic'. He admired the views of farms, villages and cities but the great rivers affected him most strongly: the delta of the Parana, the Uruguay, the Paraguay. 'What an invitation to meditation', he declared, 'what a reminder of the fundamental truths of our earth!' Among the revelations offered by this bird's-eye view, he highlighted that of the meander. 'The course of these rivers, in these endless flat plains, demonstrates peacefully the inevitable consequences of the laws of physics', he asserted; 'it is the law of the steepest gradient, and then, if everything becomes really flat, the affecting theorem of the meander'.[1]

Le Corbusier was visiting Buenos Aires to give a series of improvised lectures on architecture and urban planning. His thinking at the time was undergoing important changes.

Renowned for his architectural and urban projects for the 'machine age' that emphasize order, geometry and purity, he was seeking a new balance between the geometrical and natural, the machine and the organic. A more organic and lyrical quality was becoming apparent in his work, in his building schemes as well as in his paintings. The unbroken view from the plane left Le Corbusier enthralled at the 'biology' and 'fundamental organic life' that were revealed from on high. 'My eyes are again (they always are) turned to nature', he informed his audience at one of his lectures.[2] Encouraging them to think freely beyond academicism, he advocated gaining a similar vantage point: 'Go up in a plane above the great plains of *nature*, the nature that has made us and whose forces appear here'.[3]

Le Corbusier's criticisms of cities had long relied on biological and organic metaphors. Existing cities were rotting, stagnating, wheezing, dying. He diagnosed their illnesses and prescribed appropriate medicine or, more usually, surgery. From his aerial perspectives in South America, he deplored the diseases that had drained previously organized settlements of vital energy and resulted in their wasting away. Buenos Aires was a primary organic form of life that had outgrown its 'proper' dimensions through its rapid and unchecked expansion, according to Le Corbusier, and it now lacked the necessary organic structure. It had collapsed into decay, and he likened it to, among other things, a 'stagnant pond'.[4] Introducing his solutions in his lectures, Le Corbusier used the 'miraculous symbol' of the meander. He intended to base his propositions on nature 'in a situation where I felt the public might accuse me of charlatanism'.[5]

Le Corbusier drew an analogy between the cyclical development of the meander and creative thinking. He presented the 'law of water' as one of perpetual circulation. Water falls to the earth, bringing nourishment; what remains unused continues an inevitable cycle, flowing into the sea. But, from the aeroplane, he noted how the smooth path of water was interrupted. An obstacle broke the flow, creating an irregularity. Water was thrown to one side, then to the other. These bends led eventually to the formation of a meander whose zigzag was the result of a disturbance. 'Nature, however, does not stop; she must find a solution to everything, even to maladies as perilous as this', stated Le Corbusier. '*When the time comes, the meander is dispensed with*; the river breaks through and returns to a straight course once more.'[6] A similar process characterizes human affairs, he argued, including crises facing big cities. There is the threat of deviation, of enervation, of sinking into the silt of the meander. It is the result of a lack of human energy at the moment that it is required. But creative thinking provides the breakthrough and the original disorder is transformed into a new form, what Le Corbusier called the *law of the meander*. He attributed the insight to following the outlines of meanders during his flights above the rivers, and to reflecting on both the dead ends that can block human activities and the miraculous solutions through which they are resolved.

Le Corbusier's lectures proposed techniques for making such breakthroughs. Clear lines of circulation must be established. Streets should become great branching rivers, moving freely. Ports should be provided for parking cars. Nothing should encumber or divert the flow. It is efficient, cleansing and vital for enhancing the city's health. Architecture *is* circulation, he stressed. Le Corbusier had previously promised to establish 'water-tight formulae' for urban planning. Now he aimed to equip the machine age to 'undo the terrible rings of the meander', or rather to 'pierce the meander from

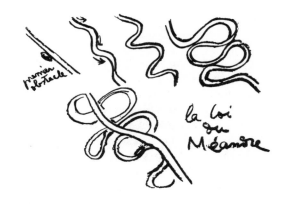

16 Le Corbusier, *The Law of the Meander* (1929).

side to side' so that 'life can again begin its wide course'.[7] In his view, learning from the laws of nature and the mathematical principles that underpin them is crucial for establishing human laws that can restore social and spatial harmony. On arriving in São Paulo, he thus inspected a map of the town and its meanders. Appalled at the confusion of curving streets, viaducts and networks of 'wormlike viscera', he announced to the city's prefect: 'You have a crisis of circulation, you can't service a diameter of 45 kilometres by making spaghetti in this labyrinth'.[8]

Yet, beneath the schemes of regulated flow and circulation, beneath the planners' concept city, other movements proliferate. The 'watertight' order leaks, overflows and is overgrown. It is haunted by the continual threat of disturbance, with Le Corbusier himself warning, 'lengths of old meanders remain, inert, unused, marshy, stagnant', along with organisms that are 'parasitic, anachronic, paralyzing'.[9] Further, the proposed order's values are challenged by alternative urban visions. Meandering, wandering and drifting are here associated not with deviations to be straightened out, maladies to be overcome, but with the everyday creativity of inhabitants. While Le Corbusier was travelling across the world demanding the demolition of chaotic knots of urban streets to enhance circulation, in his home city of Paris the Surrealists were celebrating such spaces as sites conducive to play, encounter, revelation. Tiny streets such as those of Les Halles in central Paris, so derided by Le Corbusier as obstacles illustrating the 'era of the horse' that must make way for the straight lines of the 'era of the automobile', were favoured by the Surrealists for nocturnal wanders and emotional connections through which they became places in flux, sites of possibility. Powerful psychic charges were also ascribed to threatened covered arcades such as the Passage de l'Opéra, whose 'underwater' light led Louis Aragon in *Le Paysan de Paris* to describe them as 'human aquariums'.[10] 'Washed by the waters of imagination' in this way, as Roger Cardinal notes, the city becomes 'soluble' and the location of 'astonishing metamorphoses'.[11] Opposed to the rationalizing ambitions of dominant urbanism, the Surrealists sought to explore possibilities beyond officially sanctioned channels. Through myriad paths and street-level perspectives, they aimed to chart new routes through the city, to provide alternative navigational maps based on breaking the chains that bind habitual movements and circulations, and opening themselves to other flows of passion and desire.

Railways

George Revill

Substantially a product of the nineteenth century, the railway is a defining technology of the modern world and an archetypal symbol of progress and confidence in technological modernity. Although amplified by Victorian self-aggrandizement and contemporary heritage culture suffused with nostalgia, such claims are not without justification. Few technologies can have had such an apparently direct and immediate impact, transforming and modifying the landscapes through which they run. It is not surprising that contemporaries used familiar tropes to make sense of the railway's power, impact and extent. The railway was a huge body with a main line for a backbone and arms and legs for branch lines. Railway locomotives were noble 'iron horses', destructive dragons or heroic figures from Classical mythology, locomotive drivers 'medieval knights', railway directors kings, tyrants and despots. Railway travel was often likened to flying, while stations were represented as the cathedrals of the age, 'volcanoes of life', chaotic 'towers of Babel' or theatres for social display. It is true that the railway inscribed the landscape with patterns rooted in past practice, adopting a language of architecture and civil engineering substantially from the era of canal building and drawing cultural authority for its building styles from both Classical and Gothic architecture. The planning, surveying and day-to-day management of railways owed much to eighteenth-century practices of agricultural enclosure, military survey and cartography. However, the scale and extent of railway construction produced a range of engineering and architectural structures – bridges, tunnels, embankments, cuttings, depots, warehouses and stations without precedent. Railway development also resulted in wholesale ecological change, for example, deforestation in India and the demise of the buffalo in North America, in addition to the more insidious effects on regional economies, cultures and building styles. In the UK, for example, railways were blamed for the demise of regional distinctiveness in everything from roofing materials to folk song.

As the first mechanized mass-transportation system, the railway was instrumental in the reworking of temporal and spatial relations central to the economic, social and cultural experience of modernity, known as 'time–space compression'. The railway brought cheap daily travel, rapid dissemination of information, personal communication and printed news media and uniform national time zones; it facilitated mass leisure travel, rural–urban migration and suburbanization. An unparalleled level of social mixing in the public spaces of railway stations and an unprecedented degree of geographical mobility enabled railway development to be viewed by contemporaries as alternately a threat to social order or an engine of democracy. At the same time, railways were recognized as a vital factor in the organization of economic and political spaces that forged the communication links necessary to the functioning of nation states and empires. The completion of the transcontinental railroad in the USA in 1869 was heralded as part of a global as well as national communications network

> The new highway thus opened to man will not only develop the resources, extend the commerce, increase the power, exalt the dignity and perpetuate the unity of our Republic, but in its broader relations, as the segment of a world-embracing circle, directly connecting the nations of Europe with those of Asia, will materially facilitate the enlightened and advancing civilisation of our age.[1]

Yet, perhaps most remarkable for railway development was not the confrontation and conquest of nature by culture but rather the easy and naturalistic accommodation of railways into the landscape. This is partly a product of the railway's own publicity, which

17 Albert Bierstadt, *Last of the Buffalo* (1888). The US railroads employed professional hunters and, as a result, during the 1870s, almost the entire buffalo population of the prairies was destroyed. In close collaboration with the Central Pacific Railroad, Bierstadt painted a number of pictures mythologizing the railroad's conquest of the West. In 1871 he organized a train-based buffalo hunt for Grand Duke Alexis of Russia. His complicity in killing buffalo for sport makes this image all the more ironic.

has actively worked since the early years of railway operation to order and organize the experience of landscape for the traveller. Examples may be found in many formats and genres, early railway prints showing new works and lines in images engineered to demonstrate the permanence and solidity of railway structures, the rewriting of frontier history in the American railroad pictures of Albert Bierstadt, and the multiplicity of guidebooks and posters produced to encourage leisure travel and tourism. It also results from the interpolation of the rhythms of railway operation into the daily routines of countless urban and rural communities, such that the two become so interdependent as to be perceived as a unity. Represented in such a way, writers describing English rural branch lines frequently portray them as signal markers of community and even essential elements of national identity. However, it is the railways' role in fundamentally transforming our experience of landscape as travellers that is key to this whole process.[2]

The experience of landscape from a railway train is one simultaneously of isolation and connectivity. The straight level line of the railway track and the smooth progress along the metal rails remove us from direct contact with the undulations of topography; carriage windows frame the view just as our guided progress through the landscape generates its own narrative, in perspective, sequence and distance. At the same time railway travel heightens and dramatizes the moment of travel. This experience is marked out by contrast between the frenzied tumult of the station and the quiet reflection of the railway carriage. In metaphor and materiality the railway maps out connectivities between what Proust called 'distant individualities of experience',[3] Atlantic and Pacific, rich and poor, town and country, rest and motion, nature and culture.

The railway represents a human potential to create almost unlimited energy, contrasting and complementing the natural forces against which it is pitched. In Nye's portrayal of the American railroad, its relationship with the landscape is built on a shock encounter with the awe-inspiring qualities of mechanical energy defined by an aesthetic of the technological sublime.[4] To encounter the technological sublime through the railway as a fleeting moment in the experience of landscape – the train whistle, the rush of speed, the station stop, the pause for signals – is to be cast into a pastoralized dialectic of culture and nature. Interruption of the landscape by the railway heightens the contrast between the two, demonstrates human technological capability to transform the landscape, highlights nature's precious vulnerability and ultimately indicates nature's capacity to reclaim its socialized other – technology.

Freeways

Peter Merriman

> At their best, these great ribbons of concrete, swirling through the land, give us the excitement of an environmental dance, where man can be in motion in his landscape theater.[1]

Like many of his colleagues in Britain and the United States, the American landscape architect and environmental engineer Lawrence Halprin stressed the importance of designing attractive freeways and motorways whose 'sculptural qualities' could be extended into the surrounding landscape.[2] These *man*-made constructions should be blended into the countryside through careful planning and design, while the free-flowing movements of drivers and vehicles – reflecting the original meaning of freeway in 1930 – would affect and enliven the scene. Attention should be focused on the performances of drivers, vehicles and landscapes. Drawing upon the work of his wife Ann, a well-known avant-garde performer and dancer, Halprin used techniques from dance, theatre and choreography in an attempt to notate movement in the landscape and reflect this movement in the design of freeways.

Different movements on the road may be seen to result in a form of body work, where drivers, vehicles and the spaces of the freeway and surrounding landscape are always conceptualized in relation to each other and in a series of distinct motions. Drivers' movements are regulated and managed in different ways. They are not allowed to stop, except in emergencies, and must interact with the rhythms of the outside world through a vehicle: 'a medium for thought, feeling, or action' as well as a 'conveyance for transporting people, goods, etc.'.[3] Air-

18 Two hedgehogs and a car on an autobahn near Irschenberg, Germany, 1937.

conditioning systems, tyres, glass, road signs, radios, roadside planting, landscaping, guard rails and codes of conduct are designed to mediate the relationship between the driver and his or her self, their vehicle and this outside. But as the vehicle, landscape and various rhythms become bound into the being of drivers, binaries or demarcations of outside / inside, human / machine and vehicle / freeway / landscape become problematic.

Different subjects / objects are expected to perform a variety of movements in different times and spaces: drivers are expected to proceed in a regular, orderly fashion; the road surface, signs and guard rails are expected to remain intact and in place for a calculated lifetime; different species of plants are expected to grow at specified rates, and to produce an attractive landscape in so many months and years. Different sites and processes of production and consumption, along with flows of goods, plants and animals (flows of economic and ecological capital), may be influenced by the presence and loca-

tion of motorways and freeways; with economists and ecologists identifying high-technology corridors and ecological ones. The tyre treads of vehicles transport seeds far and wide; predatory animals and birds feed off animals living on the verges and road-kill; while windscreens, radiators and wheels provide the final point of impact for many flies, rabbits and hedgehogs. The movements of these species are not costed like those of humans, whose journeys, speeds, accidents, deaths, productions and consumptions (emissions, fuel consumption, repairs) are valued by economists and environmentalists in an attempt to calculate the costs and benefits of transport policies and different routes for new roads and motorways. Freeways, which are often associated with a lack of tolls, are not free from *all* costs and implications. They come at a price, as we are constantly reminded; whether to human life, taxpayers, flies or the environment. The desire for personal freedom of mobility results in the production and consumption of these public / private spaces for enabling *and* governing the movements of drivers and vehicles. Drivers are attracted to these new freeways and motorways, but before long drivers often find themselves in traffic; those moments of driving and dwelling that are often seen to be out of place on the road.

In 1974 the unplanned movements entailed in traffic jams and accidents provided the focus of attention for two British writers who were charting the dystopian landscapes of freeways and motorways, although a quite different series of events unfold in the mysterious spaces of the verge. Peter Nichols's play *The Freeway* was first performed by the National Theatre in October 1974, and was set in the near future on the verges of a freeway in central England that was built to bypass an old motorway.[4] Hundreds of drivers become stranded in a three-day traffic jam on the freeway, underlining, while also bringing a temporary end to, the solitary nature of the motorway experience, as drivers from diverse social backgrounds are forced to cooperate and socialize on the verges. In another story from 1974, J. G. Ballard's *Concrete Island*, a quite different account is provided of the solitary, desolate spaces beyond the edges of the tarmac. Like Ballard's earlier book *Crash*, *Concrete Island* is set among the urban motorways of west London. A 35-year-old architect, Roger Maitland, veers off the motorway, crashing down an embankment onto an area of wasteland encased by slip roads. This triangular space serves as a contemporary desert island from which the injured Roger is unable to escape, despite his attempts to flag down motorists and inscribe help messages on the road signs. His wanderings on the island expose the geographies of this wasteland, as he observes the geometries of the complex interchanges, the demolished buildings covered in grass, the rubbish and wrecked cars, and encounters two vagrant inhabitants for whom the island provides a refuge from the spaces of the city. During moments of fever and drunkenness, after almost a week on the island, Maitland begins to identify the geographies and phenomenologies of his injured body with the geographies of this wasteland:

> He surveyed the green triangle which had been his home for the past five days. Its dips and hollows, rises and hillocks he knew as intimately as his own body. Moving across it, he seemed to be following a contour line inside his head . . . he thought of the strange phrase he had muttered to himself during his delirium: I am the island.[5]

Bodies, machines and landscapes become interrelated and confused, observations that have resonances with everyday freeway experiences, where the spaces of driving and the driver are bound up with spaces and materials extending far beyond the limits of one's own body, body work and traffic lane. The materials and movements associated with freeways and freeway driving reveal how cultures and natures are frequently performed together in distinct yet contingent ways and how the patterning of the landscape is an ongoing, dynamic process.

Fields

Mike Crang

That landscape in Britain is a matter of scenery, and an aesthetic way of framing the world that emphasizes a visual and detached relationship to the environment, has become something of a commonplace. Within the lowland idyll, field patterns seem so often the core of this aestheticization. And, of course, with this there is almost the repetition of reducing workers to figures in the landscape. This conversion to aesthetic objects seems echoed in their reduction by detached and objectifying scientific knowledge. I want to explore this by thinking through the technologies of working the land, and the overwhelming of actual produce and labour by abstract forces of science and capital. So I want to take two objects, one a capital good, the other a by-product, to look at how in the bounded space of the field abstract forces become concrete.

Tractor

The British soil survey has been influential in determining soil quality and agricultural land rents. But to map the quality of soil entails removing all the 'boulders' by sieving. And in this case boulders means stones greater than 25 mm. So the quality of the soil is measured by removing large infertile lumps from it – which might be rather to the point in terms of the actual nature of the land. Meanwhile, science and geography have tended to position themselves as authoritative experts telling farmers how to improve yields and, increasingly, conservation. In this spirit, schoolchildren are taught that soil erosion is best combated by techniques such as contour ploughing – that is, going around the slope of the hill so that the furrows acts as barriers to run-off, rather than up and down, where they act as channels. Which makes sense, and especially so, I remember writing down in an exercise book, when the slopes are greater than 15 degrees. But I also recall sitting in a tractor cab staring at a health and safety notice forbidding driving across inclines, especially those greater than 14 degrees.

Ironically, the notion of machines conquering natural features still figures in the promotion of these very expensive vehicles where gleaming machines are seen powering up impossible slopes. I say impossible advisedly, since watching a new display tractor fail to plough straight up a steep slope did not stop the advertisement later carrying pictures of the tractor halfway up the slope. Perhaps more remarkable is the fact that only since the 1990s have companies actually looked at what tractors were used for most of the time – to discover to their shock that they spent most of their work lives hauling loads on tracks and roads (as many a rural motorist would tell you). JCB promptly produced a roadster capable of travelling at 30 miles an hour. Meanwhile the tax authorities, who have licensed separate less taxed pink (dyed) diesel for 'off road' farm use, also raised their eyebrows. For all the macho

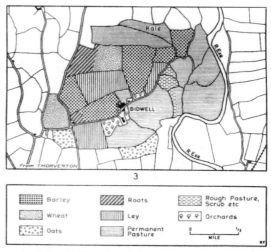

3. Bidwell (Mr. Crang) near Thorverton

Land Use (1968) of Farms to be visited

Agricultural Geography of Mid-Devon : Excursion Route
Key to all Land Use Maps

19 A Devon farm, 1968.

machinery advertising, the colloquial accounts of sales representatives tell that the real selling point for these machines is a comfortable cab – since the drivers know they will spend long hours in it. And of course the EU is currently talking about regulating how long anyone can spend driving a tractor.

Bale

While recent Government inquiries have cleared the cartel of supermarkets in Britain from profiteering from consumers, they have said little about their relative power against producers. Since the Conservative Governments of the 1980s and '90s pro-gressively removed the role of price regulation and intervention boards, privatizing the milk collection system for instance, the influence of retailers upstream in the system has grown. In terms of both quality (for which read appearance) of product and price, the dominant forces are those of the supermarkets.

Their requirements, for instance for audited processing facilities, further exacerbate the distances that produce travels – going to approved processors rather than nearby ones. Moreover, the price received by producers, as a percentage of the final cost of food, has steadily decreased. The supermarkets for their part say that they are only responding to customer wishes expressed on the till rolls.

On the farm, this can mean increased auditing by supermarkets of production techniques and imposition of changing and exacting standards for produce. It has also meant static or declining prices per unit of produce. However, with constant overheads and costs for equipment and services rising, the only 'solution' is to increase volume to provide revenue. The way to increase volume is to increase fertilizers or farm larger areas, that is, buying more land, both of which require bigger machinery, and both land and machinery usually means borrowed capital. That leads to interest charges, which need revenue. And so on. General surveys suggest that even in the mid-1990s, a time when farm incomes rose by 50 per cent or more in Britain, the return on operating capital was only some 10 per cent; but if fixed capital investment was included that figure fell to 2 per cent. At the other end of the scale, however, some types of investment in agricultural products have increased. So there is a potato futures market – trading options in selling and buying potatoes for future periods and in effect betting on future prices. This market is now more than five times the value of the annual UK potato crop.

These difficult economic situations also act in geopolitical spaces not just as functions of corporate power. It is clear that subsidized production in the EU has created food prices well over market levels. The dumping of produce and the barriers created have distorted global food trade and disadvantaged some poorer countries. It is also clear that most food trade in grain remains that with North America (with its own export-led subsidy regime and own GM corporate agendas and record levels of farm bankruptcies). Between decreasing price support (in euros) and the strength of the pound the effect has been plummeting prices in Britain. For most of the 1980s, and early 1990s, the price for wheat hovered around £120 per tonne. This is a declining real price with annual, and even weekly fluctuations, but it is well above world market rates, as US trade negotiators and consumer groups have shown. By the summer of 2000 the price had fallen to world market levels – in effect North American export price – at around £60 per tonne. Currently a tonne of baled straw is selling for £65 – so the by-product, which in the 1980s was burnt because it was too much trouble to handle, has become more valuable than the crop. Of course, farmers also have to calculate the ratio of straw to grain and the costs of handling and baling straw. But the cause is simple – straw as a bulky product with high transport costs has a relatively local market, while grain is global.

Fields then are far from just material features but are etched with these external forces. Globalized markets in the end valorize local products, while the space of the field is marked, valued and classified according to many external regimes of knowledge. The field is furrowed by many forces, only some of which go with the slope.

Trade

Tim Unwin

Above all, trade permits specialization. It allows agrarian producers to focus on the activities where culture and nature have combined to give them a competitive advantage. Moreover, trade enables total production within a given territory to be increased, even without any change in agrarian technology. In medieval Europe, the shift from largely self-supplying manorial units to an economy bound together through trade in periodic markets and fairs was thus a critical factor in enabling higher population levels to be sustained. At a much larger scale, during the twentieth century trade also enabled increasing global specialization in agrarian activity. The wine trade provides a classic example of the ways in which the interaction between nature and culture has been mediated through changing patterns on the ground.

Economic specialization has historically been facilitated by the activities of a diverse range of merchants, all of whom have sought to derive profit from their role as intermediaries between producers and consumers. Central to the activities of these merchants has been their maintenance of control over knowledge relating to the prices pertaining for particular products in different markets. As Fernand Braudel has emphasized in his description of trade in the sixteenth and seventeenth centuries,

> the great merchants, although few in number, had acquired the keys to long-distance trade, the strategic position *par excellence*; . . . they had the inestimable advantage of a good communications network at a time when news travelled very slowly and at great cost; . . . they normally benefited from the acquiescence of state and society,

and were thus able regularly, quite naturally and without any qualms, to bend the rules of the market economy.[1]

What is most significant about this claim is that mercantile profit was made possible because of the maintenance by merchants of privileged knowledge in a specific spatio-temporal context; patterns and profit were inextricably linked. Once such knowledge became more freely available, the potential for mercantile profit diminished, and those with money to invest turned increasingly to investment in production in the expectation of greater financial returns. This shift was central to the emergence of capitalist relations of production during the later seventeenth and eighteenth centuries.

Inherent within the traditional concept of trade is also the idea of particular bounded territories between which trade takes place. To be considered as trade, goods must therefore cross boundaries, and the guardians of these boundaries usually exact charges for the privilege. Hence, customs duties and trade tariffs form an integral part of any consideration of the concept of trade. In the medieval period, such charges were conceived of as payment for the protection of merchants and goods, and a way to ensure that trade transactions were indeed 'fair'. More recently such mechanisms have been used as an integral way of seeking to maintain economic and political alliances, and for those with a monopoly of power to reap the benefits from trade at the expense of the weak and underprivileged.

The wine industry has generated many examples of the role of trade since prehistory.[2] Herodotus, writing in the fifth century BC, thus provides us with a fine example of the significance of the wine trade for ancient Babylon, commenting how boats for supplying the city were built from wood and skins in Armenia. People filled these boats 'with straw, put the cargo on board – mostly wine in palm-wood casks – and let the current take them downstream'.[3] Each boat also carried a live donkey, and on arrival in Babylon the boats were broken up, the timber disposed of, and the hides transported back north on the donkeys' backs. Likewise, finds of extensive numbers of amphorae along the coasts of the Mediterranean and the rivers of western Europe attest to the extent to which wines produced in Italy were traded during the Roman period. Diodorus Siculus, writing in the first century BC, thus reports that it was possible for Roman merchants to purchase a slave for a single amphora of wine.[4]

In the medieval period, wine was one of the most significant items of trade, with Bordeaux reportedly exporting some 100,000 tons of wine a year at the beginning of the fourteenth century.[5] In the late thirteenth century, three distinct trade routes had emerged whereby producers in places well suited to wine production, but with good access to rivers and the sea, were able to supply the growing urban markets of northern and eastern Europe with wine (illus. 20). For the leading townspeople of northern Europe, wine had become a distinct part of their lifestyle, and without a climate conducive to the regular supply of quality wine in their neighbourhoods, they had turned increasingly to more southerly regions to furnish this cultural requirement. From the sixteenth century the wine trade became increasingly global in scale. Places scarcely known for their wines today became highly significant as producers and exporters for the European market. Thus Steckley noted that in 1681 sufficient wine to fill some 4.5 million quart bottles was reported by customs officials to have been imported into London from the Canary Islands.[6]

Trade agreements formed a cornerstone of economic and political policies. The

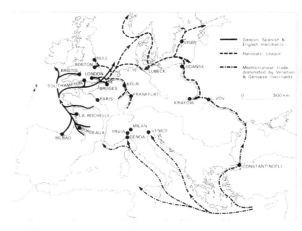

20 Main European wine trade routes *c.* 1250.

Methuen Treaties of 1703 between Britain and Portugal, for example, designed to ally the two countries in the war with Spain, also included important clauses intended to benefit the export of British cloth to Portugal, and Portuguese wines to Britain. And the wine trade continues today to play a crucial role in the global marketplace, contributing significantly to the portfolios of some of the world's major international corporations, such as Diageo.

Above all, these examples from the wine trade show that trade should not be seen simply as an economic phenomenon, but rather as an outcome of a complex tapestry of economic, social, political and cultural processes that reflect the diverse ways in which human societies seek to maintain and reproduce themselves. From the days when the first humans began to shape their cultural identities, by taking a part of nature (grapes) and experiencing the divine powers of its product (wine), people have patterned the ground with distinctive colours and vocabularies of trade.

Colonies

Felix Driver

Colonies are for ants, artists, delinquents, lepers, tourists, astronauts, nudists, pioneers, paupers and exiles – in a word, for anyone who settles, or is settled, in a site with relatively distinct boundaries. Colonists put down roots in such places, in order to cultivate the natures that are both within and without. Sometimes they take the initiative, sometimes they are cast out; often they become associated with or attached to particular parcels of land. In political terms, colonies may be outposts of empire, materially separate from though imaginatively connected to a larger space. The culture of colonialism is nonetheless articulated in a different register from that of imperialism. Empires look upward, to god, king, law; colonies are rooted in particular parts of the earth, inhabiting its patterned ground.

Colonies are made in a variety of ways, by proclamation, by treaty, by force, by trade, by cultivation, by all manner of material and imaginative effort: always, though, they are the product of a collective project of work. A colony does not exist just to be seen on a map or a chart, from afar: it is sustained through labour *in situ*, more often than not on the land itself. The romance of colonialism, as told in novels, histories and travelogues, is an epic struggle between colonist and nature: a saga of clearing, cultivating, hunting, domesticating. Thus rendered, the colony is the land and the colonizer is the plough. But colonies are made of more than individual pioneers: they are communities, with their own mores and institutions. The colony, unlike what lies beyond – outback, badlands, wilderness – is an ordered place. It may be a place of experiment or of trial:

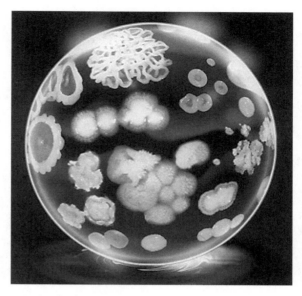

21 Bacterial colonies growing in a Petri dish.

but it is always a site where natures, human or otherwise, are disciplined.

Colonies are places of experimentation as well as order. Microbiologists cultivate bacterial colonies in Petri dishes so that they may understand better processes of organic growth and decay; social reformers establish colonies to demonstrate theories about human behaviour. The principles and methods of the colony have lent themselves to a wide variety of applications in the worlds of science and politics. The modern metropolis itself has frequently been imagined as a territory to be colonized. Over the last 200 years, the regeneration of society, the cultivation of citizenship and the reclamation of character have often been said to require the colonization of whole neighbourhoods within the city, and the planting of new colonies elsewhere – including labour colonies, model communities, new towns or indeed overseas settlements. The notion of the domestic colony as an instrument of social reform and experiment has a long and variegated history. It looms particularly large in the writings of utopian theorists, penal reformers, asylum doctors, urban planners and rural revolutionaries. For the most part, the crucial term is that of *cultivation*: moral and physical regeneration through colonization of the land.

When plants colonize, they take root in new terrain; when termites do, they build impregnable fortresses out of the materials of the earth. The European colonizers of West Africa and the Caribbean were fascinated by the termites that had got there before them, complex communities that made castles from the mud, from which to mount raids on surrounding regions. Analogies between the empires of men and those of insects abound in the writings of natural philosophers, political economists and novelists since the seventeenth century. A recurring theme is the hierarchical organization of the insect community and its human equivalent in gradations of status and class. While the termites offered one model for colonialism, it was not really the most enduring as far as the English colonists of the nineteenth century were concerned. Really to take root, colonies had to be planted, not built: that way they could reach into the earth, not merely be located upon it. Empire is about extension, but colonies are about depth.

If biogeography has long been one of the most imperial of sciences, mapping out plant and animal territories as though they were political jurisdictions, then ecology is the science of the colonial. The relationship between niche and species defines the colony, in the same way that the relationship between province and kingdom defines the empire. The biogeographer deals in distributions, while the ecologist works with communities. The imperialist maps out a territory, while the colonist inhabits nature – and is frequently unsettled by its disorderliness. The nature reserve is perhaps the most successful modern colony, a bounded and ordered space in which patterns of invasion and succession can be suspended and scrutinized – a place of experiment in the production of nature.

Continents

Luciana Martins

> Thirty years of sonar mapping and deep sea drilling now convince us that it is the continents themselves that have been the voyagers in an odyssey that has not yet finished.[1]

Continents may be lost or found; they may undertake voyages every bit as marvellous as those of the most intrepid explorers. Of all the continents, the one that travelled furthest – until it vanished from human dreams – was the Great Southern Continent. It first appeared in the speculations of the Greeks, whose Apollonian minds conceived the earth to be symmetrical; the proportion of land and water in northern latitudes had to correspond to that in southern latitudes. In the sixteenth century, world maps depicted a vast landmass believed to cover the greater portion of the high latitudes of the South Seas, showing plausibly irregular coastlines, authentic-looking place names and an array of illustrations of birds, trees and natives inhabiting its interior. In the eighteenth century, the quest for the elusive Southern Continent consumed the most daring of European navigators, including James Cook and Louis Antoine de Bougainville. Like explorers in search of El Dorado, seafarers headed south guided by an imaginary vision of an undiscovered bountiful continent. The hydrographer Alexander Dalrymple predicted that a huge landmass would be found 'in the intermediate spaces between the Cape of

Good Hope and America, and the westward of the last, between it and Papua; the one opposite to the Atlantic, the other to the North Pacific Ocean'.[2] Dalrymple was to be disappointed: after two expeditions to southern latitudes, all Cook was able to chart were the tracks of his vessels criss-crossing vast oceans punctuated with tropical islands. And it was on one of these islands, during his third voyage, that Cook met his own end.

For Europeans, voyages through space were also voyages through time. Whatever travellers could not understand – unfamiliar social mores, languages and habits – was deemed to be primitive or savage. In the process, a geographically and naturally remote other was fabricated by the Enlightenment, an antithesis to itself. But the novelty of the experience of travel could not easily be contained: constantly unsure of where they were, who they were and what they knew, voyagers unsettled metropolitan certainties and fed new utopias.[3] Could new continents really give clues to Europe's past – or future?

The fabulous geography of the Great Southern Continent, for instance, was enriched by legends of giants inhabiting the far ends of the earth. Various books of the Old Testament mention humans of gigantic proportions: races of giants before the Flood, those contemporaries of Moses or simply peoples of unusual stature or strength. During the Renaissance chronicles of discovery included reports of the existence of giants in the New World, confirming a widely held theory suggesting that people were physically bigger the nearer one got to the North and South Poles. Following Pigafetta's description of the natives of Tierra del Fuego as Patagonians in 1520, their 'gigantic stature' was depicted in several travel accounts.

The link between giants and the New World triggered numerous speculations

22 Depiction of 'giant' Patagonians published in A. J. Pernetty, *Journal d'un voyage fait aux îles Malouines* (1780). Pernetty accompanied Bougainville as a chaplain in his South American voyage during 1763 and 1764.

about the human past. In the work *El Paraíso en el Nuevo Mundo* (1655) by the Spanish scholar Antonio de Léon Pinelo, for example, the existence of giants was said to provide evidence for human habitation of the new continent before the Flood, suggesting it was the site of Paradise.[4] But above all giants had a strong hold on the popular imagination. In France and Britain this excitement was revived by a description of the Patagonians in an anonymous account of the voyage of the *Dolphin* around the world under Commodore John Byron in the second half of the eighteenth century: 'Their middle stature seemed to be about eight feet; their extreme nine and upwards; though we did not measure them by any standard, and have reason to believe them to be rather more than less'.[5] This growing interest in the Patagonians had a tremendous impact on the publishing business. Old books revived and new books were published because of the *Dolphin*'s encounter with the 'giants', arousing not only popular curiosity but also the interest of philosophers and men of science.

The 'age of reason', however, proved fatal to the legend of the Great Southern Continent, as well as to the Patagonian giants. In the Admiralty's official collection of travelogues compiled by John Hawkesworth, *An Account of the Voyages Undertaken . . . by Commodore Byron, Captain Wallis, Captain Carteret, and Captain Cook* (1773), the Patagonians were authoritatively reported to be seven feet (2.1 m.) tall at the most. At the same time, the dream of a Great Southern Continent faded from view, as the tracks of Captain Cook's vessels failed to trace its shores. Readers feasted instead on reports of Pacific islanders whose amphibian character both astounded and disturbed their sense of the natural order of things. The Patagonians, meanwhile, were transformed from giants into degenerates; at the uttermost ends of the earth, where nature seemed so radically different, explorers anticipated finding extraordinary human beings, and if this couldn't be gauged by their size, some other measure of difference had to be found. As Johann Reinhold Forster – who accompanied Captain Cook on his second voyage – bluntly put it, 'I believe the nations inhabiting the frozen extremities of our globe to be degenerated and debased from that original happiness, which the tropical nations more or less enjoy.'[6] The status of the Patagonians as primitive barbarians was reiterated by Charles Darwin, following his encounter with the inhabitants of Tierra del Fuego in 1834: 'I never saw more miserable creatures; . . . What a scale of improvement is comprehended between the faculties of a Fuegian savage & a Sir Isaac Newton – Whence have these people come? Have they remained in the same state since the creation of the world?'.[7]

It took three centuries of intermittent contact with the inhabitants of the far southern 'ends of the earth' for Europeans to lay the giants to rest. The dream of the Great Southern Continent also gradually sunk from view. From the nineteenth century to this day, however, Europeans have been trying to get to terms with the vastness of the South Seas. The continental eye looks for an immense landmass, and when it cannot be found sees only a void; the islander knows more about the routes and currents that criss-cross the seas, and the treasures that are waiting to be found.

Battlefields

David G. Passmore

Scattered throughout the heavily forested valley slopes of the Prümerberg heights, to the east of the Belgian town of Saint Vith, are clusters of shallow depressions that denote a Second World War battlefield. These are the remains of foxholes and bunkers dug by troops of the American 7th Armoured Division facing the advancing German army during the Ardennes offensive of December 1944, commonly known as the 'Battle of the Bulge'. A small roadside memorial marks the locality where bitter hand-to-hand combat delayed, but could not prevent, a breakthrough and assault on Saint Vith. The visitor to this place can walk among the dugouts where defending troops met the attack on the late afternoon of 21 December, and can survey a wooded landscape that is unlikely to have appeared very different to the combatants; its patterned ground stands in atmospheric and moving testimony to those who died here.

The defence of Saint Vith formed only one of many engagements fought throughout the narrow wooded valleys of the Ardennes during the offensive of 1944, but (and excluding the rebuilt houses and bridges of the region) relatively few of these have left a visible trace on the modern landscape. The same is true of most battles fought throughout human history and many, perhaps most, readers of this book will live in the vicinity of a place that, at a particular time in the recent or distant past, constitutes a battlefield. These limited spaces are landscapes that have the capacity to exert a powerful hold on our attention. But, for most people, the experience of the historic battlefield is conditioned by the heritage industry, and here the focus of attention tends to be places where the scale of battle and / or the outcome has assumed particular importance; where military reverses, attritional stalemates, decisive victories, heroic resistances or gallant defeats have been culturally and historically designated as significant. Armed with detailed knowledge of the engagement (the strategic context, the terrain and weather, the participating forces, the course of the battle itself, its boundaries, timeframe and sequencing, the consequences), the battlefield visitor is guided (often literally, through footpaths, viewpoints and on-site information boards) through an experience of landscape as the site of major events in human history. Here the block-diagram style of battlefield map, which reduces combat to abstract vectored symbols, has become a necessary and familiar tool of battlefield interpretation (illus. 23), although some landscapes may still feature the physical remains of fortifications and scars of battle, which provide a ready point of focus.

Military geographers and geologists have contributed much to the analysis of the landscapes of battle, especially with regard to the circumstances of geology, terrain and weather that act to condition, facilitate or obstruct military operations. However, the resonance of the historic battlefield is also contingent on our personal intersection with places that have hosted the extremes of human experience. Yet geography has been much less troubled by what can be

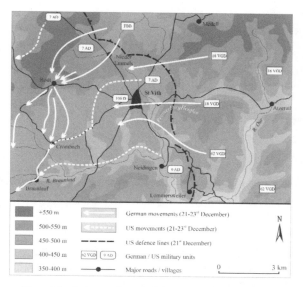

23 Map of the Ardennes forest at Saint Vith, Belgium, showing disposition and movements of units of the US and German army between 21 and 23 December 1944, during the 'Battle of the Bulge'. *Key to unit identities*: 7 / 9 AD – 7th / 9th Armoured Division; 106 D – 106th Division; 18 / 62 VGD – 18th / 62nd Volksgrenadier Division; FBB – Führer Begleit Brigade.

known of former battlefields from the perspective of the combatant, and in seeking to inform our understanding of the broader physical context and course of a battle, military geographers and the heritage industry run the risk, ironically, of distancing us from the battlefield as lived by the participants. In his celebrated analysis of the battles of Agincourt, Waterloo and the Somme, for example, the military historian John Keegan reminds us that many of the combatants will have directly experienced and fought (perhaps briefly) in only a small part of the battlefield.[1]

In order to glimpse the 'face of battle' for individuals or groups of participants, Keegan draws on a wide range of battlefield circumstances (including terrain, tactics and equipment), as well as the written narratives of those involved, and it is the latter that assume particular importance for exploring the warrior experience of the increasingly large-scale battles of the twentieth-century World Wars, which ranged across three-dimensional landscapes of air, sea and land.[2] Indeed, the spaces that have hosted air and sea battles are likely to have indeterminate boundaries and lack any enduring frame of reference; here the act of studying the wrecks of ships and aircraft is perhaps the most immediate means of engaging us with the cockpits, turrets and hulls that framed the personal experience of battle for airmen of the twentieth century and the sailors of this and earlier times.

Study of the material remains of battle (including personal effects, equipment and perhaps even the remains of those who died) usually requires excavation, and hence it is archaeology, with its investigation of patterns *beneath* the ground, that is doing much to illuminate the battlefield experience of individual combatants. Witness, for example, the tracing of individual US cavalrymen across the battlefield of Little Big Horn (Great Sioux Reservation, 1876) through the recovery and analyses of buried rifle cartridge cases.[3] But archaeologists are also beginning to seek a deeper understanding of the relationship between warriors and landscape, recognizing here that battlefields are places that are encultured by the act of war, and that the decision to fight in any particular locality may be dictated by cultural concerns as much as technological requirements or tactical necessity. Carman, for example, draws a contrast between the level and relatively featureless ground typical of medieval and earlier battlefields from the terrain of hills and valleys contested by armies of the seventeenth to nineteenth centuries.[4] These perspectives remind us that as places of cultural significance battlefields are liable to be perceived differently by differing populations, and that these concerns may be particularly acute when one of the warring parties is fighting on home (familiar) territory, or is campaigning across alien terrain.

Maintaining a focus on the personal experience of combat and its cultural context is therefore a means by which we can begin to access the human face of battle across all scales of battlefield, whether these constitute relatively small-scale engagements or the mechanized and frequently international (globalized?) scope of battles in the twentieth-century World Wars. In the latter case the term 'battlefield', with its implicit concern for terrestrial landscapes, begins to lose its immediacy since engagements ranged over larger three-dimensional spaces of air, sea and land that are less readily bounded. Perhaps instead we should begin to think in terms of 'battlespheres' that are created and transformed by acts of war, and in bringing the individual experience of combat to the fore acknowledge the resonance of places associated with violence, trauma and loss.

Dust

Phil Dunham

> If I should die, think only this of me:
> That there's some corner of a foreign field
> That is forever England. There shall be
> In that rich earth a richer dust concealed;
> A dust whom England bore, shaped, made
>   aware,
> Gave, once, her flowers to love, her ways
>   to roam,
> A body of England's, breathing English air,
> Washed by the rivers, blest by suns of
>   home.
> Rupert Brooke, from *The Soldier* (1915)

So the story goes, when the Anglo-Welsh soldier-poet of the First World War, Edward Thomas, was asked what he was fighting for, he picked up a handful of dust from the ground and replied 'this'. Scientific definitions of dust have traditionally centred on particles. Grain size, texture, mineralogy: it is a language of solids and points. Yet, as this example shows, the same desire for fixity is evident in many expressions of what might be termed the cultural entrainment of dust. Typically, the imagery of dust is used to convey a strong sense of social or cultural identity, often through the suggestion of clear-cut division. For many, dust symbolizes the distinction between belonging and exclusion, the familiar and the foreign, the living and the dead and, by implication, the social and material. Depending on the context, the idea of dust may be deployed as a signifier of proud nationhood (as opposed to foreign 'inferiority' or incursion), of age and decay (as compared with youthful vibrancy) or of a slovenly indifference to dirt and disease (as against the ordered 'rightness' of cleanliness and personal hygiene). Or it may be used to invoke the cold, inanimate realities of the 'physical landscape', as opposed to the warm flesh of the living (usually human) body. In each case, dust is used to mark some kind of boundary between Self and Other, and thus to epitomize the kinds of binary opposition that have dominated traditional Western understandings of 'our place in the world'. In Rupert Brooke's sonnet, *The Soldier*, for instance, dust forms a central motif in a careful juxtaposition of contradictory elements (familiar–foreign, living–dead) which, like the assertion by Edward Thomas, serves to reproduce a powerful sense of English national identity. Likewise, in Christian theology, dust marks the boundary between life and death: the imagery of God creating 'man' from the dust on the ground (Genesis 2: 7) and the emphatic 'dust to dust' of the funeral oration, highlighting not only a strong connection, but also a clear distinction, between human beings and the physical world they inhabit. For Christians, dust connotes the physical remains of the body, left to decompose quietly in the churchyard once the soul has been liberated and the 'breath of life', imbued by God, has been extinguished.

Yet, in truth, dust resists the modernist ennui, the weariness of classification, the strain of keeping things fixed. Try as we might, the attempt to consign (and confine) dust to its 'proper place'[1] – literally and imaginatively – is invariably thwarted, not least because of the tendency for dust to remain 'suspended' (in every sense of the word). Dust is at once both material and immaterial, characterized as much by its spacing, its hollow connections, as its solids and points. Dust ebbs and flows, settles and rises, repeatedly blown out of place as it is swept up, entrained and deposited by the flow of the breeze. Dust forms clouds and plumes, storms and hazes. It is seldom fixed in time and space. And as it transforms, dust not only moves but also betrays movement through space, yielding intricate impressions and traces as all manner of events and encounters are revealed by the dust they throw up. Dust is no respecter of boundaries, whether real or imagined. Rather, it is apt to expose and subvert the contrivance of order. For instance, some 9.8 by 10^6 tonnes of wind-blown material were deposited over England during the great fall of Saharan dust in 1903, which raises the interesting possibility that Edward Thomas based his allegiance to England on a handful of African dust.

Far from upholding the conventional distinction between the social and the material, dusty narratives of culture-nature ought therefore to unsettle these categories in ways that emphasize their inherent instabilities and the flows and connections between them.

Take, for instance, the body. It is well known that much of the dust we encounter (especially in the home) is in fact 'us'. More correctly, it consists of tiny fragments of dead skin that have peeled and flaked from our bodies. Moreover, the outermost layers of human skin are made up of dead cells that are themselves in the process of becoming dust. In relation to the central theme of this book, therefore, dust raises questions about what (if anything) is consistent or whole about our bodies, and where (and indeed whether) a line can be meaningfully drawn between the human and nonhuman worlds. But perhaps more than this, dust questions the extent to which these worlds can be adequately represented through the confines of language. The enigmatic qualities of dust in this respect were never lost on Edward Thomas who, in the story with which we began, eventually allowed the dust to slip through his fingers, symbolizing his deep uncertainty about what 'This England'[2] – the idea for which he was to lay down his life – actually meant. And it was the strain – and ultimate failure – to fix 'This England', to capture its essence, that lay at the heart of Thomas's literary career; from the tortured precision of his early prose, through the fragmentary staccato of his countryside diaries, and into the strange, unresolved enigmas of his poems:

> Even so the lark
> Loves dust
> And nestles in it
> The minute
> Before he must
> Soar in lone flight
> So far,
> Like a black star
> He seems –
> A mote of singing dust
> Afloat

> Above,
> That dreams
> And sheds no light.[3]

A salutary reminder to those of us who try to 'fix' through writing: to be motes of singing dust that dream and shed no light. Perhaps that is all we can hope for too.

Pollution

Ismo Kantola

On 24 May 2002, after more than twenty years of heated debate and intense campaigning, the Parliament of Finland decided to permit the building of a fifth reactor to be added to the nuclear power generating capacity of four plants, 750 megawatts each, already in operation in the country since the end of the 1970s. In the debate that followed the parliamentary decision, the concepts of pollution and progress played an important role. However, the debate also showed that the power to define the meaning of these concepts rests heavily in the hands of a relatively small group of people who are assigned the authority of an expert.

One of the founding intellectual resources of this expertise of progress and pollution through which experts assert their authority to define meaning can be called logical empiricism.[1] This form of knowledge relies on the logical consistency of linguistic expressions together with a supposed correspondence of the concepts with the world 'out there' (whether observed and experienced or not). In this type of knowledge, there is a practical necessity of 'black boxing' unsolvable and frustrating questions and dilemmas, as well as an imperative for limits on questioning in general. As a sociologist I see pollution, as well as any kind of environmental problem, as a socially constructed problem. Its emergence consists of struggles about conceptual and semiotic framing as well as about the power to define the proper mode of thematization of the problem(s). What interests me is the place of black boxes within environmental debates – and in alternative foundations for expertise that do not necessarily abandon 'science'.

In a recent article on the sociology of technico-instrumental research, Terry Shinn criticizes rather severely what he calls 'the new orthodoxy of the sociology of science'.[2] Among the targets in his critique of the 'orthodox school', he pinpoints the relation of humans with nonhumans – and well-known studies by Bruno Latour, Michel Callon and Steve Woolgar that allege that the human / nonhuman relation is fundamental to the making of new knowledge in science and technology. As an alternative to the new orthodoxy, Shinn proposes a study of technico-instrumental research that takes more seriously the existing division of labour in science and technology. Converging understanding of the world 'out there' is not brought about by human actors communicating with the nonhuman or by a simple mechanism of diffusion, but instead by 'multiscient' individuals capable of shuttling among various fields of science and technology. The resulting knowledge is precisely not the sort that is verified by its logical consistency, nor is it just a matter of trust and commitment, but rather something whose truth can be demonstrated.

My re-elaborated proposal, perhaps somewhat at odds with Terry Shinn's analysis, is: actually there are three types of knowledge that we use in orienting ourselves in this modern world. One of these is technico-

instrumental knowledge, the truth of which is demonstrable. This must include not only technical instruments but also accounting systems and other media that function satisfactorily and demonstrably well. The second type of knowledge is analytical, its truth being verifiable as the logical consistency of propositions concerning a certain well-defined area of reality. The third type of knowledge is based on trust and commitment to action that is bound to make true an idea or a plan. This type of knowledge materializes itself in collective action, in something that could well be called a project or sometimes more justly a movement.

Each type of knowledge has deficits. Analytical knowledge must presuppose correspondence with its premises and certain parts of the real world. In order to do so, creators of this knowledge must put unsolvable questions in black boxes, which means committing to a tacit consensus among the respective experts not to take up any of these black boxed issues. In science, there is still a lingering awareness of some of those problems. However, when analytic knowledge is combined with technico-instrumental knowledge and practices – in order to provide means for projects and movements essentially based on pure trust and commitment – a reminder of the black-boxed issues is no longer tolerable. Taking scientific expertise as a basis for the legitimation of decision-making pre-requires forgetting the black-boxed basics. As a result of this amnesia, expertise no longer has restrictions on its knowledge, and can be used to exert authority in any situation.

I would like to maintain that modern environmentalism has to a remarkable extent grown (and still keeps growing) out of the reopening of the black boxes of science. Relative to black boxing is the externalization of economic, social and environmental

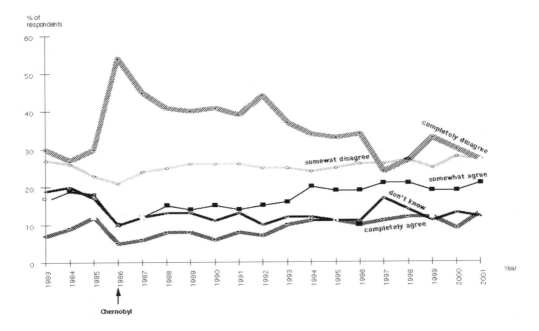

% of
respondents

completely disagree

somewhat disagree

somewhat agree

don't know

completely agree

Chernobyl

Year

24 Finnish attitude percentages on the public opinion survey assertion: 'The probability of a major nuclear power accident is so small that there is no reason to be concerned about it'. Figures are collected annually.

impacts in defining an accounting or measurement system. Once accessible for reopening and re-thematization, both the externalized impacts and the black-boxed problems serve as fuel and a *raison d'être* for new, critical and alternative projects and movements. However, neither can the challengers themselves escape the necessity of setting limits to critique and questioning once they want to convert their knowledge into action.

In Finland, the twenty-five-years debate about and campaigning for nuclear power shows an interesting shift as to the strategies of the disputing parties. The proponents of a parliamentary permission for additional nuclear-energy capacity have shifted from economic arguments to environmental ones. On the other hand, the critics of nuclear-power-based energy supply have shifted from environmental to economic arguments. This has become possible thanks to increased understanding of economic accounting of energy and the advancement of other types

of technico-instrumental knowledge. The n-campaigners focus on the black boxes of coal-powered energy-production, while the anti-nuclear campaigners expose externalities and inconsistencies in the economy of nuclear power. While there is, perhaps, a common basis for argumentation on the technico-instrumental level, the disputing parties have thus far succeeded to dodge confrontation around the black boxes containing nuclear waste and carbon dioxide.

Perhaps the non-human actors of today are communicating beyond experts, directly to lay people, in the form of environmental problems that are resulting from the modern technico-scientific governance of the physical world. Knowledge created by technico-instrumental research can be used both to advance harmful projects and to benefit the search for remedy. It can be used for maintaining the status quo, but also to overthrow it.

Crucial for a successful and purposive use of the technico-instrumental knowledge will be a revaluation of the trust-and-commitment-

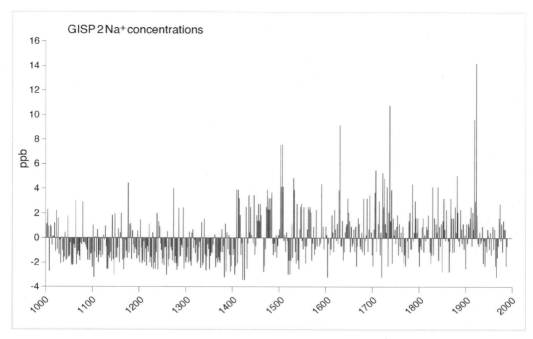

25 Reconstruction of annual (July–June) air temperatures for GISP2 for the period AD 1000–1987.

based knowledge that has had such a decisive role in implementing a nuclear-power-driven energy economy in a small country like Finland. Thus far the parliamentary discussion preceding the decision in favour of nuclear energy has been based on observing the logical consistency of an unquestioned, given selection of scientific minutiae.

Climate

Alastair Dawson

In recent years, publication of research arising from the United States (GISP2) and European (GRIP) ice-core drilling projects in central Greenland has revolutionized the way in which we think about climate change.[1] In respect of the so-called Little Ice Age, the academic community received a severe jolt after the publications of Kreutz

and Mayewski, and of Meeker and Mayewski, who presented a chronology of sea-salt deposition for the Greenland ice for approximately the last 1,500 years.[2] These writers made particular use of sodium (NA+) concentrations recorded in the ice as a result of North Atlantic storminess changes (illus. 25). Their analysis showed very clearly that NA+ concentrations and hence North Atlantic storminess remained low during the medieval warm period (MWP) but was abruptly terminated about AD 1400 by a sharp increase in NA+ concentrations. North Atlantic storminess increased markedly at this time, and the researchers have showed that it has remained at high levels ever since. Unlike the temperature chronology, there is no indication for the NA+ chronology of a change in climate at the start of the twentieth century. Are we therefore to argue that we are still living within the Little Ice Age? In respect of North Atlantic storminess (itself a measure of the North Atlantic Oscillation [NAO]) the Little Ice Age has not ended – yet in terms of air temperature it has!

During the 1970s quantification in geography was the rule. This presented a problem with respect to the Little Ice Age, since it was not an easy exercise to gather together the appropriate instrumental weather data that could show when this time interval began and ended. For Scotland, it was almost impossible. The general preconception about the Little Ice Age was that it represented a period of temperature cooling following the period of medieval warmth and that it ended at the start of the twentieth century. Yet opinions differed. For example, the *Oxford Companion to the Earth* refers to the Little Ice Age as 'beginning sometime in the 13th and 14th centuries and lasting until the end of the 19th century . . . [it] was a period of generally colder climate . . . [whose] effects can be detected over most parts of the globe'.[3] One consequence of this style of thinking is that particular

intervals of the earth's history (in this case the Little Ice Age) are interpreted on the basis of a single parameter of climate – in this case temperature.

The Greenland ice cores also provide a record of air temperature change. The derivation of this chronology is, however, complex since it relies upon the use of the oxygen isotope chronology measured within Greenland ice and the conversion of the oxygen isotope measurements to air temperature values. This derived air temperature record is generally regarded as one of the kingpin records of climate change for the Northern Hemisphere. One might expect, therefore, that a sustained decline in air temperatures recorded in Greenland ice implied a period of climatic deterioration across the Northern Hemisphere and certainly across the North Atlantic region. Similarly, records of air temperature warming recorded in the Greenland ice are

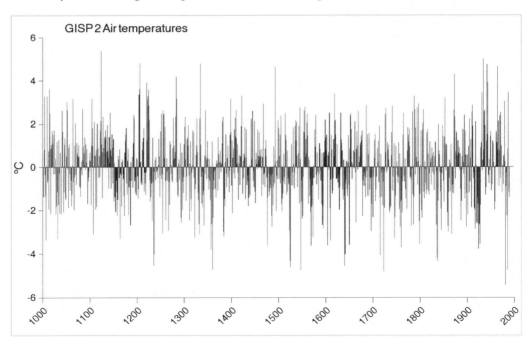

26 Reconstruction of annual Na+ values for GISP2 based on statistical interpolation between 587 datapoints.

frequently used as a surrogate for climatic amelioration elsewhere. When the Greenland air temperature record is examined in detail, however, the major episodes of climatic change generally assumed to have taken place over about the last 1,000 years show themselves less clearly (illus. 26). For example, the Little Ice Age air temperature data for the GISP2 ice-ore drill site in central Greenland exhibits extreme inter-annual variability. Where then is the Little Ice Age in the Greenland ice-core record?

There are two factors that may inform us further. First, it is important to remember that the isotope concentrations preserved in ancient and compressed Greenland snowflakes represent a record of air temperature change well above the ice surface in the lower troposphere. In fact, the oxygen isotope concentration data can be regarded as a surrogate for snowflake production over central Greenland. Secondly, it is important to recall the role of katabatic winds across central Greenland that originate over the centre of the ice sheet and move outwards towards the coast along topographic depressions. One can imagine air temperatures in central Greenland buffered by the effect of katabatic winds, which serves to diminish the signature of regional changes in climate. These observations serve as a warning to those seeking to define the start and end of the Little Ice Age that they are 'treading on thin ice'!

Where does this leave us in our task of recognizing the Little Ice Age in climate history First and foremost it takes us back to the beginning and the slow, meticulous procedure of gathering together instrumental records of past weather together with documentary information from letters and diaries. Yet very few of these records of past weather and climate have been investigated. This is largely because the passage of three decades of scientific progress since the 1970s has not

been accompanied by a significant increase in interest in past weather and climate. To a large extent, this is because the field of historical climatology lies in academic 'no-man's land'. It is absent from most university curricula of Geography, History, Earth and Environmental Science. The most up-to-date thinking on climate change processes in the North Atlantic region involves ocean currents and thermohaline circulation. Periods of climatic cooling are generally associated with a slow-down or shut-down in thermohaline circulation (THC). Past periods of warmth are associated with an acceleration in the circulation of heat and salt across the North Atlantic. One might therefore expect that the so-called Little Ice Age may have represented the most recent shut-down of THC across the North Atlantic. It is ironic, therefore, that the documentary and instrumental records of past weather and climate in Scotland may prove to be invaluable in the reconstruction of this most recent complex and fascinating period of the earth's climate history.

Lakes

Laura Cameron

Stop of interest

Beside the Trans-Canada Highway in the Fraser Valley of British Columbia, Myrtle Ferguson gestures out towards the green orderly fields where Sumas Lake used to be. 'There – we swam before breakfast, we swam before lunchtime . . . we swam again in the afternoon and had a swim before we went to bed.'

Scent plumes. This is my cue and I land softly

on the papery skin and tracery of blue veins that is her outstretched hand. Split the skin, probe, repeat. Ah, there. Very still now, the warm blood pools. I wait, then suck until my belly bloats.

Commuters surge past. A Government sign describes a story of progress – the agricultural benefits of what was called the 'Sumas Reclamation Project'. This skeletal official history of the Sumas Lake drainage of the 1920s is reinforced by the intensively managed floodplain and echoed in waterscapes cum landscapes – the Fens, the Nile Delta, the Zuider Zee – around the planet. A founding story for a nation. A topography, too, of forgetting.[1]

Fly now; so heavily, slowly. Alight to rest, digest, sending a slow trickle of pink water drops down the side of the fence.

Sumas Lake was a flood lake, frustrating the map makers, expanding during Spring freshets and winter rains as its tributaries swelled. The flooding Fraser River, which drains one-third of British Columbia, once fed tremendous amounts of water into Sumas Lake. In 1894, at its 200-year flood level, the lake stretched twenty miles between mountains five miles apart. At low-water time local people grazed cattle and sheep around the lake edges. A stopping place for migratory wildfowl, a spawning route and habitat for fish – the drainage of Sumas Lake represented one of the major losses of wetlands along the Fraser River in the twentieth century.

Lake gone? But rainwaters and floodwaters return, over spilling the dykes – to wet the egg I came from, to wet the eggs I will lay on lake-bed soil. Yes, some come back, joining those more fond of dark waters, culverts clogged by detritus, stacked tires.

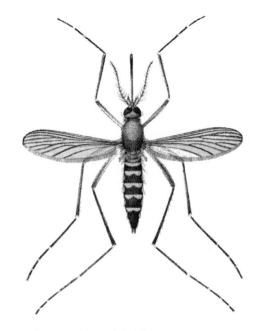

27 *Aedes vexans* (Meigen), female.

'Mighty Mosquito Must Migrate' to the 'wilds of Potsdam' sang the newspapers during the Great War, praising the workers near the Lake who, acting as courageously as the women of Great Britain, 'stuck to their fruitpicking despite the fierce offensive of the mosquito'. The political desire to create farmland was aided by new scientific entomologists, experts in identification and extermination. United against the mosquito, the Provincial and Dominion Governments furthered a virtual geopolitical campaign that involved one of the first aerial mappings of mosquito populations in Canada and the targeting of Sumas Lake as a hotbed of mosquito insurrection.

Aedes vexans – I? I – a lake, its right to exist.

The Stó:lō, the Aboriginal people living in the valley, called the mosquito 'Qwá:l' – a name too for a Sumas warrior. According to one story, mosquitoes once were sparks, the burnt remains of the cannibal giant Saskts who set upon a group of children after they failed to share their food. The children managed to outwit the giant, pushing it into a fire, and they transformed the sparks into mosquitoes as mementos of Saskts. While written narratives, like histories, tend to rely on time – the time-line of dates – to talk about events in space, oral traditions tend to employ the place names of spaces to talk about events in time. Yet children of an oral culture, sent by the colonial government to residential schools where they were forbidden to speak their own languages, often lost place names, ways to evoke the stories, meanings, origins and pleasures in their landscape and waterscape. What happens to stories when places, like lakes, disappear? One woman recalled: 'I went to school before the lake was drained and when I came back, it was gone.'

We travel miles, evenings are best – exodus, up, over. Light is lovely, factories working late, suburbs, lamps, firesides where storytellers gather, young bodies, old.

Like the lake, many of the people who lived there were understood as unfit neighbours, requiring domestication. Without a treaty, the Stó:lō were forced onto ever tinier reserves, creating more dry space for non-Stó:lō settlers. Without consultation, Sumas Lake was drained. In 1915, a few years before the lake drainage, the 92-year-old chief of the Sumas Band at Kilgard, Selsmlton (Ned), spoke to the joint Dominion-Provincial Royal Commission on Indian Affairs. He began with the stories that he had been told: 'I know the old people used to say that the white people will be shoving you around all over this open prairie to get our food.' Chief Ned went on to judge that most of his reserve was subject to overflow at high water. Yet, referring to the lake's important fish habitat, he did not want to have the land dyked 'because that will mean more starvation for us'.

It's the eggs that need blood. Bronze they will

be, marked with polygon patterns, beautiful, hatching with rising waters, at home there, as larvae, as pupae, emerging on the surface film to fly, frenzy, mate.

The waters of Suman Lake are perhaps more latent than permanently gone. Even now, 80 years after the initial drainage project put to work some of the biggest pumps then draining land in the British Commonwealth, the agricultural and residential lands continue to be pumped. If the drainage stopped, the water would, without doubt, return.

Lakes bring dangers too . . .

Salmon are sometimes found in Lake Bottom drainage ditches. Sturgeon are sighted swimming back and forth in front of the Pumphouse following ancient routes to home waters. Before the drainage, shore birds at Sumas Lake were observed destroying great numbers of mosquito larvae: fish fry, dragon flies, salamanders, parasitic worms and bats were known mosquito predators. Possibilities, other stories remain here, reconnecting us to another sense of place and the challenge of sharing it.

So – how many bites of memory do you require?

Fire

Stephen J. Pyne

How should we think about fire? An answer is not obvious. It is testimony to the immense significance of fire that humanity has for so long chosen not only to anthropomorphize it but to grant it a substantive identity it does not deserve. Early philosophers considered it a god, or at least theophany, the manifestation of a god-like presence and power. The Aztecs called it Huehueteotl (or 'Dios Viejo', the Old God), and the Hindus, Agni, along with Indus the most venerable of their pantheon. The ancient Greeks, and the ancient Chinese, labelled it an element. For Western civilization it then morphed into a declination of lesser substances like phlogiston and caloric before ending as a subservient chemical reaction, the rapid oxidation, usually accompanied by flame, or other substances. Today it no longer claims reality as an autonomous substance. Rather, fire is a phenomenon that derives from its circumstances. It is what results when heat, fuel and oxygen combine under suitable conditions. It has no reality apart from the physical circumstances that make it possible. And that, in brief, is equally the lesson of its intellectual history. The definition of fire has changed with its cultural circumstances. It takes its character from its context.

In this way, fire enters many subjects, yet claims none uniquely as its own. The other elements – air, water, earth, even wood – have a hard materiality. While they also have a chemistry and are compounds of many substances, one can pick them up, carry them to another setting, push and plunge and pummel them. One can fill a football with air and kick it. One can fill a bucket with water and haul it to a field. One can pick up earth and dump it elsewhere. One can leave them alone, untended, and find them again later. But one cannot pick up fire, as fire. You carry its fuels, upon which it glows or flames – you pick up embers, smouldering branches, a flaming matchstick. Remove that fuel and the fire dies. Shut off its air or cool it and the fire will go out. Other 'elements' have intellectual disciplines and academic departments to study them. Fire does not. It is, in truth, not an

element at all except that its unblinking importance makes it elemental to human life.

The time has come perhaps to re-centre fire. The reason is context. If fire is its surroundings, those surroundings are almost wholly biological. Life created the oxygen that fire craves, life created the fuels that feed it, and, in the guise of humanity, life progressively oversees the kindling that sparks it into existence. Here is where a re-centring of fire packs its punch: it compels us to shed the simplistic notion that 'fire is a tool'. If it is a tool, it is an odd one, and a tool that exists only because of its setting. An axe exists in its own right: a fire does not. An axe cannot morph into something else as it moves from a carpenter's shop to a woods; a fire can. Clearly, people have 'used' fire and hence it may be considered as a technology. What kind of technology is it?

Several kinds. There is fire as a tool, fire as a tamed 'species', fire as a captured ecological process, or at least these are the most common conceptions. Consider each in turn. Tool fire embraces 'tool' in its everyday meaning. Flame sits on a candle as a claw hammer sits on a handle. It applies concentrated heat and light. Of course one has to feed it wax and ensure that it has ample oxygen, while a hammer neither consumes the wood of its handle nor demands air; but there are good reasons to treat such fires as a tool in the vernacular sense. What one wants is the heat and light. It is thus possible to substitute another tool for this one, to use heated coils and electric lights, for example, instead of flame. Or to put the 'flame' into a chamber that disaggregates it into the most elemental parts of combustion and then apply its heat to power prime movers.

Tame fire works differently. It depends more acutely on its context. Such fires work within a domesticated, usually agricultural setting: they are the fire equivalent of domesticated species such as cows, horses and sheepdogs. They do a variety of tasks, much as a horse may pull a plough, draft a surrey and carry a rider. They may burn the pruned limbs of fruit trees, the ditches around a farm, the fallow of a field. But their power is only as great as their surroundings and these are very much shaped by human contrivance. They are, in fact, fire-variants of kept creatures: they must be bred, selected, trained, nurtured, housed, harnessed to particular tasks, kept on a leash. They are harder to substitute for. Replacing the tame fire is like substituting a tractor for a draft ox. It can be done, but the consequences ripple through the farm.

Captured fire more resembles a caught animal, like an elephant that can be directed to useful tasks. Its 'wild' properties are what make it valuable. In this instance, its 'wildland' or coarsely managed context are what define the fire and sustain it. People let it loose, like a cheetah trained to the hunt, and allow it to roam. Its success depends on timing and of course on setting. It can, quickly and unexpectedly, go feral or turn on its nominal guardian. Yet its value is unquestioned: it can challenge wildfire on its own grounds, without meticulous preparation. It can substitute a partially controlled process for an uncontrolled one. It is how, over long millennia, humanity has turned uncultivated lands to productive purpose. But as an ecological process, it is not readily replaced. No combination of chainsaws, bulldozers and wood-chippers can do what it does. While a technology, it is hardly a tool in the common sense, and attempts to characterize it as such must fail.

All of these technologies, moreover, depend not only on their environmental setting but on their relationship to humans. None of them could even exist without a human agent. Those relationships run a gamut: tool fire is a device, tame fire a symbiosis, captured fire an alliance, and there are others less prominent. Fire cannot be as readily separated from its user as the naïve image of a tool suggests. It is easy to take a candle away, less so field fires, and still less prescribed burning because the web of relationships increases. Subtracting fire may be as powerful as adding it. A removed hammer may affect a nail. A removed field fire may unravel an ecosystem.

Instead, fire-as-biology recommends another strategy. It focuses on the overall context, social as well as biological. It envisions fire as a catalyst, a synthesizer of those surroundings. It argues for thinking of fire control as a variety of biological control, much like integrated pest management. It shifts attention from mechanical acts such as starting and stopping fires, and toward the interconnections that make fire possible, shape its behaviour and determine its outcomes. It forces people to accept their role as fire creatures because it is we who (nearly) close the biological cycle of burning.

Fire-as-tool suggests that the problem is to put fire in or take it out. Fire-as-process suggests that the problem is to decide what fire's context should be, and then determine what kind of catalytic fire-induced jolt might best serve that context; that fire is not merely a tool to reduce fuel so much as combustibles are a means to get the kind of fire a biota requires; that our role as fire-keeper is more complex than that of tool-maker because it involves ecological relationships as well as tasks. That fire, while no longer considered an element, remains elemental.

God

John Polkinghorne

To believe in God in the sense that the three great monotheistic religions of Judaism, Christianity and Islam affirm is to believe that reality is one and that it makes total sense because it is a divine creation. The landscape of theology is the whole universe; its timescale is the whole spread of cosmic history, both past and to come; and its fundamental explanatory principle is grounded in the operation of the will of a divine Agent.

For the believer, the rationally beautiful order of the physical world, which induces in its scientific explorers a deep sense of wonder, testifies to the divine Mind that has ordained that order. Behind the fifteen billion years of cosmic history, which have seen a ball of energy turn into the home of self-conscious beings (the universe become aware of itself), lies the fruitful will of its Creator. This divine purpose has been expressed from the beginning in those laws of nature whose fine tuning (the anthropoid principle) alone has permitted the subsequent development of carbon-based life.

Thus, it is believed, nature testifies to the God who holds it in being. Nor is culture silent. The Creator is One who is worthy of worship, for God is also the ground of the true, the good and the beautiful. Human culture, just like human science, is, at its deepest level, discovery and not invention, a response to the way things are. Profound moral principles – such as love being better than hate or that persons are always ends and never merely means – are neither disguised evolutionary survival strategies nor useful social conventions. They are discernments of reality, for our ethical intuitions are intimations of God's good and perfect will.

Aesthetic delight is also a form of encounter with reality, for it is a sharing in the Creator's joy in creation. Belief in God endorses the validity of both the impersonal investigations of science into the pattern and structure of the physical world, and also the insights of individual experience into that world of value that is the context of personal living. Another dimension of that world of cultural reality is the encounter with the sacred presence of the divine, to which the world faith-traditions bear testimony. In these ways, theistic belief is able to integrate our natural / cultural experience of the many-layered reality in which we live. Science and religion, nature and culture, are perceived theologically as complementary aspects of that one great Theory of Everything, belief in God.

So great and all-embracing a vision is not, however, unproblematic. The greatest challenge that faces belief in God is the problem of the evil and suffering in the world. Here seems to be so many black threads woven into the pattern of creation. Believers and unbelievers alike are aware of the problem that this poses and no one could suppose that there is some simple, one-line answer to its deep perplexity. In responding, theists have to find a path between two unacceptable and extreme pictures of how God might relate to creation. One is the picture of a God who does absolutely everything, a Cosmic Tyrant whose grip on events never relaxes. The other picture is of a God who does nothing in particular, the indifferent Spectator of cosmic history. If God is the Source of goodness, and so the Source of love, both these images must be false idols. The Creator cannot be the Tyrant because the God of love must give some due degree of independence to the creatures who are the objects of divine love. They must be allowed to be and to make themselves, even if this implies allowing the act of a murderer or the incidence of a cancer. But the God of love cannot be just a bystanding Spectator either. In some real way, the Creator must be active and involved in the travail of creation. To use a memorable and powerful phrase, God must be involved to the point of being 'a fellow sufferer who understands'. The monotheistic faiths have, over many centuries, sought to understand their experience of God in ways that can accommodate this more profound image of divinity, with its implication that, while all that happens is allowed by God, not all that happens is in accordance with God's beneficent desires.

One final challenge to theism remains to be discussed. Our study of cosmology tells us that the long-term prospects for the universe are bleak. Eventually, after many more billions of years, its history will end either in the bang of cosmic collapse or the whimper of cosmic decay. Carbon-based life, together with all culture, will have disappeared altogether before this dismal end. What, then, are we to make of theism's claim to make *total* sense of what is going on? In the end, will it not all prove to have been 'a tale told by an idiot'? This challenge leads us to consider a final affirmation about God that the monotheistic faiths each want to make in its own way: that God is the ground of a true and everlasting hope, the One who can be trusted not only in life but in death also. They believe that the last word does not lie with mortality, either human or cosmic, but with the eternally steadfast faithfulness of God. The evolutionary pattern of our presently experienced world is that of the death of one generation to make way for the life of the next generation. Belief in God implies that there is a more profound and ultimate pattern to reality than that, for it places their trust in the final, hopeful pattern of death followed by resurrection to eternal life, a new life lived in the merciful presence of God.

Water

Vic Baker

We humans are composed of 70 per cent water by weight. Science was born when one of us, Thales of Miletus, speculated around 600 BC that water is the material cause or essence of all things. Similarly, our planet, Earth, is covered in area by 70 per cent liquid water, shrouded in clouds of water vapour and capped at each end by accumulations of water ice. Yet it was only in the late 1960s, when Apollo astronauts looked back from the moon upon their home planet, that realization was made of the great mistake in naming the world. Thales may have been overly simplistic in considering all things to be made of that of which he himself was composed, but his guess was a good one. The element, hydrogen, whose oxide is water, is indeed the most abundant element in the universe as we currently know it. However, Thales' successors continued to accept that the earthy surfaces upon which they walked and the landscapes that they viewed were appropriate for the name of the world that they inhabited. Viewed from the rest of the universe, the situation is quite clear: the name of our planet should be Water, not Earth.

About the same time that Thales was musing about what everything was composed of, Lao-tse in China was teaching that the primordial essence of all, the T'ai-chi or Tao, the Great Ultimate, or motivating force of the universe, was unknown and unknowable. Out of this mysterious unity, however, came the tension of two opposites, yin and yang, which are natural forces permeating all that exists. The cold force of accumulated yin became the element water. Water is the first element of this cosmology and it is first in the Western mind as Thales showed. That we are also mostly water, in composition or essence, leads one to wonder about how we view a world that is also, in essence, water. Put a cellular membrane around some water and we have the makings of primitive life. Modern biochemistry traces human origins through phylogenetic trees to just such ancestors. After these billions of years, are we not just water coming to a scientific contemplation of ourselves, the universe that is water, just as we are water?

Science seeks understanding of the world. It has been remarkably successful in that quest, emulating the original lucky guess made by Thales. Some have claimed that this success derives from a peculiar point of view about the world, a view that Thomas Nagel called 'the view from nowhere'. Presumably this detached viewpoint has produced spectacular successes ranging from quantum mechanics to molecular biology. However, it cannot apply to any scientific study of people and water. The reason is obvious, once you think about it. It is people (scientists) who must take this view. Despite the grandest claims of the artificial intelligence enthusiasts, the doing of science is likely to be a human activity for some time to come. (Thankfully I can be spared the prospect of sharing discoveries with robots.) Scientists can either admit that they bring a viewpoint to their studies or they can engage in the pretence that they have no viewpoint, despite the heritage outlined above. As Aristotle wisely observed, we all have a metaphysics, especially those of us who claim not to have a metaphysics, for that claim is itself a powerful kind of metaphysics.

The two viewpoints of people in relation to water are (1) aquarian and (2) piscean. The aquarian sees the world from the outside as an object to be explained. Its facts serve to confirm or deny that explanation, and explained truth provides the power with which to generalize, justify, control and manipulate. The aquarian must separate from reality to avoid bias in generating objective truths so that the resulting controls and manipulations are unhindered by nonscientific motivations. In contrast, the piscean sees the world subjectively as an opportunity for understanding. Its facts serve as clues to stimulate guesses as to its nature, leading to more refined understanding and better guesses. The world becomes almost a sacred place of which the piscean is a part, rather than an austere laboratory in which to test sacred theories.

Floods are one of the extremes of water. They are flows unusual for their rarity and immense magnitude, and sometimes they are damaging to people and their activities. The aquarian views floods as a collective phenomenon to be explained. A theory as to their statistical distribution in time and space can be formulated in unbiased mathematical terms and tested against a few decades of measured streamflow at a gauging station. Extrapolating from the sample of streamflow, the aquarian can generalize to the ideal of the 'hundred-year flood', using this as a criterion for the design of protective works and for the imposition of regulations intended to prevent the hazardous consequences of damaging floods. The theory of the aquarian tells how nature is, and the results of aquarian science tell how people are to adapt to that view of nature.

The piscean sees floods as unique phenomena. Although too dangerous to experience directly, the signs of the most extreme past flood occurrences provide reality indicators that can be documented and interpreted. While a theory poses what the aquarian wishes to say to nature, the interpretation of these flood signs is the expression of what nature says to the piscean. The conveyance of this message to those at risk from floods is intended to stimulate public action in response, as opposed to regulating its response by law. The piscean approach would emphasize communication of what has happened and thus might happen again. The aquarian approach communicates a theoretical construct, the '100-year flood', which has nothing to do with real years and treats 'flood' as the mere number produced by a statistical extrapolation. The aquarian requires a response, which may well be wrong if the theory is flawed. The piscean promotes responsibility in regard to partially understood reality, such that revised action will be required in light of further experience.

Water science has often been justified in aquarian terms, but there is nothing intrinsically unscientific about a piscean approach to science. Because there can be no 'view from nowhere', we need to make a choice about how we will view water. Will it be (1) from an unnatural, separate perspective (aquarian), or (2) from a total reality of which the perspective is a part (piscean)? The facts of our composition and evolutionary heritage show that (1) is unreal and artificial. The problems of our limited resources and fragile environment make (2) all the more relevant for human progress.

Oceans

Julian A. Dowdeswell

The blue of the oceans is the most clearly identifiable feature on the Earth's surface viewed from space. Deep-sea environments, however, are among the least well known on our planet. For example, the floating ice shelves of Antarctica, more than 300 metres thick and fed from the interior of the Antarctic Ice Sheet, provide an almost impenetrable carapace over unexplored seawater-filled cavities the size of England and up to about 1,000 metres deep.

The oceans – past, present and future – are a fundamental component of our dynamic Earth. Life on our planet is widely agreed to have begun in the oceans, emerging onto land only about 350 million years ago – less than 10 per cent of Earth's history. Today, the interactions between ocean and atmosphere are a major control on our weather, and changes in the nature of ocean circulation will influence climates of the future. The oceans have also provided routes for early human migrations and exploration of the

28 Sea ice covers much of the high latitude oceans.

earth's surface and, more recently, for international trade and as a theatre for the conduct of war.

The oceans make up more than 70 per cent of the earth's surface. They have an area of 360 million km^2 and a volume of about 1,350 million km^3.[1] The deepest water is over 11,000 metres, in an ocean trench near the Philippine Islands. Ocean waters vary both vertically and horizontally in temperature, salinity and chemistry, and in the amount of biological productivity that they sustain. About 75 per cent of ocean water is between -1 and 5°C in temperature (when pressure effects have been accounted for) and salinity averages about 35 parts per thousand.

The configuration of the oceans has varied at all timescales. Waves and tides change ocean–surface conditions and sea level over minutes to hours. Ocean warming and glacier melting have raised sea level by up to 20 centimetres over the past hundred years. The growth and decay of large continental ice sheets over glacial–interglacial cycles during the last two million years or so has caused sea level to rise and fall by more than 100 metres with a periodicity of about 100,000 years. New ocean basins have developed and older basins have been consumed over hundreds of millions of years by the plate-tectonic processes that link the earth's solid crust with the underlying viscous mantle. The present shape of the ocean basins and continents, and their positions with respect to the poles, are ephemeral in the context of Earth history.

Surface and deep-water currents, influenced by the Earth's rotation and radiation balance, transfer mass and energy within and between ocean basins. Ocean–surface currents are driven mainly by the Earth's major wind fields. By contrast, deep-ocean currents are influenced most strongly by density differences between water masses – hence the term *thermohaline* circulation, combining the temperature and salinity components of water density.

The sea floor in deep-ocean basins, located several kilometres beneath the water surface, is often a very low-energy environment. Levels of potential and radiative energy are very low, because abyssal-basin floors are usually extremely flat, cold and dark except close to tectonically active mid-ocean ridges. The slow rainout of rock and biogenic fragments from the ocean onto its floor provides an almost continuous and undisturbed sedimentary record in such locations. The chemical and morphological characteristics of micro-organisms and fine-grained rock particles taken from deep-ocean basins have been used to reconstruct the environmental changes that have taken place over the past few millions of years of Earth history. The time-resolution recorded in any core is dependent on sedimentation rate and the degree of mixing by bottom-dwelling organisms. Environmental data varying in resolution from hundreds to thousands of years have been extracted from core material that is amenable to the range of dating methods available.

These deep-ocean archives of past conditions have provided information on the magnitude and rate of change in a number of environmental variables, including sea-surface and deep-water temperature, ocean productivity, and the build-up and decay of ice sheets. Such proxy evidence on the nature of past climates has shown that many key environmental parameters have undergone rapid shifts in the past, rather than changing slowly through time. Thus, the thermohaline circulation of the North Atlantic Ocean, for example, appears to have switched on and off abruptly a number of times over the last 100,000 years. The notion that climate can change abruptly after passing complex environmental thresholds between different relatively stable states is a fundamental one. It has made the understanding of the way that the Earth's environmental system works a priority area for scientific research in a world where the levels of so-called Greenhouse gases are rising rapidly as a result of human industrial and agricultural activity.

Finally, although deep-ocean basins are being mapped with unprecedented accuracy by the latest generation of marine-geophysical bathymetry systems, the oceans remain arguably the least known environment on Earth. Only a few years ago, hydrothermal vents or 'black-smokers' were discovered, located on deep-sea mid-ocean ridges, providing energy for sea-floor organisms through chemosynthesis rather than conventional photosynthesis. Further surprises in terms of geological processes and organic life probably remain to be discovered in Earth's oceans. A new generation of autonomous underwater vehicles is being deployed in, for example, trenches in the deep-ocean floor and beneath the sea ice and ice shelves of the high-latitude seas, in order to continue probing unexplored areas of this very hostile environment. At the same time, scientific measurements continue to monitor the ocean environment in better-known locations, in order to detect changes in ocean conditions that may affect modern climate.

Ice Sheets

David Sugden

'Whether we accept what our imagination must suggest or pause at the actual facts which have been discovered, this great ice-sheet is unique; it has no parallel in the world, and its discovery must be looked upon as a notable geographical fact.'[1] So wrote R. F. Scott after the initial forays onto the Antarctic Ice Sheet during the *Discovery* Expedition of 1901–4, where he was impressed by the uniformity of the high-altitude ice plateau backing up against the Transantarctic Mountains. H. T. Ferrar, a geologist on the same expedition, captured the essential characteristics of an ice sheet as the 'uniform cloak of ice and snow of unknown extent which covers land of continental dimensions'.[2] At the time Ferrar used the term 'Inland Ice', following Scandinavian use of *Inlandsis* which had come into usage following F. Nansen's first crossing of the Greenland Ice Sheet in 1888.[3] The latter term made sense where the ice sheet lay inland of the coast, as in much of Greenland, but gradually lost ground in the face of Antarctic experience of ice extending beyond the coastline. Scott was right; astronauts in the space shuttle highlighted the Antarctic Ice Sheet as the single most obvious terrestrial feature on Earth.

It is difficult to convey the sense of scale of an ice sheet and the stunning impact of its surface environment so inimical to human activity. As recently as 2001, I hopped on to a Twin Otter aircraft for what I expected would be a short flight from McMurdo Sound across the Ross Ice Shelf, only still to be airborne some three hours later. When deposited in the Ford Ranges in West Antarctica, our group of four were humbled and concerned to realize that we were the only humans within a radius of more than 1,000 kilometres. And then after a season of just snow and ice there is the wonderful shock of realizing that you are returning to the normal world when you first notice the proximity of temperate climes by the smell of their vegetation. But these experiences of an ice sheet are cushioned by advanced technology and obscure much of the depths of the experience. There is no substitute for the diaries of the initial travellers. Read of the shock that Nansen experienced when he saw temperatures on the Greenland Ice Sheet fall off the bottom of his thermometer;[4] the ever shortening diary entries as E. H. Shackleton and companions struggle with resistant, granular snow and windchill associated with persistent outward-blowing katabatic winds as they approached the South Pole in 1909; the balancing of human and natural factors as they make the life-saving decision to turn back, having travelled 1,200 kilometres and reached within only 155 kilometres of the target;[5] the way the balance was tipped against Scott's doomed party in 1912 by colder than average weather;[6] the human cost of experiencing gale-force katabatic winds for 340 days in one year;[7] and the experiences that underlie the naming of *Inexpressible Island*.[8]

Our knowledge of the surface of the Antarctic Ice Sheet improved over the subsequent century, but so far removed is the ice sheet from human experience that we accept a situation where there are parts still less well mapped than the far side of the moon. In places, radio-echo sounding has added a third dimension and revealed the nature of the bed, but there are still areas the size of Europe with only a handful of profiles. The dome of the ice sheet is more than 4,000 metres high in the centre and of comparable thickness. The ice accumulates on the ice-sheet surface, mostly near the coast, and declining to rates equivalent to the driest deserts in the centre. The ice flows out radially, most dynamically in the form of ice streams that are rivers of fast flow with speeds of hundreds of metres per year. Varying basal ice temperatures control sliding processes and produce an abundance of subglacial meltwater in particular places, including subglacial Lake Vostok, which is

the size of Lake Ontario. The ice is discharged into the sea through the periodic calving of icebergs, some of the latter commonly exceeding the size of UK counties. The Northern Hemisphere can boast its own smaller ice sheet in Greenland, 3,300 metres in altitude; it differs from the Antarctic ice sheet in that much of its border ends on land and thus loses ice through surface melting.

Both current ice sheets are well integrated into human experience. To geographers, ice sheets are dynamic landscapes and land-forming agents; to glaciologists they are physical entities; to geologists they are sedimentary rocks verging on the metamorphic at depth; to astronomers they are collecting devices for meteorites; to oceanographers they modulate the thermohaline oceanic circulation; to biologists they provide an extreme challenge to all manner of life; and to climatologists they are control switches of world temperature and, through ice cores, the source of an unrivalled archival record of past climate. Above all, they catch the human imagination. The words *Antarctic Ice Sheet* in a research project catch the attention of the media and, some would argue, perhaps also of the research councils.

Had this book been written 18,000 years ago, the entry on ice sheets would have been very different. An Antarctic-sized ice sheet covered North America as far south as the latitude of New York, and smaller ice sheets extended over the UK as far south as the environs of London and from the Scandinavian heartlands into the Netherlands, Germany and Siberia. Global sea level was 120 metres lower than present because of the volume of water frozen into the expanded ice sheets worldwide. Our European ancestors were squeezed into southerly climes where images of their tundra world are now preserved in caves, some with entrances below present sea level.

The understanding of ice-sheet behaviour is at an exciting stage. Observations of the beds of the former Northern Hemisphere ice sheets gleaned over 150 years provide an unrivalled insight into the way that ice transforms the landscape. Now there are computer-based simulation models designed to represent the long timescales of ice-sheet growth and decay, and an explosion of high-resolution remote-sensing information from current ice sheets to calibrate the models at a level of sophistication inconceivable only a few years ago. The bringing together of these different approaches is leading to decisive advances in understanding ice-sheet behaviour, the links with climate and the way that ice sheets modify and interact with the earth.

Sun

Denis Cosgrove

Heliography is perhaps older than geography. By this I mean that picturing the sun as a surface – as patterned ground – and understanding its form and motion are among the most ancient of human arts and sciences. Devices for observing, measuring or refracting solar phenomena are the most enduring, moving and monumental landscapes on earth: Stonehenge, the pyramids at Giza or at Palenque, the temples at Angkor Wat in Cambodia or at Konark in Orissa. In New Mexico, the Anasazi people placed stone slabs before spiral petroglyphs on Fajada Butte in Chaco Canyon, so that a dagger of sunlight might mark the summer solstice. Through patterns cast by the sun on earthly ground, terrestrial time and space are measured and mapped. The raised column, pillar or obelisk originates as a gnomon, the basic device for measuring time-space by the shadow cast by sunlight. Indeed, the Egyptian obelisk's curious tapering shape and pyramidal cap may represent the sculpting of solar rays into earthly stone. These vertical signs mark the essence of place – a point in space differentiated from nature and identified by human intervention.

If the presence and absence of sunlight mark patterned ground on earth – geography – both naturally and through human work, what of patterns on the sun itself? Our capacity to study the surface of its globe is severely limited. For the human eye it is briefly possible at dawn and dusk, when the solar disk, viewed at a low enough angle for atmosphere to shield its glare, appears roseate or gilded. At these times, conventionally moments of mystery, contemplation and prayer, the sun appears as a perfect circle unmarked by any surface variation. In wintry northern climates, behind thick layers of cloud, the sun may appear as an opalescent disk riding in the sky. Otherwise, in the brightness of day, as the sun performs its service to life on earth, it quite literally blinds us. By an uncanny inversion we 'see' it only as a black disk etched as an after-image on the retina of the closed eye. Among those who have studied and written most movingly on the sun's appearance, Galileo and Milton went blind. The English artist J.M.W. Turner transformed the meaning of painting trying to capture in deep layers of pigmented oil the visible sun. He died whispering 'the sun is god'.

Little wonder that the sun is mapped more frequently as symbol than as science. Most parsimoniously, the sun appears on maps or in spatial illustration as a golden circle, perhaps with smiling face or with flames leaping from the edges of his disk. Children everywhere bring this image into their earliest drawings of home and childhood spaces – 'the sun has got his hat on, and he's coming out to play'. The sun is consistently figured as male: Aten, Helios, Apollo. His diurnal and annual arcs through the cosmos have provided the basis for the most elaborate architectural and decorative schemes, too obvious a symbol of that unity of power and beneficence that every ruler seeks to embody to be ignored iconographically. Virtually every sovereign has grasped for the sun, embodying it to articulate the idea of rule: in early modern Europe none more directly or consistently than Louis XIV, the *roi soleil* of France. Where the royal court had once circulated around the realm as the sun rotates through a geocentric cosmos, Louis sat immobile at Versailles, gilded centre of a heliocentric France. From his Hall of Mirrors great axes inscribed each cardinal direction. Primary among these was the line that ran from west to east, passing through his throne room to terminate at the horizon, where a golden statue of Apollo's chariot sinks, half submerged in a lake that signifies the Western Ocean. Louis' inheritance echoes through modern France in the concept of *la gloire* – glory – a solar term, which remains that nation's assumed inheritance, and which every French head of state feels obliged in some way to express.

Mere humans may not look at such glory – it flames forth in rays of blinding light. In Baroque churches it is not uncommon to find a small hole strategically located in the roof, through which a piercing shaft of sunlight, rendered visible by slowly circling dust particles (once thought to be the very atoms of creation), inscribes the solar passage onto a meridian arc drawn on the floor, or differentially illuminates a sculpture or sacred image in the imitation of divine light. In the most dramatic such plays of light and shadow, the hole is drilled into a dome, its light acting as the principle player in a

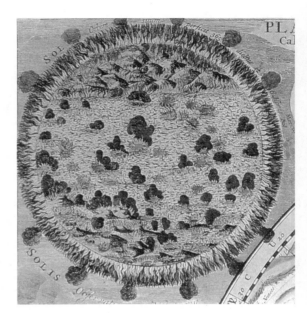

29 Christopher Scheiner's map of the sun of 1635 reproduced as an insert within Carel Allard's map of the southern sky, *c.* 1700.

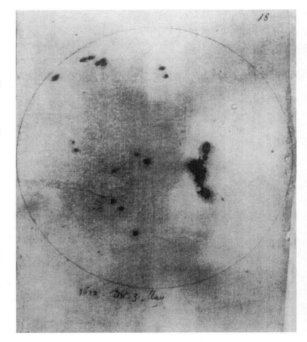

30 Galileo's image of sunspots burned directly onto paper through the telescope.

painted drama of global illumination by faith. The earliest attempts actually to 'map' the sun also date from the seventeenth century and emerge from the same culture. Christopher Scheiner, a German Jesuit scholar, disputed with Galileo primacy in observing spots on the sun's surface. So profoundly contrary was this to the prevailing belief in the purity of solar fire that Scheiner was dissuaded from publishing his discovery for fear of ridicule. (If he lost in this sense to Galileo, he gained in observing the sun indirectly, thus saving his eyesight and becoming the first person to recognize that human sight is the imprint of light images on the retina.)

Scheiner's observations are graphically recorded in a 'map' of the sun of 1635 (illus. 29). From the round disk, oriented by the cardinal axes, fires leap into the element of ether. Solar geography consists of three parallel zones. Those towards the poles appear to be land, while the central zone has an oceanic quality. In every zone fires burst forth from volcanic craters, their smoke accounting for the spots revealed by the newly invented telescope. This wonderfully imaginative illustration, widely reproduced in the margins of world maps in the succeeding years, might be contrasted with Galileo's famous image of 1613 produced by directing sunlight through the telescope onto paper (illus. 30). Here the sunspots appear as burns on the white surface. Production of such a map through mechanical means without the draughting mediation of the human hand was a significant contributor to its scientific warranty.

It is through the mediation of ever more sophisticated machines of vision that we have been able to examine and illustrate the solar surface, now known to have a complex and dynamic geography of energy fields, waxing and waning across its vast spaces.

Such knowledge has served only to increase our wonder at this blazing source of life. So the sun remains a powerful stimulus to the imagination. In her art installation *Red Sun*, Diane Thater used video monitors and a DVD player to present digitally reprocessed NASA photographs of the sun's surface. These had been broken into primary and secondary colours, recombined and distributed across a bank of nine screens to create bloody patterns on the fiery solar surface, establishing a conversation between the energy directed through video and the primal power of the sun itself – a truly contemporary heliography.

Water
Circulating Waters, Circulating Moneys, Contested Natures
Erik Swyngedouw

In the summer of 1998, the South-east Asian financial bubble imploded. Global capital moved spasmodically from place to place, leaving cities like Jakarta with a social and physical wasteland where dozens of unfinished skyscrapers are dotted over the landscape, while thousands of unemployed children, women and men roam the streets in search of survival. In the meantime, El Niño's global dynamic was wrecking havoc in the region with its climatic disturbances. Puddles of stagnant water in the defunct concrete buildings that had once promised continuing capital accumulation for Indonesia became breeding grounds and great ecological niches for mosquitoes.

Malaria and Dengue fever suddenly joined with unemployment and social and political mayhem in shaping Jakarta's cityscape. Global capital fused with global climate, with local power struggles, and with socio-ecological conditions to reshape Jakarta's social ecology in profound, radical and deeply troubling ways. Just a year earlier, Thames Water Inc. had advertised its part takeover of Jakarta's water supply company, celebrating the fact that the company is satisfying the thirst of 8 million city dwellers. I kept wondering where the other 7 million inhabitants get their water!

The above examples illustrate how the excavation of water circulation and of water as a cyborg, a cybernetic organism that is simultaneously technological and organic, permits relating material and symbolic processes, real and mythical conditions, local and global dynamics. Water is of course biochemically vital, embodies deep social meaning and cultural value and internalizes powerful relations, both socio-economic and physical. The socio-natural production of cities is indeed predicated upon some sort of circulating water. The multiple temporalities and interpenetrating circulations of water (the hydrological cycle, dams and reservoirs, canalization and distribution networks of all kinds, treatment and pumping stations, the flows of investment capitals, etc.) illustrate the perpetual metabolism and mobilization of water. Moreover, water worldwide is rapidly becoming a problem of gigantic dimensions. More than a billion people have no access to some sort of reasonably potable water, while millions are displaced as mega-dam projects keep on feeding the modernizing dreams of local and global elites. Mega-cities in the developing world suffer from immense water shortages, while the water metabolism in developed cities begins to threaten the very metabolism of urban life as pollutants of all

kinds (but notably nitrates) challenge the very sustainability of the capitalist city and the metabolism of social and biological life.[1] Of course, water also carries powerful symbolic meanings (health, purity, naturalness), which in recent years have been successfully 'mined' by a burgeoning global multi-billion dollar mineral water industry.

The cyborg flow of H_2O relates all things / subjects in a network, a rhizome, connecting the most intimate of socio-spatial relations, inserts them in a political-economy of urban, national and international development and is part of a chain of local, regional, national and global circulations of water, money, texts and bodies.[2] These multiple metabolisms of water are structured and organized through relations of power, socio-natural power; that is, relations of domination and subordination, of access and exclusion, of emancipation and repression. And these social power relations become embedded in the flow and metabolisms of circulating water. The circulation of water produces a physical geography and a material landscape, but also a symbolic and cultural landscape of power. The waterscape is a liminal landscape where the cyborg character of the transgression between the social and the natural is perpetually emptied out, filled in again and transformed.[3] This circulation of water is embedded in and interiorizes a series of multiple power relations along ethnic, gender and class lines. These situated power relations, in turn, swirl out and operate at a variety of interrelated geographical scale levels, from the scale of the body upward to the political-ecology of the city to the global scale of uneven development. While water is captured, sanitized, bio-chemically metabolized to become 'urban' drinking water, it is simultaneously homogenized, standardized and transformed into a commodity and into the real–abstract homogenized qualities of capital circulation and money power in its manifold symbolic, cultural, social and economic meanings. The struggle for water and the contested nature of the uneven access to water turn the metabolism of water into a highly contested terrain that captures wider processes of political-ecological and economic change.

In Third World cities, for example, the elites, clustering around the water reservoirs, had and have unlimited access to water. Water access gives them a significantly longer life expectancy and presents valued symbols of cultural capital and power. Permanently irrigated tropical gardens separate their often militarized urban oases from the urban desert that surrounds them, while ornamented fountains in the court-yard testify to their social and cultural distinction. Nevertheless, water-related illnesses and deaths are the prime cause of infant mortality for most of the world's population.

Evidently, the social struggle around water is the result of the deeply exclusive and marginalizing political, economic and ecological processes that drove the expansion of the city. The urbanization process itself is, indeed, predicated upon the mastering and engineering of nature's water. The ecological conquest of water becomes, therefore, a necessary attribute for the expansion and growth of the city. At the same time, the capital required to build and expand the urban landscape itself is also generated through both the political-ecological transformation of the city's hinterland and the global financial flows of investment banks and lending institutions. When the Londoner drinks the water of Thames, it is exchanged for money, turned into capital and partly circulated back into Jakarta's uneven geography of water distribution.

31 Informal water vending in an Ecuadorian city.

In short, the urbanization of water and the social, economic and cultural processes associated with the domestication of water brought access to nature's water squarely into the realm of class, gender and cultural differentiation and made water subject to intense struggle for control and / or access. The commodification of water, in turn, incorporated the circulation of water directly in the sphere of money circulation and capital accumulation, making access to water dependent on positions of social power. This hybrid flow of water, whose biological use-value is central to the sustainability of life, has indeed acquired a substantial exchange value that permits new forms of capital accumulation; nature turned into an accumulation strategy. Needless to say, the inevitable tension between the need for water and the private appropriation of or control over water has and will continue to unleash profound social struggles. And the central questions, of course, that animate such conflicts and mobilize the bodies of men, women and children squarely revolve around 'who has the right to nature?', 'who has the right to nature's water?' and 'who has the right to the city's waters?'

Pollutants

Anna R. Davies

Passions run high in relation to the practices of genetic modification between those who see the technologies as the Holy Grail for future society, offering life-enhancing functional foods – such as 'golden-rice' manipulated so that it contains Vitamin A to combat malnutrition – and those who perceive genetic modification of crops to be a fundamental challenge to natural evolution, forming a qualitatively new generation of pollutants.

Geographically, genetically modified (GM) products now pervade sites of production and consumption in many countries, including the USA, China and Argentina. In contrast, the UK has put the commercialization of transgenic technology in the production sphere on hold, at least for the time being. Instead field sites have been selected and are being used to test the impacts of certain genetically modified crops on the environment. Despite this apparent moratorium, intense conflict still surrounds the future of GM crops in the UK.

In Weymouth, Dorset, magistrates acquitted seven protestors of aggravated trespass in

32 GenetiX Snowball launch action, 4 July 1998.

2001. The previous year they had dressed as grim reapers and 'decontaminated' field test sites 'polluted' by GM crops. These protestors form part of a loose network of resistance to crop gene technology in the UK that has emerged from established environmental organizations such as Greenpeace and more amorphous Direct Action groups. Like the Weymouth Seven, other anti-GM groups, including GenetiX Snowball, have also been involved in 'decontamination' events. GenetiX Snowballers are campaigners for non-violent civil responsibility around the issue of gene technology, which they see as unwanted, unnecessary, unsafe and irreversible. Dressed in protective suits, face masks and gloves, Snowballers designate GM crops as 'biohazards' and destroy a symbolic number of plants taken from test sites. Even within the small scale of the field test sites the GM crops are seen as genetic pollution, where pollution is envisaged as more than purposively constructed 'matter' out of place.[1]

Anti-GM demonstrations function on a number of interrelated levels: as visual 'media events' to raise the public profile of GM issues; as Direct Action, or 'civil responsibility', to protest against the failure of democratic procedures to engender positive socio-environmental development; and also as essentially moral forums to engage with GM crops as 'pollution' where official scientific and political processes do not recognize them as such. It is the final aspect – the challenge to establishment designations of 'pollution' and 'pollutants' – that is particularly interesting since it presents an opportunity to reconsider both the notion of pollution, *what* it is and *who* is involved in establishing it.

Scientific definitions of pollution have been a significant element of environmental policies from the early developments in air quality control to the current concerns with matters such as global climate change. In the GM arena scientific practice, in its various guises, has a pivotal role in both defining the techniques of GM and establishing its impact on society and environments. Yet scientific definitions of pollution are also social statements, which are dynamic and reflect patterns of power. This is not a new idea; pollution has been consistently used as a potent metaphor to inscribe social hierarchies and societal norms and values (or rituals and taboos) beyond environmental concerns in health, welfare, crime and punishment and in gender and race relations. Over the last century, however, the social bases inherent in the construction of pollution have been eclipsed by technical calculations and scientific measurements. There is little explicit engagement with fundamental assumptions concerning human / nonhuman interactions and, returning to the work of Mary Douglas, this leaves considerations unarticulated about what it means to be 'natural and 'in place' or 'unnatural' and 'misplaced'.[2]

Issues such as global climate change, BSE (or mad cow disease) and GM crops, with their inherent uncertainties, have however brought into focus the role that values play in establishing parameters for pollution and in making judgements about the nature of nature and what matters about the location of matter. A fundamental aim of resistance groups such as GenetiX Snowball is to make explicit, and ultimately challenge, the hegemony of privatized technological innovation in the realm of GM crops and consequently force a more transparent debate about socially situated discourses of science and morality in the UK. The development and use of GM then provides an opportunity to engage with the explicit embeddedness of defining the 'other', in this case pollution; raising the hackles of judgement inherent, but often unnoticed, in environmental

policy. On the one hand, GM protestors do express fears of biophysical harm and the potentiality of novel risks to human and non-human environments, which are characteristic concerns of environmental science and dominant in environmental policy making. On the other hand, these anxieties are closely allied to unease with political processes that legitimize essentially commercial GM activities and ethical concerns that see the splicing of genes as morally wrong.

The naming of 'pollution' is political and has a geography and a chronology – a time and place – constructed dynamically through cultural interactions between people and in relation to non-human environments. At the boundaries of human understanding, such as GM technology, environmental science cannot function as the single authoritative arbiter in establishing definitions of pollution and should be part of wider discussions about the nature of governance, democracy and power. That the Weymouth Seven were acquitted lends weight to their construction of GM crops as dangerous 'pollutants', where pollutants are conceptualized in extra-scientific terms. Yet when faced with the wider geopolitics of free trade and global capitalism this may be a small victory only temporarily stemming the spread of new transgenic patterns on the ground. It is far from certain that the blinkers surrounding the formal practices of establishing what qualifies as a pollutant, and what does not, are being removed and replaced by a more transparent and discursive process of designation. What is certain is that for more expansive processes to emerge in the field of GM crops these debates have to be removed from the laboratory and placed firmly in the public arena.

Trade

Ian Cook

A seed contains inside its coat the history of practices such as collecting, breeding, marketing, taxonimising, patenting, bio-chemically analysing, advertising, eating, cultivating, harvesting, celebrating, and starving.[1]

Once they're picked, they start to die. Twisted off the stem. Just as they've 'turned'. From fully green, to green with a yellow streak. By farm workers. On a platform made from scaffolding. Welded to a trailer. Pulled slowly along avenues of trees. By a tractor. Jerked about. As the wheels follow undulating tracks in the baked mud. Under the hot sun. Shaded by leaves splaying out from the treetop. Leaves that shade the fruit growing around that stem. In a column. 'Turning' fruits at the bottom and flowers at the top. These eighteen-month-old trees will soon be felled. The leaves have finally succumbed to 'bunchy top'. The sprayer can't reach them. Twenty feet up. Where eight 'pickers' are leaning precariously off that platform. Four a side. Jerked around. Slowly moving. Looking for those colour changes. Cupping the bottom of 'turning' fruits. Carefully twisting them off. Each a good handful. Placing them in crates for the packing house. Trying not to let the white latex oozing from their peduncles drip onto their skin. It's nasty. We're on a papaya farm. Picking fruit for the export trade. To the USA and Europe. 'Fresh'. Sold in mainstream supermarkets. 'Product of Jamaica'.

It's 1992. We're on a 50-acre farm. Where sugar cane used to be grown. Great House, sugar factory, rum distillery and slave hospital ruins at the centre of the farm. Equipment rusting away inside. The farm manager's house built in the ruins of the overseer's. Traces of the agricultural, export-oriented, plantation society that Jamaica was set up to be. When world trade was in its infancy. In the 1500s. Much has changed since then. But this land is still devoted to export agriculture. Jamaica is still an impoverished country. The farm workers are descendants of enslaved African people. The farm's owners and managers aren't. But at least they're not still farming cane. That's a horrible business. Backbreaking. Seasonal. With unpredictable yields and prices. No predictable or steady income. Grinding poverty. With that connection to slavery days. Now reliant on preferential markets.

33 The cover of a 1992 marketing leaflet for Jamaican papaya.

Quotas. An uncompetitive industry kept afloat. But threatened by the WTO. The 'free market'. And from EU expansion. Involving countries with no colonial obligations. Changing voting patterns. On international trade agreements. For sugar. And bananas. Jamaica needs to diversify exports. To service its debts. To tackle rural poverty. By identifying niche markets. Overseas. For high value commodities. Like tropical fruits.

Judging by advertisements in those markets, these fruits just appeared in the trees. Pure nature. Picked. Wrapped. Packed in a box. All the same. Size. Shape. Colour. Look. Ripeness. Taste. Price. Available twelve months of the year. Standardized. Like cans of beans. But this is a 'nature' that can't be understood separately from trade. After Columbus found papaya in the West Indies, its spread worldwide followed the colonial exploits of the Spanish and Portuguese. Its copious, durable seeds travelled well. Germinating and becoming naturalized in tropical environments with plenty of rain and fertile, well drained soils. In the wild, or in people's backyards, papayas are far from uniform. They can be monsters! Ten pounders. There are male, female and hermaphrodite trees. Males pollinate. Females produce round fruits. Hermaphrodites produce smaller, pear-shaped ones. And papaya trees can change sex with changes in climate. The size of fruits is inversely proportional to the height of the tree. Soil nutrients affect the taste. But the ones on the supermarket shelf are all the same. Commercialized. Standardized. Most notably in the *Codex Alimentarius*. The food code. FAO, WHO, WTO codifications. Designed to marry world trade and 'consumer safety'. Via global trading standards.

Carica Papaya L., aka the 'Solo', is one such papaya. Taken from Jamaica and Barbados to Hawaii in 1911. Hawaii's only commercially grown papaya by 1936. Setting the standard for others to follow. Growing papaya for the Japanese and US West Coast markets. But also selling the seeds. Knowledge. Expertise. For others to grow the Solo. Elsewhere in the tropics. To boost exports to other wealthy markets. Markets too far from Hawaii. Like the rest of North America. Europe. From places with the right conditions, connections and needs. Like Jamaica. Which has to do things 'properly'. To break into those markets. Using 'advanced' agrotechnology and agro-chemicals. Training and supervising pickers and packers. To be careful. Accurate. On time. Or else. Washing. Checking. Grading. Filling standard 4 kg gross – 3.5 kg net – boxes. With fruits of the same size. Twelve of 290 g. Ten of 350 g. Seven of 500 g. Or thereabouts. Depending on retailers' specifications. ASDA wants 12s. Tesco, 10s. M&S, 7s and 8s. Flown to Miami or Gatwick. On BA. Air Jamaica. Regular flights. Taking tourists home, and / or making diasporic connections. Not like Brazil. The source of 90 per cent of Europe's papayas. By sea. There's little choice. There's not so much air traffic from papaya-growing regions. A longer journey. Fruits picked a little earlier. Which may not ripen properly. Or too late. Which might be over-ripe on arrival. Variable quality! A big problem.

And what about papaya consumers? Who pick them off the shelf. Exchange them for cash. Take them home. Ripen them. Cut them in half for breakfast. Scoop out the seeds. Sprinkle lime juice on the flesh. Eat it. Perhaps. A taste of the tropics. One per person. Solo consumption! Four fruits to go today. Or is it three? If you count the lime. Recommended daily intake. Papaya aids digestion, too. But that's not all. Chewing gum. Toothpaste. Contact lens cleansing fluid. Indigestion remedies. Canned meat. Leather goods. Shrink-resistant woollen fabrics. Vegetarian cheese. More complex commodities. Containing extracts of papain. That white latex you wouldn't want to drip onto your skin. Because of its protein-digesting enzymes. Commercially farmed. Another part of the papaya trade. Its nature far from pure. Or simple. So what are you paying for? If you buy papaya? It's not a discrete thing. By any means.

Airports

Mark Gottdiener

Airports are touchdown spaces on our planet for human vectors that criss-cross the globe. Terry Gilliam's postmodern remake of *La Jetée*, '12 Monkeys' (1995), depicts the end of the world resulting from the transmission of a deadly virus by one man carrying a brief-case with a round-the-world aeroplane ticket. According to recent research, air travellers are twice as likely to catch a cold as those people who remain on the ground on the same day. Air travel, then, involves the movement of organisms that range from the human and animal to the microscopic. Airports are the transitory collecting bins for these life forms. Anyone travelling can come into contact with organic life from anywhere else on the earth.

Landing at the Helsinki-Vantaa airport in Finland one day, I watched out of the window while my plane taxied to the gate. A large field of grass and weeds lay adjacent to the tarmac. As if on cue, a rabbit emerged from the field and slowly approached the runway. 'Is it going to jump in front of the plane?', I thought. How many rabbits hopped back and forth between the jets, I will never know, but it was clear that this airfield was

also an ecological domain inhabited by several species. Bunnies pose no risk to air travel, however; birds do. About forty years ago, until flocks of gulls were managed effectively by airport authorities, birds caught in jet engines were responsible for several catastrophic accidents. Now JFK International Airport, in the New York City region, advertises its falconry program. The raptors are used there to keep the gulls from invading jet space. Mechanical flight intersects with organic flying objects because both inhabit the same terrain.

Many airports today are gigantic places carved out of territory that is usually located in the hinterland of massive urban regions. The Denver International Airport, in the United States, stretches out over 53 square miles including 28 miles of underground pipes and fibre optic cables that service the planes; Hong Kong International Airport is built on a 3,000-acre island off the coast and possesses the largest passenger terminal in the world, a single building of 5.57 million square feet. Now most airports are more like cities than simply terminals. They possess their own mini-climates, ways of life, 'urban legends', accidents, crimes, hotels, serendipitous encounters, fast food services, gourmet dining, spiritual centres, retail shopping stores of every conceivable kind, casinos, conference rooms and business facilities.

The airport / aeroplane environment, which many of us inhabit frequently, produces negative effects on the planet. Many of these are 'problems', and are well known, such as the issue of noise pollution. Heathrow, located within the London metropolitan area, for example, shuts down at midnight because nearby residents cannot tolerate its noise. The dumping of fuel prior to landing has also been labelled a serious environmental issue in recent years. There are, however, effects of the airport / aeroplane environment that we are just beginning to discover because of our previous failure to conceptualize that system as a separate dimension of living and working on this planet. Only now are we increasingly turning our attention to the realm of air space and the consequences of massive human habitation within that domain.[1]

Perhaps the best illustration of this shift in conceptual thinking, the elevation of the airport / aeroplane environment as a separate subject, concerns the issue of 'contrails'. At five or more miles high, all jets produce frozen water vapour from their exhaust. These long parallel lines are known as 'contrails', and they act very much like clouds. Areas of the globe that experience frequent fly-overs possess a numerous and steady cover of contrails. Atmospheric scientists have long suspected that such artificial cloud cover creates pollution problems, but, until recently, no definitive study has been able to extract its effects.

Immediately after the events of 11 September 2001 all commercial aviation in the United States was banned. Scientists at the University of Wisconsin used global satellites to discover that contrail activity consequently suffered an enormous decline. They had long predicted that this artificial air cover would lower daytime temperatures in areas of frequent flights because the contrails would block out sunlight during the day. At night they surmised that these same vapour trails would hold in ground level radiation, thereby increasing nighttime temperatures. With a full commercial travel ban in place for 72 hours, the scientists predicted that the reverse effects could be actually measured. That is, in areas of frequent fly-overs, daytime temperatures should spike measurably *above* average, while measurements at night would be *below* average. As reported on 9 August 2002, their

predictions were correct, and the effect of contrails was confirmed.[2]

We enter the airport / aeroplane environmental system only as temporary residents. Consequently, we have not, until recently, conceptualized the full measure of how that system affects the planet. Understanding that more than 2 billion passengers fly by plane annually helps to place this emergent environment in perspective. It is composed of increasingly bigger territorial touchdown places, that is, airports; the vortexing of immense populations from air space to the ground on a daily basis; hundreds of thousands of daily flights via jet planes that needle their way through the atmosphere and interact with insect and avian life along with the chemical composition of the air itself; the spewing of fuel and water vapour pollutants across thousands of miles; flying garbage and frozen waste from eight miles high; and, not the least, the rapid vectoring of micro-organisms via human host carriers that criss-cross the globe and, consequently, the connecting of disparate human populations in ways that are both unintended and, in many cases, damaging to health.

Site

Sites appear to provide a ground on which to form an understanding of the patterns of the world. They can provide a firm basis for looking at the world, and set the scene for the things that take place here. Very often such appreciations see sites as being bounded and identifiable spaces. In this sense, sites can be both the process through which knowledge about the world is gained, as in fieldwork, and also the target of such knowledge, as in the field. The site, in both senses, is clearly demarcatable. Except, when we read the pieces in this section, we find that they are not quite so clear, or stable, or bounded. Sites are mutable, porous and covered in flows (see previous section). In this sense, they are places of concentration and intensity of process and energy. In the study of nature, the idea of locations having a special importance follows partly from the production of scientific method. Here we have a number of locational requirements: for sampling and for our identification of exemplars. The former suggests that we can accurately extrapolate from the small scale (the sample) at a site to the larger population, and this idea is implicit in realist conceptions of analysis where the small scale is studied and is regarded as a microcosm of, and a pointer to, the large. While such philosophies of science stress the context of the site, others stress the representativeness, where the site is used as a useful example of a phenomenon and where we are supposed to extrapolate from this to the wider landscape. Of course, we have a problem here. If the site is used as exemplar, then it is, by definition, *not* representative; our hypotheses limit our search for 'type-sites' that in turn produce and fashion our hypotheses. In this section, we can begin to speculate about alternative ways of thinking about the ground on which our patterns of the world are built. Thus, if we think of sites such as churches and refuges, we can begin to ask about spaces of safety and beauty in the world around. Now, site is about certain kinds of processes and energies. Take tors, for example, that not only create markers on the tops of hills, but become the focus of our attention. Then there are places that have ghostly significances, figures that walk through the site from a bygone era, as we ourselves also walk through sites that seem somehow to evoke their pasts: be they ghosts towns or old hospitals. In this world, sites are recognized as being made, perhaps by government intervention, perhaps by floods, perhaps in violence, perhaps in peace, but always in the midst of entanglements between nature and culture.

Mountains

Greta Rana

35 Machhepuchhare, the fishtail mountain, Pokhara, Nepal – 'a mystery'.

Mountains should be admired because they are there, yes, but more so because they present an arena with indefinite limits in which to play out our delusions of human grandeur. For those who see themselves as heroes / heroines, there is the challenge of the unknown – the fields of permanent snow that may or may not hide a crevasse or come tumbling down as an avalanche, spraying the atmosphere with a kaleidoscope of colours and leaving behind the aching and limitless silence of death. Indefinite space, mountains can be a gateway to the indefinite space of eternity.

There are logical, scientific reasons to admire mountains. Geologists are usually entranced by the idea that the rocks tell a story going back into the limitless reaches of time. And in the areas that the snow doesn't cover all year long, you can find the lichen, the great survivor through eternity: if only it could speak!

Once on the top of a mountain you have the heavens above you and around you – the world spread out below. The rippling vistas, ridge upon ridge stretched to the very edge of the earth. The very highest mountains give the added edge of hypoxia and perhaps hallucination. Is that why the great sages believed that eternity was to be found on the roof of the world, as they looked across the sky and through the fields of stars? They weren't to know that the stars might have been quite unsparkling at close quarters. For them it was a never-ending ocean of light. For lesser mortals, there was always the belief that long-lost creatures stalked the heights, and hence came the yetis and big foots of the mountain world.

These creatures bridge the gap between the divine and the human in the mountains. They bring us down to earth, into our own space, because the particular type of creature seen or unseen depends upon the mountain region you come from – it defines you. The yeti stalks the Himalayas and Hindu Kush and 'big foot' the Appalachians.

All this comes from a deep human belief that mountains are not quite what they seem. They're a mystery. Those parts of mountains that are still clothed with virgin forest seem to have eyes that look at you when viewed from afar. Inside the forest, it is easy to believe that there are caves somewhere that will take you down into the belly of the earth and that there are flora and fauna that we don't even know of, parts of planet earth we have never seen. Because, of course, we believe that mountains come from the earth's belly. The collision of the continents and the pounding of the frontiers of the ocean floor thrust these giants up into the sky, section by section, creating fault after fault and, in consequence, the possibility of future upheaval. One day, of course, whether we witness it or not, it could all be quite settled, a honed down range of mountains, and the earth's geomorphological perspective might be quite different from what we see today.

Beyond these, the mountains of myth and legend, are the mountains of the worker. These present quite a different picture from that of the mountains of the sage and the climber, the mere adventurers into the territory of the spirit or the territory of human endeavour. These are the mountain people who are limited to their terraced fields of maize or buckwheat and hardier vegetables and villages with defined boundaries, defined by tradition or superstition and watched over by spirits both friendly and unfriendly, the whisperers hidden in caves who need to be placated so that you can bring the harvest home and survive the winter.

From their perspective, the mountains have well-defined patterns; the patterns that define my fields, your fields – the boundaries of stupendous successions of bounded terraces containing their lives, their lifestyles, their next season's meals and community occasions.

Such defined boundaries are sacred, sacred because of the food they produce and because of the very sanctity of the soil that nurtures the mountain dweller. Their products are used to survive and to offer to the gods in worship, rituals that go back in time to the era of cave paintings and animism because they seem to have worked, because they bring out the fruits of the earth from the harsh mountain soils year after year, century after century – will it last?

Other defined boundaries, of course, are not so sacred. They contain a lake or a view, a famous mountain – there are famous mountains that, in their own right, have just as big a pull as film stars. Actually to have climbed one of them is almost as good as getting a famous autograph or rubbing shoulders in a crowd milling around the celebrated. These are the mountain areas for tourists, the areas that provide one with a place within a mountain area in which city dwellers can be in the mountains with almost the comforts of home – roughing it without actually having to meet the exactitudes of the normal mountain dweller who negotiates survival on a daily basis in the most difficult areas of the earth. The tourist can always go home. The tourist treads latitudes and longitudes for pleasure,

36 Dudh Koshi Valley, Nepal Himalayas – 'a hoard of treasures'.

discarding them and leaving them behind at will.

When mountains occur on the earth, they usually do so in quantity. They are a range. Sometimes they have a hoard of treasures. In such cases, the human animal with its exploitative industry will rip out the goodies in enormous quantities – until they have exhausted the very womb of the earth. They then trade the riches it has taken millennia to form for the essentials – for plastic trash and the expendable paraphernalia of 'modern' life – usually on unequal terms of exchange.

Thus the riches of the mountains reach the cities; the jewel captured in the rock that tells a story will end up in a shop window. There are those who believe that the shop window sets them off beautifully, because they've never seen the jewel's original environment of ice and rock against a necklace of stars, or felt the awesome power that forged it all out of the earth, thrusting upwards against time.

Thrusting upwards, unseen, unless the earth quakes and the glacial lakes burst the ends of their moraine dams and come down, 'asha asha' all falling down, collapsing in the thunder that drowns even the sounds of the perpetual mountain winds. For the mountains will grow until nature dictates that they will stop thrusting upwards and the winds and elements pound them into plateau. Only then do mountains cease their relentless vertical endeavour and begin to enjoy the birds and animals from a lost horizon. They settle and we perch – humans who will never rest until the last refuges on earth are filled with their clutter. Until then, mountains are the last refuges of sanity. The places into which one can escape, knowing it's hard to follow.

Fields

David Matless

A field is such a pretty thing
Green nettles grow and orphans sing
Lost child at play beneath God's sky
Yet finds delight by bird and bee

Tho' life may ne'er reclaim a death
Depletion passes with the year
A child makes all the fallow sing
A field is such a pretty thing

Anon., Victorian

On an average English December afternoon a crow alights on a furrow to pick the worms in winter wheat. Low sun outlines the rookery. Cawing proceeds. The farmer's rag-on-a-stick deterrent may as well be indoors for all the good it does. Gunshot from the wood is far enough away. Below sodden clay millions live.

Beasts eat and excrete soil for the wheat to rise. A few will not be missed. A parked car mists by the gate. Vapour trails ignore the field. Death for life at the turn of the year. The farmer is at tea.

Scarecrows may be mock human (rags on a cross), plastic bags waving in wind, twirling orange and black squares, mock guns banging every so often, a fence hung with dead birds. It is rare to see a human in a British field. Exceptions: walkers (may skirt the edge), workers moving machines in isolation, owners checking the crop, gang labour imported with scarce rights.

In 1952 James Fisher accounted for English *Birds of the Field*, finding crow (*four types*), starling, finch/bunting (*seven*), weaver (*two*), lark, pipit, thrush (*three*), owl (*two*), falcon, goshawk, goose (*six*), plover (*two*), gull (*four*), rail, pheasant (*four*):

> When all is quiet and sunny on a day of May or early June, almost anywhere in the farming lands of England, a cheerful liquid trickling song may be heard, dropping from the higher branches . . . This is the song of the goldfinch, an amiable bird.

Fields sang in a manner from charming (sparrow) to stuttering (fieldfare), up to and including full ecstatic quivering (skylark). Succeeding decades bring a different census, the lark descending. The suburban garden grows rich in contrast.

As a field of knowledge knows what it is not, so fences and hedges and things less tangible mark the edges of land that may thus be called a field. The medieval open field of the English Midlands was as edged and subdivided as a hedged West Country patch. The latter may be retained; the former has been owned and fenced from existence. Trans-historical field classification according

36 Forrabury Common, Boscastle, Cornwall, June 2002. In the foreground the Celtic field system of 'stitches', in strip cultivation in summer and under common grazing in winter. In the background the former Board of Trade and coastguard lookout on Willapark Point, over the Atlantic Ocean.

to ecological richness is of doubtful value for those caring enough to be anthropo-centric.

A field is made of plants put in order. Who doubts that wheat enjoys the sun? See how it waves.

If the soil carries the answer, authorities differ on optimal treatment and maintenance. Dr Thomas Barrett followed Charles Darwin's *Vegetable Mould and the Earthworm*:

We have written a book in an endeavour to create a mental picture of the most important animal in the world – the earthworm. When the question is asked, 'Can I build topsoil?' the answer is 'yes'. And when the first question is followed by a second question, 'How can I do it?' the answer is 'Feed earthworms'.[1]

Male and female in one body, earthworms enjoy comparative immortality in the absence of predators or chemical agents of death.

Yet so many things besides worm work can happen in a field; adolescents told us what they did and saw:

It is nice to get out of bed onto grass. The raindrops sound nice when you are inside, and my Dad says there aren't so many leaks nowadays. [*Camp*]

People bring their cars and offer things. The farmer bought a new car with the money, and said it was muddy here anyway. [*Sale*]
People watch people playing instruments and dance about. A lady said it was like Hawkwind, but she was quite old. It goes on for days. [*Festival*]
I didn't know cows were that big. I got the radio man's autograph, and saw a lady holding bees. People like looking at machines, mostly the men. [*Agricultural Show*]
In the country the fields had food in them, but now there's a playing field, and they make the dogs go in the sandpit. We have swings and goals. [*Play*]

Fields may also feature customary practice. An Eastern Counties custom, recorded by folklorists in the 1920s and, according to some, an adaptation of fire ritual concerning energy in darkness, has young men on Old Year's Night ascending sugar beet or turnip heaps to throw the harvest. Hurling may last for up to one hour. Distance and direction are unimportant.[2]

All of this used to be fields: I could walk as far as the eye could see.

All of this used to be fields: So much more happens now we have some space to live.

Fieldwork

Vic Baker

In science, humankind has found its philosopher's stone. Science progresses towards truth because it employs a method of rational activity proven to achieve success. It was this method that led the theorizing genius of a young Isaac Newton to discoveries about matter and force that revolutionized understanding of the universe. In such understanding one is guided by the searchlight of scientific theory, illuminating the darkness of nature's reality, just as one is also constrained by the strictures of objectivity – or so the conventional view would have things.

There is also the voyage of discovery, in which the adventurer is stimulated by the subjective experience of his or her direct contact with reality. How much of Charles Darwin's great synthesizing of the biological world was born on the voyage of the *Beagle*, and how much derived from his vast knowledge of biological principles? For the theoretical physicist the 'field' consists of idealized entities, impossible to experience directly, such as quarks and quantum singularities. The earth scientist, by contrast, can bodily enter the field of his or her enquiry. Herein lies a dilemma: does the becoming or being part of that which we study diminish our objectivity and thereby impair our science?

On popular numberings of the greatest scientists of all time, the only geologist to be included, usually way down the list after a few dozen physicists and a score of chemists and biologists, is inevitably Charles Lyell. As the 'Newton of Geology' Lyell provided a method for study of the past, and championed it in his popular book *Principles of Geology*, published in numerous editions throughout the late 1800s. One reasons most objectively, Lyell admonished, by confining enquiry to that which can be solidly verified by one's own experience: processes in evidence today are most likely to have been responsible for effects generated in the past. Armed with this principle, the science of geology can be placed on a firm theoretical basis, perhaps even close to the status of physics. Speculations about unwarranted extreme processes are readily discounted; only observations of the present can reliably serve as guide to what one can know of the past.

Had Lyell and his contemporaries been exposed in the field to the cataclysmic flood landscapes of central Asia or the Channeled Scabland of Washington state, this 'principle of uniformitarianism', as it came to be named, would have been far less likely to have exerted such a strong influence in the earth sciences. As one stands on one of the great gravel bars of the Channeled Scabland, among the giant current ripples up to 10 metres high and composed of coarse gravel and boulders, looking up at scoured bedrock on coulee walls, the dynamical processes of the responsible cataclysmic flooding engulf the observer. One feels a part of such great floods, and ideas about their operation spring to mind in regard to natural patterns observed and documented. All seasoned field investigators know of similar experiences, and this was how inspiration for his flood theory came in the 1920s to J. Harlen Bretz, as he took groups of his students on field trips to the Channeled Scabland. That Bretz's flood theory took nearly half a century to gain acceptance by the scientific community shows the hold that the methodological and the theoretical have on the scientific mind. Had his uniformitarian critics bothered actually to visit the field, Bretz insisted, there would be no scabland controversy.

Fieldwork is a semiosis, that is, a continuum of interaction involving the scientist with the systems of signs or clues encountered in the natural world. These signs relate to one another causally, as fossils relate to the living organisms that preceded them, and the signs also trigger perceptions and ideas in those who are open to their message. In this way the palaeontologist sees the association of fossil organisms with sediments that indicate the past environments in which the organisms lived. The coherence of numerous such observations leads to the formulation of hypotheses that account for what presents itself to the field observer. Only trivially does one come to the field to test preconceived notions. Imagine Sherlock Holmes telling Dr Watson: 'I have a hypothesis to test my dear Watson; drat, it was falsified; try again, wrong again; onward, testing to infinity!' No, one goes to the field the way that Holmes goes to a crime scene: to be inspired toward notions of reality far more productive than those that could be preconceived.

Arguably the greatest geologist of all time was Grove Karl Gilbert, who studied river processes in the American West during the late 1800s and early 1900s. Gilbert made a sharp distinction in scientific methodology between 'theorists' and 'investigators'. The former he held to be interested in finding the facts that would sustain their theories, while the latter were interested in the quest itself. For the investigator like Gilbert, facts that overthrow some prevailing theory are always the most interesting. The investigator is one, 'fertile in the invention of hypotheses', and the source of these hypotheses lies in anomalous phenomena observed in the field, colligated with analogous relationships to other field observations stored in his or her memory.

The theoretical physicist studies systems that are presumed to represent the essence of what is important to the operation of the universe. The field geologist, geographer or ecologist, on the other hand, studies nature as it is, without the idealized designation as to its underlying system. In explaining the world, the theorist speaks to it. In the field, the investigator lets the world speak to her or him. Consider the simple act of describing field experience by means of a map. I have heard more than one physicist remark on the unscientific simple-mindedness of the placing of lines on maps, merely describing an inert reality that can more readily be copied by objective mechanical sensors. In this case, the implied ignorance lies not with the field mappers, among whom only the most naïve would act like objective mechanical sensors. Rather, the ignorance lies with those so impoverished in connection to reality that they could conceive of such a dull and unrewarding field experience. Those passionately devoted to the art and science of field mapping know that mapping is the recording of semiotic experience, relating the connections in space (and time for the geologist) suggested by conversation with the natural world. Interpretative mapping might emphasize patterns of ecological diversity or temporal sequences of geological strata, but no automaton would produce such interpretations, since they are triggered by human interaction with the world, and communicated in understandable form to fellow investigators.

Hospitals
Alphonso Lingis

I had somehow managed to get a ticket. Only 25 were sold for each performance. Downtown Rio, the control centre where in high-rise buildings the staffs of corporations and banks work by day, was now deserted. We stood inside the iron fence of the old disaffected hospital, which crouched between office buildings, awaiting demolition.

Finally the doors were opened. We stood in the dimly lit entrance hall; on either side of us on one-metre-high boxes stood Yahweh and Lucifer, two old men wearing robes of coarse cloth. Lucifer argued that Job was pious because Yahweh had showered him with all terrestrial blessings. Yahweh accepted the test that Lucifer proposed. The lights that illuminated them went off and they vanished in the darkness. Screams were heard; then Job and his wife pushed through us, the wife wailing over her children, lifeless in her arms. They staggered down the corridor. We followed. In niches along the corridor stood robed figures chanting a dirge.

We arrived at a huge room, no doubt a former lecture or demonstration hall, but plaster lathes showed through patches of the wall that had been damaged by rain. Two rats fled as we approached, scrambling into the wall. The wife rushed back and forth shouting, shaking her fist heavenward. Job sought to console her and silence her blasphemies. Two bare-chested men descended upon Job, stripped him naked, then disappeared. Job's wife climbed up onto the balcony, raising her arms up to the darkness above, shouting out her misery and her defiance before her fate. She descended, left the room and staggered up a staircase. As we turned to follow her, Job, streaming with sweat and blood, pushed through us. Most of us cast down our eyes before his nakedness; a young woman swooned, was caught by others before she fell. Another, an old woman, reached to hold Job, her own eyes red with pain.

Upstairs, we made our way along an open portico: across the courtyard we could see windows of the empty hospital, although we had read that one section of the building was still functioning: terminally ill homeless people whom the police collected from the streets at night were brought there to die. In some of the windows we could see skulls and skeletons as used by medical courses. As we crossed over a catwalk, we contemplated a procession below us, a priest carrying a cross followed by flagellants chanting a *Dies irae*.

We found ourselves in another large room, no doubt a former medical ward. Now there was but one stripped metal bed. The ceiling was bare of plaster and the rain had blackened the walls. Small black bats careered through the dim light. Job collapsed on the bed. One after another three of his friends approached, dressed also in those timeless coarse robes; they expressed shock over his state. Job's wife, shaking in anguish, urged them to do something. At length Job stumbled out of the bed, his body marked by red lines from the bare springs of the bed, covered with scabs.

He staggered out into the corridor; we followed him. The corridor was very narrow, and there were planks set on sawhorses all its length so that we were pressed against the wall. One after another, the friends of Job strode across the planks. They recognized that they could not console him since his afflictions continued unabated. They told him there must be some explanation for the disasters that had befallen him. Finally each raised the question whether Job had not offended the Law, if only inadvertently, unknowingly. They elaborated their arguments, striding up and down the length of the planks.

One after another they left, and Job struggled on down the corridor. We found him in a small circular room, where most of the plaster had fallen from the ceiling and walls. The bare lathes were visible like bars of a cage. In the centre was a raised metal table. Over it was suspended a bright light. This was the former surgery room of the hospital. We had to push together around the walls; the room was soon hot and the air dead. Job lay on the table, his naked body dripping sweat and blood on the bare metal of the table. After some time the door opened again, and we recognized Yahweh, whom we had seen at the entrance at the beginning, in the celestial dispute with Lucifer. Job turned on the table, then shifted off it and turned his questions to Yahweh himself. But Yahweh was now himself in rags, covered with festering wounds and blood. He stood there for some time, with nothing to say. Then he left; the door closed behind him.

Job hesitated only long enough to catch his breath, then turned to the door and opened it. The corridor outside was now thick and opaque with luminous fog. One could see nothing through it. Slowly Job entered it. Into some kind of deliverance? Into madness? Nothing suggested an answer to our question. The light and fog slowly dissipated.

Finally we ourselves left through the dim and empty corridor, descended the stairs, crossed the now empty courtyard; looking up all the windows were dark. But we knew that in one wing of the building lay destitute people, dying.

Outside the streets were deserted. In the office buildings that walled them there were floors illuminated where cleaning staff were working. I walked toward the bay and then down the broad park that borders it, hearing occasionally birds rustling in its luxuriant trees. Then I penetrated the long tunnel still full of fumes that led to Copacabana. When the tunnel was bored, Copacabana became the most famous beach in the world. Only three blocks wide, walled on the right side by cliffs, Copacabana is the single most congested urban area in the world. But now it is inhabited by lower-middle-class people in its crowded apartments; the rich, the elegant shops, clubs and discos, have moved to Ipanema and beyond. In fact it was now

rather safe to walk alone; the pickpockets and muggers are gone at this hour when the tourists are asleep in their hotels. I walked mostly in the street; on the sidewalks people, whole families, were sleeping fitfully sprawled on flattened cardboard boxes. Some of these people, I thought, have AIDS. I reached Avenida Atlântica; beyond, the beach sparkled under the moon before the black, rumbling ocean.

Wilderness

Charles Warren

> What would the world be, once bereft
> Of wet and of wildness. Let them be left,
> O let them be left, wildness and wet.
> Long live the weeds and the wilderness yet.
> Gerard Manley Hopkins, *Inversnaid* (1881)

Wilderness isn't what it used to be. Human perceptions of the wild and untamed natural world have evolved almost beyond recognition since wilderness was seen as a fearsome and terrible place, the appropriate location for the temptations of Christ. As recently as the eighteenth century, 'wilderness' referred to barren, treeless wastes, and civilization was almost synonymous with the subjugation of nature. Wild was bad; tamed and useful were good. Even in the early days of conservation, only 'useless' land was granted scenic protection. Today we have come full circle: the wilder the better. What was worthless has become priceless. The place of satanic temptation has become a sacred temple.[1] What previous generations understood as 'development', 'progress' and 'improvement' – the utilization and transformation of nature for the betterment of society – are retrospectively cast as rape and pillage. These days, Mother Nature is no longer to be cowed into submission to fulfil the material aspirations of humankind, but is to be loved, cherished, honoured and obeyed. The transformation from negative to positive is complete, and that from slave to master (or mistress) nearly so. This is exemplified by calls to develop 'an ethic built upon respect for the authority of nature and wildness'.[2]

Concurrent with this perceptual revolution has been a steady evolution in our views of the place and role of *Homo sapiens* within the 'natural order'. From the Enlightenment onwards, we have been being progressively demoted. Judaeo-Christian conceptions of a transcendent deity have been challenged by neo-pantheist, Gaian notions of a more material, biotic divinity. In this schema, we are no longer the pinnacle of a divinely created order, responsible to Father God for our actions. Instead, we are simply a part of the holistic integrity of Mother Earth, doing her inscrutable bidding for the good of the planet. No longer lords of all we survey, now we are mere cogs in the ecological machine, albeit frighteningly powerful cogs (or spanners?) with the potential to derail the machine altogether. A practical outworking of these profound perceptual transformations has been the inexorable rise and rise of green priorities and biophilia in societies worldwide, as traditional anthropocentric outlooks have been challenged by ecocentric, 'Earth First' ethics. Where once the land's highest calling was productive use, now the greatest accolade that can be conferred on an area is to be selected for *non*-use – wilderness areas, national parks, nature reserves and the like.

Wilderness, then, is not what it used to be in our minds. Nor is it the way it used to be in physical terms. Once upon a time, long, long ago, the world was unmarked by the activities of people, but now a human signa-

ture can be found from pole to pole, and from mountain top to deepest ocean, even if only in trace form. Biological and physical systems have everywhere been altered, and in this sense we now live after the end of nature. As this unpalatable truth has confronted us with increasing force, so there has been progressive loss of faith in the long-standing view that a 'hands off' approach is best for wilderness areas. For better or worse (and it is frequently worse), human actions have so changed the environment that total non-intervention is rarely a sensible option because it would often lead to the 'wrong' result (i.e., not what society wants, either aesthetically or ecologically). In its current state, nature needs nurture. Ironically, 'to have nature be "natural" requires constant human intrusion'.[3] It is, anyway, unavoidably true that non-interference in nature is no more an option for us than for any other species. Having done our worst to it, we are now honour-bound to do our best for it. Frequently, this will require not a 'hands off' but a 'hands on lightly' approach.

Whatever state wilderness may now be in, conceptually or physically, it is hard to over-

37 Grand Teton National Park, Wyoming, by Ansel Adams.

state the power and significance that the *idea* of wilderness has had in Western culture during the last two centuries, especially in North America. The writings of Thoreau, Muir and Leopold, the poetry of Wordsworth, the landscape painting of George Catlin, and Ansel Adams's iconic photographs of the American West – all have been important in shaping perceptions of wilderness as an objective reality to be encountered 'out there'. Now, however, it is widely recognized that wilderness – and its big sister 'nature' – are cultural constructs, states of mind.

[Wilderness is] entirely the creation of the culture that holds it dear. . . . [It] serves as the unexamined foundation on which so many of the quasi-religious values of modern environmentalism rest. . . . [Wilderness represents] the false hope of an escape from responsibility, the illusion that we can somehow wipe clean the slate of our past and return to the *tabula rasa* that supposedly existed before we began to leave our marks on the world.[4]

This cultural construction of wilderness arose in parallel with the increasing distancing of society from nature that accompanied progressive urbanization. The call of the wild is an unappealing summons for those who spend their lives coaxing a living from the land. As Aldo Leopold wryly observed, 'wild things . . . had little human value until mechanization assured us of a good breakfast'.[5] Wilderness can exist only as a counterpoint to civilization.

Wilderness areas continue to evolve, both perceptually and actually, constantly being shaped by dynamic natural processes, by cultural forces and by interactions between these. The realization that for some people – Australian Aborigines and North American 'First Nation' peoples, for example – so-called wilderness areas are ancestral homelands has further destabilized cherished, frontier-born notions of wilderness. Critics use this to argue that the whole concept of people-free wilderness areas is 'morally repugnant, ecologically incoherent, intellectually indefensible and politically dubious'.[6]

Does all this mean that the wilderness concept is past its 'sell by' date? Most certainly not. Conceptually speaking, a cultural construct it undoubtedly is. Physically speaking, landscapes and ecosystems have been so altered that 'true wilderness' in an absolute sense is effectively extinct worldwide. But these realities are perhaps less important than the fact that a *sense* of wilderness (or, probably better, wildness) can still be found across vast tracts of the globe. These are the places where, even though traces of human influence may be found, the landscape as a whole has not been humanized, the places where the human notes are drowned out by nature's symphony. Arguably, it is this neo-wilderness perception of a nature where nonhuman processes reign supreme that needs to be safeguarded, rather than some of the more purist or fundamentalist conceptions of 'natural' that depend on chemical or genetic purity. The lure, the wonder, of wild nature and its power to inspire does not depend on its existing in some antediluvian state of untrammelled perfection. It comes from the humbling yet uplifting sense of 'nature in charge' – the perception that people are visitors just passing through.

The raw wilderness gives definition and meaning to the human enterprise.[7]

In wildness lies the preservation of the world.[8]

The wilderness is dead. Long live the wilderness.

Parks

Tariq Jazeel

> Through these gates you enter a Protected area. The animals, birds, trees, the water, the breeze on your face and every grain of sand, are gifts that nature has passed on to you through your ancestors so that you may survive. These gifts are sacred and should be protected . . .
>
> Portal inscription at Yala National Park, Sri Lanka

And so I contemplated Yala National Park's portal inscription as I entered through its elaborate gate. We were in the park by 6.30 am. Yala is beautiful at this time. Thin daubs of sunlight scatter themselves over the slumbering landscapes. The birds and monkeys find their voices and slowly begin to animate the tree-tops. Within an hour or so the jungle pulse is alive, and this is one of the best times to spot wildlife in the park. Now the bears, leopards and elephants emerging freely from their nocturnal residences are enticed by the cool morning temperatures. By 9.30 am we had seen our first leopard. We saw it in the road as we navigated our four-wheel drive through the parks' network of precarious dirt tracks. The leopard darted into the thickets. Obeying park rules we stayed in the vehicle and cut the engine so as not to scare it. We remained silent and motionless. Fifteen metres or so up the track the leopard crept stealthily through the thickets and on to the sandy road, his powerful, muscular shoulders elevated above his sleek frame and his head poised in perfect balance, blinking lazily as he crossed.

As with many other parks the world over, Yala National Park, deep in the arid south-east of Sri Lanka, sets aside a space for 'nature'. Encounters such as this are the lifeblood of the park attracting thousands of visitors annually, yet they also point to interesting and complex relationships between the human and nonhuman world. Yala's portal inscription quoted above brings to mind the suggestion of the environmental historian William Cronon that 'the nature we study becomes less natural and more cultural'.[1] Yala is a space of wildlife preservation and observation, a space of recreation. However, observing Cronon's plea, Yala also articulates particular cultural expressions of the taken-for-granted realities that 'nature' points to, and, moreover, the position of humans in relation to the natural world. These very relationships are signified by this landscape's emparkment. As Cronon might suggest, the park is a 'perfect place for meditating on the complex and contradictory ideas of nature so typical of modernity'.[2] Our separation from the landscape through the vehicle, our inability to alight from the vehicle for fear of startling the leopard, and our overwhelming impulse to capture this moment photographically, all suggest that, as humans, we are participating in a highly regulated relationship with the nonhuman world. We are witness to a natural world that unfolds before our eyes in this park. Here, at this particular moment, as I crane my neck to peer out of the vehicle at the leopard, '[t]he two concepts, nature and culture, can only exist in dialectical relation to one another . . .'.[3] We are 'cultural', the leopard embodies 'nature'. But what is the history of these taken-for-granted assumptions about the separation of culture and nature, and to what extent do they apply in Yala National Park?

The relationships referred to above actually find their roots in Yala's colonial history. To the British, Yala's overgrown jungles were devoid of culture and economy in the mid-nineteenth century. The spread of civilization was achieved by the heroic subjugation of 'unruly' and 'savage' nature, and in 1898 the Yala Game Sanctuary was established. Hunting was considered a noble and romantic pursuit that civilized this corner of Ceylon, which was described by British administrators in 1873 as 'mostly forest and low jungle, infested by wild animals and fever haunted'.[4] Yala's emparkment fixed in space relationships of power, proprietorship and morality between the human and nonhuman world; relationships intensely European in origin that have, over the years, reinforced the juxtaposition between nature and culture. Today we tame the leopards and elephants with our camera lenses and environmental management policies rather than with our rifles and hounds. In fact, the origins of the park in areas of western Europe lie in the practice and perfection of horsemanship and martial skills. A visceral space of muscular challenge and violence, the European binaries of culture / nature, and civilization / savagery were performed in parks. At the margins of aristocratic country estates, where the landed lord sought to position his cultural self in Edenic allusions to pastoral life, here the wilderness that lay beyond the garden was a space where hunting and military parties could satisfy their voracious appetites to civilize nature.

But parks are, of course, a worldwide phenomenon. As Yala has emerged as one of Sri Lanka's most famous National Parks it has evolved to articulate some uniquely Sri Lankan *cultures of nature* that unsettle these discourses of emparkment that separate culture and nature so powerfully. In a country where Buddhism is so predominant that it has been drafted into the written constitution, nature is not so unproblematically distinct from culture. Yala overlays an ancient Buddhist civilization. Here the past

38 The view from the top of Akasachetiya in Yala National Park.

is made present by the abundance of renovated, but ancient, Buddhist ruins. Just half an hour after our leopard encounter we went to climb the rock at Akasachetiya. On top there is an ancient rock pool and the remains of a 2,200-year-old *dagoba*, and at the base there are caves with Brahmi inscriptions. After a short, steep, twenty-minute climb we were at the summit enjoying breathtaking views over the park. In the distance we could see the gleaming white towers of Situlpahuwa temple in the interior of the park, to which 50,000 Buddhist pilgrims travel each year.

I was conscious that the jungles between here and there, and then beyond, were sanctified, as Yala's portal inscription told us. Yet there was something peculiarly normal about being up here; an awareness of how experiences of being in the world are so rooted in Buddhism in Yala. An awareness of having to recast my conception of what 'religion' means in a society where religious philosophy has long since cemented its relationship with social reality. In Yala Buddhist discourse settles over every rock, tree and river. The interleaving of archaeological ruins with the fabric of the park, and the ability of visitors to experience and connect physically with these ruins, are reminders that Buddhism does not separate humans from the natural world. In 'Sinhalese', the language of the Sinhala

Buddhist people of Sri Lanka derived from the ancient Buddhist script Pali, there is no direct translation for the word 'nature', neither is there one for the word 'landscape'. In Yala National Park 'culture' and 'nature' cannot be separated from one another as easily as we might first think. Here the modern spatiality of the park collides with pre-modern Buddhist discourse and tradition to both enable and unsettle under-standings of the relationship between two supposedly autonomous spheres – the human and the nonhuman worlds.

Farms

Michael Mayerfeld Bell

> If life in harmony with Nature is a primal
>   law,
> And we go looking for the land where we'll
>   build our house, is anything
> Better than the blissful country? . . .
> Where can we sleep, safer from biting
>   envy?[1]

Thus wrote Horace of farm life, and many have observed as much in the millennia since he took to the hills above Rome to savour the pleasures of 'moving rocks around and digging a bit in the soil'.[2] Farm, farm, farm – the word itself is something to savour, a purring word with a warm finish, as a vintner might say. It is a word of contentment with a satisfying 'aarrr' sound that buzzes nicely in the English speaker's throat, and then brings the lips together in a gentle linguistic smile.

Some of that contentment may be the unconscious pleasures of cultural puns, of fortuitous resonances of farm with other words and meanings. A farm is a place of the *arm*, of honest toil with the honest earth, of the body and its connections with the wider body of nature and nature's supposedly guileless, primal truths. A farm is a place *far* from us, a place of inevitable distances, that we must travel to in the mind for it is never where we are, although it is what we truly *ar*, and thus is equally a place of the head and its imagined communities. A farm is a *real*m, a region of our property and command and the free reign of geo-graphic individualism. A farm is *fam*ily too, minus the tinkling adornment of the 'ily' but plus that lovely buzz, giving it the *ar* of he*ar*th and he*ar*t and equally speaking to a Christmas-tree sense of wholeness and centredness and w*arm*th. It is a plain and *fer*tile word, deep and loamy in our imaginations.

Compare farm to the brittleness of agri-culture, with its hacking 'ag' and 'gri' and polysyllabic stutter. Who wants to be an agriculturalist when you could be a farmer? There is no licence, we imagine, in the direct wholesomeness of farm for the neologisms of corporate cultural conglomeration: agribusiness, ag industries, ag products, ag exports, ag engineers, ag equipment and Conagra. Rather, it suggests an invitation to the active practice of an identity, with a double buzz: farmer.

But the hacking side of farm has always been a part of the rural scene. As Horace wrote in his epistle 'to the foreman on my farm',

> Let's have a contest, steward, to see which
>   one
> Can defend the farm: the man by whom it
>   is run,
> Or the man by whom it is owned.
>
> For I say that living in the country makes a
>   man happy.

You say the city. Small wonder, that one discontent
  With his own lot prefers another's.[3]

Small wonder indeed that it has so often been the one who owns the farm and does not work it who is so easy in praise and defence of its natural safety from envy. The farm has long been imagined as labour-less – labour in the sense of compelled and alienated exertion – and thus a matter of the ecology of pleasure and not the economics of exploitation. Millions, nay, billions, have long found it otherwise and have left the land for the city in search of more humane contentments.

The tension between these two natures, that of ecology and that of economy, is to be found in the history of the word itself. Farm, for all its apparent Anglo-Saxon ring of ancient and intrinsic authority, originated in the legal and fiscal of the Norman landscape order. Farm is a Middle English word, adopted from the French *ferme*, itself a phonetic descendent of the Latin *firma* meaning a 'fixed payment'. For Middle English speakers, a 'farm' meant 'a fixed yearly sum accepted as a composition for taxes or other moneys to be collected; also, a fixed charge imposed on a town, country, etc. to be collected as taxes within its limits'.[4] A 'farmer' was a leaseholder, legally obligated to pay an annual fee, perhaps for the right to toil in the soil or perhaps for some other right. The original surety in the word farm did not derive from the land and its moral firmament but rather from the firm, death-and-taxes unavoidability of the economic.

And so it remains. As much as we would desire it otherwise, a farm is a legal arrangement within the world of capital and its dull obligations, its guile and its biting envies. A farm is fundamentally a business, among its other fundamentals, as all farmers who manage to keep their land must know, and as farmers are wont to remind politicians, romantics and other visitors from the city.

But what a business. As the old joke goes, want to make a small fortune in farming? Start with a large one. With returns on capital as low as a percent or two on even the farms generally deemed successful, it is no wonder that rural folk by their millions and billions have left to seek their fortunes small and large elsewhere. In the United States, the 1980s are often spoken of as the years of the 'farm crisis', when low commodity prices coincided with a bursting of a farm real estate bubble. But farming has been in financial crisis since the first scratchings 10,000 years ago.

This raises the question of why anyone at all keeps at it. It cannot be for the money, for there has been powerful little of that in the social history of the farm – at least powerful little that has stayed with the farmers. Many have kept at it because they have been compelled to by the social arrangements of their time and place, of course, and many are still so compelled. In the developed world, however, there is little of that constraint today, and indeed the number of farmers there continues steadily downwards, as everyone knows. As everyone knows: but let us not ignore that millions yet remain on the land even in the rich countries.

They are there because of another nature and its pleasures. They are there because the crops they are trying to grow are not only those of grain and gain, of corn and money, but as well that sweeter fruit that we have always sought in our ecologies: the self. There may be little of appeal to a Horace in such a mechanized and chemicalized self-ecology, but this is local knowledge, the most local of knowledge. Farmers are no different from the rest of us in searching for not just any self, but a natural self apart, so we hope and trust, however quixotically, from the guile and envy of grain and gain. The special gravity by which the farm holds our cultural imagination ultimately originates from the pull of this molecular tension – ecology / egology / economy – in all our lives and the many natures created thereby.

Bogs

Calvin Heusser

When the composer Hector Berlioz introduced the minuet 'Will-o'-the-Wisp' in his opera *The Damnation of Faust*, he chose a bog context to invoke the mysterious, nocturnal goings-on in the setting between Mephistopheles and Faust on the plains of Hungary. Depicted by flickering lights hovering at nights in moonlit mists, the 'Will-o'-the-Wisp' brought on an unwordly atmosphere of sorcery for demons to bewitch Marguerite, Faust's beloved. The scene captures the widespread belief over centuries past of bogs as places where evil spirits gather, an attitude that still continues in many places.

Instances of human remains disinterred from bogs adds substance to the conviction that bogs are home to sinister activity by unearthly creatures. The discovery of Tollund man by peat cutters in 1950,[1] disinterred from a Danish bog after having been preserved for some 2,000 years, adds fuel to the imagination. The body, partially clothed with headpiece, was in an excellent state of preservation, even with facial whiskers strikingly unchanged. From the rope noose around his neck, however, it was clear that he had been hanged, possibly part of a sacrificial rite, and was dispensed with simply by being left to be consumed by the generative peat. Had he wandered into the bog to be set upon by spirits?

Modern practice identifies a bog as strictly a landscape feature and leaves any spiritual connection to the supernatural. The name bog, Celtic in origin and meaning soft, is generally referable to the poorly consolidated, quaking sphagnous mat and its surroundings, whereon humans or wild animals are likely to sink and disappear below the surface. Bogs occupy basins frequently found in terrain at higher latitudes, or in mountains, where ice sheets were prominent millennia ago. They can also be extensive in maritime regions subject to cool, hyper-humid oceanic climate.

Bogs are remarkable as repositories of past human–environmental interaction. Artefacts discovered in the peat, involving pottery, goblets, ornaments, clothing and household furniture, depict life styles during the Stone, Bronze and Iron Ages. Bog peat acts as a preserving medium for artefacts that were part of past cultures by virtue of its poor oxygen content, acidity ($\sim$PH 4) and toxicity, which are restrictive to bacterial activity and decomposition of residual organic matter. The tempo and style of human activity since the termination of the last ice age (Wisconsin / Weichselian glaciation) are in part tied in with fluctuating rates of peat growth associated with climatic change. Recurrence surfaces in the bog stratigraphy illustrate variable intervals of wetting and drying related to growth and stagnation.

An interesting case of changing conditions at the bog surface as related to agriculture concerns the Somerset Levels in raised bogs at Glastonbury in south-west England. During the Bronze Age, trackways needed to be constructed as a means for negotiating boggy terrain during the cooler, wetter Sub-Atlantic period (2,800 years BP), following the relatively warm, dry Sub-boreal (5,000–2,800 years BP). But later the trackways, dating by radiocarbon between 2,900 and 2,400 years

BP, proved difficult to maintain and were progressively overrun and ultimately interred by rapidly deposited layers of un-humified peat. Rising groundwater in the end caused the fertile agricultural plain, including settlements at Glastonbury, to be abandoned.

Plant microfossils, particularly pollen and spores, and macro-remains identified in peat significantly supply a basic archive for reconstructing vegetation and climatic parameters at different stages of human development in the post-ice age era. Migrating over de-glaciated ground, Palaeolithic hunter-gatherers early on invaded tundra to hunt and butcher mastodon and other megafauna as sources of food now extinct. Nomadic in their way of life, they were extraordinarily adaptive at this time, when July temperatures in northern Europe are estimated to have been as much as 7°C lower than today. Over a span of approximately 10,000 radiocarbon years, humans further adjusted to the ensuing changes of climate: the warmth of the early post-glacial period, then the subsequent cooling with fluctuating climatic episodes during Neo-glaciation in the late post-glacial.

Bog pollen records disclose the forest expansion of birch, pine and hazel (*Corylus*) at first, followed by mixed oak (*Quercus*) forest containing elm (*Ulmus*), lime (*Tilia*) and ash. Using stone axes and fire, Palaeo-lithic man endeavoured in a limited way to open the forests; however, it was not until the Sub-boreal period that upscale forest clearance was underway and that Neolithic farmers began to tend the land for agriculture and animal husbandry.[2] Pollen of ruderals, for example, dock (*Rumex*), plantain (*Plantago*), goosefoot (*Chenopodiaceae*) and cereal grasses (*Triticum*), indicative of cultivation of the deforested land, mark the clearance event. Records from Britain over the past 2,000 years, encompassing the Roman, Anglo-Saxon and Norman periods, reveal the cultivation of

rye (*Secale*), hemp (*Cannabis*) and flax (*Linum*).

Fossil pollen data from eastern North American bogs show related trends in vegetation and climate. The American Indian did not attempt to clear the land except for the use of fire to establish pathways, to flush out game for hunting and for opening up limited areas for planting. Peat burning seems to have been in the early post-glacial, as indicated by amounts of charcoal in samples of bog peat, and is seen in the Americas as far south as Tierra del Fuego.[3] It was not until European man arrived in America, relying heavily on iron tools, that forest clearance was undertaken on a large scale. Evidence for this event is commonplace in pollen records, shown by the expanse of ragweed (*Ambrosia*) and the presence of dock and plantain. In fact, wherever European commerce has influenced places distantly removed from Europe – for example in Japan – pollen of dock and plantain are often manifest in the latest bog deposits.

Over the centuries since foreign immigrants first colonized the Americas, humans have been witness to a constantly changing scene. Land-use patterns during the twentieth century have increasingly altered, exacerbated mainly by industry and by the inroads of urban sprawl upon the original agrarian society. In the Lower Hudson valley, north of New York, atmospheric pollen surveys show that herb pollen (ragweed and grasses) has been decreasing, as open habitats in farmland are replaced by suburban housing combined with a steadily rising population.[4] The changes have also been sudden, as unexpected chestnut blight and Dutch elm diseases illustrate. The decrease of chestnut pollen in the uppermost horizons of regional bog peat matches the decline in chestnut trees. Introduced into New York City in 1904, the pathogen spread rapidly, so that by 1915 it virtually destroyed this highly prized timber tree over its entire extent.

39 Humans and apes in Tim Burton's *Planet of the Apes*.

Humans

Robyn Longhurst

The *Planet of the Apes* films invert the purportedly natural hierarchy in which humans are considered superior to (nonhuman) animals. They depict humans being caged and tortured by apes. The films are social commentaries on the way that humans treat animals and the all-too human frailties of humankind. The recently released version (2001) of the film, directed by Tim Burton, begins with a clear division being drawn between humans and apes (although several different simian species coexist in the planet's ape society). Apes rule the planet with an iron fist and humans are despised. Humans and apes, it appears, belong in clearly separable categories. As the narrative unfolds, however, this division between humans and apes is destabilized on at least three counts.

First, everyone – humans and apes – speaks a common language, English. This is a major change from the original *Planet of the Apes* film of 1968, which was directed by Franklin Schaffner. Second, the most 'human' character in the film is the chimpanzee Ari (played by Helena Bonham Carter), who believes that all species were created equal and joins forces with the outcast humans. The human hero, Captain Leo Davidson (played by Mark Wahlberg and described by the film reviewer Roger Ebert as 'a space jockey type, trained in macho self-abnegation'), is depicted as less human (and humane) than Ari.[1] His basic motivation is to get off the planet, and he seems unconcerned about the friends he leaves behind.

Third, and perhaps most importantly, the division between humans and apes is destabilized through an intra-species romantic triangle. This triangle develops between Ari, the sympathetic female chimpanzee, a female human blond rebel named Daena (played by Estella Warren) and the male human hero, Captain Davidson. Interestingly, Davidson is less attracted to the 'sexy' human Daena than he is to the compassionate chimpanzee Ari. This inter-species love triangle results in the first on-screen 'on the mouth' kiss between human (Davidson) and chimpanzee (Ari). It is a beauty and the beast encounter, but viewers are left in doubt as to who is the beauty and who the beast.

Interestingly, the romantic connection between Davidson and Ari never develops into a sexual relationship. As Ebert points out, the film 'could have dealt with the intriguing question of whether a man and a gorilla having sex is open-mindedness, or bestiality (and, if bestiality, in both directions?)'.[2] It could have, but it doesn't. It is a 'cautious movie'. Undoubtedly, the portrayal of human–ape sexual acts would have provoked viewers to question radically some of the more usual social, discursive and bodily lines drawn between humans and apes.

Planet of the Apes (both versions) encourages audiences to think about what it means to be human and how humans establish their difference from animals. The film illustrates that humans and animals are not clearly separable. It is possible for animals to engage in behaviours and display traits often associated with humans (such as agency, resistance, empathy, compassion). Likewise, it is possible for humans to engage in behaviours and display traits often associated with animals (such as fleshliness, barbarism, carnality, cruelty). The discursive, social and bodily boundaries between humans and animals are blurred, relational, unstable and impossible to secure.

This insecurity of boundaries makes it difficult to pin down the meaning of the term 'human'. Should a definition of 'human' rest on a set of common bodily, genetic and chromosomal features, or on a capacity for rationality, emotion, agency, consciousness, self-awareness and language, or perhaps on something entirely different? In the final instance, it is difficult to say.

One of the reasons why is it is difficult to say is because knowledges about humans and animals, and the relationship between the two, are constructed differently at different times and in different places. For example, whereas hunter-gatherer societies have tended to view the distinction between humans and animals as permeable,[3] Western scientists and philosophers have tended to view the distinction as stable and firm. As Anderson has noted, in the seventeenth century, 'while both humans and animals were believed to be capable of physical sensation, Descartes deduced that since animals lack reasoning capacity, their sensations are merely "bodily" (physical / mechanical), of which they can't be "aware" or "conscious"'.[4] Not only were humans and animals conceptually separated at this time, but humans came to be elevated above animals. For the most part, humans have oppressed and dominated animals, and this continues today.[5] These power relations create different 'patterns on the ground'.

Encounters between humans and animals shape and are shaped by spatiality. They are emplaced. To return to the example of *Planet of the Apes*, the original film is set on earth but in the future. It is based on the fear of a human-induced nuclear holocaust. The recent version is set on another planet and is based on the fear of a human-induced genetic holocaust. In the two films, the social relations between humans and apes unfold in different directions, forming different 'patterns on the ground'; humans and apes are 'in place' and 'out of place' at different times and in different spaces.

The taxonomies that fix humans get sketched differently, temporally and spatially. The ways in which we live our lives in the world cannot be separated from our understandings of who we are and who we are not. In the final instance an answer to the question 'what is human?' can never really be fully decided. The most useful option might be to allow the question to remain open and to be alert to the differing ways in which this question is answered by different individuals and groups at different times and in different places and spaces.

Islands

Beth Greenhough

Islands have long featured in popular culture as places where people find themselves. For island nations, this relationship between place and identity is linked to specific ideas about island spaces. Bill Bryson suggests that, for British islanders, their island home is intimately tied up with their national identity:

The British have a totally private sense of distance. This is most visibly seen in the shared pretence that Britain is a lonely island in the middle of an empty green sea . . . I can remember after I had been living for about a year in Bournemouth . . . looking at a map . . . [and] being astounded to realise I was closer to Cherbourg than I was to London. I mentioned this at work the next day and most of my colleagues refused to believe it. Even when I showed them on a map they frowned doubtfully and said things like 'Well, yes, I can see it is closer in a strictly *physical* sense', as if I was splitting hairs and that really *a whole new concept of distance was required once you waded into the English channel* – and of course, to that extent they were right.[1]

While, as John Donne famously stated (1623) 'no man is an island', numerous literary and script writers use islands as locations to explore and isolate what might be termed 'human nature'. William Shakespeare's *The Tempest*, William Golding's *Lord of the Flies* (1954), Daniel Defoe's *Robinson Crusoe* (1719–20) and television programmes such as the widely syndicated *Survivor* and the bbc's *Castaway 2000*, are just a few examples of the programme makers' use of island locations as a device to isolate and examine their cast(aways). Underlying these fictional and staged experiments is the belief that encounters with islands may give clarity to human nature. Similarly, cartoonists have employed islands as a staging device in which to isolate and satirize human characters.

All these social experiments share the assumption that the experience of being cut off from civilized society causes people to revert to some kind of natural type. Island tales are almost always stories of the triumph of man over nature as in *Robinson Crusoe* and *The Tempest*, or of the triumph of nature over

40 W. K. Haseldon's cartoon appeared in the *Daily Mirror*, 15 April 1926.

civilized man, as in the *Lord of the Flies*. This role that islands play as social and cultural laboratories is a direct reflection of how our understandings of the world are tied up with our sense of time and space. Despite living in a world where communications technologies make the possibility of being marooned on a desert island highly unlikely, we are conceptually limited by our natural human capacities. Islands can define the boundaries between nature and society through the assumption that some internal, essential, human nature is exposed when we become isolated from the rest of the world.

Nowhere is this more apparent than in the work of the naturalist Charles Darwin, whose theory of evolution drew directly on this assumed relationship between islands and natural types. Alfred Russel Wallace, one of Darwin's associates, notes how islands like St Helena, 'when first visited by civilised man', formed 'a kind of natural museum or vivarium in which ancient types . . . have been preserved from the destruction which has overtaken their allies on the great continents'.[2] This image portrayed islands as passive and unchanging places, which, like Steven Spielberg's film *Jurassic Park* (1993), offered geographical snapshots of another time or age. The notion that remote oceanic islands were self-contained spaces, isolated from a rapidly industrializing civilized world, made them particularly good reference points for defining the nonhuman, natural world. Islands were viewed as simplified laboratories for the investigation of natural processes. Using evidence from the geological record, Darwin and Wallace set out to prove that the distinctive flora and fauna of the Galápagos Islands, among others, gradually evolved when plants and animals were isolated from the mainland population. From these island studies Darwin developed his theory of the survival of the fittest, now known to us as the theory of *natural* selection. Unconsciously, perhaps, Darwin and Wallace were echoing and re-enforcing those fictional myths and stories about islands; islands are the places where all kinds of individuals revert to their true forms.

However, the isolation of islands is a highly relative quality. Darwin's own journeys are testimony to the temporary and fragile status of island isolation. Once discovered an island is never truly isolated. Islands are always linked to the mainland by the gaze of the outsider, the television viewer or scientist. After all, islands would be a meaningless category without continents with which to compare them. Darwin needed to compare his island specimens with nearby continental examples to illustrate how differences or variations between them could have evolved during periods of geographical isolation. Equally, the cartoons and fictions set on islands would have little meaning if they did not have some relationship or connection

with the world beyond the boundaries of the island, something to which their audience can relate. It is this paradox, the fact that the isolation of islands is only significant at the point when they are no longer isolated, that defines how islands become meaningful spaces.

Hence the British need to persevere with 'the shared pretence that Britain is a lonely island in the middle of an empty green sea'.[3] British identity is tied up with maintaining the myth of isolation even in the face of an ongoing connectedness to the outside world. Arguably the notion of islands as spaces of isolation is far more a product of such cultural understandings than natural types. In short, islands are examples of how we use the world around us to define our identities, to find ourselves: islands are a convenient cut-off point for drawing lines between civilization and nature, human and nonhuman species, British islanders and the rest of the world. It is therefore perhaps not surprising, as Bill Bryson noted, that crossing the boundaries of island spaces requires a 'whole new concept of distance'.[4]

Beaches

Yvonne Rydin

> Here I am, before the sea; it is true it bears no message. But on the beach, what material for semiology![1]

For many parents, Alfie and Annie-Rose will be familiar characters. Alfie is about three years old and Annie-Rose is his toddling baby sister. In one of Shirley Hughes's picture-book stories, the pair are taken on their first trip to the beach. After a long car journey, they finally get their first glimpse of the sea. But before that, they can smell it. That curious mix of ozone, decaying seaweed and salt will be familiar to anyone who has been to a British beach; do other beaches smell the same? It is a uniquely evocative smell. Nowhere else smells the same. It can carry memories of similar childhood holidays. It tells one exactly where one is.

But the sensual effect of being on the border of land and sea is not limited to smell. All the physical senses are involved. There is the touch of the sand or rock and of the water. For those brave enough, there is the roller-coaster motion of the surf. For the more timid, there is the coldness of tidal water splashing over feet, pulling the sand away from under toes as it retreats. If the sun shines, there is the warming, even burning effect of solar radiation. In more inclement weather, there is the feel of the wind and rain. There are the sounds of those waves and of sea birds. The salt of the air finds its way into the taste of days on the beach, usually along with sand. All these sensations will be behind any vision of the beach, captured in myriad postcards, photographs and paintings. They all add up to the unique experience of otherness offered by the beach. Every part of us is bombarded with information telling us that we are somewhere very different from our normal landside existence.

After all, holidays – even day trips – are supposed to be different. Holidays are at a physical remove from home, in accommodation that is different from the flat or house we normally occupy. And we do different things on holiday. The diurnal rhythm is different, the food, the ways of occupying ourselves, even our clothing are usually different. Otherwise it would not be a holiday. And on the beach these differences are at their most extreme. We sit on rocks or sand. Clothing becomes practically non-existent. Or for some

41 A British beach in August.

there is the fancy dress of wet-suits, making swimmers and surfers look like seals in the waves. On a beach, everything has to be different because of the direct engagement with the elements: the earth, the water, the wind, the sun. This is an exciting opportunity and yet this otherness can also be threatening and disruptive. So those who visit the beach often find themselves trying to domesticate it.

Of course, as soon as we go to the beach, we shape and change it. Part of this is the simple presence of people in a new location. We are not part of the ecosystem of the beach and its capacity for absorbing us is limited. When the film *The Beach* came out in the 1999–2000, it portrayed the idyll of a few on a tropical beach. When people sought to visit the actual site of filming, their very presence put pressure on the beach and threatened to reduce its idyllic qualities. Much beach management is about trying to manage these pressures and the damage that results, removing litter and waste and returning the beach to its pristine condition, supplementing the twice-daily cleaning that the tides provide.

But part of our effect is deliberate. It is about reducing the very difference with everyday living that attracted us in the first place. For too much difference is uncomfortable and threatening. In many ways, we want to change the beach. So families set up camp on the beach, surrounded by wind shields and insulated by deckchairs and other padding. We re-create aspects of domestic life with picnics and barbecues. Recreational aspects of domestic life are also brought onto the beach. Families and groups play football, cricket and frisbee, all activities more reminiscent of the park, playground and garden. Even building sandcastles will be an activity that children have practised in their sandpits at home. The sight of families trying to re-create home life in this terrain of otherness can be humorous but also touching. For there is still the attempt to engage with the otherness of nature. They are handling the tensions of seeking, recognizing and trying to cope with a different terrain.

How far can this tension be maintained? With more use of the beach, the willingness to tolerate the un-domestic, the other, seems to reduce. Water quality must be 'safe', not different, implying considerable infrastructure development to treat any emissions into the water near the beach. We come to expect the facilities of urban development. Toilets, cafés, changing rooms and huts, shops, entertainments. At this stage, the beach becomes just the location for the beach resort. Concrete and wood replace sand and rocks. One can walk the promenade or boardwalk without touching sand; one can walk out over the sea along the pier. This is not the beach, the area that is repeatedly washed by the sea, but the seaside, the essentially urban counterpart to the beach.

However, the fundamentally untameable character of the beach is always there. The land can be developed but water is a more resistant medium. Indeed in its more hostile moments, it is destructive of development. Beaches are created by the erosive force of water movement against the land and this is an ongoing process, which can be held at bay only by considerable engineering effort and then only temporarily. This movement of water is a threat; it can flood; it can drown.

Yet it is this movement – its sound in the crash of waves, its appearance as the light moves over the shifting water, its distinctive smell, its swelling in surf-crested waves – that attracts us to the beach in the first place. A boundary between water and land, but also between the everyday and the holiday, the domestic and the natural, the stable and the shifting, the safe and the dangerous. The beach and our holiday experiences on it capture the deep ambivalence of our desire to be in close proximity to natural features. It is the shoreline between threat and attraction, between the desire for difference and the fear of it.

Deserts

David J. Nash

Afar in the Desert I love to ride,
With the silent Bush-boy alone by my side:
Away – away – in the Wilderness vast,
Where the White man's foot hath never
    passed . . .
A region of emptiness, howling and drear,
Which Man hath abandoned from famine
    and fear;
Which the snake and the lizard inhabit
    alone,
With the twilight bat from the yawning
    stone;
Where grass, nor herb, nor shrub takes
    root,
Save poisonous thorns that pierce the foot;
And the bitter-melon, for food and drink,
Is the pilgrim's fare by the salt lake's brink:
A region of drought, where no river glides,
Nor rippling brook with osiered sides;
Where sedgy pool, nor bubbling fount,
Nor tree, nor cloud, nor misty mount,

Appears, to refresh the aching eye:
But the barren earth, and the burning sky,
And the black horizon, round and round,
Spread – void of living sight or sound.

from *Afar in the Desert* by Thomas Pringle (1834)

Wilderness. Emptiness. Drear. Famine.
Drought. Barren. Burning. Thomas Pringle's
lyric poem describing his travels through the
Kalahari Desert eloquently summarizes some
of the most common, and largely negative,
perceptions of arid regions.[1] Deserts have
been considered 'areas to avoid' for much of
history because of their extreme climates and
lack of surface water and food. The ancient
Egyptians, for example, regarded 'the desert'
as an inhospitable and dangerous place where
gods, wild animals and the dead held sway,
terming it the 'Red land' (in contrast to the
'Black land' of the Nile). Indeed, one of the
words used by the Egyptians for 'desert' is the
same as that used for 'foreign land'.[2] More
recently, 'Western' media coverage prior to the
conflicts in the Arabian Gulf and Afghanistan
focused as much upon the extremities of the
environment and the difficulties in engaging
in battle in arid places as to the rationale for
war itself. Constructions of deserts are, however, frequently contradictory, clouded by
conventional wisdom and romanticism, and,
more significantly, differ between individuals,
between cultures and with space and time.

The Threatening Desert versus the Sheltering Desert

You must love the desert, but never trust it
completely. Because the desert tests all
men: it challenges every step, and kills
those who become distracted.[3]

One of the most frequent perceptions of
deserts is that they are threatening landscapes,
associated with environmental crises such as
desertification, rampant soil erosion and over-
exploitation of natural resources. This view is
so prevalent that it has almost acquired the
status of conventional wisdom, even among
workers involved in development in such
areas.[4] However, public and scientific perceptions of issues such as dry land degradation
have not remained static and serve to illustrate the varying ways in which deserts are
visualized and constructed. When the series
of widely publicized droughts and associated
famine struck the Sahel in the 1970s, it was
reported that people were suffering and dying
as a result of adverse climatic conditions.
Populations were viewed as being effectively
helpless in the face of a hostile environment.
As research into the evidence for, and processes of, desertification progressed, however,
blame for land degradation shifted away from
'natural' explanations and was focused
squarely upon 'cultural' activities. Rather than
being the passive victims of a harsh environment, inhabitants of desert-marginal regions
were viewed as actively promoting their own
demise by employing inappropriate land use
practices. Images of bare tree-trunks, stripped
of their branches in the quest for fuel wood,
replaced those of wind-blown dust and
encroaching dunes. The situation in the 1990s
changed yet again to a more balanced view
of the issue, whereby the United Nations
Convention to Combat Desertification now
defines the problem as 'land degradation . . .
resulting from various factors, including
climatic variations and human activities'.
Explanations for desertification had shifted
from the natural to the cultural to produce a
blurred understanding of the 'problem'.

Changing perceptions of desertification
are also associated with changing responses.
These range from ambitious 'expert-led' projects, such as the Great Green Wall created in
northern China to 'reclaim the desert', to

more local-level approaches to land management involving indigenous populations, such as those used in the south-west Kalahari. This shift in emphasis reflects the fact that deserts cannot simply be viewed as threatening places but are also (using the widest definition of the term 'desert') home to around one-fifth of the world's population. Desert inhabitants often have very different views about their environment, but, more significantly, perceptions of the desert differ both within individual communities living in the arid zone as well as between desert and extra-desert dwellers. To the inhabitants of arid regions, 'the desert' is often perceived as an austere rather than a necessarily dangerous environment. Deserts are very attractive to parents in urban centres who may send their children to live with Bedouin tribes to harden their souls and allow them to enjoy the 'freedom' offered. There are, however, major disparities in wealth between urban and rural populations. While nomadic desert dwellers may benefit from the perceived openness, freedom and shelter of the desert landscape, their lifestyle is far from idyllic.

The Timeless Desert versus the Dynamic Desert

In the desert you have time to look everywhere, to theorize on the choreography of all things around you.[5]

In addition to the opposing tropes of benevolence and threat, deserts are portrayed on the one hand as endless seas of constantly shifting sand in films such as *Lawrence of Arabia* (1962) while at the same time being viewed as vast, timeless, unchanging landscapes in 'coffee table' volumes. Neither is, of course, strictly the case. The popular image of 'the desert' as an endless expanse of sand-

dunes is a highly misleading one. Dunes are important landscape features in tectonically stable, relatively low-relief deserts such as those of Australia, but become of lesser significance in more tectonically active, high-relief areas where erosional and water-related features dominate. For example, 43 per cent of the Sahara Desert is occupied by mountainous terrain, with only 28 per cent covered by dunes.[6] Images of the desert as portrayed in films like *The Good, the Bad and the Ugly* (1966) may therefore be more appropriate than those of *The English Patient* (1996), but even this generalization is dangerous given the considerable spatial landscape variability within and between different deserts. Climates in different arid regions also vary substantially. The classic 'Hot' desert, as typified by the central Sahara and the Arabia peninsula, may well occupy 45 per cent of the global arid zone, but it must be remembered that so-called Cold deserts account for around one-quarter of the total. These include places such as the Gobi and Turkmenistan deserts, where mean monthly winter temperatures drop to well below freezing.

In contrast to the conventional wisdom that deserts are stable and unchanging environments, the world's arid zones have been, and are, highly dynamic spaces. For example, the Sahara Desert was almost completely covered by grass and shrubs as geologically recently as 5,000–6,000 years ago, when Sahelian vegetation extended as far as 23° North. Climatic changes occurred around this time that led to higher summer temperatures and lower precipitation, and resulted in a switch from grassland to the present arid landscape. Many deserts are much younger than conventional wisdom suggests. Deserts are also highly responsive to climatic changes and natural climatic variability at the decadal and even inter-annual level. For example, the received wisdom that the margins of the world's deserts are expanding as a result of problems such as pervasive aridification has now been largely discredited. Desert margins retreat and advance as desert vegetation responds to interannual variations in rainfall. Even the normally bare linear dunes of the Namib sand sea had a healthy cover of grass in the year 2000 following an unusually wet austral summer.

Deserts may appear threatening but are home to countless millions. They may appear to be timeless places but many are relatively young. They may appear to be static and unchanging but are highly dynamic spaces. Whether they are indefinite spaces very much depends upon the viewpoint and timeframe of the observer.

Floods

Julian A. Dowdeswell

Less than 200 years ago, the Biblical Flood still dominated the interpretation of many geological phenomena. The emplacement of perched boulders high above modern sea level was credited to the Flood, before it was understood that Quaternary glaciers had deposited such large 'erratic' blocks after eroding and transporting them sometimes hundreds of kilometres from their source. Today, floods resulting from high-magnitude and often prolonged rainfall are regarded as important agents of landscape change.

John Wesley Powell, one of the first geologists to explore western North America, described a flood as follows in his book of 1895, *Canyons of the Colorado*: 'As the storm comes on, the little rills increase in size, until great streams are formed . . . and now the waters,

loaded with these sands, come down in rivers of bright red mud, leaping over the walls in innumerable cascades.' However, quantitative measurements of the processes taking place during floods, and their rates of operation, are difficult to obtain directly. Instrumentation is susceptible to damage or destruction and data are lost. As a consequence, the processes operating at high river discharges are often understood mainly through computer modelling of flow hydraulics or by reference to the effects of floods through the later examination and interpretation of flood deposits.

The magnitude of past floods can be assessed by the dimensions of the erosional features that are produced – the huge Channeled Scablands, which cover about 40,000 km² of southern Washington State, produced as the retreating North American ice sheet unleashed vast lakes of previously dammed glacial meltwater,[1] or the immense canyons observed on satellite images of the surface of Mars.[2] The series of floodmarks on many bridges provide a historical record of the height reached by flood waters, although this is a rather crude metric, taking no account of changes in drainage-basin characteristics such as shifts in land-use or flood-amelioration schemes. Today, the size of a flood is often estimated statistically through its return period: the length of time within which a flood of a given discharge will be repeated in a specific environmental setting.

The geological modification that takes place during floods can be viewed in the context of either instantaneous landscape change – for example, how much wider or deeper a river channel becomes during a flood – or relative to the time that the landscape takes to recover its pre-flood dimensions – dependent on the rate of channel fill and bank rebuilding. In some cases, an environmental threshold may be passed, and the landscape reaches a new equilibrium shape with the processes acting upon it.[3] Longer-term landscape change is the result. Climate change, whether natural or anthropogenic, will also affect the magnitude of storms. The severity of flooding experienced and the rate of landscape recovery will, therefore, vary through time.

These views of what constitutes a flood relate to the natural rather than the human environment. A flood is one thing to an earth scientist, but quite another to an insurance-company executive or a reporter! Today, floods are featured in the television news regularly, with the amount of air-time often dependent on the number of (Western) casualties. Here, it is the human rather than physical consequences of floods that are the principal focus of attention.

This has often been so in literature and film portrayals of floods too. Take D. H. Lawrence's *The Rainbow* (1915):

> With preternaturally sharp senses she heard the movement of all the darkness that swirled outside. For a moment she lay still. Then she went to the window. She heard the sharp rain, and the deep running of the water. She knew her husband was outside.

Similarly, in the film of 1984, *The River*, the growing threat from continuing rain, together with its potentially disastrous consequences, are related closely to the people affected.

There are exceptions, however. George Eliot, in *The Mill on the Floss* (1860), makes observations on the geomorphological consequences of floods that would not be out of place in a (particularly well-written) geology textbook:

> Nature repairs her ravages – but not all. The uptorn trees are not rooted again – the parted hills are left scarred: if there is new growth, the trees are not the same as of old, and the hills underneath their green vesture bear the marks of the past rending.

This prose contains an important geological implication – that the stratigraphy and sedimentology making up the sedimentary record demonstrate the effects of past floods, even if these are concealed beneath the modern subaerial landscape. It also gives the sense that time is needed for the landscape to recover from the effects of flooding.

In the context of future change in particular, floods will continue to affect both the natural and the human landscape, at a magnitude and frequency that will be dependent on the environmental shifts that the earth experiences through global warming. The scientific predictions of the *Intergovernmental Panel on Climate Change (IPCC)*, and, indeed, futuristic visions such as the unceasing downpour in the Los Angeles of 2019 in Ridley Scott's film *Blade Runner* (1982), provide continuing reminders of this. The prediction of flood magnitude and timing using mathematical process-form models, the assessment of flood hazards to those living and working in threatened areas, and the calculation of the insurance risks and economic consequences of flooding, provide a clear example of the interface between a view of floods based on physical science and human relevance.

Dams
Nina Laurie

Big Dams started well, but have ended badly. There was a time when everybody loved them, everybody had them – the

Communists, Capitalists, Christians, Muslims, Hindus, Buddhists. There was a time when Big Dams moved men to poetry. Not any longer.[1]

The continents and names change but everyone remembers their generation's big dam 'mega project'. For me it was the Aswan high dam on the Nile, for those who came a little later the Itapu dam bordering Paraguay, Brazil and Argentina. More recently, we have heard about the Malaysian Pergua dam, and currently debate rages over damming the Namarda in India, the Biobío in Chile and the Ilisu in Turkey.

As with the names and locations, the representation of the big dam has shifted over time. With the years fault lines in the mega-project dream have unsettled the straightforward techno-fix place of dams in 'development'. The modernization of the 1950s, inherently bound up with ideas of 'taming' water for drinking and commercial agriculture and 'harnessing' its power for hydroelectricity, has been questioned. By the 1970s the fascination of achieving the damming of an enormous river like the Nile was tempered by the problems associated with stagnant water: malaria and the rapid spread of freshwater lilies where bilharzia larvae live. Cheap hydroelectricity from the Itapu dam used in the expanding Brazilian car manufacturing industry was gained at the cost of complex geopolitical negotiations demanded by a tri-nation project. By the time of the Pergua, Namarda, Ilisu and Biobío dams, negative representations of big dams have come to be dominant.

The Pergua dam has become synonymous with the corruption of tied aid, since 'development funds' were given in return for arms contracts. The Namarda, Ilisu and Biobío dams have come to symbolize the struggle of indigenous people and ethnic minorities against the loss of their lands, and threats to their livelihoods and cultural heritage. These struggles have become emblematic social movements rallying international support, often by emphasizing women's struggles against the (masculinist) poetry of engineers.

The anti-dam movement, as prevalent in the industrialized North as in countries of the South, currently dominates water politics. The movement has culminated in a visible shift in donor support for dam projects highlighted by the recent World Bank-funded independent study on the worldwide impact of dams. Focusing on the world's 45,000 biggest dams, the 404-page report by the World Commission for Dams indicates that the positive impacts of dams are exaggerated.[2] The many negative impacts of dam building are given centre stage, since the report highlights the displacement of 40–80 million people, which often affects the most vulnerable. The report's main recommendation is that no dam should be built without the agreement of the affected people.

42 Women in Cochabamba, Bolivia, helping to block a road as part of the protests against a new water law and against the takeover of the Municipal Water Company by Aguas de Tunari, an international water consortium whose main partners were International Water – the global arm of the UK water company NorthWest Water and US company Bechtel.

43 'No to the privatization of wells'. This became a crucial issue in the Cochabamba water uprisings from January to April 2000, as people tried to protect their historical water uses and customs from marketization.

In the context of 'anti-damism' a new language is emerging to interpret the shifting relationship between 'nature' and 'culture' in water management. In popular literature 'de-engineering' dams is replacing an older language of the 'damed machine river'.[3] Environmental and social concerns are outweighing demands for cheap electricity and water. So, in the light of these shifts, what has happened to the poetry of dams and the men who made it? What has happened to the male engineers whose walls were emblazoned with photographs of big dams representing regional and national development dreams? What happens to their standing in their communities, their access to power and their masculine subjectivities when their dream dam project is abandoned because international donor interest has shifted?

These men and their dreams do not disappear. Some become frustrated, some resist, while others struggle to reinvent their dreams under different guises, shaping them to fit with different versions of the modern that are in vogue with funders.[4] The internationalization of current dam politics is as much about the struggle over which dominant masculine subjectivities can produce the most successful version of 'the modern' as it is access to water.

It is only in the context of an embodied understanding of dam politics, and the investment in particular development dreams represented in this politics, that we can begin to explain seemingly contradictory contemporary development scenarios. Scenarios where, for example, in Cochabamba, Bolivia, support for a big dam was successfully mobilized by a rural–urban alliance in order to resist World Bank-led water privatization packages and oust an international water company.[5]

Engineering dams is not new. For thousands of years ancient settler communities developed complex social relations around irrigation systems that facilitated habitation in mountains and dry deserts from the Andes to the floodplains of the Ganges. Today networks of ancient irrigation systems and dynamic social rituals underpin many forms of communal water management in countries of the South. Such networks blur the nature-culture dichotomy. Under an international donor ideology of 'socially inclusive' (neo)liberal development, community-managed micro-irrigation is currently promoted as a sustainable alternative to the big dam. This shift involves a subtle yet frightening change in language. Under donor support for micro-irrigation, enhancing social and natural 'capital' is equated with indigenous knowledge and spiritual respect for the waters of the earth. The poetry of big dams is being replaced with the poetry of the market, and I'm not sure that I want to live in a world dominated by either of them.

Churches

Robbie B. H. Goh

A likely candidate for the *ur*-church might be the Old Testament stone that marks the encounter between man and God – hence Jacob's divine visitation (Genesis 28: 18–19) is commemorated by a stone, which marks the 'Beth-el' or 'house of God'. This is not far from the etymological roots of 'church': the Greek *kuriakon*, the Lord's house (*Oxford English Dictionary*). Yet the edifice of the church – its man-made status as a physical dwelling place of God analogous to human dwellings – is fraught with problems, as King Solomon recognized: 'But who is able to build [God] an house, seeing the heaven and heaven of heavens cannot contain him?' (2 Chronicles 2: 6). God's altar is inimical to, or only minimally tolerant of, human artifice: 'An altar of earth thou shalt make unto me . . . And if thou wilt make me an altar of stone, thou shalt not built it of hewn stone' (Exodus 20: 24, 25).

The seemingly irreconcilable opposition between transcendent God and material church thus leads to two dialogically opposed patterns of the church: on the one hand the primal and natural church that signifies God by invoking the realm of nature; and on the other hand the magnificent church edifice that signifies God through ornamentation and the grand scale of construction. These two opposing ideas are further complicated by human interventions: the human structures and ideologies that are invariably mixed up with the church's spiritual project. The natural and grand churches thus also respectively imply two competing social identities: man as a part of the natural world created by God, and man as part of the institution that draws its earthly and social authority from the heavenly authority of God.

Grand church structures like the European cathedrals of Romanesque and later times (Durham, Lichfield, Notre Dame in Paris, St Paul's in London) explicitly evoke the triune God with architectural elements such as trefoils and three-fold entrances; their cruciform layouts serve as reminders of the crucifixion of Christ, while their soaring spires direct attention heavenward. Yet at the same time these also serve to demonstrate the power and wealth of the Church, as well as the social importance and wealth of the community – the church building as 'witness to the hopes, fears, aspirations, wealth or poverty' of the parish.[1] Other architectural elements, such as the fleur-de-lis and Palladio-inspired Corinthian columns, point to borrowings and influences from specific cultural and historical moments, and to a symbolism as much concerned with socio-political as with spiritual power.

This symbolism of institutional authority accordingly confers on the church a role as the parish's or community's centre for social activities. In practical terms, the sheer size of the great church makes it conducive for large social gatherings, and many churches have a basement or purpose-built adjunct hall precisely for activities such as celebratory meals, jumble sales, raffles and bingo. The economy

44 A 'Turf Church', Iceland.

of such church spaces – effectively the only large halls appropriate for gatherings of several hundred people, apart from expensive commercial spaces such as hotels and theatres – adds to the social and moral authority of the church as the central space within the local community. The church as important social space has been commemorated in such well-known artistic representations as Peter Paul Rubens's *The Triumph of Christ over Sin and Death*, Giovanni Paolo Pannini's *Cardinal Polignac Visiting St Peter's* and Pieter Bruegel's *The Battle between Carnival and Lent*, as well as in many of the images and discourses from contemporary popular culture.

The institutional and social functions of such church structures are contested by an opposing notion, of the church as a 'natural' space rather than a large and stately edifice, invoking a transcendent Deity through the unconstructed openness of nature rather than through the allusions and symbolism of ecclesiastical architecture. Such natural churches are not surprisingly often politically opposed to the institutional Church, and imply an oppositional social identity – uncluttered and free from prevailing social prejudices and authorities. Thus, in eighteenth-century England, the 'strange way of preaching in the fields' practised by John Wesley, the founder of the Methodist Church, was a means both of circumventing the control of the Established Church, as well as of creating a form of religious praxis that was socially open, accessible and flexible.[2] Similarly, the 'open chapels' of colonial Mexico – courtyard-like structures that were simultaneously a part of the official church structure, and yet also apart from it, relatively unstructured and flexible – represented an engagement with the very different religious traditions and social structures of the colonized natives.[3]

The idea of the natural church, and the image of the church as relic or object outside the realm of human society, persist in the art and culture of the age of European industrialism and modernization. Hence Michael Angelo Rooker's *Interior of Ruins, Buildwas Abbey, Shropshire* (c. 1785), which depicts a group of rustics in unselfconscious activity, leaning against the aisle columns as they prepare their food, while their dogs play in what used to be the nave. The weeds topping the gallery and capitals give these the appearance of natural features like cliffs or crags. Similar treatments are seen in Thomas Girtin's *Kirkstall Abbey* (1802), John Sell Cotman's *Croyland Abbey* (1802) and other landscape paintings. In poetry, William Wordsworth's 'Lines Written a Few Miles Above Tintern Abbey' refuses to describe directly or in any detail the titular abbey, so that it appears to merge into the 'green pastoral landscape' that is the implicit church of the speaker as 'worshipper of Nature'.[4]

This pattern of opposition between natural and institutional churches seems to be part of the logic of creative destruction through which the idea of the church evolves – a logic inherent in Christ's challenge to the Pharisees: 'Destroy this temple, and in three days I will raise it up' (John 2: 19).

Villages
David Matless

Village: A scale of meaning, often tinted with community; regularly small in anatomy; set in country or, if in the town, pretending to a like spirit of belonging; a site set apart for living a true life; a site of inbreeding and bestial manners, of forelock tugging and pathetic servility; a commune of persons made whole in equality and harmonious with a fruitful earth belonging to all and none; a place for microcosmic stories and the ravelling of lives.

Commuter village: Here people sleep, wake, drive, work, drive, eat, relax and sleep. Place fosters ease on summer evenings and weekends. Winter brings reports of stifling domesticity. One car per adult becomes the norm. Amateur dramatics and local history take wing. The ardent cultivation of a social scene may exclude those engaged in cultivation for a living. Not all villages with commuters are commuter villages; at some point the social geographic balance tilts. Years of funded research have failed to pinpoint the turning. Class, land, ancestral demographics are all in there somewhere. Buses are rare. By day one walks in whole deserted streets.

Deserted village: The traveller in the English Midlands may remark upon bumps in the pasture, evident in low sun. Summer evenings and winter afternoons show former places. The 'Lost Villages of England' fostered a melancholy scholarship post-1945, field historians and geographers bringing home lost local civilization. Why turn to Rome when such relics lay by the roadside? Ridges and furrows mark sites of cultivation and building, settlements ended by monastic expansion, monastic dissolution, landlordly expulsion, disease and the general decline that has befallen places down the ages. Standing in a lumpy field the historian ponders injustice and equality, freedom and servility, a world better than today, a world grimmer by far, gathered under pasture.

English village: A particular ideal diagnosed by Ronald Blythe in 1969 as constituting a 'national village cult'. Contains church, trees, public house, green, pond with ducks, people. All seem at ease. Yet what the admiring or critical observer sees as simplicity may harbour frightening complexity. Lions in the garden, worms in the bud, something rotten in the State, something nasty in the wood. An ideal critiqued and mocked as long as evoked, and evoked for a startling range of ends. All political ideals gather here, wildly opposed visions of the good life serving to suggest something more than simply pleasant, though pleasant simplicity is difficult enough on its own; see *Commuter village*.

Estate village: Also referred to in histories of ownership as a closed village. Often possessing architectural coherence. Coats of arms may be stamped on houses; all live under the sign. Historically admired by conservatives, loathed by socialists. Radical village ideals may echo the estate village in their pervading sense of order, with the squire naturally lopped and ownership in common. Village and land are evidently connected; see also *Deserted village*.

Gated village: Commerce gathers folk into community as attractive resorts spring up. Primarily a North American phenomenon. Hot Springs Village, Arkansas, boasts eight eighteen-hole golf courses and a luxury of facilities. Who would not aspire to a life 'Natural, beautiful, peaceful' yet also 'private and secure'? Circles are squared through a property-owning 'government of the people' fostering the 'natural rhythm of life'. This is all-year-round stuff, not just during time off. Time is always on in the gated village. Such people are indeed 'Welcome to Heaven on Earth'.

Fishing village: A village on the coast living in part via the capture of fish. Authorities distinguish settlements defined by occupation: 'Without actually doing it nobody knows what working in the sea is like'.[1] Seeking testimony in song, Charles Parker and Ewan MacColl recorded Yarmouth herring fisherman Ronnie Balls for their BBC 'Radio Ballad' *Singing the Fishing* of 1959: 'If you fish for the herring, they rule your life'. Many UK fishing villages have declined with falling numbers of fish and fishermen. Causality is complex, a chicken and roe story of Government, markets, technology and stocks. Fishing villages, given attractive harbours, may draw the tourist, becoming service centres of another kind.

Holiday village: A place of ordained fun. Commonly of chalets, possibly of caravans, maybe of apartments, certainly for just a week or two. Village spirit is fostered among people temporarily thrown together by choice via the provision of entertainment. Residents may be discouraged from leaving the site. Barriers are not impenetrable but village and surrounding country sit in a state of limited osmosis. Attendants disport in distinctive gear, at once clowns, policemen, friends and targets. Postcards are available, often in startling colour. In recent years kitsch nostalgia has accrued around the Hawaiian ballroom, the monorail and the glamorous grandmother. Specialist events are held to boost trade in fallow winter months.

Mining village: Occupational community dependent upon mineral extraction, chiefly coal in the UK, but also lead, tin, etc. Do not see *English village, Commuter village*. Inland version of fishing village. Systematically dismantled by UK Governments in the 1980s and '90s in battle against organized labour. Severe socio-economic difficulties. Celebrated community culture, attracting determinedly sensible nostalgia, not yet of the kitsch variety. Slag heaps make the ridge and furrow of the next millennium.

45 Skegness Model Village, Lincolnshire. Clockwise from top left: entrance kiosk; fire station; bathing pool; general view.

Model village: Comes in two sizes. *Large*: the product of philanthropic and reformist dreams of community and social and moral improvement. Ironically Nonconformist.

Small: miniature Lilliputian, English village by kit, the adult visitor dwarfing imagined life. Children relish the chance to rampage a settlement. Perhaps the most interesting of all village types. Often found in seaside resorts. The visitor grazes candy floss while contemplating the quiet life. Shops are labelled with rude proprietorial names.

New England village: See *English village*; wooden housing, actual snow.

Open field village: Three fields, strips, Court Leets, no hedge bother. Laxton survives in north Nottinghamshire; C. S. Orwin made his name here. Common medievally. See also *Deserted Village*.

Shopping village: Found in airports. Cultivation of temporary feeling of consumer community via the purchase of odd items. Economy residents view the international bourgeoisie at conspicuously useless conduct. Shopping is the new hunting; see also *Estate village*.

Urban village: Realm of happy contradiction. Residents dream that everybody knows their name. Bizarre surveillance fantasy among those unable to cope with atomized world.

NOTE: The geography of the village tends to particular patterns, with some arrangements of living breaking the shape. Forms of understanding have historically been drawn to clear, nucleated, properly edged form. Do not see: shack settlement, ribbon development.

Home

Yi-Fu Tuan

Home is a place that offers security, familiarity and nurture. In degree of artifice, it can be a clearing in a vast tropical forest and, at the other extreme, a flat in a high-rise building in the middle of a metropolis. In size, it can be a bedsitter (a studio in American English) and, at the other extreme, the planet Earth. Home is usually a fixed place and geographically specific – this house, not that, this valley, not that. Usually, but not invariably. For a caravan on the move can be a home to nomads, and retired people in North America are known to consider their mobile home their real home, which they move (drive) from one location to another as their mood dictates, or as the seasons change.

Consider the three key words that define home. First, security. Home is shelter or haven. Implied is something that is not home and that lies outside of it. Home, no matter what its size, is thus a bounded space. A clearing in the forest, a house, a neighbourhood, a city, a nation state and the planet Earth are all bounded spaces, beyond which lie the unknown, the threatening, but also the exciting. Human beings, like all animals, need to feel secure, a feeling that

(for human beings) can be guaranteed by fences and walls, lines protected by magical rites or military force, but, at the most basic level, it is simply the awareness of clearly drawn limits, for with such awareness one knows whether one is still within them, and so can adjust one's state of mind, alert or relaxed, accordingly.

Second, familiarity. Home is the familiar place where difficult and stressful choices no longer have to be made since, thanks to prior experience, one knows just where things are and what to do: for example, that's the most dependable water hole, that porch offers the coolest shade, that news-stand is where one can count on getting *The Economist* or the *New York Times.* Familiarity provides psychological security – a desirable outcome – but it can also lead to boredom. Hence the periodic need to go beyond home to the space of adventure and danger. In many traditional cultures, women were more or less confined to the home. Such confinement, ostensibly to protect women and make them feel safe, can actually exacerbate their anxiety and fear by making the outside world seem ridden with threat. On the other hand, it can also exaggerate the appeal of that which lies beyond.

Third, nurture. Home is essentially nurturing. That may well be the heart of its meaning, for nurturing presupposes security and the support of the familiar. In the safety and familiarity of home, human beings are able to recover in body and spirit. Food nurtures, and it is available in the home place, as it may be elsewhere, with, however, this difference: in the home place, one knows just where to find it when one needs it. Nature is the ultimate source of food. Not surprisingly, certain tribes of hunter-gatherers in the Congo basin see not only their temporary shelters in the clearing but the tropical forest itself, so generous in its provisions, as home. For modern city dwellers, food is to be found in the fridge and in the neighbourhood grocer's. They know that it comes from nature – often nature in distant parts of the world – but they seldom know how exactly it ends up in their local store and, finally, in their fridge. Hence, sensitive city dwellers, for all their pride in their gadget-rich penthouse, may feel periodic tremors of anxiety; and perhaps for this reason they may contribute to environmental causes that seek to protect their (and everybody's) larger home – the planet Earth.

Home allows us to rest. Within its borders, we can end our vigilance, relax, and even shut our eyes and sleep. The human meaning of home is especially deep, in part because we, unlike other animals, undergo a prolonged period of immaturity during which we need ample rest under the protection of home and caring adults. For this reason, the home of our childhood tends to resonate more poignantly than do the homes that we have occupied as adults. Another reason for home's deep resonance is that it is where we recover from sickness. This is not true of other primates (baboons, monkeys and apes), whose sick members are obliged to trail their fellows as best they can, the alternative being abandonment and death.

Home is a thoroughly humanized, socially constructed world, and this is true even for the hermit, who, however far he ventures into the wild and wherever he settles, necessarily carries in him and with him all the cultural habits and tools (including language) that he acquired in childhood and youth. Language is the universal tool for place-making, and language is, of course, social. Hunter-gatherers are unique in creating their homes primarily by means of language – that is, by naming and telling stories about the animate and inanimate things that surround them. Even in the most

sophisticated societies, people must use words to plan and build a home; moreover, after its completion, what the occupants say to one another, and about the spaces they share, makes a real difference to their home's ambience. Security, needless to say, is socio-psychological and not just a matter of strong walls. As for nurture and care, they are provided by people, and a well furnished home is one that facilitates such provision. Social also is the division of labour in the maintenance of home. In most societies, the interior is women's domain. Women furnish, decorate, sew, clean and cook. Men look after the home's larger physical structures and exterior space.

Home that can be directly experienced - not just seen, but heard, smelled, and touched - is necessarily a small and intimate world. It is this direct experience that gives home its power to elicit strong emotional response. Human beings, however, are also endowed with imagination, which can extrapolate 'home' far beyond the directly experienceable – house, neighbourhood and towns – to such large spaces as region and nation-state. A whole country, even one of continental size, can then become home, or homeland – and homeland, even more than home, is a guarantor of security and nurture. Hence homeland can command a people's ultimate loyalty, which is the offering up of their own life in its defence.

Shelter

Charles Gordon and Rob Shields

> Before I built a wall I'd ask to know
> What I was walling in or walling out . . .
> from *Mending Wall* by Robert Frost (1915)

Adam's hut in Eden must have been the barest shelter – for what would he have sought shelter from in a paradise? Not fierce animals, or weather, or even God himself. This is why there are no shelters mentioned in the story of the Garden of Eden; and thus architecture and building rank among the first professions.

The minimum required of any sort of building is that it offer some sort of protection for someone or something from someone or something else. Shelter is primordial – less than a 'hut', just a lucky overhang of rock that hides or protects, a high drift of snow deflecting the wind, dense overhead foliage, or a lean-to of branches cutting the rain. Anything more sophisticated takes on other functions; it becomes 'a house', 'a barn' and so on.

But consider the simplest 'bus shelter' for waiting passengers. If production, particularly food production, refers to getting the energy needed for survival from the natural environment, shelter refers to one means by which the loss of that energy is slowed down and managed. Yet even the most basic, functional shelters give us a hint that all shelters have an ulterior motive, to provide shelter from only specific dangers and provide a refuge to ends that are socially determined. Shelter is rarely limited to thermodynamic and safety functions. Embellished in the form of the roofs over train platforms, the basic function of protection from the elements is quickly developed into an important statement of technological prowess or social

ambitions. Shelter is one way in which the fluid patterns of social organization are maintained and concretized through a material intervention in the environment – to continue with our example, a bus shelter allows commuters a momentary respite from wind at a bus stop in an exposed location.

What is at stake in these interventions in the human–environment relation? Some theorists in countries with cold climates have asked whether there is a human right to shelter? A traveller taking refuge in the bus stop of our example but intending to continue, on foot, mounts, by their occupation, one small challenge to the social organization of shelter. Shelter from the threat of violence and from fear of others can quickly turn the humble 'bus shelter' into a miniature version of 'bunker architecture', replete with surveillance cameras, panic buttons, bullet-proof glass and uncomfortable features that *deny* shelter to those, such as the traveller, who would seek to shelter from the wind or rain for too long. Real-world 'shelters' are thus more hospitable to some than others. Much of European and North American public space and infrastructure highlights the systematic denial of shelter to specific classes of person.

Shelter has an institutional and irrevocably political context. It is argued by many progressive social groups to be among the most basic human rights. Any group, from family to community to society, can be understood from the way that it organizes itself to distribute or deny shelter to its members, much as it organizes health care, consumption and, particularly, production. We can sum up the issues involved as follows:

- What is being sheltered? Individuals; organizations or artefacts?
- What are the actual dangers and / or perceived risks? 'Nature'; other species;

other members of the same species –
and from outside or from inside the
group?

– What are the means of shelter? Symbolic
or concrete?

These factors combine to create a 'mode of
shelter' specific to a time, place and culture.
It is as characteristic of society as the mode
of production, and we can read a society by
its shelters. Nevertheless, it is assumed within
many forms of thought that the ultimate
goal is to protect the self, and the maintenance of the physical body will subvert any
other values. But there are many situations
in which the choices for survival privilege
group or artefact over the individual. (We
often assume that the survival of the individual is a value that supersedes all others. In
fact, cultures prescribe the choices to be
made in terms of survival and shelter.)

In many forms of cultural prescription
over survival and shelter, it is all too easy to
construct the 'user', whether an individual or
group, as a passive, adapting creature, suffering or enjoying the shelter provided to him
or her. But many are alienated from the shelters imposed upon them. The kind of activity
idealized in the film *The Great Escape* (1962)
represents the work of resistance to an environment designed to be controlling. More
generally, escape is one of the major responses
to the mode and means of shelter. That said,
short of escape there are many ways in which
people attempt practical or aesthetic resistance to specific shelters or to social modes of
shelter; the most obvious are interior decora-
tion, on the one hand, and graffiti, as might
be the case in our example of the bus stop,
on the other.

Attempts at resistance may founder on the
class or material realities of shelter. Shelter is
unevenly distributed; any given shelter may
be partial and unequally hospitable to uses

and users. If, as mentioned at the beginning,
shelter is as crucial to individuals and societies as production, then it can be argued
that the concepts of powerlessness, meaning-
lessness and the separations from self and
species that characterize alienation characterize the relations to shelter as well.

Shelters as humble as those at a bus stop
or over a railway platform tell us about the
values of a culture and the social mode of
shelter; they also tell us about the world that
people encounter and decisions they take in
the course of their everyday lives. Only in a
utopia, a return to the Garden of Eden where
we would have no need for it, would we boast
that we have solved the problem of shelter
beyond further debate.

> This man, with lime and rough-cast,
>   doth present wall,
> that vile wall, which did these lovers
>   sunder . . .
> Shakespeare, *A Midsummer-Night's Dream*

Tors
Christopher Tilley

> And now we made for the top [of Kilmar
> Tor]. It was more like scaling the ruined
> walls of a gigantic castle than a hill.
> Boulders are piled on boulders, as if
> dropped from some Cyclopean hand . . .
> Wander yourself over these great moors . . .
> and see if you do not find yourself, after a
> while searching for meanings, seeing
> resemblances, and hearing voices such as
> you never saw or heard before.[1]

From the prehistoric past to the present, the
tors or granite rock outcrops appearing on

the hilltops of the moors of south-west England have had an enduring human fascination. Even though, relatively speaking, they are small and insignificant in height, they do indeed appear as immense, majestic and mountainous to an observer on the moor. The apparent hyperbole used in their description by many writers such as Folliot-Stokes is indeed justified. Tors have a striking visual power and dramatic quality out of all proportion to their actual size. Although the rocky tors occupy only a small part of the surface area of the moors, they dominate the landscape. Visitors come today specifically to see the tors, to climb on them, walk between them, gaze at them, photograph them and enjoy the panoramic vistas. The visitor to Dartmoor may purchase the *A to Z of Dartmoor Tors* with descriptions of each.[2] Truly to know these landscapes is to know these tors and the relationships between them. To acquire an intimate knowledge requires walking between and around them at different times and seasons, for their identity alters according to when, and from where, and how they are approached.

For some romantic writers the tors have a dreamlike quality freezing the past in the present with spiritual and magical powers, places inducing contemplative thought. For the British army, the tors and the mosaic of stones and bogs that surround them provide an ideal training ground for search and rescue and invisible movement. For visitor or upland farmer alike they provide vital reference and orientation points in the landscape. Tors punctuate these upland landscapes. Each have their own names, shapes and forms, their own particular identities. They mark place and inscribe themselves on human memory in multiple ways.

Individual rocks within the rock masses often exert a particular fascination in terms of the aesthetics of their forms, shapes, textures,

weathering lines, quartz and mica inclusions, and the lichens growing on their surface. Mostly grey and dull, the rocks may glow rose-pink at sunset, transforming their appearance. Sometimes the sunlight glints brilliantly on mica inclusions visible only from particular angles and directions at particular times of day and seasons of the year. The manner in which the rocks may appear for an instant and then disappear in the swirling mists so commonplace on the moors animates the rocks. But the tors exert their fascination in relation to the human body not only because of the look or monumental appearance of these stones, but because of the way in which they feel, the sounds of the wind hooting and howling through them from different directions, the smell of the stones and the earth and vegetation surrounding them. A sense of awe and wonder for these places, notwithstanding a modern rational geological explanation for their formation, continues.

Made up from the hardest granite capping the hills and ridges, they are composed of lenticular blocks of granite, with gently rounded surfaces, resting horizontally on each other, with the individual sheets often being of great size. They sometimes rest precariously on each other, hence the name logan (logging or rocking) stone. Although granite is very resistant to erosion, the fantastic shapes of the high tors owe their form to the fact that, as the granite was cooling and crystallizing from its molten state, horizontal and vertical cracks and joints appeared running at right angles to each other. These caused the rock to split naturally into cubes and rectangular blocks, dividing the mass into columns separated by openings and fissures. Weathering and the freeze–thaw action of ice in the past have both rounded these joints and enlarged them. The top stones of the highest tors are frequently riddled with solution hollows or

46 Showery Tor, Bodmin Moor, Cornwall. In the foreground part of a massive Bronze Age ring cairn surrounding the tor is visible. Rough Tor is visible beyond.

basins, some of which are permanently filled with water. These may be so perfectly regular in form that they appear to be carved, a significance that may have been recognized by prehistoric populations.[3] These basins are frequently interconnected by channels and erode over the lips of the rock to create incredible arc-like shapes when seen from below.

Tors are characteristically surrounded by extensive areas of tumbled blocks of stone and fallen slabs below them, known locally in Cornwall as 'clitter'. Such areas make walking extremely slow and arduous, sometimes impossible. There are often numerous voids and chamber-like spaces amongst the tumbled blocks on the upper slopes. Accumulations of clitter sometimes form distinctive streams running down the hill slope and bands crisscrossing it. The clitter masses have their own particular fascination: spiral and circular and oval shapes are visible within them when seen from particular places, only to be lost from sight again when one moves within the stones.

While to a modernist rationality all these stones are inanimate, we can surmise that to prehistoric populations they must have been places of overwhelming ancestral spiritual power and significance. The moors of southwest England are depopulated today. In prehistory we know from the presence of numerous stone circles, stone rows, burial cairns and settlements of round houses that these areas were densely settled.[4] People built their houses amongst the dense clitter masses on the hill slopes. They oriented the doorways of their houses to face towards important distant tors, and built cairns on the hilltops in, among and around them.[5] They surrounded individual dramatic stones with ring cairns or moved stones away from large earth-fast stones or 'grounders' to emphasize their forms, and may even have rearranged boulders in the clitter masses to enhance pre-existing shapes, arrangements and forms.[6] The rocks to them were, as they remain for us, vital resources with which to think, to act and to relate. Although tors are unaltered features of the landscape, their overriding significance has always been cultural, connected with the human events and stories, memories and myths with which they are imbued.

Caves

Sarah G. Cant

Sitting quietly in the dark, I remain motionless, then blink. I blink again, but still I cannot see. This thick, black treacle-like darkness completely surrounds me, darker than a moonless night, timeless. There is no visible distinction between my body and the space that I am in. This darkness seems endless. I move an arm. My limb cuts through the pitch-black space freely then bruises suddenly as it impacts upon a hard, textured surface. I hear the faint sound of moving water, somewhere in an unseen distance, and sense a cool breeze across my face. There is no other place on earth, no other space within nature that is quite like this, like a cave.

For those who may accidentally find themselves in a state of sustained underground lightlessness, some say sanity exits quickly as the dark filters obscurely into the body and hallucination becomes easy. Bright colours appear to dance before the eyes and the cave may encourage a paranoid state. One gruesome cave myth circulating below ground claims there was once an explorer, lost in a cave, alone, lamp-batteries dead, who began to think that the cave was talking to him. Then his left foot, encouraged by the speaking-cave, began to pick on his right foot. When rescuers found the troubled caver, he had cut off the 'offensive' left big toe with his penknife, in order to stop the argument.

Fortunately, I am not alone and I have an electric lamp (that works) attached to my yellow caver's helmet. I have chosen to be in this state of complete darkness temporarily. With a swift flick of a switch, eyes blink and a beam of pale light casts this way and that as I move my head. The light falls onto rock, shiny here, muddy over there and 'wave-scalloped' nearby. My light picks out puddles of muddy water on the floor, short stalactites dripping from the passage roof, and mud-besmeared overall-boot-helmet-clad caving companions, appearing one by one as lamps are switched on. Contemplating this under-earthly space of cave, I am struck by the immensity of my surroundings and the stories that mingle to create this special kind of space, under the ground.

In every direction I am surrounded by limestone. A colossal mass of rock-with-a-history permitting the existence of caves. This immense story began once upon a (deep) time, at the bottom of an ocean. Limestone, a sedimentary rock borne of death – layer upon layer of decomposing marine life, compressed and consolidated over time. Between the disappearing ocean, the layers of rock and the uplifting shifting fracturing that later takes place (geology, geomorphology), cracks appear and limestone landscape develops an intimate relationship with hydrological process. As water leaves the surface-world of sunshine, showers and clouds, it seeps and courses underground, finding its wily way into the cracks and gaps between faults and bedding planes. Acid-charged water eats away rock, widening gaps, enlarged further by abrasive shards washed in from above and carried along, underground. And so the physical space, the hole in the ground, shaped by the actions of water on limestone, comes into existence, but remains largely hidden – only nature knows about these extensive absences within rock, below a surface landscape of earth, trees, grass and sky. There are some clues on the surface, the wide-open mouths shouting from limestone plateaus and hills 'I am a cave!' But surface-nature is often secretive, saving the best delights for those dedicated enough to seek them; the tiny cave openings 'cunningly hidden in a shakehole in the barren moorland' that hardly suggest 'the succession of galleries and pitches which extend beneath the rocky valley beyond'.[1]

As I sit in the cave, I recall how I reached this spot, a journey of climbing, walking, crawling, climbing, squeezing, crawling, walking (upright once more – hurrah!). My body moved slowly through this rock-bound, intriguingly shaped, often surprisingly beautiful, sometimes muddy, sometimes cold-water flowing in, ever-changing dark space of cave. My very presence amongst this subterranean system of passages, shafts, caverns, stalactites, stalagmites and streamway brings them into existence, as my caving technology (lamps, ropes, ladders, helping hands, fellow cavers) allows me to set foot in the hidden spaces that are caves. Indeed, for many a cave is a 'natural cavity in rock underground or leading underground, frequently restricted to those openings capable of entry by man [sic]'.[2] Caves are 'half human achievement, half nature's'.[3] Caves are not simply part of a physical geography of limestone rock, water, calcite and mud. Darkness and moving human bodies intermingle with natural cavity to reveal human geographies of presence, encounter and exploration, shaping the subterranean spaces we know as caves.

The presence of cavers – those who explore caves – became organized and systematic at the end of the nineteenth century, as rambling, climbing and natural history societies (later 'caving clubs') ventured underground in search of new places to explore, and the word 'speleology' was invented to describe cave-science. But if the caver 'makes the cave', what were the places of Stone Age dwellings, the settings for ancient Greek myths, the lairs of medieval dragons, the sites of fairy tale where hobgoblins and trolls would hide? These places of myth, legend, fear, desire and curiosity are also caves – they too reside within the same physical geography of limestone. So do the caves that

47 Harry Savory's photograph of John Hassall at the Spur and Wedge in Wookey Hole, 1913.

are lit brightly with electricity, with a path, guard rails and a guide who points out stalactite curtains named 'the flitch of bacon', stalagmites topped with orange iron ore called 'poached eggs', and human-face-shaped rock formations. But while there are many different stories that layer upon layer, rock-strata-like, shape caves beyond literal form and space through the physical and imaginative presences of the sensing, feeling, knowing, defining human body, caves, those holes below ground, have become coded by ease of human access. There are 'show caves' for tourists who absorb cave stories in a large, managed place, and 'wild caves' for cavers experiencing a hard-to-reach place. Wild caves exist everyday within nature, but more so at the weekends, when bodies clad in cavers' attire venture underground.

As I stand up, and we slowly begin to make our way back up to daylight, I do not feel (too) scared underground. There is a strange comfort in knowing that my limestone surroundings adorned with stalactites and mud are part of something deeper in time, much bigger in presence, gathering meaning as human bodies move through these intimate spaces within the earth, layers of story, interpretation, experience. I am at ease in caves – as long as my lamp is working and I am not completely alone . . .

Zoos

Kay Anderson

I feel distinctly uneasy in confined spaces, or to put it more precisely, in spaces of confinement. Take me to a sweatshop, as a colleague once did in Chinatown in New York, and the workers who labour under conditions of other peoples' choosing are not the only bodies sweating. The example of the asylum also comes to mind. This space reins in the wills of those who fall to one side of that feint line dividing the 'sane' and the 'mad' that barely conceals its own insecurity.

But in the case of the zoo, one's unease is not only with the visibly obvious and palpable – the brute fact of incarcerated life displayed for all our humanly senses. The bizarre world of the urban zoo enacts a more intriguing detention than that. For unlike the prison and the asylum, the sweatshop and other grim spaces of confinement, the contemporary zoo *conceals* the traces of human creation, and certainly any visible manifestation of power. The infrastructures that make possible today's zoo attempt a perception of freedom, not an image of mastery. Moats rather than bars.

Much like our gardens, which we strive to look casual and uncontrived – where there is a programmed organization of plants positioned according to height, character, colour of bloom and leaf, timing of sprout, bud and show – the zoo embodies a longing for human *in*visibility within the very act of nature creation.

The zoo is an intensely contradictory space, all the more captivating for its rich and fragile paradoxes. Allow me, therefore, to dwell for a moment among the strands of culture / nature that stitch together this peculiar 'patterned ground'.

The zoo, then, is a world of nature typically located at the heart of that proud prop of 'civilization' we call the city. It is simultaneously a space for recreation, as well as education. Spectacle is juxtaposed with science. Visitor surveys tell us that many people arrive full of expectation, and leave disappointed if not depressed. 'Where are all the animals?' is a common lament. Most zoos today run breeding programmes for endangered species, while publicly acknowledging that the natural home of such species, 'in the wild', is itself thin on the ground. The seminal zoo archetype of Noah's Ark lives on in many a zoo director's daydream (and also in mine: 'if only the animals had missed the boat', I have found myself fantasizing). Animals in the zoo are not domesticated, but nor are they wild. They are not hybrids, but nor do they ever fully embody their species either.

Think also of those pallid descriptions of exhibits that hang on the beast's enclosure. This is 'Millie the Macaw' whose relatives in nature come from the space coloured red on the world regional map. They condescend to not one, but both sides of the divide of keeper and kept that define the urban zoo.

In the post-Taliban city of Kabul, where universal human suffering goes largely unre-

48 'Home and Away at the London Zoo' by Britta
Jaschinski, 1996.

ported, the most emaciated of captive lions
receives the most specialized of care. Marjan
has counterpart celebrities in most of the
world's zoos (whose fate we can compare
with millions of less charismatic farm animals
gripped by foot and mouth disease in the
United Kingdom during 2001). The more
scary and elusive in nature, the more allur-
ing in captivity. Belinda the Bird-Eating
Spider participated for years in hypnotherapy
programmes run by London Zoo to help
people overcome their fear of spiders, and
is now pinned to a corporately sponsored
display board. Guy the Gorilla of London
Zoo, who died of a heart attack after having
dental work in 1978, is now memorialized
in a statue. Jumbo the Elephant, star of
London's imperial collection and mother
figure of many colonial zoos, is the name
given to millions of soft toys and oversized
aeroplanes.

These are just some of the characters who
have earned a badge of distinction in a space
where, more generally speaking, a specimen
stands in for a species (and other species
are weeded out in their entirety). This is the
camel. This is the field cricket. Zoo animals
as body doubles. A kind of national reference book. Though in today's zoo, animals
live in simulated ecosystems (echoes of
Harrods' Floral Hall) rather than dedicated
'houses' (echoes of human domestic arrangement). Never mind that many free animals

live in particular places as much through
contingency as species adaptation.

Of all the abundant juxtapositions within
the space of the zoo, think of the performa-
tive and the captive, the vital and the inert.
By way of example, there are the strategic
stagings on offer at the zoo. 'Not to be
missed' at London Zoo are: Feeding Time
at the Lion's Den, Dinner Time at the
Penguin Pool, Elephant Care and Animals
in Action. Hand-rear a Porcupine. In summer be sure not to miss Snacks for Snakes
(of whole, dead animals!). Frenetic activity
in the midst of captivity. Inmates on the
move, throbbing and pacing, all the more
so against forces that confine them.

The zoo is a space that activates most
all of the human senses – seeing, hearing,
smelling, touching. A day at the zoo for
human audiences is redolent not only with
vistas, but odours, the mediation of touch
and the unaccompanied voices of the animals'
very own live album. Visual perception as
multi-sensory experience. The zoo as a
sensorium. So also do confined animals
affect a dense mix of human feelings. Fear,
repulsion, attraction, awe, guilt, wonder,
disgust, embarrassment, shame and empathy
are among them. These are emotions that

49 'A Gorilla's Grip, Berlin Zoo' by Britta Jaschinski, 1996.

rise up, not serially, like a string of beads or a succession of assembly-line cages. But, rather, all at once, in a resounding muddle.

The tensions in enclosures that gather together the animal and botanical universes – including zoos, animal circuses, wild animal and safari parks, aquaria and nature theme parks – are infinitely intriguing in themselves. They call up the rich contradictions in our relation to whatever it is we call 'nature'. It's a world to be at once conquered and preserved, occupied and liberated, rendered intelligible yet all the while excessive to what can be known about it. It's a world to which we advance, precisely because we can retreat. Engagement at a distance. Conditional immersion. Such is the impossible paradox of 'controlled intimacy' at the heart of the nature enclosure.

Police Stations

Nick Fyfe

'Pigs', 'blue locusts', 'raw lobsters': critics have always been keen to blur the boundaries between nature and culture in their search for derogatory epithets to describe the police. Yet, with a curious kind of symmetry, the discursive constructions invoked by the police to describe and make sense of the spatial and social worlds they encounter rely on similar entanglements between nature and culture. Indeed, 'cop culture' is characterized by readings of society and space that deliberately destabilize the divisions between the human and nonhuman worlds in ways that clarify the functions and legitimize the actions of the police. Take the territory surrounding police stations, 'the ground' as officers call it, which is perceived to be fraught with physical and

moral dangers. It's a 'jungle', a place 'in which a thief may harbour with as great secrecy as wild beasts do in the deserts of Africa or Arabia', a world continually on the brink of chaos that only the police are able to save from sliding over the edge. It is a world of morally impure areas, dirty places populated by 'rubbish' and 'toe-rags'. 'Welcome to the Arsehole of the World . . . the bowels of the earth' is a typical greeting to newly arrived officers at a police station.[1] But these characterizations of the spatial and social patterns of 'the ground' enable the police to make sense of their role in terms of a deeply moral enterprise. Surrounded by these 'dirty places', the police mission is one of 'cleaning them up', acting as 'refuse collectors, sweeping up the human dross', tackling the 'cancers', which can spread unless met with the cleansing agent of forceful and persistent police attention.

In stark contrast to these discursive constructions of 'the ground', police stations represent a safe haven, a refuge from the dangers that lurk outside. Here officers are relaxed and confident because this is police territory and anyone brought in is forced to accept absolute police control over their bodies: 'The bottom line is that they've got the power, yea? Like one of them said to me out there, "you keep your mouth shut in here, because we can do whatever we want to you in here".'[2] Yet, paradoxically, as places of physical safety, police stations pose dangers to the cultural identity of officers. Given the importance of adventure and machismo to how the police define their role, those officers who work within the safety of the station are known as 'station queens' who, unlike those 'asphalt cowboys' or 'hard-chargers' out on patrol, cannot cope with the dangers of the masculine preserve of the street.[3]

Ironically, however, few of the people arrested by patrol officers and brought into police stations are dangerous. They are the 'world's dross' and 'rubbish' made up largely of drunks, vagrants, shoplifters and prostitutes. Once within the police station, however, they become 'prisoners', 'bodies' or simply 'police property'. 'Prisoners' rarely pass through the public domain or front region of a police station, which exists on one side of the station office counter where strong normative sanctions regulate what is regarded as the 'correct performance'. Rather they are taken directly to the private domain or back region of police-controlled space, isolating the prisoners on police territory. With its mix of 'custody suites', interrogation rooms and cells, this back region is patterned in ways that are of crucial symbolic importance. In the 'custody suite' prisoners are routinely forced to hand over all their property, partly to remove items with which they could harm themselves but also stripping them of a sense of personal identity and self-esteem: 'They said they had to take all my stuff, said they had to take my wedding ring off. I wasn't having that – I told them there was no way they were having it, and they said they'd take it off by force'.[4]

While being questioned in interrogation rooms, prisoners are forced to participate in rituals that are as much about maintaining a sense of the moral superiority of the police in the face of the animal-like cunning and deviousness of prisoners as they are about allowing a suspect to tell their 'side of the story'. But it is the spatial confinement of prisoners within cells that provides the starkest example of the interplay between human and dehumanized worlds within police stations. Locking a 'body' or 'police property' in a cell gives the police complete control over a 'prisoner's' access to warmth, exercise, food and drink. For those labelled 'obnoxious', pleas for water are ignored until they are prepared to 'tell the truth' – 'Once I was in there and I was dying of thirst I had to have some water and I rang the buzzer again and again but no one came. I had to drink the water out of the loo'[5] – and requests for blankets are dismissed: 'The inhuman "prig" is never really perceived to need a blanket simply because he is "an animal" and in the wild, animals seldom use blankets!', explained one officer.[6] By contrast, those who cooperate are labelled 'good as gold', and may receive cigarettes, books or opportunities to exercise. Prisoners within police stations thus become entangled in a symbolic struggle in which their human needs are appropriated for a game of 'rewards and punishments' that only the police can win.

Boundaries

Anssi Paasi

Political boundaries have become naturalized to such an extent during the twentieth century that our perception of political spaces normally begins from their essentially bounded character. While they often have the appearance of arbitrary natural lines on maps and in atlases – although representing fixed cultural patterns – their construction is always based on human action and decisions. They are exploited in governance as markers of territoriality, that is, to make a distinction between those located inside and outside a community, a distinction that usually takes the form of constructing physical barriers with clear locations or defining symbolic boundary lines to separate certain social groupings. While political boundaries can be based on natural features such as mountains, sea shores or rivers, their justification in social life is linked with questions of political loyalty, inclusion / exclusion, identity and citizenship.[1]

Boundary narratives are manifestations of social power. They are normally based on history and often celebrate past victories. The patterns of cultural life and their inherent meanings are often understood as being grounded in physical nature. This is excellently illustrated by the novelist Georges Perec:

Countries are separated from each other by boundaries. Crossing a boundary always touches one's mind: the imagined outline takes the material form of a wooden barrier, which is never located in the place which it is thought to represent, but some tens or hundreds of metres to one side of it or the other. Yet it can change everything, even the landscape. The air is the same, the soil is the same but the road is no longer entirely the same, the graphics on the signposts have changed, the bakeries are not the same as those of a moment ago, the loaves are a different shape, the cigarette packets that have been thrown on the ground are different . . . The boundaries are lines, lines for which millions of people have died. Thousands of people have died because they did not succeed in crossing a boundary. Survival depended merely on passing some ordinary river, small hill, peaceful woodland . . .[2]

National boundaries, whether representing predominantly the patterns of culture or nature, usually have a deeply emotional role in collective memories. Sometimes, as in the case of the more than 1,200 kilometres of the Finnish-Russian border, a sterile barbed-wire fence running through uninhabited forests, the boundary has become a crucial medium on both sides for the constitution of international relations and representations of the neighbouring state. This makes it far more than just a winding line that stretches over vast distances. It is superficially a 'pattern on the ground', but it is also a significant element in the social and political consciousness of the citizens living on both sides. State boundaries, of which there are more than 300 in the contemporary world, are therefore crucial elements in national ideological landscapes, and it is this that creates their relatively fixed image.

Political boundaries have always been crucial symbols and institutions in the control and governance of territories. The current 200 states are divided internally by a number of administrative, cultural and symbolic borders that exist among some 500–600 ethnic groups or nations. Boundaries have been constructed by various hegemonic groupings, and numerous ethnic groups all around the world are struggling to construct their own bounded territorial spaces, often using the 'borderless' cyberspace as a medium for this struggle.

Rivers, mountain ranges and seas are used effectively to divide and control human interaction, which attaches deeply human and political meanings to these basically physical elements. Boundaries may thus be important in assigning cultural meanings to physical landscapes, simultaneously conferring on these physical elements the attributes of natural, fixed and eternal patterns.

The patterns of nature do not follow the more or less closed land boundaries, and they are regularly crossed without difficulty by birds and other animals that have their own patterns of territorial behaviour. A fitting example is the border between Finland (and the EU) and Russia, which, while strictly guarded, is crossed by many great predators such as lynx, wolverines, bears and wolves, so that the numbers of border crossings actually observed and recorded run into several thousands every year. Interestingly enough, it is the Finnish Border Guard Service that compiles the statistics on these crossings at the same time as maintaining strict control over the flows of people and goods!

Boundaries between states and political blocks are important in geopolitics because they also divide natural resources such as oil and fresh water. These elements will probably be crucial for future questions of war and peace in the Middle East, for example. Cultural and natural patterns also coincide in the fact that the emerging global consciousness of environmental and pollution problems has forced us to reflect on the porosity of political boundaries.

The patterns emerging from culture and nature have also become fused in the rhetoric of geographers regarding political boundaries. Academic research was important for the invention of boundaries, and scholars have been in a crucial position in producing and giving meanings to these elements, which effectively display the links between power, knowledge and 'geo' elements. Since the late nineteenth century the State has been understood as an organism, in the spirit of the emerging evolutionism, with boundaries as its 'membranes'. This naturalistic interpretation was a continuation of a long tradition that divided boundaries into 'natural' and 'artificial' ones. Since the Middle Ages nature was used in a deterministic spirit as one crucial argument for the 'correct' location of political boundaries, an idea that was based on the interpretation of the power of natural law, setting out at times from religious arguments that regarded good, natural boundaries as God-given. This division remained important up to the Second World War, after which a more realistic interpretation gained in prominence.

State boundaries in particular have lost much of their significance in a globalized world dictated by new forms of geo-economics and information economics that give priority to mobility, speed and flows of various kinds. This will question the static territorial patterns that have usually been linked with cultural and political boundaries in nationalistic thinking. Boundaries will continue to be important as instruments of governance even in this more dynamic international territorial system, however. All political boundaries – including those that reflect natural patterns – are processes that are constructed and given their symbolism by human beings. The challenge therefore lies in finding ways to study not only boundary lines or border landscapes as such but also the practices and power relations that produce boundaries and are part of the creation of all dividing lines.

Natural Resources

Michael Watts

Petroleum, it is sometimes said, is the economic bedrock of our hydro-carbon civilization. The fuel of modernity, oil is an archetypal global commodity, the repository of unimaginable wealth ('black gold') and part of the largest business on earth. To be an 'oil nation' is to have discovered El Dorado in your backyard. Oil, quipped the Chief Executive Officer of ARCO, *is* money. It also happens to be filthy, black and foul-smelling. It squirts 'obligingly up into the air', noted the great Polish journalist Ryzsard Kapucinski, and 'falls back down to earth as a rustling shower of money'.[1] More than anything else, petroleum is a sort of lie: it reveals the profound mystification, the paradoxes and that contradictoriness that surround natural resources in our modern world.[2]

What exactly, then, is natural about petroleum? Well, it's naturally oily. It is a flammable liquid that occurs as a product of geo-physical and biological processes of great historical depth. A by-product of pre-human geological history, oil is deposited in subterranean formations and consists principally of a mixture of hydrocarbons with traces of nitrogenous and sulphurous compounds. In practice, of course, the composition of what passes as petroleum varies quite considerably, as one might anticipate in view of the heterogeneous circumstances associated with a 600-million-year history of sedimentation and organic decomposition. Oil's natural properties, one might say, are unstable and variegated.

Petroleum is customarily extracted through drilled wells, pumped along pipelines and refined into different 'fractions' or components. The science and practice by which oil is explored, located, pumped and fractionated has, in the last 150 years, deepened and proliferated to the point where it is now part of a massive engineering and technical infrastructure. The oil industry is now dominated by the 'majors', a cluster of transnational and highly diversified energy companies. It is sometimes said that oil drilling was invented by E. L. Drake when he sunk his now infamous 21-metre well in Pennsylvania in 1859. But several hundred years before the birth of Christ, the Chinese were sinking 1,100-metre wells to exploit petroleum for a multiplicity of purposes. Surface oil deposits had been used as asphalt and as a sealant by the Sumerians 3,000 years before the Chinese! Oil's natural-resource use spans, in other words, a vast swath of human history. Currently, oil and related gas exploitation covers two-thirds of global energy needs. More than three-quarters of all known reserves of petroleum are found in eight oil exporting countries.

Petroleum is the quintessential modern natural resource. It is present in and produced by nature, and a material source of wealth that occurs in a natural state. But this is a contradictory and non-sensible claim on its face. Oil is natural insofar as it resides in its Jurassic bedrock. But it is not immediately accessible or useful; it presupposes human knowledge and practice (drilling, exploring, refining). Oil's wealth is not conferred solely by natural process but rests upon an appraisal – a state of knowledge and practice – that is social, technological and historical. Petroleum is profoundly *of* nature – it is typically subterranean and has peculiar biophysical properties. And yet its naturalism is expressed and understood in quite determinate ways; how differently would the Chinese bureaucrat of the first century BC and the twentieth-century hard-rock geologist have described petroleum's natural properties!? Petroleum's 'resourcefulness' is not natural at all. Its expressive form as wealth, the defining property of a resource, presupposes acts of transformation, distribution and use – which, incidentally, was very different for sixteenth-century North American Indians than for a twenty-first-century Louisiana petro-chemical industry. Petroleum as a natural resource rests, then, on particular meanings of natural (for example, theories of biophysics) and particular renderings of resource (for example, theories of wealth predicated on scarcity and natural limits).

But there is another realm in which natural resources must operate, namely the social imaginary: in other words, how oil is rooted in the imagination of people living in the specific historical and social circumstances of its use and deployment. Oil as a natural resource carries it own mythos, also shaped by place and time. I currently inhabit a petroleum age in which, from the vantage point of the oil-importing North Atlantic economies, oil stands in a specific relationship to the mosque and the Arab world. For oil-producing states, petroleum provides the idiom for nation-building and the financial wherewithal for modern development (think, for example, of the petrolic ambition of a great modernizer like Shah Palavi in Iran). Oil is inextricably bound up with unimaginable personal power (Rockefeller, Nobel, Rothschild, the Sultan of Brunei), untrammelled corporate hegemony ('the Seven Sisters') and a history of spectacular imperial violence and war. Did not the long and dark tentacles of oil appear in the catastrophic demise of the twin Trade Towers in New York? Was not Osama bin Laden a product of oil as much as of Wahabbi Islam? Was not the Ayatollah Khomeini's revolution in 1979 fuelled by oil-inspired resentments and grievances? Need I mention Enron? Oil and Islam, war and violence, corruption and power, wealth and spectacle, scarcity and crisis are, in our times, seemingly all of a piece.

Petroleum's symbolic and mystificatory powers are ubiquitous. Oil, says Kapucinski, creates the illusion of a life without work, life for free; petroleum 'expresses perfectly the eternal human dream of wealth achieved through accident'.[3] Oil wealth is a sort of gigantic lottery. One need turn no further than the White House to confirm petroleum's reach, its bravado and fetishistic powers. President George W. Bush, after all, is an oil man from Midland, Texas; he has surrounded himself with oil men, and is currently engaged in a war to protect oil, a war that cannot be grasped outside the long history of American geopolitics in which the protection and acquisition of this most singular of natural resources has been the cardinal principle.

A natural resource is, then, a technical, symbolic and economic assessment or appraisal of the biophysical realm that is deployed in particular ways for particular purposes through particular practices.[4] Natural resources are not, any more than nature itself, intrinsically static or scarce or fixed because these technical, cultural and economic assessments are dynamic and changing. In contemporary America or Europe, oil is a particular type of commodity used, exchanged and fetishized in quite precise ways. It is a bundle of natural (biophysical), productive, cultural and economic relations.

To speak of a natural resource is to utter a peculiar sort of contradiction. Natural resources are not natural in any simple sense; and neither are their resource characteristics that reflect particular forms of extraction, transformation, use and fetishization. It is altogether appropriate to recall that petroleum is popularly referred to as 'black gold'. But gold after all isn't black. And neither are many forms of oil. They are colourless.

Central Places

Trevor Barnes

A central place is any location that offers a service or a product to its surrounding market region. That location might be New York, with its myriad of businesses and business types that serve the United States and even the world, or it might be Stratton in north Cornwall, with its three pubs, a butcher, a corner store and a newsagent that serve only the villagers themselves, and not even all of them. The task of central place theory is to delineate the geographical relationship among different central places, that is, to recognize a patterned ground.

It was in Mr Westlake's A-level geography class at St Austell Sixth Form College in Cornwall that I first saw the pattern. Mr Westlake was not much of a teacher, rarely holding our attention, and his presentation of the theory part of central place theory left little residue. It was only when he distributed Cornwall county maps with pieces of tracing paper so that we could plot the distribution of different sized towns (central places) and later join up the dots that I began to see the point (literally). Amazingly, a spatial pattern emerged. Larger towns like St Austell, coloured post-box red on my tracing paper, were geometrically encircled by the small forest-green dots of surrounding villages such as Sticker, St Dennis and my own one of Par. I was stunned that I could see order within the chaos of a Cornish county map. It seemed like black magic. Also, I was stunned that a theory we learned at school could apply to where I lived. Par was simply home. How could it be a theory?

That tension in central place theory between, on the one hand, a compelling geometry and, on the other, a compelling lived experience is also found in the lives and works of the theory's modern founders, two Germans, Walter Christaller (1893–1969) and August Lösch (1906–1945). On the surface, central place theory is about finding an abstract spatial order, and represented for Christaller and Lösch by the geometry of a hexagonal lattice. Patterned ground means for them the geometrical purity of a regular polygon. The trouble, though, is that polygons are not pure. The messy details of geography and history, of life itself, of lived experience, intrude. Not just pattern is important. So is the ground on which it is inscribed, and which muddies an otherwise spotless spatiality.

Christaller, the geographer, found pure geometrical order early on. He said:

I have always liked drawing . . .When I was twelve, I was given the Debes atlas. I came to see the hexagons through my drawing – only the lines were not always straight. But then on small-scale maps they always were!

His doctoral dissertation published in 1933, *Central Places in Southern Germany*, was a continuation of his childhood obsession with drawing lines and making hexagons.[1] In March of that same year, though, Hitler became Chancellor. Pursuing *Lebensraum*, Hitler sought to expand dramatically Germany's territory, first through annexation and later by *Blitzkrieg* military tactics. In planning their new territories, Christaller's central place model provided exactly the geographical template that the Nazis sought. They wanted both industrialization and a return to a Teutonic rural ideal, and Christaller's hexagonal scheme, linking rural villages with industrial cities, provided precisely for this possibility. From 1940 Christaller was employed by Konrad Meyer, who headed the Planning and Soil Office, which was part of the Reich's Commission for the Strengthening of Germandom operated by the SS under Heinrich Himmler. The task was to draw up plans for reconfiguring the geography of Germany's eastern conquests ('General plan of the East'), primarily Czechoslovakia and Poland, and, if successful, Russia itself. Christaller was given special charge of planning Poland using central place theory (illus. 50). As Christaller said,

Because of the destruction of the Polish state and the integration of its western parts into the German Empire, everything is again fluid. . . . Our task will be to create in a short time all the spatial units, large and small, that normally develop slowly by themselves . . . so that they will be functioning as vital parts of the German Empire as soon as possible.

The ground on which it was enacted, however, soiled the central place pattern that Christaller envisioned for Poland. To create the new hexagonal landscape, 4.5 million out

50 Christaller's central place model of a metropolitan region.

of the 10.2 million Poles living in the country were removed through relocation, deportation and extermination.

The other founder of central place theory, the economist August Lösch, was far less sympathetic to Hitler, and, unlike Christaller, never swore an oath of allegiance to him. In 1933, after Hitler took power, Lösch complained in his diary that 'everybody dances now to the whistle of that one fool. In this Germany, only creatures are still tolerated. But I am hoping and working for *that* Germany which will come thereafter.' That said, like Christaller, Lösch hankered after pure pattern, which again he thought was best represented by the nested hexagons of central places. That pattern did not necessarily already lie on the ground, though, but was as much as anything a rational ideal and moral benchmark for which to strive. As he famously wrote in his book *The Economics of Location*, 'The real duty of the economist is not to explain our sorry reality, but to improve it. The question of the best location is far more dignified than determination of the actual one'.[2] While Lösch's pattern was never as grounded empirically as Christaller's, nonetheless it was informed by Lösch's historical and geographical context. For Lösch, Germany's hope in the face of 'that one fool', and the tumultuous period preceding his

ascendancy, lay in upholding the purity of reason. Reason represented the moral alternative to the 'contemptible' and 'destructive' 'chaos' that otherwise reigned.[3] Central place theory was so important to Lösch because it derived from, and was the crystallization of, reason. In this sense, central place theory made as much a moral claim as it did a geographical and economic one. Lösch died shortly after the war from privations suffered by upholding this moral claim about pattern against the grounded chaos that surrounded him.

It is easy to be bamboozled when seeing spatial patterns, and to think that their symmetry possesses inherent meaning. Certainly, I thought that the central place hexagons of Cornwall whispered secrets as I plotted them as a sixth former. Had I been paying attention to Mr Westlake, however, I would have recognized that in addition to the pattern, there is a need to recognize the ground in which they are embedded and gain significance. It is not only patterned ground that is important but also a grounded pattern.

States

Michael J. Shapiro

The provocation for this piece is the story 'Indian Country' by the Native American writer Sherman Alexie. For Alexie, contemporary Indian presence is both geographically and ethnologically ambiguous. The story's main character, Low Man Smith – a writer and doubtless a stand-in for Alexie – describes himself in one of the story's conversations as one who is 'not supposed to be anywhere'.[1] Moreover, his Indian-ness, along with that of other Native American characters, is highly diluted; a Spokane, he speaks and understands no tribal languages, was born and raised in Seattle, and has visited his own reservation only six times. If viewed pictorially, the 'Indian country' that emerges in Alexie's literary landscape would have to be a few faintly visible colour flecks on a map of the western states of the United States. Tellingly, the precarious and obscure visibility of that country is reinforced throughout the story's dialogues by continual challenges to traditional Indian practices of intelligibility. For example, when Low Man asks an older Indian, Raymond, if he is an elder, Raymond shifts to a non-Indian idiom: 'elder than some, not as elder as others', he replies.[2]

The dimly etched and ambiguous Indian country that Alexie's story maps is the result of a history of effacement. In this brief account of the remapping of former Native American provenances in the West, my focus is on a particular photograph (discussed below) that testifies to an important juncture in the process. First, however, I want to point to other genres, produced at significant historical moments in the process through which Euro-American representational practices played a role in the historical displacement of the Native Americans from the landscapes of the continent. One of the first that comes to mind is Cotton Mather's 'Exact Mapp of New England', an illustration in his narrative of New England church history, *Magnalia Christi Americana* (1702). There, 'apart from two tribal choronyms in the heart of New England's dominions – Nipnak Country and Country of Naragansett – there are no further signs of actual Indian presence'.[3]

Mather's representational violence was both historically and geographically near the beginning of the process of effacement. Subsequently, while the westward expansion of the US was displacing Native American inhabitants and recoding their lands, their

genres of landscape representation were being ignored. Euro-American textual practices devoted themselves to the new state's 'ethnogenesis',[4] its growing and totalizing continental presence. For example, a century and a half after Mather's symbolic conversion of New England into a Christian imaginary, James Fenimore Cooper was contributing to a symbolic erasure of Indian presence in the Western landscape. In an essay contributed to a coffee table book about 'picturesque' landscapes, he begins by noting that his essay is meant to enlighten those who cannot travel and must therefore be content to derive their information from 'the pen, the pencil, and the graver'.[5] He goes on to contrast an American landscape, which has 'an air of freshness, youthfulness, and in many instances . . . rawness',[6] with the landscapes of Europe 'on which are impressed the teeming history of the past'.[7]

Contrary to Fenimore Cooper's conceits, the seemingly youthful and raw landscapes of the West contained a rich history, which he was unable to discern because he wholly neglected an Indian perspective. As the anthropologist Keith Basso learned, when he was taught Apache cultural geography by native informants,

> For Indian men and women, the past lies embedded in features of the earth – in canyons and lakes, mountains and arroyos, rocks and vacant fields – which together endow their lands with multiple forms of significance that reach into their lives and shape the ways they think.[8]

To appreciate the epistemic and historical significance of western landscape for Apaches, one would have to fill in a glaring omission in Fenimore Cooper's list of genres of representation. Rather than 'the pen, the pencil, and the graver', the western Apache's 'place worlds' (Basso's expression) are collectively experienced through orality. The naming of places is commemorative; it expresses significant episodes in tribal history. When the names are subsequently invoked in daily conversations, the landscape re-emerges in commemorative enactments aimed at producing tribal solidarity. Accordingly, Apaches practise a 'history without authorities'.[9] Their landscapes are place worlds that contain a 'teeming history' of *their* past and are invisible to those who rely on built structures and on genres of writing. As Basso puts it:

> Long before the advent of literacy, to say nothing of 'history' as an academic discipline, places served humankind as durable symbols of distant events and as indispensable aids for remembering and imagining them – and this convenient arrangement, ancient but not outmoded, is with us still today.[10]

Fenimore Cooper's scripted account of western landscape is therefore of a piece with the process through which the imposition of a European state model of social and political organization 'over-coded' the prior affiliations that were to become a vanishing 'Indian country'. Shortly after his Eurocentric reading of a landscape that he never visited, some photographs of western landscapes were taken. Although they appear to be simple recordings of landscapes, they participated in the expansionist process through which the West was settled, 'tamed' and effectively inscribed, as the State recoded the landscape, turning it into a white provenance and a resource that would aid in the process of industrialization.

From the Native American point of view, the mapping process, of which the photographs were a part, was an antagonistic cultural encounter. As Alan Trachtenberg puts it: 'The act of mapping and naming was, in the eyes of the Indians, an act of trespass, not upon property but on religion, upon the sacred itself. The white man's maps threatened a whole way of life.'[11]

A photograph by William Bell (illus. 51), one of the photographers accompanying Lieutenant George Wheeler in his survey of the lands of 1871–3 west of the one hundredth meridian, records an exemplary moment in the process of trespass. Black Elk wrote his commentary on what was left of the Indian country in 1930. His remark captures well the process through which the 'Indian country', upon which Alexie reflected in his story, had become so diminished. Given his eloquence and veracity, Black Elk deserves the last words in this piece: 'They have made little islands for us and always, these islands are becoming smaller.'

51 Grand Canyon of the Colorado River, Mouth of Kanab Wash, looking west.

Refuges

Sophie Watson

A seventeenth-century English jurist, Sir Edward Coke, inscribed in law that complacent aphorism that took more than 300 years to destabilize. In the *Third Part of the Institutes of the Laws of England* (1628, chapter 7, p. 162) we find: 'For a man's house is his castle *et domus sua culque est tutissimum refugium* (and each man's home is his safest refuge)'. Almost 350 years later, the Housing (Homeless Persons') Act 1976 recognized otherwise. The argument from nearly a decade of feminist activism that home (or even castle) was imbued with different meanings and experiences for those who dwelled within now meant that battered women could apply for public housing as homeless. The recognition that sex, gender, bodies and power mattered had finally unhinged this happy couplet of home and refuge. For women the home had at last been revealed to be sometimes the unsafest place of all.

A more contingent and relativistic idea of refuge can be found in a religious text – *The Book of Common Prayer*, Psalm 104, verse 18. Drawing on metaphors from the natural world we find: 'The High hills are refuge for the wild goats and so are the stony rocks for the conies'. But how do we know from the outside when one being's refuge is another's prison?

Symbolic attachments and imaginative worlds create a sense of home, so too does a sense of safety and security. Outward signs of belonging or fear may be hard to discern or read. The walls of the homes or castles that make up the visible infrastructure of our cityscapes, that seem to provide protection against external tensions and stress, may in fact be walls that confine and hide the violence enacted within. Domestic violence articulates a state of disconnection, isolation and invisibility. Prior to feminist campaigns to change police practice and the law, domestic violence was seldom reported and legal or police intervention was rare. A violent act that would have been prosecuted in the public realm of the street or outdoors was recoded when committed at home as a domestic private affair and police were reluctant to intervene. The lack of alternatives for women who did report violence, owing to limited financial independence, no alternative housing options and infrastructures of support, meant that many returned home to encounter further bouts of battering. Such a conundrum gave police further ammunition for their passivity and lack of intervention – 'they all go back home eventually anyway' being a common refrain. Domestic violence was further trivialized through everyday discourses like 'a domestic tiff' and comic media representations of home life with the 'henpecked' or misunderstood husband being provoked to react.

Politicization of domestic violence meant a shift from disconnection to connection. A network of refuges was established in Britain during the 1970s following the exposure of domestic violence after the establishment of the first home for battered women in Chiswick, London. Like wildfire the idea spread and Women's Liberation groups around the country spontaneously emerged to campaign for the rights of battered women to be given shelter and refuge from domestic violence. Pressure was exerted on local authorities to grant dwellings, and funds were sought to run them. By the mid-1970s most large towns and cities had refuges or women's aid groups and a national federation of women's aid with paid, full-time staff had been set up. Up and down the country, large run-down family homes, men's castles and refuges were transformed into chaotic secret hideouts where up to twenty women and their children were crammed into shared rooms and communal kitchens and bathrooms. The collectivity of shared living and shared experience of domestic violence opened up, through the space of the refuge, a new subject position of the survivor as opposed to the victim. Through the articulation of new discourses of violence a new category of woman, a new identity – the battered woman – was created. In articulating the needs of the battered woman in the arenas of the State, new interests, rights and responsibilities were also formed that in turn shifted normative understandings of gender and sex practices.

The network of refuges and the form of political organization of women's aid has been a non-hierarchical one, laterally connecting places across the land through informal and formal connections, nationally and globally. This was a network of flows and knowledges hidden from sight but active and vociferous. These refuges known and visible only to those involved in domestic violence personally or politically thus made new patterns on the ground. These were powerful patterns whose significance could be recognized only when it mattered. New walls were thus constructed out of former homes and castles, and these were walls that offered protection. Women who worked or lived in a particular refuge were often the only ones with access to it. Contact by outsiders, even other actors in the arenas of the State, could be made only by telephone, and visits to refuges were not encouraged. New boundaries of public and private space, of visible and invisible walls, were thus being drawn along gendered lines. The secrecy of the whereabouts of the refuge, where secrecy meant safety, offered an interesting counterpoint to the secrecy of the violence practised in the privacy of the home, where secrecy meant fear.

At the same time as domestic violence articulated a new space of collectivity and connection and of common interest and experience, embedded within these very forms were points of disconnection. Although feminists struggled hard to make the refuge a space of empowerment for women, black and Asian women in Britain saw the women's aid movement as predominantly white and middle class. Race and class intersected in complex ways to produce new spaces of exclusion and conflict. While white middle-class women could negotiate arenas of the State with ease and familiarity, black women encountered racist responses. It has taken more than two decades for there to be serious recognition that bodies are implicated and inscribed with the particularities of race and culture that are implicated in the violence that women experience.[1] Such a recognition implies a new kind of refuge politics for the next century and new patterns of intervention and response.

Enterprise Zones

Henry Wai-chung Yeung

Where on earth can we ground a harmonious blending of human technologies and natural landscapes? Not too many places indeed. The following illustration is one such place – a science park in which 'great minds think alike' in a highly pleasant natural environment. Science parks, however, are not the only places where land is enclosed for industrial development. Many other varieties of 'enterprise zones' exist today: industrial parks, industrial districts, technology districts, special economic zones, export processing zones and new industrial spaces. While it is true that these terms and descriptions of engraved human landscapes emerged and became popularized in our imaginations in different historical periods during the twentieth century, they all represent a peculiar form of territorializing and entangling physical landscapes.

In their various spatial and social formations, enterprise zones are truly a form of limited space through which nature is made to produce via entrepreneurial practices, and through which these very practices are transformed by the physical environment. These zones are not stand-alone human objects that happen to be erected on specific landscapes. Rather, they are products of immense interactions among different forces of production (e.g., capital and labour) and, more important, between nature and its multi-faceted cultural counterparts. Take the development of specific 'enterprise zones policies' as an example. They emerged from the new economic development policy under Margaret Thatcher in the UK in 1981 and from similar community development initiatives in the USA during the early 1980s and France during the mid-1980s (note: the development of similar special economic zones and export processing zones in developing countries since the 1960s, e.g., Malaysia, Mexico and China). Policy makers and urban planners saw these enterprise zones as a new and innovative means to resolve problems of industrial restructuring and economic decline in inner cities and rural communities in advanced industrialized economies; they represented the emergence of a new wave of enterprising culture and entrepreneurship under the hegemonic influence of neo-liberalism and market-based economic strategies. By the early 1990s, there were more than 3,000 such zones in the US alone and another 28 in the UK.[1]

In what ways are cultural practices and physical landscapes mutually constitutive to produce different varieties of enterprise zones? In the first place, enterprise zones are spatial outcomes of enterprising discourses and location-specific policies that demarcate specific locations in inner urban areas or rural communities for the revival of economic growth and / or the enhancement of job creation. They are usually about a few hundred hectares in size. Many of these zones would experience significant administrative transformations, which entailed one-stop agency and procedure to enable the establishment of new entrepreneurial firms. They also involve some sort of institutional innovations through which there is a shift from central State to local policies. In order to attract dynamic firms to locate in these enterprise zones, generous tax and other fiscal incentives are offered to offset the initial locational disadvantages, or simply to out-compete other enterprise zones and localities. There are also stringent eligibility criteria for new firms in terms of their establishment status, employment potential and extent of technological innovations.

On the other hand, nature can influence the territorial formation of various types of enterprise zones significantly. The attraction of the physical landscape can operate through at least three ways: accessibility to major transport networks; aesthetic appeal (e.g., lakes or seafronts); and the geographical imaging of the landscape. First, accessibility in terms of relative time and cost is crucial to new firms locating in enterprise zones because many of them have industrial linkages that are stretched far beyond the spatial boundaries of their inhabited zones. In fact, empirical studies have found that most firms in enterprise zones tend to serve customers and obtain materials from suppliers who are often located outside their zone. This spatial phenomenon of external dependency has something to do with the intentional creation of enterprise zones that indirectly reduces the likelihood of agglomeration economies. Spatial accessibility becomes a critical determinant in most enterprise zones in the US and the UK. The role of nature here is to influence how accessibility can be realized under different physical and environmental conditions.

Second, the aesthetic appeal of specific territorial zones can be so important that nature becomes a crucial marketing point for these zones. In other words, the condition of nature in these zones can make or break their futures. Why is that so? The demand for an aesthetic working environment is nothing new. What is new is how nature is reproduced in such enterprise zones as science parks to present a 'naturalistic feel' of working and playing in nature. Green landscaping is the virtual camouflage of most science parks today. In other industrial parks, picturesque landforms are always welcome and entangled together with standard and flatted factories, and recreational and residential facilities. For example, Jinji Lake in the Suzhou-Singapore Industrial Park in China was cleaned up and reconstructed to create a new sense of place – a 'natural' park within an industrial park.[2]

Third, the geographical imaginations of the enterprise zone landscape can enhance the success of specific zones dramatically. After China opened its door to the global economy in 1978, four coastal cities were chosen in which to establish special economic zones with the purpose of attracting international investments. The coastal location of these four zones has contributed to an 'open' and 'progressive' image of China's special economic zones; these coastal zones have served as the 'estuaries' into which global capital can flow. Their maritime nature also underscores their symbolic interactions with the global economy as defined historically by Imperial China's opening of only selected coastal ports to external trade.[3] Equally compelling is the Silicon Valley story. The Californian stretch of high-tech zones from San Francisco to Santa Cruz, passing through San Jose, has become recognized globally as the epicentre of the American Dream – enormous prosperity, great entrepreneurship and unlimited opportunities. The Silicon Valley is now clearly synonymous with global success in high-tech riches. This makes it really hard for us to imagine the fact that California's success is equally grounded in the wealth of nature.[4]

To revisit the illustration above, enterprise zones represent specific human endeavours to produce a kind of patterned ground that straddles nature and technology. Through this process of producing new spaces, we may be consuming nature in such dramatic ways that the human–nature pendulum is grossly tilted in favour of our unlimited wants and desires. Enterprise zones are after all landscapes of desire and innovation – they are sites of creative destruction in an economic sense; they are also locales for human–environment interactions.

Town Halls
Nicholas Low and Brendan Gleeson

Over three weeks in 2001, 19,000 people thronged to Melbourne Town Hall to hear scholars, statesmen, scientists, writers, advocates and athletes from all over the world provide an extraordinary and critical disquisition on the condition of the world and Australia's place in it. These lectures, celebrating the centenary of federation, provided a vehicle for unmediated public discourse outside the commercial and political forums of what is sometimes called debate. Cogent arguments were expressed that cut right across the patterned ground of established ideology. There was an uplifting sense of relief in the audience as speaker after speaker tore away at the carapace of Australian complacency encasing the bowels of national and global life: the market. Something had changed.

Town halls, remember, created the market at the intersection between the ecological organization of nature and the institutional organization of human society. They once marked the operational centres of patches of ground disturbed by agriculture. The town hall, with its clock and its market, signalled the dawn of the modern, bringing both the relentless optimism of the day and the denial of the unknown. In the medieval gloaming, nature was experienced, often feared. In the busy intercourse of the market, nature was consumed. And from the town hall, it was regulated.

Town halls provided for the most basic needs of human occupation: paths and sites of exchange of the 'produce' of local nature moulded for human occupation and use. Out of sight of grand history and politics, town halls created the rules of the market. Industry and machinery developed, and the town was transformed into a place of power coming from money rather than arms. With national and international trade, town halls grew very large, and attempts were made to equip them with the pomp of castles and cathedrals – with mildly ludicrous results: *bourgeois gentilhommes*. The town hall as an institution had outgrown its neighbourhood, and its occupants looked for power elsewhere.

When the townsmen with their wealth gained power in the state they brought with them ideas about their civic institutions. National bourgeois governments took on the task of constructing national markets and subjecting social life to their rules: 'the great transformation'. The town hall clock was moved to the parliament building (recall the famous clock tower at Westminster). The nation and state, once dominated by landed aristocrats, came under the sway of the new media of money, the market and the regulation of time. Regulation in places gave way to the regulation of space.

In the late twentieth century, having exhausted the possibilities of national markets, states took on the task of creating global markets shaped for the purposes of vast capitalist enterprises. The town hall as a regulatory institution moved out of its urban integument first to the nation state, and from the State to the global sphere. The World Trade Organization is today nothing more than the world's town hall. The patch of ground disturbed by humanity is no longer local. Filaments of connection are being installed to organize the global construction and consumption of the whole of nature: fuel, water, the atmosphere, oncomouse and featherless chicken. Everybody interacts with anybody by chat and by trade. All that is solid travels by air. Internet – yes of course – but you can't eat electrons. The growth of movement ever further, ever faster, is exponential. Everything is shaped for consumption, then everything is consumed.

So what is left? The town hall remains a place in a placeless world. Why move if everything is the same? The difference of neighbourhoods (in competition) is what globalization craves. A global world is not a homogeneous world. It is a divided world – bloatedly rich, starvingly poor and most of what lies between. Qualitative difference too has to be nurtured, and if it isn't there, created. So every town hall is busy crafting themes of difference to advertise to the world. But then so is every private corporation.

The people's corporation has a more important function to perform. Town halls still embody the spirit of democracy, social protection, political innovation and critique of the orthodoxy of governance. In Australia they are sometimes places of apology to the Aboriginal people for past genocidal practices. Perhaps paradoxically, in view of their origin, they are also the places where ecological protection and the regulation necessary to achieve it are most clearly taking hold in the world today. Local Agenda 21 was contained in a very short chapter in the Rio Declaration – almost a footnote to a document shaped by nation states. Since the Earth Summit of 1992, the environmental stature of local government has grown.

The world looks not to Brasilia or The Hague for inspiration but to Curitiba and Groningen, whose successful transformation of local transport is famous worldwide. There are global networks of town halls. The International Council for Local Environmental Initiatives (ICLEI) serves 'a worldwide movement of local governments' to achieve tangible improvements in global environmental conditions. More than 6,000 local councils in 113 countries have made a formal commitment to Local Agenda 21. Global communication disseminates critique and alternative practice.

Towns were made possible by sustained agriculture and sustained society and, in creating local markets, town halls had to recognize the social and natural conditions of their existence – connected as it is to the social and natural patterns on the ground. The global market, however, is blind, insensate. It responds only to the stimulus of the moment. It has no organ that could possibly become aware that humanity is consuming its own body. It is generating none. National

52 Melbourne Town Hall in 2002, displaying a poster advertising 'National Sorry Day', a perpetual reproach to a national government that refuses to apologize for the Australian genocide: the forced removal of Aboriginal children from their families over a period of 150 years.

states have given themselves up to the service of the market. But town halls still exist, in place, at the boundary between humanity and nature – a seemingly residual and anachronistic position in a market-dominated world.

Town halls can act as levers to shift entrenched and ineffectual patterns of governance. The market has developed to its limits. New institutions are needed to protect the environment and they are being forged, haltingly, patchily, in the world's town halls. Town halls will never replace nations and international governance. History does not go into reverse. But there will be local action – globally coordinated.

By the second half of the twenty-first century we will see a revision of the market that recognizes ecological limits. If living standards are to improve for the poor, we will have to see an upsurge of local production for local consumption. Town halls supply the test-beds for the new machinery of governance to make these ideas happen. Just as the idea of 'government by the market' started with the town hall, so the idea of environmental governance is taking place locally and spreading internationally. The age of the market will come to be seen as a primitive, dark night of the environment. Yet a new twilight is enriching us with its colour.

Slums
Gareth A. Jones

Occupying steep hillsides, marsh borders or the green buffers around airports, slums are visible reminders of a city's poverty and ecological fragility. Denied nature, nature is constantly invoked to represent the slum. In common speech slums spread like sores, cancers, mushrooms, weeds, cut scars into the landscape or somehow float as 'islands of squalor'. Slums always invade hillsides, creep up valleys, encroach upon better-off areas or are absorbed into the city in some ill-defined process of organic succession (illus. 53). Left untouched, slums fester and decay: slum is a corruption of the word slime.

Seduced by miasmatic theory which held that illness resulted from poisoned air caused by rotting matter, sweat and excrement, planners in nineteenth-century Latin America embraced an understanding of the city as a 'product of nature' long before

53 Children of the *suburbio* (suburb), Guayaquil, Ecuador, 2001.

Robert Park's theoretical refinements decades later. If, in the city as organism, the metabolism of arterial roads provided circulation, botanical gardens the lungs, food markets the stomach, libraries the brains, the slum was the armpit or anus. Slums were scripted as impure, dirty, diseased, sites of physical and moral decay. The slum was simultaneously 'unnatural', compared to the bucolic imagery of pure nature, and too close to nature for the aspirant modernist ideals of the *mission civilisatrice*.

Then, the solution was to tame or clear the slums. A writer in Rio de Janeiro in 1904 described the victory of man over slum / nature / culture / history:

> A few days ago, the picks, intoning a jubilant hymn, began the work of the Avenida Central's construction, knocking down the first condemned houses . . . we begin to stride toward our rehabilitation. In the collapse of the walls, in the crumbling of the stones, in the pulverisation of the earth, there was a long groan. It was the sad and lamenting groan of the Past, of backwardness, of Shame. The colonial city, filthy, backward, obstinate in its old traditions was weeping . . . but the clear hymn of the picks . . . [was] chanting, in their unceasing, rhythmic clamour . . . the victory of hygiene, good taste, and art!'.[1]

Nature, however, could sometimes lend a hand. Aldous Huxley provides an unsympathetic account of the fate of Belize's slums in 1930:

Walking through the streets, one saw but little traces of the great calamity of 1930, when a hurricane blew the sea in a wall of water right across the town. A heap of bricks, it is true, was all that was left of the principal house of God; but Mammon, Caesar and the Penates had risen fresh and shining from the ruins. Almost all the private residences and all the government offices, all the shops and warehouses, had been rebuilt or repaired. The town as a whole looked remarkably neat and tidy. Even a tidal wave may have something to be said for it. It does at least clear away the slums. Our governments and municipalities are less brutal; but they are also, alas, a good deal less effective.[2]

Times have changed, a little. In his Doomsday prognosis of nature unchecked, Robert Kaplan describes the journey from airport to downtown Conakry:

The forty-five minute journey in heavy traffic was through one never-ending shanty-town: a Dickensian spectacle to which Dickens himself would never have given credence. The corrugated metal shacks and scabrous walls were coated with black slime. Stores were built out of rusted shipping containers, junked cars, and jumbles of wire mesh. The streets were one long puddle of floating garbage. Mosquitoes and flies were everywhere. Children, many of whom had protruding bellies, seemed as numerous as ants. When the tide went out dead rats and the skeletons of cars were exposed on the mucky beach. In twenty-eight years Guinea's population will double if growth goes on at current rates. Hardwood logging continues at a madcap speed, and people flee the Guinean countryside for Conakry. It seemed to me that here, as elsewhere in Africa and the Third World, man is challenging nature far beyond its limits, and nature is now beginning to take revenge.[3]

Kaplan's children-ants follow a long tradition of bestializing the slum. In 1966 Sam Schulman told readers of the *New York Times* about 'the rudest kind of slum, clustering like a beehive around the edges of any principal city in Latin America' in which people live 'almost like animals, the tugurio's residents are overwhelmed by animality' in 'urban poverty's abyss'.[4] The popular image of the slum remains one of wandering pigs, goats, chickens, of vicious dogs and vermin. In some parts of Latin America the word for mouse hole, *ratonera*, is also slang for slum.

Today, these slums must go through 'upgrading' or 'regeneration'. The front cover of a recent World Bank report entitled *Cities without Slums* shows an open sewer winding between houses. Under the logo 'Working together to change faces of poverty', four smaller photos show smiling, half-naked children, perhaps threatened by the sewer, the dangerous nature, flowing past their doors. With enough political will, fiscal management and security of tenure we are told that this nature can be 'tapped', and thereafter, pictorially, nature disappears to become infrastructure and community projects. Upgrading the slum means re-odourizing the slum. Ironic, since a mainstay of the slum economy is washing clothes, the lack of clean water compensated by impregnation with flower-scented soaps. In Mexico, shops in slums sell eggs, tins of tuna, fruit, matches and candles, as well as a range of washing powders, disinfectants and air fresheners.

54 The Favela of the Rats, Recife, Brazil, 2000.

Garden Cities

Joe Kerr

Going door to door in the slums are groups of clean-cut evangelical missionaries and Avon ladies. Cleanliness is next to godliness and it comes with a hint of pine and rose water.

The representation of the slum as animal/nature draws on a range of senses (illus. 54). In Recife, there is a small *favela* among a complex of sugar mills and biscuit factories. The air is permanently filled with the sweet smell of sugar that claws at the throat. The *favelados* need sugar in order to work, but with it come the rats. The Favela do Rata is known for the smell of sugar and the size of its rats. The inhabitants take what precautions they can. Babies sleep in cots suspended from the roof supports to prevent the rats from biting them or worse. First thing in the morning, they beat the tin roofs to dislodge the rats; at night they leave out food to attract them outside and put acid down the drains. To take a photo I climbed a high wall but lost my footing and fell forward, narrowly missing the bloated body of a dead dog. From the stomach cavity an exodus of rats scattered into the decomposing rubbish that lay all around. The daily battle between sugar-fortified rats and undernourished *favelados* is difficult to capture in a photograph, but I am always reminded of the smell whenever I think about slums.

On visiting the first-ever garden city of Letchworth, one could perhaps be forgiven for confusing its winding avenues and picturesque homes for the authentic relics of a pre-industrial community; its founders would certainly have appreciated such a mistake, since this is exactly the effect they were aiming for. But a mistake it would nonetheless be, for Letchworth Garden City was founded only a century ago, when Britain was still a great industrial power.

However, this would not only be a case of mistaken identity, but of mistaken intent also. For despite its archaic appearance, the garden city was a wholly original and innovative contribution to the emerging discourse of Modernism. While its meandering streets, carefully planned to accommodate the pre-existing topography, and its humble Arts and Crafts architecture, designed in sympathy with vernacular traditions, might seem a world away from the mechanistic and standardized urban solutions proposed a generation later in France and Germany, nonetheless it sprung from a utopian impulse that was no less ambitious or far-sighted than those more illustrious visions of the future. In particular, it offered a seductive alternative to what was perceived as the disastrous sundering of nature and culture that industrialization had imposed on the new urban proletariat. While strenuous efforts had been made since the mid-nineteenth century to ameliorate the worst horrors of urban life, by 1900 many reformers had become convinced that the city itself was beyond redemption, and that only some form of re-engagement with the soil could offer salvation for a physically and morally corrupted society.

It still seems improbable that a radical blueprint for a de-urbanized future has lain concealed in the gentle Hertfordshire landscape for the better part of a century, but beneath the spreading canopy of Letchworth's mature and abundant trees lies the first real attempt of the twentieth century to address the intractable urban problems inherited from the nineteenth century. On reflection, it is hardly surprising that the first coherent model for solving the ills of the industrial city was developed in what was then the world's most advanced industrial economy. But in its physical appearance at least Letchworth seems to be looking backwards rather than forwards, hence the ease with which its far-reaching influence has often been overlooked.

To explain why an exemplary community of the future should look uncannily like an idealized medieval town, one has to consider the peculiar nature of the British critique of capitalism from which the garden city movement emerged. For despite the presence in Victorian London of so many philosophers of total revolution, in this country the opponents of industrialization largely sought 'a peaceful path to real reform', to quote the subtitle of the founding text of the garden city movement, written by Ebenezer Howard in 1898.[1]

From the early nineteenth century, when concerns over the human cost of industrial expansion were first voiced, there had developed a consensus among reformers from either end of the political spectrum that the rise of capitalism had destroyed all that was good about pre-industrial society. Therefore, for them, it made absolute sense to look to the past to redress the ills of contemporary society. It was after all William Morris, almost alone among Victorian social agitators in having actually read Marx, who imagined a future in which greater London had been largely destroyed, to be replaced by tranquil countryside and harmonious village communities of the kind it had previously subsumed. It was only a small step from Morris's fanciful vision in *News from Nowhere* of 1890 to Howard's proposal a decade later actually to build a network of new low-density communities, established on agricultural land at a distance to existing cities and planned for a strictly limited optimum size.

Howard was a polemicist and not a designer, and so his book is somewhat vague about actual patterns on the ground. However, he was able to convey in highly effective (because non-specific) diagrams the principal ambition of his proposals, which was to effect the reconciliation of town and country. What is unprecedented about Howard's particular brand of futurism is that it is neither pro-urban nor pro-rural. Indeed, he is quite careful to list both the advantages and disadvantages of both. But, as his famous diagram 'The Three Magnets' demonstrates, the aim was to combine the benefits of both, while excluding their shortcomings. Thus it would be wrong simply to dismiss the garden city as yet another bucolic utopia, for it contained all the necessary elements of urban life,

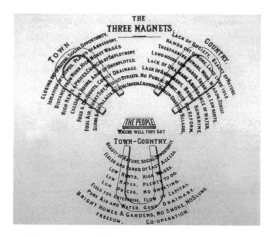

55 Ebenezer Howard's 'The Three Magnets'.

but placed in a direct relationship to the land. Ironically the more radical aspects of garden city theory, including the public ownership of land and the inclusion of all social classes within a single community, were of little long-term influence, while its physical form as established by Howard's architects proved easily adaptable as a model for the kind of speculative suburban development that Howard and his followers deplored.

There is no escaping the fact that the garden city was proposed not as a solution to the underlying causes of industrial malaise but merely as a panacea to its physical symptoms, and it was the failure to develop a political critique in tandem with its social critique that was to be its downfall. Given that Howard's supporters were a motley mixture of wealthy philanthropists, Quaker chocolate manufacturers, Christian socialists and the like, the lack of a political focus is not too surprising. Indeed, the only consensus of opinion that united them was the pressing need for some measure of social reform – that, and a firm belief in the redemptive value of returning to the land, not least because working the soil implied the avoidance of more seductive earthly pleasures.

It hardly needs to be said that, in its own terms, the garden city movement was a total failure, despite the establishment of several garden cities and garden suburbs in the UK, and across continental Europe and America. But I still find these bold pioneering communities fascinating, not least because their physical landscapes are so revealing of the moral landscape of Britain at the turn of the last century. For on the one hand we can read in them the particular ethical concerns of Victorian society, particularly the separation of culture and nature, yet on the other we can also see a real attempt to engage with and influence the modern world. However

naively utopian it might be to negotiate the future with a vision of the past, nonetheless the garden city was concerned with such real issues as urban alienation, class division and gender inequality. Letchworth and its successors have often been dismissed as smug havens for holier-than-thou liberals, but whatever the truth of such criticisms, I would never carelessly dismiss such a brave and ambitious attempt to redress the horrific consequences of unbridled capitalism.

Towns
Matthew Gandy

The idea of the town as a model form of human settlement rests ultimately on the promotion of a particular set of social, political and aesthetic values. Writing in 1956, for example, the former chief architect for the London County Council, Frederick Hiorns, despaired at the 'monstrous pseudo-urban confusion' that characterized modern cities and called for the resurrection of historic traditions in town planning in order to counter the 'neglect of the reasoned, self-effacing urban directive which is the essence of civilized living'.[1] Yet this search for spatial harmony reveals a profound ambiguity between the idea of the town as a form of historical continuity and the modernist impulse towards the reordering of spatial and social relations.

The modern idea of the town is closely bound up with a nostalgic design ethic rooted in the promotion of aesthetic harmony between nature and human artifice. Although towns have historically most often emerged as regional market centres for agricultural produce, the modern town, as it has developed in the post-garden city era, is more frequently invoked by architects and planners as a small-scale social and ecological utopia. The British New Towns, for example, were an anachronistic design solution to the problems of post-Second World War urban malaise. The 'respectable' working classes were siphoned off from the dilapidated and over-crowded housing stock of the inner cities to be rehoused in planned communities that owed more to the ideals of Victorian social engineering than to any real engagement with the dynamics of urban and industrial decline. The creation of new towns such as Basildon, Crawley and Stevenage formed part of a wider urban dynamic of inner-city abandonment, the promotion of new consumption norms and changing working-class aspirations.

The development of a conservative, family-oriented urban form reached its apotheosis in the post-war suburb with its strictly topi-arized division of space. The ideology of the 'suburb' is closely bound up with the chang-ing meaning and character of town life as an alternative to metropolitan forms of modern-ity. In North America, the so-called New Urbanists of the 1990s advocated model settlements as a market-driven design solution to the social and environmental malaise of post-war urbanism. The promotion of towns is clearly both a design ethic and at the same time an ideological construct developed in opposition to the perceived failures of modern cities. For many proponents of 'ecological urbanism', the city is itself seen as a mori-bund spatial form to be superseded by a hi-tech Jeffersonian idyll of networked semi-rural settlements. Yet the emerging dynamics of global urbanization involve a heightened emphasis on human interaction and have confounded technologically driven post-urban projections of the future. In all these accounts, however, the town and the city are

56 Williamsburg, Brooklyn: a town within a city?

treated as atomized elements within a wider spatial plane that remains epistemologically opaque. The possibility that the fate of towns and cities is interlinked is suppressed within a design-oriented conceptual schema that fails to recognize the structural factors that lie behind the shaping of urban space.

The ideological divide between town and city is perhaps most starkly illustrated in relation to different conceptions of violence and social cohesion. In the United States, for instance, historical data on violent crime suggests that large industrial cities such as Chicago, Pittsburgh and New York have been consistently less violent than the small- and medium-sized towns of the rural South. The contemporary violence of small-town Louisiana, for example, can be related to the long-term effects of a brutal plantation economy on every aspect of social life.[2] As for hate crimes directed against ethnic and sexual minorities, there is a very different geography of safety to that implied by the conventional town-city schema. Manchester's 'gay village', for example, is nestled in the heart of the city as a distinctive and vibrant social community rooted in the greater freedoms and social tolerance associated with metropolitan culture. This is, of course, a very different kind of 'town' to that envisaged in the conventional tropes of urban design, but it does nonetheless highlight the frequent elision between the ideas of town and community in the description of human settlements.

At the heart of the ideology of the town is the sense that towns represent a more authentic type of human experience. In his elegiac essay on the French new town of Mourenx, written in 1960, Henri Lefebvre reveals his ambivalence towards the brave new world of post-war urban reconstruction. Lefebvre's encounter with the pristine concrete geometries of Mourenx is suffused with a deep sense of melancholy and disorientation. Whereas the nearby old town of Navarrenx is conceived quite differently as 'history and civilization in a seashell'. The winding streets evoke 'a thousand-year old community which was itself part of a wider society and culture, ever more distant from us as the years pass by'.[3] 'This small town', writes Lefebvre, 'with its craftsmen and shopkeepers, in its well-established context of peasantry and countryside, is vegetating and emptying, like so many other dying villages and towns'.[4] In this context Lefebvre uses the contrast between old and new towns as a means to explore the ambiguities of modernist urban design. The motif of town life emerges as a bulwark of social and cultural authenticity against the faceless momentum of global capital and the mandarins of urban renewal.

The apparent superiority of town life is often erroneously conceived to be little more than a matter of scale, but the differences owe more to status, meaning and ideology. The idea of the town is as ambiguous as that of the city. Towns can invoke a rich legacy of culture, history and collective memory. Neighbourhoods within cities can acquire the characteristics of a town or village, and they may even retain something of the original character of former settlements absorbed by metropolitan growth. Yet at the same time the innate conservatism of the ideology of the town can become translated into fear, intolerance and social exclusivity.

Ghost Towns

Dydia DeLyser

In the late 1930s Walter Knott, owner of a boysenberry farm and chicken-dinner restaurant on the outskirts of Los Angeles, set out to build a 'ghost town' from scratch. Assembling a collection of deliberately distressed false-fronted buildings, his motives were two: first, to entertain those waiting in the long lines at his restaurant, and, second, to inspire those same patrons with the ideals of the pioneering Americans who had come before them – ideals he thought could be conveyed by the ruins of a mining town. By the time Knott completed his work, ghost towns had become a natural part of the western American landscape, and, in these often popular tourist attractions, the tumbledown buildings had become accepted lenses through which to view the country's glamorized frontier past. But, Knott's conscious creation apart, such landscapes were anything but natural, their windows on the past anything but clear.

Emerging only in the twentieth century, most ghost towns have their roots in the abandoned mining camps of the American West. After the California Gold Rush of 1849, many mining towns faced a reality of unrealized profits. Failed ventures, these towns were described by early commentators such as Mark Twain simply as abandoned camps – anything but places that tourists would be likely to visit. In *Roughing It* he wrote of such towns, ' they stood, as it were, in a living grave . . . isolated and outcast from brotherhood with their kind'.[1] In Twain's time such towns were dead camps, not ghost towns.

Places with names like Tombstone, Skidoo, Aurora and Bodie all once greeted the dawn of promised prosperity, pledged primarily by the pursuit of gold. Of many, little remains but a landscape gashed and scarred by excavations, their extractive industry long since silent. Although the buildings may be reduced to splinters, their hilly slopes still lie littered with mine dumps and tailings – the discarded surface rock deemed not worthy of further analysis and too barren for even the hardy desert plants. But while some consider a 'ghost-town phase' a predictable part of the life cycle of a mining town, such failed or abandoned mining camps did not become ghost towns over night, or simply by virtue of their abandonment.

Devastated by the failure of their mining enterprises, and abandoned by almost all of those who had inhabited them, ghost towns, for a time, lay isolated. In remote towns where it was too difficult to stay, it was difficult also to leave, and many former inhabitants abandoned not just homes and jobs but also possessions of all sorts. Littered with such detritus, the towns themselves stood, scattered across the deserts and mountains of the American West, everything decaying only gradually in the dry western climate. For decades such abandoned towns

were difficult (or nearly impossible) to reach, and for most there was little interest in trying. But beginning with the rise of automobile tourism in the 1920s, many of these towns became newly accessible. After the Second World War, with the wide availability of army-surplus Jeeps, and the parallel rise of off-road travel, even remote ghost towns became reachable. But they also became *desirable* as destinations: as their abandoned buildings and discarded possessions grew older, interest arose in these artefacts of another age, and ghost towns came to be seen not as the abandoned camps of Twain's time, but rather as windows onto a romantic past.

The critical element lay not in these towns' abandonment but rather in a link to an evolving mythology of the American West. Long a focal point in the abstract for the American imagination, the mythologized West became linked not just to abstract and imagined spaces, but to real places – to ghost towns.[2] Promulgated through the media (in newspapers, fiction, film, television and art), Western landscapes became associated with notions of freedom, self discipline and high-spirited independence.[3] And ghost towns, tangible survivals of the western frontier, places with rough and rowdy reputations born of their raucous mining pasts, became places that tourists could visit to access those intangible ideals.[4]

Some ghost towns discovered that their old reputations could provide a new source of income. Worth more dead than alive, Tombstone, Arizona, once offered itself for sale, lock, stock and barrel as a film set.[5] Restructured as it is today around the OK Corral (made famous in films by the hyped shoot-out that took place near there), and rebuilt to allow buildings to appear even more decayed, Tombstone (like so many other ghost towns) now has a thriving tourist

57 Bodie. California's decayed buildings and deserted landscape often evoke images of the mythic West familiar from film and fiction.

business, its streets ringing with re-enacted gunfights and lined with souvenir shops, restaurants, hotels and re-imagined saloons.

The former gold-mining town of Bodie, California, followed a different course: dedicated as a California State Historic Park in 1964, today no hotel houses visitors, no saloon serves sarsaparilla, and no gunfights are re-enacted. The remaining buildings, still filled with abandoned possessions, stand weathered by time and the elements, but also, in their own way, meticulously preserved. According to Bodie's policy, buildings are maintained in a state of 'arrested decay' (holding them to their states of 1962): nothing will be restored to newness, nor will anything be allowed to lean all the way into collapse. Even with its daily maintenance work, the result is heralded as the West's most 'authentic' ghost town, and many of Bodie's 200,000 annual tourists praise the Park's natural appearance while expressing disdain for Knott's ghost town, never realizing the extent to which Bodie's – along with all other ghost towns – are continually created landscapes.

When Walter Knott built his Orange County ghost town, he sought to 'give the visitor an unmistakable feeling that he stands in the presence of some of those climactic happenings so vividly described by . . . Mark Twain',[6] even though Twain's understanding of an abandoned mining town was quite different from Knott's. By the 1940s ghost towns had been transformed: from the remnants of failed extractive industry and towns where few cared live, to what one Bodie visitor called 'portholes to the past', evoking images of the mythic West to thousands of tourists who visited them, their apparent decay often as consciously created as their glorious pasts.

Cities

Mark Gottdiener

Las Vegas is the most successful desert habitat developed by humanity, but it can also be considered a precursor for life on other planets. Like some Antarctic research station, life support must be imported. Every piece of lettuce, every tomato destined for casino buffets, must be trucked in from a distance. Closer in analogy to Mars than Antarctica, every drop of water must be piped in from sources exterior to the region. Built by multi-national corporations and individual high rollers on the premise that 'a fool and his money are soon parted', Las Vegas represents the new urban landscape where both the human-built environment and nature reach their respective limits.

To call Las Vegas a 'city', would be a mistake. Just as in the case of all other urban areas in the United States, and, in many cases, elsewhere around the globe, the built environment has taken on the form of a multi-centred metropolitan region.[1] The historical central core has lost many of its functions to the benefit of surrounding areas constituted as more specialized centres in the regional array. Suburban nuclei are not 'edge cities', as the uninformed journalistic accounts would have us believe. City modes of development and typically city modes of interaction have little to do with these built spaces. The new form of space is an integrated yet dispersed regional conglomeration of strip zoned roads, multi-laned highways, abandoned factories and new spaces of manufacturing, old commercial buildings and new consumer spaces; of immense, sprawling residential areas and clustered town houses or apartment buildings, of struggling central city shopping and immense regional malls, mini-malls and market spaces; and, interspersed among these functionally specialized multi-centres are green areas, polluted brownfields, grass lands, undeveloped plots, factory and abandoned mall spaces turning to decay.

Some academics argue that this new form of space first discussed in 1985 is most characteristic of Los Angeles.[2] Nothing could be further from the truth. Multi-centred development corresponds to the emergence, in the United States, of the de-industrialized, late capitalist phase of social organization.[3] This regional pattern is characteristic of New Jersey and Connecticut, of the Atlanta region, the Washington, DC, area, of Chicago and Buffalo, as it is of Los Angeles. Perhaps the area that exemplifies not only the new form of the built environment, but also the new, 'postmodern' mode of money making is Las Vegas itself. Indeed, urbanists have been 'learning from Las Vegas' longer than places like LA.[4] When people fly into Las Vegas, they very rarely stay in the historical central city. The popular tourist area, which accommodates more than 20 million visitors a year, is located *outside* the city on a boulevard extending north–south called 'The Strip'.[5] All the new casinos, especially the mega-resorts that have turned Las Vegas into the third most popular tourist attraction in the world, are situated in the multi-centred regional array known as Clark County.

Residents of south-western urbanized spaces have often reported missing domestic pets that have seemingly disappeared without a trace from fenced-in backyards. It was not until the 1980s, more than a decade after most people in the United States called the suburbs rather than the inner cities their home, that public officials acknowledged a growing coyote problem. Suburbanites were warned to watch over their pets, especially cats, which the scavenger canines found particularly tasty. Meanwhile, in the inner city, residents were struggling with rat populations that had seemingly exploded as large sections of the urban landscape were pillaged by the twin forces of abandonment and renewal. Nature, it seems, had been seeping into the concrete jungles of the human-made environment by bits and pieces over the years. As tightly knit and heavily populated central cities gave way to the new form of space, a multi-centred regional environment interspersed with empty land and built up nodes, this interface between the constructed and the natural multiplied and expanded to a regional scale, like some aggressively scalloped shoreline.

Nature punching its way into the new space produced struggles that were fought at the most micro level – between home owners and biological pests. Suburbanites waged a continual battle with carpenter ants, termites, wasps and hornets. Even plants, the most passive of earth's creatures, were sometimes marked as aggressors. Dandelions, crabgrass and generic 'weeds' were no longer to be tolerated, but instead wiped out with the use of biological warfare that possessed an alarming toxicity to humans at certain concentrations.

With approximately two million permanent residents, the Las Vegas region exhibits all the contradictions of living on a mass basis in a place never intended for permanent human habitation. Heavy winter rainstorms produce flash flooding in the centre, obliging all traffic to halt and in some cases even requiring that drivers abandon their cars completely. Producing lawns becomes a constant battle against biological pests and desert climate. Immense quantities of water are required to give the landscape that 'ideal' colour of green. Here, in Las Vegas, like future space colonies, natural forces must be controlled completely. Neither urban planners nor housing developers have given thought to living *with* nature. Housing types must conform to normative considerations, many of which are borrowed from ideas developed in temperate, seasonal environments. Water must be secured in ever increasing supply rather than conserved. The automobile, not public transportation, must remain the dominant mode of travel. Open space signifies the need for more development, not the creation of parks, green spaces or wilderness buffer zones. In Las Vegas, as in most of the south-western states, the ratio of park acreage to residents is the lowest in the USA. If the concept of conservation means a mechanism by which we can rediscover nature, in a sense, and begin the task of living with the natural environment in greater balance, then this path is decidedly the one not taken by our land-hungry process of low-density regional development. During the current phase of late capitalism, the city has disappeared in favour of a new form of space, the multi-centred metropolitan region. Within this expansive array, nature is an intruder and an inconvenience to be battled with rather than an ally that is respected for its life-supporting powers.

Suburbs

Nancy Duncan

American suburbs have long been considered neither wild nor wholly artificial, hybrid places where the boundary between humans and nature is most obviously blurred. Suburbs are romantically regarded as places where people can commune with nature. The dissolution of the human–nature boundary, however, is far from complete. Zoonosis, the 'inadvertent infection of humans with an animal pathogen',[1] is one of the more frightening embodiments of nature in suburbia today. Lyme disease, the most common vector-borne disease in the USA, is also found in Europe, Asia and Australia. Of reported cases, 80 per cent are in the north-eastern USA. In certain counties up to 50 per cent of ticks have the organism and 60 per cent of the backyards surveyed had infected ticks. If not discovered in its early stages, Lyme can become a dreadful, debilitating disease. The multi-system, intermittent and migrating symptoms of (late stage) Lyme include auto-immune disorders, chronic arthritis, fatigue, sleep disturbance, memory loss, backache, neckache, headache, chest pain, mood swings, paranoia, cognitive and attention problems, suicidal depression, paralysis, myalgia, neurologic and cardiac problems, dizziness, deafness, vision problems and (rarely) death.

Ixodes scapularis, the black-legged tick, a dirt-dwelling, blood-sucking arthropod the size of a poppy seed is the vector of the insidious *Borrelia burgdorferi*, a bacterium, a silvery, undulating, shape shifter that evades the immune systems of its host / victims by changing its genetic composition in as many as thirteen recombination events over a period of days using different repertoires for each species of host. In order to enter a human body, the bacterium must first have been hosted by at least two other species within which it takes various different shapes and forms. More than 16,000 cases of Lyme disease are reported annually as *I. scapularis*, the tick, embeds itself in the skin of suburban dwellers. Ticks lie in wait for their victims in the damp grass and woodland edges of suburban backyards. The keystone hosts of *I. scapularis* are the 30 million white-tailed deer, increasingly viewed as the scourge of American suburbia. Also implicated are warm, wet springs and white-footed mice, from which juvenile ticks obtain the organism, and oak trees, whose annual production of acorns influences the size of the mouse populations.

When Europeans began to settle in eastern North America there were far fewer deer. Thick forests are not ideal environments for them. Woods interspersed with farms are much better. Native Americans had cleared some farmland, but they also hunted. The settlers cleared more of the land, but they too were hunters. By the early twentieth century, deer were close to extinction in much of the eastern United States. Consequently, some states banned hunting and restocked. Although rapid suburban development of rural areas during the twentieth century reduced the rural habitat for the deer, they have now become so well adapted to recently reforested, large-lot suburban land use patterns that they thrive as never before. Wooded patches, open fields and gardens are a perfect combination for deer. If hunters were not allowed to shoot hundreds of thousands of them every year, and cars did not kill nearly as many, large numbers of the deer would starve. Deer management teams organize mass shootings. In some places, especially where much of the population has had Lyme disease, deer hunting sparks bitter battles between deer-feeding nature lovers and their angry Lyme-suffering neighbours. In many places, because of high human population densities, hunters are restricted to bow hunting and are unable to reach the deer that browse contentedly on suburban lawns. Other methods of culling tend to be expensive and largely ineffective. Exporting is virtually impossible, for nowhere do they say, 'bring me your deer'.

The landscape of American suburbia is changing as a result of the 'deer wars'. An 'us against them' mentality is producing two-metre-high electrified wire or stockade fencing and enormous patios. A nascent enthusiasm for replacing the ubiquitous American lawn with habitats for songbirds, butterflies and small mammals has been dampened. Deer-unfriendly plants are rapidly replacing those that deer love. Wooded lots are cleared to deprive mice and deer of their favoured woodland edge habitats. Deer are destroying the understorey, obliterating habitats for ground-nesting birds and rare songbirds; there are not enough seedlings to replace dying trees. Signs point to the evolution of new and less leafy landscape tastes. A *New York Times* journalist declared:

> The hot look for summer gardeners now includes masking tape, long sleeves and multiple pairs of socks, children, dogs and lawns are liberally doused with pesticides, long cherished gardens lie fallow, even down payments on houses have been walked away from. At least one backyard has been pre-emptively covered with asphalt.[2]

Gardening services provide Hispanic day labourers to risk the dreaded disease in place of the frightened home owners. The unwelcome ecological lessons learned by sufferers from the Lyme and 'Lyme anxiety' epidemics have reinforced older, more contemplative approaches to nature as 'other', something to be viewed at a distance from the windows and roadways of suburbia. Those who favoured a *laissez-faire* approach to nature, those formerly dedicated to hiking and gardening, those who moved to the countryside to engage actively with nature without resorting to chemicals, those who disdain rural working-class hunters but now welcome them on their properties, all are waking up to new sets of choices in their unstable relations with nature.

The sprawling suburban land use patterns so conducive to deer, and consequently their

ectoparasites, are clearly traceable to the extinction of wolves, bears and big cats, the building of railroads and highways, exclusionary zoning, small patchy conservation reserves and easements, planning instruments and institutions, environmental legislation, ecological theories and strategies, time and other resource commitments to anti-development measures, the history of nature appreciation as cultural capital and quests for privacy as a central liberal individualistic value. This long established nexus of processes and orderings is so broadly and deeply incorporated into the physical fabric of suburbia, so thoroughly stabilized through the support work of tangled sets of cultural, institutional and ecological interconnections, that it has proven largely resistant to all but minor management techniques and 'personal protection measures'.

Tracing the multiple conditions and consequences of the deadly spirochete (bacterium) *B. burgdorferi*, one is led down many well worn and some newly charted pathways, for example, the deciphering of the *B. burgdorferi* genome; the discovery of the amazing properties of the blood of western fence lizard hosts, which kills the spirochete in ticks, thus protecting many western US suburbanites from the deadly Lyme cycle; and tick-eating guinea fowl pecking about on some suburban lawns today. These construct radically heterogeneous webs of human and nonhuman agency – differentially competent, differentially accountable.

Humans and *Bb* coexisted peacefully for many millions of years. By about 1980 in certain suburban landscapes, however, humans had created the ideal patchy 'patterns on the ground' for *Bb*, white-tailed deer, ticks and their other hosts to thrive:

> Lyme disease is not epidemic because people raped the land, massacred other

species or despoiled their biota. Rather, it happened because people loved nature and became nostalgic for unspoiled settings; they tried to heal land they had exploited and ease urban crowding and blight. To a cynic, the emergence of Lyme disease confirms the adage that no good deed goes unpunished. To a naturalist, it is proof that an ecosystem's complexity almost always exceeds our power to grasp it.[3]

Suburban nature / culture is evolving in some unexpected ways; older fears of wildness and a desire to gain the upper hand in the backyard wars by fair means or 'fowl' are likely to produce some new landscapes and landscape tastes – at least until the hostile, entangled, indeed profoundly embodied, relation between *Bb*, its keystone and secondary reservoir hosts and humans once again become disentangled.

Farms

Lewis Holloway

> . . . his father's farm was splendid enough to be painted in oils[1]

Farms as fixtures in the landscape descend from an economy of letting (farming) out land on annual lease for a fixed payment; land was held 'in farm' from at least the thirteenth century in England. The process of farming out set into a noun, a farm, with a number of implications for how farms tend to be understood. First, it seems that farms structure much rural landscape with the apparent fixities of farm buildings, fences, walls and hedges. Farms are thus presences in

rural landscapes: traces of labour, land-ownership patterns and investment. Second, for the enumerators of agricultural censuses (and in much agricultural geography), farms are fixed as 'holdings', business units and regulated enterprises. Third, as sites for locating cultural and economic visions, farms have borne heavy symbolic loads for both farming and non-farming people. Farmed land, for example, is frequently positioned as 'natural', in opposition to the urban; those who farm are regarded as closer to nature. Numerous individual and collective attempts to get 'back to the land' or to 'nature' have thus centred around farms, imagined as icons of tradition, rootedness and belonging, and reaffirming a persistent association of 'self-sufficiency' and agricultural work with moral and physical health. Other visions of agriculture have produced the 'model' farm of the Victorian 'high-farming' period, a version of how farming should be done in newly privatized, post-enclosure farmscapes, or the farm-as-just-another-business, imagining the farm as an efficient factory floor. Although set in very different discursive contexts, the farm more or less fixed in the (physical and imaginative) landscape, as a set of fixtures pinning landscape down, or as an ideal state, is an enduring political, academic and ideological object.

Despite this sense of fixity, however, farms act as mechanisms for holding together, or apart, streams of things that are fluid, that flow into, circulate around and move away from the farm. Much of a farm – its slurry pits, silage clamps, grain stores, milk tanks, fences, gates and fertilizer bags – is there to engineer the movements of heterogeneous organic and inorganic things bound up with and necessary to farming as well as with each other: nutrients, animals, manure, milk, money, diesel, genetic material, soil, plants, water and so on. As attempts to hold together a fluidity of substances, nutrients, capital, bodies and energies, farms are damming mechanisms, attempting to stabilize and regulate flows by imposing order in space. Farms need multiple and constant movements, combinations and recombinations of many and varied things, in order to effect their continuation as farms. They are thus assemblages of the material and immaterial, positioned and existing in relation to each other: land, machines, animals and plants, and knowledges, skills and finance. Agricultural labour is what holds things together in relational patterns occupying multiple time frames that are simultaneously often rhythmically seasonal, follow the trajectory of 'progress' espoused by agricultural science, and encapsulate inter-generational, sedimented relations between people, farm and sometimes particular strains of livestock.

Farm assemblages are, however, precarious, being open to disruptions that bring things together, or let them fall apart, in the wrong places and times. Unwanted things – becoming pests, diseases, weeds – insinuate themselves into the assemblage. Uncertainties – the weather, the market, mechanical failure – present risks. Materials – pesticides, slurry – escape their intended containment, becoming out-of-place pollutants in other systems. In response, farms encapsulate strategies for holding together / apart that become conventional (the application of agro-chemicals or veterinary science) or are seen as alternative ('organic' farming or animal homeopathy) in particular times, places and discursive frameworks. Whichever, in their relations and material connections with other spaces, such as abattoirs, fertilizer factories, organic certification agencies, Farmers' Markets and international commodity markets, farms become enrolled through contracts, accreditation and regulation into particular strategies of holding things together or apart in specified ways.

These strategies signify a requirement to arrange things in farmed space, even if the 'conventional' and 'alternative' do so in different ways, and are the subject of debates over what farms and farming should be. The so-called factory farm may not accord with many idealized visions of farming, although as an ordered machine it achieves certain effects.

In these ways, farms might be seen as existing within particular ways of ordering or channelling things and fluidities to obtain certain movements and combinations at certain times, rather than as a priori fixtures; farming is achieving the right relations between things. These things are themselves complex. As just one example, farm animals are both physiologically, atavistically rooted in 'nature' and the encultured embodiment of domestication and breeding, their emergence fixed as pedigreed and certified genealogy, and given cultural and economic significance in the showground or sale ring.

Yet in the same way that farms can move from being land held 'in farm' to being iconic constructions or ordered assemblages, they are always open to becoming something else. In some cases, the holding together fails and its parts drift away to mingle with others. Abandoned upland farms, for example, are haunted by shadows of past lives, work, noises and smells. In other cases, strategies of business reproduction and the meaning of farming are radically changed, as when farms become leisure spaces, tourist attractions or hobby farms. Or, perhaps, for example as farm parks, become simulacra of 'real' farms in assembling equipment, livestock and styles of farm work as 'heritage'. And the work of farm assemblage can be shattered by catastrophic failure. After the slaughter of livestock associated with the UK outbreak of foot-and-mouth disease in 2001, are farms that have been 'culled-out' still farms? For farmers, at least, they may not be so; 'Farming is passed down, or it should be. A farm is built up for generation after generation, and when it starts to slip and go – you feel an absolute failure. That's what you feel.'[2] Farms can slip and go. So, following a cull, and remembering an achievement of holding together worthy of immobilizing as art, 'The Lockerbie farmer came into his barn in the evening after the killers had disinfected everything and gone. And standing there, in the silence, he may have remembered the days when his father's farm was splendid enough to be painted in oils.'[3]

Floodplains

Richard Tipping

Much of what today we recognize as acculturation, such as urban living, writing and literature, trade and the trappings of ostentatious religious belief, was facilitated through an extraordinarily intimate but frequently fraught engagement between people and rivers on floodplains. It is an old story, as old as the earliest 'civilizations' themselves, 4,000–5,000 years ago, clustered close to rivers that were quixotic in nature, sometimes benign but too often cruel, in Mesopotamia, the 'land between the waters', in the Indus valley or slightly later on the banks of the Nile. It is a familiar story also, but with new twists and resonances for modern societies.

Floods from rivers create floodplains, transporting silts and sands from higher ground and dumping them as broad level layers infilling valley floors. These are transformative landscapes. They evolve, are never static and change with a dynamism that is reflected in the societies that depend on them. Sedimentation can concentrate flood deposits as natural levees bordering the channel, and these ridges can then lock or confine the channel to one route. But river channels can also wander over floodplains by meandering, or slice dramatically across them by a process called avulsion, attacking and eroding the floodplain edge, broadening the floodplain and redistributing sediment across it. Over time this thick veneer has a complex four-dimensional sedimentological architecture reflecting the multiplicity of sediment sources, from one or several active river channels and from bordering slopes, varying depositional energies as river flow increases or decreases, and contrasting environments that range from active and abandoned gravel-filled channel fills to marshy, organic-rich backswamps.

In the large river systems of the Near East, floods originate in headwaters hundred of kilometres away from the prehistoric cultural *foci*. The riverine nutrient-laden mud appeared like gifts from the gods to early societies. Hapi was the Nile god, adorned with a headdress of aquatic lotus plants. These Near Eastern floodplains are narrow strips, since floodwater is dissipated rapidly (see illus. 58). Villages had been the way of life in the Near East from before the end of the last glaciation, but the effects of an agriculture confined to floodplains led to agglomeration and early 'cities'. In this way also floodplains were transformative, permitting and supporting the emergence of entirely new social structures. Architectural differences in buildings at excavated sites speak of emergent hierarchies in these Near Eastern 'cities', unlike comparable developments in the Indus valley, as kingdoms and empires were established. Yet the buildings reflected the reasons for their success with alluvial mud brick, and temples

58 The River Euphrates in its middle reaches, on the Syria–Turkey border, is a major feature with a 5-kilometre-wide floodplain between low hills. On the floodplain, villages were established that developed over time into artificial occupation mounds called tells. This tell, in the middle distance, began life in the Chalcolithic period, was abandoned at the end of the Akkadian empire 2,000 years ago, but was reoccupied subsequently as a trading centre and focus for farming.

– and water itself in the hanging gardens at Babylon – raised high in celebration.

But floods can be violent events, transforming landscapes in instantly destructive ways, and the relation between rivers and people has now to be, as ever, a respectful and uneasy one. Flood myths are common in all floodplain cultures, embedded within the earliest epic of Gilgamesh and echoed in the Bible, based however distantly and distortedly on real events retold to keep alive the memory and to warn for the future: Sumerian societies in Mesopotamia and the lowland Maya of central America were both strongly fatalistic, mistrustful of nature. Today we develop more scientific, more statistically assured measures of flood prediction, but are surprised (and governments threatened) by changes in flood magnitude and frequency that exceed our expectations. Perhaps flood myths persist because they

purposefully describe worst-case scenarios that are not seen in our more complex mathematical estimates.

Near Eastern societies developed on floodplains that had existed before people. Elsewhere, floodplains grew and expanded because of people. In prehistoric Greece, in small montane catchments, farming on valley sides led intermittently to soil losses and the creation of valley floors for continued settlement. The connectivity between slopes and floodplains in these small systems enhances the relation. In one view, to the farmer in the hills, this is land degradation, but of course to the farmer on the floodplain there is only a wondrous transformative gain.

If floods were feared as destructive forces, then the failure of the river to flood was disastrous for early empires in semi-arid landscapes where farming would be unfeasible were it not for floods. Everything came from floods, the seasonal restoration of nutrients in the thin and nitrogen-depleted soils as well as water itself. In many catchments, flooding was for most of the time predictable. Methodologies were established for recording flood altitudes on the Nile 4,000–2,000 years ago. Whether this zeal for measurement is associated with failing floods is unclear, but at this time documented famines in Egypt and the collapse of the Akkadian empire in Mesopotamia have been associated with much new palaeo-environmental evidence for increasing aridity. This was the end of the Homeric 'golden age' throughout the eastern Mediterranean. Soils became parched; along the lower Tigris and Euphrates floodplains salt levels possibly rose to toxic levels; and dust whipped off the floodplains was dumped in the Red Sea. Physical change was accompanied by loss of confidence in the future on the Nile:

> Indeed, the Nile [still] overflows, yet none plough . . . [because] Everyone says: 'We do not know what will happen throughout this land'.
> *The Lament of Ipuwer*, probably *c.* 2,000 BC

The reliance on floods was total. In periods of stable climate, rivers were more benign. Initial attempts by settlers to constrain and confine floods became, with ingenuity and perseverance, irrigation schemes, and with increasing confidence the rivers were regulated by sluices and check-gates, water moved by *shadoofs* and animal power. The transformations from natural landscapes were extraordinary. Floodplains were sliced up with checker-board canals and ditches, and became human-made in ways that astonished even a seasoned observer like Herodotus, from a culture that was

not floodplain-based, on visiting Egypt in the later fifth century BC. The agricultural techniques were simple, but the intensification of farming generated the surpluses that drove the cultural changes.

The techniques developed away from these Near Eastern heartlands in later centuries in western Europe could not be significantly different because rivers behave in similar ways everywhere. However advanced society becomes, on floodplains ambition must be grounded on a few simple physical realities. In western Europe, because rain falls everywhere, floodplains were integrated into larger farming systems. They were not the sole focus of attention. Integration meant recognizing the same exceptional productivity on floodplain soils that typified Near Eastern communities, but for growing grasses for grazing rather than for bread. Floodplains in western Europe were locked into systems of daily and seasonal transhumance and the circulation of nutrients between pasture and field. Breaking this cycle, as in the later medieval period when ambition for crop growing intruded onto floodplains and reduced the balance between animals and arable, led in part to catastrophic failure.

Today, floodplains are again transformative landscapes. In rural England they are the places to put people, in neat 'dormitory' villages that look from the air like ancient Ur. They are the sites of urban sprawl and industrial development, which look like nothing that has been before. But even when regulated, straightened and strait-jacketed, rivers will misbehave. Floodplains will remain as precocious and unpredictable as they have always been.

Hills

Sue Hamilton

The topographic qualities of hills are often perceived in purely functional terms, such as providing defensive places for the siting of castles and forts. Hills are much more than this. In the sacred geography of the Saami, the indigenous hunters and reindeer herders of northern Scandinavia, the foremost landscape features were (in descending order of frequency) hills, mountains and lakes.[1] Hills form part of cultural space, both as acknowledged but unaltered 'natural' landmarks, and as locales on which monuments and domestic structures are built. Together with other distinct topographic features such as rock outcrops, mountain peaks, valleys, bays and inlets, hills are part of the spinal character of the landscape.

Hills are the high points of the landscape, and through their domination of the skyline (be they covered in trees, or in open ground), they provide a sense of place to the communities of their environs. The outlines of distinctively shaped hills are easily identifiable from a distance, and form highly visual backdrops to lower-placed sites and settlement. There is an inevitable heightening of the visibility of any monument placed on a hill. Such 'openness to vision' is contradicted by the increased physical remoteness of sites on hills. This reinforces concepts such as 'unreachability', sanctity, exclusiveness and elevated status in relation to the structures, communities and persons that are located on distinct or remote hills (e.g., temples, monasteries and hermits). These concepts are prevalent in myths of landscape where priority is given to the vertical axis in space – with hills and mountains 'marrying' the sky (the world of gods) to Earth (the grounded world of mortals).[2]

The early farming societies of north-west Europe (fourth–second millennia BC) provide numerous examples of the role of hills in the social and symbolic organization of the landscape. Large burial mounds (Neolithic long barrows and Neolithic and Bronze Age round barrows) were strategically placed on prominent hills to be viewed from hill slopes, lower hills and valleys below. The long-distance views that hilltops command were also utilized. Long mounds were oriented to prominent topographic features either by pointing to them or by running parallel to them. Such a pattern occurs in the orientation of Neolithic long cairns in the Black Mountains of Wales. These cairns have a complete lack of regularity with respect to their compass orientations, but are consistently oriented with their axes either running parallel with major rivers or, more often, pointing to the prominent spurs and hills of the Black Mountains.[3] In this way hills were not only physical but also ideological boundaries to community territories.[4] This concern with connecting-up and referencing 'natural' hills and other dominant features of the landscape indicates a prehistoric structuring and understanding of the 'world' that straddles the modern Western world's conceptual division between 'natural' landscapes and humanly used space. This 'interplay between 'culture' and 'nature' created a sense of immutable 'God-given' order and thereby reinforced prevailing social structures.

A blurring between natural topography and constructed architecture is famously evinced in the siting of Silbury Hill (in the Avebury region of southern Britain). It is the largest artificial prehistoric mound in Europe. It was built during Neolithic times, is some 40 metres high, is calculated to have used three million person-hours in its construction, and is situated to attract the eye from the Neolithic hilltop monuments of its surrounding region.[5] In other cases natural hills are 'appropriated' and disguised by architecture. The largest Bronze Age cairns of Bodmin Moor, Cornwall, were heaped over high rocky outcrops ('tors'), and draw upon natural 'ancestral' powers by enveloping the outcrops in hill-like cairns.

Monuments on hilltop locations are magnetic to the human eye and thereby invite the onlooker to journey to them. Their positioning promoted, and made visual, pathways and rights and rites of passage across the landscape.[6] British Bronze Age round barrows are often associated with chains of hills, so that on arrival at one set of hilltop barrows another group appears on the next skyline. This 'chaining mechanism' would have been particularly important to societies that made regular journeys across landscapes (moving animals between pastures, regularly relocating arable fields / clearings or exploiting dispersed resources). The hill forts of the first millennium BC in southern Britain provide an example of another type of use of hills to connect places. Many are on hills that provide long vistas of 'other' landscapes and resource zones. These privileged viewing points enabled the hill fort users to monitor rights of use and passage across landscapes.

The physical shape of distinctive hills and their accreted stories of use are pre-eminent to their importance. Many dramatic hills have deep-time biographies of human use as a result of a recurrent interest in concurrently respecting and adding to their 'ancestry'. The banks and ditches of British hill forts surround and yet respect the remnant banks and ditches of earlier Neolithic enclosures. The layout and entrance orientation of hill forts regularly takes account of the locations of the preceding Bronze Age burial mounds that are sited on the same hills. Monuments are often placed on hills that have a history of being

places for votive offerings (including the modern ritual of walkers, adding a stone to hill summit cairns).

Hills can also be a by-product of large-scale human activity over thousands of years of in situ activity. The Neolithic and Bronze Age tells of western Asia, south-eastern Europe and North Africa are 'artificial hills': stratified mounds of archaeological deposits that have built up through the repeated demolition and re-levelling of the mud-brick houses of ancient villages and towns. Artificial hills can also be the outcome of prodigious community rubbish collection. For example, the British Bronze Age rubbish middens of East Chisenbury, and Potterne (both in Wiltshire) include the by-products from feasting on a massive scale. Today, East Chisenbury forms a diffuse hill, and was long taken to be a natural topographic feature.

Hills can take many forms of colour, texture, profile and gradient, depending on their geology and vegetation, and the differential effects of weathering. Archaeological remains are best preserved on hills that have been traditionally maintained under pasture. Evidence of past settlement and agricultural activity survives where buildings were terraced into hill slopes (e.g., the post holes of the Bronze and Iron Age roundhouses of southern Britain) and where cultivation terraces were constructed. Hills that are cleared of vegetation suffer denudation, and the slighter remains of settlement (artefacts and shallow postholes) are generally 'lost' from ploughed hills and hill slopes. Substantial amounts of hill wash (colluvium) – sediments and associated displaced artefacts (e.g., pot sherds) – that have accumulated in the valleys of southern Britain since Neolithic times indicate that here the hills and hill slopes were the first wooded places to be cleared for farming. Down-slope movement of sediments can, however, fossilize some of the activities that took place on hill slopes. The boundaries of ancient tilled fields still remain through the trapping and accumulation of hill-wash against their original hedge and fence boundaries (the later prehistoric lynchet systems of lowland Britain).

Hills cannot be abstracted from human affairs. Our personal and cultural identity is bound up with the topographic places that we visit, know of and live within. The unravelling of the construction, use and erosion histories of hills, and of the various impacts of hills on individual communities, lies at the boundaries of the disciplines of anthropology, archaeology and geography. Any exploration of the significance of hills to past and present peoples must give equal importance to the roles of 'altered', 'domesticated' hills, and 'unaltered', 'natural' hills in cultural perception.

section three

Matter

In the Preface, we have already hinted at the extreme difficulty of understanding the material world as one thing. Should we see it as a collection of elementary particles coalescing to produce different organic and inorganic structures? Should we see it as the simple fact of being alive, now that that the definition of life has become so thoroughly blurred by discoveries about what constitutes life's basic constituents? Should we see it as a prosaic 'nonhuman' background on which every-thing 'human' floats? Should we see it as that ever-present shower of dust, rising and settling in the air and every now and then illuminated by a ray of light?[1] The possibilities seem endless.

But what can be said is that currently there is a great deal of interest in trying to rework materiality born out of a sense of uncertainty that a stable definition of 'matter' could ever be reached. This interest runs in four directions. One is towards trying to take the object world more seriously in its own right, a direction that has ended up with a collapse of the analytical distinction between humans and nonhumans as actors. Action is what has to be studied, which implies not trying to decide in advance what sort of agencies might be doing the action. The second is towards re-placing the material. Distinctions between large and small, global and local, macro and micro become primitive artefacts whose stubborn persistence needs to be explained in an interconnected world in which circulation and differences in speed, and the new kinds of track and trace metrology that accompany them, are the predominant forces.[2] The third is towards attempting to understand the degree to which what we understand as material is mediated by our own imaginative images of it. Matter becomes a kind of 'lyric substance'[3] involving all kinds of touching moments.[4] The fourth is towards the invention of new political and ethical vocabularies that can come to terms with the new liaisons prompted by techno-scientific elaboration, which has placed us in a kind of moral purgatory.[5]

The entries that follow all display these kinds of directions as they try to trace out new materials that involve a whole range of different sensings of the world. The flight of bees mixes with the creak of the pub sign swinging in the wind. The new transgenic reality knocks up against jungles and wildlife. Waves are found in the atmosphere as well as at sea. Cities bear comparison with lichen. Nations become mountains to climb. Humans become shadows of nonhumans. Food transmutes into 'nature' and back again. Moraines fish for compliments. Viruses infect everything. Patterns turn into ground.

Bees

Ted Benton

As I recall, 16 August 1995 was a warm, sunny day. I was sitting in an open glade among hawthorn scrub in Wat Tyler Country Park, a former industrial site in the east Thames Estuary. Most of the former estuarine marshes in this district have disappeared under layers of London's domestic and industrial waste. Its ponds, areas of scrub, meadow and heathy grassland are interspersed with more formal picnic areas, a café, craft studios and a miniature railway. Its nutrient-poor soil, favourable climate and lack of agricultural activity have resulted in as rich an ensemble of wild animals and plants as any in the county. For invertebrates, along with other similar 'post-industrial' sites in the area, it is of national importance.[1]

I had chosen to eat my sandwiches on the grass next to a patch of Red Bartsia (*Odontites verna*). As I sat and watched a couple of workers of a common bumblebee species foraging on the Bartsia flowers, I heard a tell-tale high-pitched 'buzz'. This is what I had undertaken the two-hour rail journey (with five changes of train!) from my home in north Essex to hear. The sound signalled the arrival at my Bartsia patch of a single worker of the rare 'Shrill Carder Bee' (*Bombus sylvarum*). A local naturalist had discovered the bees – thought to have already become extinct in the county – at this site the year before. I had been told that Red Bartsia was its 'favourite' forage-source.

By coincidence, this event was connected by a complex social, political and geographical sequence with the 'Earth Summit' held half a world away in Rio in 1992. Among the agreements reached at the Summit were a convention on biodiversity and a series of chapters outlining steps to 'sustainable development' known as 'Agenda 21'. By 1995 the UK Government had followed up its Rio commitments with a 'UK Biodiversity Action Plan'. Among a select elite of rare and endangered species singled out for special attention were five bumblebees. Recent surveys had shown alarming declines in several bumblebee species, but in the case of these five the situation seemed particularly dire. A national Bumblebee Working Group was set up, and it was soon realized that the Shrill Carder Bee was very close to extinction. The Essex population, it now seems, formed part of one 'macropopulation' of which, it appeared, only four remained in the whole of the UK. Under the devolved 'Local Agenda 21', a local Biodiversity Action Plan was contrived to coordinate research and conservation for the Essex bees.

Interestingly, due to the efforts of countless amateur naturalists, the flora and fauna of Britain are among the most comprehensively studied in the world. Equally interestingly, the first draft of the Shrill Carder Bee Action Plan consisted mainly of elementary truisms. It was assumed that, along with much of our wildlife, the bee had been devastated by the ravages of agricultural intensification: the destruction of flower-rich meadows, grubbing out of hedgerows, draining of wetlands and saturation of the land with chemical poisons. This assumption was consistent with the survival of the bee in non-agricultural urban sites, such as Wat Tyler, and Ministry of Defence training areas (the other relic populations), and, so far as it goes, is probably true enough.

What was not explained was why the Shrill Carder Bee was close to extinction, while other species – although no doubt also significantly affected by agricultural change – remained relatively common and widespread. It was soon realized that virtually nothing specific was known about the mode of life and ecological requirements of the bee. The great pioneer of bumblebee students, W.F.L. Sladen, had written a few passages on the Shrill Carder Bee in his classic work of 1912, but subsequent academic writers had done little more than crib his account.[2] In Essex, despite intensive field work, we had observed only workers (not queens or males) and only in August! Only close observation and many hours of intensive 'field' work would discover some of the immensely complex web of interconnections between, on the one hand, human material and cultural practices and, on the other, the lives of the multitude of other species – in this case bumblebees – with which we precariously, and often unknowingly, coexist.

Thus, a recent study by Saville *et al.* has exploded the simple-minded 'foraging efficiency' model of bee behaviour.[3] Bees from a closely monitored nest were not found foraging closer than 250 metres from the nest, despite the presence of patches of suitable flowers much closer. Subsequent 'electronic tagging' of bumblebees has shown that they travel much further than had previously been thought, and can re-locate their nests over distances as great as 10 kilometres. It seems that the ecological relationships of bumblebees are far more complex than is commonly allowed for. Inspired by this study, and recognizing the importance, now, of urban habitats for bumblebees decimated by agricultural change, I concentrated my studies on bumblebee movements in a fragmented *urban* landscape: the large provincial town where I live.[4] At least twelve species – all but the rarest of the species found in the county as a whole – survive in parks and gardens, but also in 'despised' urban locales, such as along railway tracks, along footpath margins, in neglected allotments, uncultivated open spaces, blighted development land and along the banks of the river that runs through the town. Only one

59 Suburban gardens in Colchester; a habitat for all the common bumblebee species.

such site is formally designated and managed for nature conservation.

The really striking thing is how this mosaic of habitats happens to meet the diverse ecological requirements – suitable flowering plants for nectar and pollen from February to October, mate-location and nesting sites, places to hibernate undisturbed, and so on – of all these species. This mosaic has arisen and still persists as an unwilled and contingent outcome of the history of the town. One continuing threat to such habitats is a residual urban park aesthetic, for which all unmanaged diversity is 'untidy', and whose vision of perfection is even lawn grass with neat rows of 'lollypop' trees. But this can be, and is being, effectively challenged. Much more powerful are the intensifying pressures for urban 'development', aided by Government proposals to 'streamline' the planning process. Meanwhile, a powerful rural lobby is actively protecting its privileges, directing developers from 'green field' to 'brownfield' sites. The patchwork of urban habitat is under threat as never before.

There is now an urgent need to spread awareness of the enormous value of despised urban locales: they harbour a diversity of wildlife far outstripping what remains in the impoverished arable monocultures that cover most of the English agricultural lowlands. Moreover, they are, literally, on the doorstep of the people who live in our most densely populated towns and cities: their actual and potential amenity and educational value could not be exaggerated. They are an indispensable habitat, both for the bees and for urban humans. They need to be defended from those whose pursuit of profit neither knows nor cares about either.

Pubs

Diane Watson and Tony Watson

Stop Traveller! This wondrous sign explore
And say, when thou hast viewed it o'er,
Grantham, now two rarities are thine:
A lofty steeple and a living sign.

60 The Beehive, Grantham, Lincolnshire.

The traveller visiting the Lincolnshire town of Grantham is unlikely to miss the fine steeple of St Wulfram's church. It stands as a bold sign of the wealth and importance enjoyed by this old market town when England's ecclesiastical masons were making their mark on the country's landscape. It can also be read as a sign of the more general human urge to shape the physical world through cultural efforts that might stand alongside, if not rival, the natural shaping of the world. Ancaster stone was taken out of the ground and thrown up into the sky to direct human attention heavenwards. But stone from those same quarries later went into the making of the Tudor pub that still sits in the shadow of St Wulfram's. Many of the inn's customers would have been illiterate, and to help them remember it and to make it possible for them to arrange assignations on its premises, it had attached to it the sign of a pig. To this day, people arrange to meet each other 'at the Pig'. But more of that shortly. What about the living sign referred to in the above rhyme?

Whereas the public house with the sign of the pig presents to the traveller only a representation of a pig, the rival hostelry of The Beehive, only a few hundred metres further away from the church, signals its existence to the world with a real hive – a hive of living bees. This is set within the branches of the tree outside the pub. Also attached to the tree is a plaque displaying the poem that compares the wondrous living sign with the glory of the church's soaring spire. In this living pub sign, we might say, is the perfect blending of the human and the animal, the cultural and the natural. The hive is a joint product of the carpenter and the bee.

Shortly after arriving in the town from the south, and a mile or so short of the Pig and the Hive, the traveller may catch sight of a painted sign on which large sparkling snowflakes fall past a black cow. This is a delightful visual joke. It subverts the conventional assumption that a pub called The Spotted Cow must once have been owned by someone possessing a cow with distinctive hide markings. It also sidesteps, or leaves implicit, allusion to that popular 'hey diddle' in which 'the cow jumps over the moon'. It is almost worth going into the pub to celebrate the humour of the witty sign painter. He or she too has made their mark by crossing boundaries, mixing 'the cultural' of the sign-painting craft with 'the animal' of the grazing animal. But even in the cow itself, there is a blending of culture and nature, as there was in the beehive. The cow is a *domestic* animal – bred out of nature by humans, for human purposes.

As in towns and villages across the country, one can map the ground of this Lincolnshire town with reference to its pubs. We might direct the traveller: 'If you come into the town from Melton Mowbray, bear right at The Sir Isaac Newton, pass the Springfield Arms, turn left at The Spotted Cow, go straight on past The Reindeer, The Fox and Hounds, The Recruiting Sergeant, The Goose at the Bank and turn right at The Angel and you'll find the Pig on your left.' Yes, we are back to The Pig.

For almost two centuries 'the Pig' has been formally called The Blue Pig. And elsewhere in the town there is a Blue Bull, a Blue Cow, a Blue Dog and a Blue Horse. In the past there were many more such pubs, the Blue Fox and the Blue Ram among them. And, yes, there was a Blue Man too – a single human presence among the animals. The 'bluing of the pubs', as we might now label it, resulted from a political mapping of the ground of Grantham in the early nineteenth century. Sir William Manners was a lord of the manor with strong Whiggish political aspirations. His political colours were blue and he required all the inns, alehouses or taverns on his territory to 'fly his flag', so to speak. In these places one would be offered a drink of 'blue ale'. Such a drink was an inducement to vote in parliamentary elections for Whig candidates. This was a time, remember, when voting occurred in public. Where you drank, in effect, located you on the town's political map.

61 The Blue Pig, Grantham.

Other names, like the Lord Harrowby, The Gregory Arms and, indeed, The Manners Arms, located drinking premises on the town's landowning map. The Manners Arms has now disappeared. And it would seem that William Manners was not altogether successful in influencing election outcomes in the town. Nevertheless, his son, F. J. Tollemache, did become a celebrated Liberal MP for Grantham. For a century or more, a statue to Tollemache has been as prominent a landmark in the town as that of another famous son of the town, Isaac Newton. But, unlike Newton, Tollemache did not have a public house named after him – until recently. The former Co-operative department store, another part of the town's history, has been converted by the Wetherspoon's chain into The Tollemache pub. But what of that other famous Grantham politician, Margaret Thatcher? There is no public house named after her. This is in spite of the recent appearance of a pub close to the house where the famous lady grew up. But, for some reason, they called it The Nobody Inn. The ground has been mapped – for the present at least.

Pigs

Nigel Clark

'The situation of few parts of the world are better determin'd than these Islands are, being settled by some hundreds of Observations of the Sun and Moon.' So Captain James Cook RN claimed of New Zealand (Aotearoa) after his first circumnavigation.[1] Cook has often been viewed as the archetypal Enlightenment hero, a man who turned enlightened thought into action. And nowhere could the act of enlightening be practised with such purity of purpose than at the farthest reaches of the globe; regions that, in the words of Cook's shipmate George Forster, 'had hitherto lain plunged in one long night of ignorance and barbarism'.[2]

These days the age of European expansion has lost its gleam, and we are more likely to view the staking out of these already-inhabited lands as the start of a long and painful imperial project. In many senses this a welcome change, but there is also a risk that the inversion of enlightened adventure into more gloomy saga still takes much of the Enlightenment's ordering impulse at its word. For one of the most illuminating things about the 'grid of intelligibility' that descended upon Europe's Antipodes in the eighteenth century is precisely what escaped it.

While the voyagers of the age of scientific exploration busied themselves in a rigorous 'pinning down' of newly encountered land forms and life forms, they also triggered events that would escape visibility, defy mapping and confound intelligibility. I refer, in particular, to the seeding of new-found lands with exotic life. Observing of New Zealand on his first visit an absence of '4-footed animals, either Tame or Wild, or signs of any, except Dogs and Rats',[3] Cook set about making amends on both succeeding voyages.

As well as planting a range of crops, he introduced breeding pairs of goats, sheep and enough hogs and sows to conclude 'that there is little fear but that this country will, in time, be stocked with these animals, both in a wild and domestic state'.[4] In the case of the pigs, he was quite correct.

The practice of introducing biota to distant regions followed on from the early experience of colonizing the eastern Atlantic archipelagos – the Canaries, Azores and Madeiras. Here, Europeans had been pleasantly surprised to find that plants and animals from home could thrive in novel environments. As Europe's maritime adventures extended globally, it became common to seed remote islands and coastlines with livestock, as an insurance policy for possible shipwreck and as provision for later stopovers or settlements. So conventional was this practice that Cook may have been beaten to the first landing of pigs in New Zealand. The French explorer Jean François-Marie de Surville is now thought to have left hogs and sows in 1769 – the year of Cook's first visit – possibly in gratitude to Maori who helped his crew recover from scurvy.

Pigs – *Sus scrofa domestica* – are in many senses the ideal biotic colonists. Hardy, mobile and omnivorous, they convert a higher proportion of the food they eat into consumable flesh than any other of the large domesticates. While their diet of concentrated carbohydrates and proteins sooner or later brings them into competition with their human counterparts, this tends to be less of a problem in the early days of settlement, when there is often an abundance of these food groups in the wild. The capacity of pigs to fend for themselves, combined with their prolific breeding patterns, meant that 'swinish multitudes' often moved in advance of European colonists in much of Australasia and the Americas, providing a vital food source in the lean years of establishment. But these same colonizing qualities also pose a threat to existing ecosystems, especially in regions unaccustomed to hoofed browsers. Grubbing up roots and seeds, pigs can open up dense forest to sunlight, at the expense of existing biotic communities and to the advantage of subsequent invaders – both human and nonhuman. As has been concluded of Cook's introduction of pigs to New Zealand: 'so well did they survive that, if it weren't for hunters and dogs, their descendants would have reduced the landscape . . . to a ghostly shadow of itself'.[5]

In this sense it is tempting to view pigs as the seeds of empire; proxy imperialists set down to do the groundwork for the establishment of a new European order. But in condemning the spatial history of enlightenment in this way, we run the risk of resurrecting it, in its negative image. If the narrative of enlightened progress is understood as the demarcating of civilization from wildness and the subsequent pushing back of this line, then what seems to be most interesting about the dissemination of exotic livestock is the way that it willingly confounds this logic. For Cook, like every pig-planting voyager from Columbus onwards, anticipated that his domesticated porkers would not only run wild, but that many would stay wild. Mapping the frontier into existence, with one hand, he set about blurring it with the other, by unleashing elements that effectively crossed Western thought's great divide *in the wrong direction*.

And the pigs themselves made the most of this opportunity. While their relatives on the European home front were subjected to 'improvement' through systematic breeding, in the biotic underworld of the periphery pigs escaped this genetic disciplining. Random variations and repressed genetic traits flourished: in their new environment wild boars and sows grew long-legged, sharp-snouted, slab-sided and razor-tusked. And as if to flaunt their disdain for the frontier still further, the pigs of the colonial periphery would return to haunt civilized life, scavenging crops, preying on new-born farm animals and mating with their domesticated counterparts.

But there is another sense in which enlightenment at ground zero seems divided against itself. Anticipating New Zealand being 'settled by an industrious people',[6] Cook nonetheless foresaw the flourishing of pigs in their wild state most immediately as a boon for 'the Natives'. He landed his hogs and sows at a distance from Maori settlements, otherwise, in his words 'all our endeavours to stock this country with useful animals were likely to be frustrated by the very people we meant to serve'.[7] In the process, Cook relinquished any chance of gratitude or return. Maori accepted the gift of pork with gusto, becoming keen hunters and affording a prominent place to pigs in their own inter-tribal gifting.

Subsequent history, ecological as well as socio-political, has obscured the magnanimity of Cook's gesture. Like the behaviour of the pigs themselves, the gift of swine overran the circle of exchange, exceeding calculation, and thus defying the logic of reason itself. In this sense, at the instant when it should have been most true to form, enlightenment reveals something more generous or generative than our spatial histories have chosen to recognize: a furtive element that critical Western commentators may yet flesh out and feast upon.

Humans

Myra J. Hird

One could argue that the entire feminist philosophical project pivots on a commitment to challenge the assumption that 'mankind' is homologous with 'humanity'. Philosophical and political endeavours to name the gender of the speaking self and, indeed, the gender of that which is spoken, have tended to assume that sexual difference exists.[1] While the vicissitudes of gender are forever dissected, material sexual differences remain fixtures of our social landscapes, grounded apparently in 'nature'. In this short space I want to explore sexual difference as an implicit dimension to definitions of 'humans'. I will suggest that our confidence in the immutability of sexual difference is ill-founded. To do this, I will explore the constitution of sexual difference through intersex, transsex and biology.

It is well known that nonhuman living organisms exhibit an enormous range of 'sexual' and 'non-sexual' characteristics – male seahorses get pregnant; most species on Earth reproduce without sex. Male pipefish get pregnant on the underside of their bellies. Many species are either male and female simultaneously or sequentially. Many types of fish and other species change sex back and forth depending on environmental conditions.[2] Among humans, intersex conditions (a variety of conditions in which humans contain traditionally defined female and male characteristics such as chromosomes, hormones, gonads and / or genitals) affect approximately 1.7–2 per cent of the world's population, making sex diversity more common than either albinism, Down syndrome, cystic fibrosis or some ethnicities.[3] However, living evidence of sex diversity among humans is so traumatizing to the Western world that a newborn with ambiguous genitalia is considered a 'social emergency' and children are surgically reassigned into *either* girls or boys. What incites the medical community to favour extremely intrusive surgery for anatomical conditions that these doctors themselves admit present no functional or medical dangers?

People with intersex conditions challenge the immutability of sexual difference upon which Western political, economic and social structures are built, and we continue to choose non-consensual invasive surgery over the abundant sexual diversity found in nature. Nonetheless, the incorporation of a surgically assigned 'female' involves a determination as to the constitution of femaleness. Any definition of 'woman' that retains any corporeality must be able to define that corporeality and this is exactly where the problem begins in definitions based on 'sex'. A woman identified with an intersex condition (or any woman for that matter) may have any combination of partially or totally surgically created vagina, labia and/or breasts. She may or may not be able to reproduce sexually. If being female does not entail the possession of particular anatomical parts, then the artificial creation of these body parts is inconsequential.

Our current assumptions about the constitution of 'sex' struggle with this implication. Transsexualism effectively argues that if gender can be learned then 'womanhood' and 'manhood' are available to anyone with the capacity to learn. Many transsex people contest the assumption that one must be born with one particular set of genitals to *be* of that sex, or that genitals correspond to 'knowing' sex or gender at all. The experiences that are claimed to be typically female (menstruation, childbirth, etc.) are shared by only a minority of people identified as female on this planet. The experiences shared by most people who are identified as female are carrying firewood, hauling water and working on assembly lines – activities not reliant upon morphologic constitution.[4]

But what of those humans who are confident that their non-intersexed, non-transsexed bodies are unequivocally sexually dimorphic? Far from supporting this 'organic chauvinism',[5] contemporary analyses of biology suggest something far more interesting. The 'sex' on which we base our discussions of 'sexual difference' is not absolute. There are many variations: XXY, XXXY, XXXXY, XXYY, XXXYY to name only a few. All foetuses spend their first six weeks in an XX womb and her amniotic fluid, undergoing the same development until the release of testosterone for most XY foetuses. Yet while the genomes (chromosomal make-up) of no two people are identical (except for identical twins), the genomic make-up of all people is identical to within one per cent.[6] The differences we hold so dear (hair colour, skin tone, etc.) and on which so much of our social organization is based ('sex'-segregated sports is an obvious example) are minuscule in comparison with our biological similarities. The only thing that does not exist is a pure (Y or YY) male. There has been a case of a boy born with an XX configuration, however. This boy's ovum split several times before being fertilized by sperm, providing further evidence that parthenogenic reproduction extends to humans. So human reproduction may yet resemble the kind of 'reproduction' most popular on this planet, which requires no sense of 'sex' at all.

The cells in our bodies engage in constant, energetic reproduction.[7] Indeed, the millions of microbes that exist on, and in, our bodies make our traditional definition of ourselves as single organisms highly problematic. Our cells also provide asylum for a variety of viruses and countless genetic fragments. And none of this interaction requires any bodily contact with another human being. Further questioning the assumption of sexual difference, mitochondria (organelles containing enzymes that regulate the reactions that provide energy for cells) contain DNA that is entirely inherited from the mother. This means that *most* of any human being's DNA is inherited matrilineally.

In contrast to the minimal amount of specifically sexual reproduction that some human beings engage in, each of us engages in constant reproduction including *recombination* (cutting and patching of DNA strands), *merging* (fertilization of cells), *meiosis* (cell division by halving chromosome number, for instance in making sperm and eggs) and *mitosis* (cell division with maintenance of cell number). Moreover, we constantly reproduce our own bodies as an essential feature of autopoiesis. We reproduce our own livers every two months, our stomach linings every five days, new skin every six weeks and 98 per cent of our atoms every year. Our human bodies live in a permanently fertilized state, with only our egg and sperm cells qualifying as sexed (haploid): most of our cells are intersex (diploid). And 44 of our 46 chromosomes are completely unrelated to sexual difference.[8]

Far from revealing sexual dimorphism, at every material level, human bodies practise a wonderful combination of intersex, reproduction and heterogeneous exchange with the environment. At this bodily level, we resemble most of the living matter in four out of the five kingdoms on this planet that reproduce without sex.

Moon

Denis Cosgrove

Why is the man in the moon a man? Does he make for a lunar human geography?

There is neither man nor woman, indeed no human face at all, on the lunar surface. The man, or rather men, who, briefly, were *on* the moon found not a face but a complex and specific physical geography – a selenography – that has now been charted at scales comparable to earth-surface mapping. The surface of the moon is a battered, angular landscape, etched in monochromatic greys where the absence of atmosphere distils light into unimaginable harshness and makes kilometres-distant, 1,500-metre-high mountains appear mere hillocks an hour's walk away. In its intense, metaphysical light, the most difficult thing of all to grasp on the moon's surface is spatial scale, a *human* geography. The reason for this is the absence of anything that offers what was once called 'the measure of man' – no softening atmosphere, no colour, no plants or animals . . . no faces.

But scientific knowledge of the moon's physical geography has not destroyed its enchantment. Its *human* geography is located here on earth. We still find romance in the soft light it casts over nocturnes, are entranced by the cold shadows of a moonlit night, moved to reverie by the coloured tones of the lunar disc. The moon can still catch us utterly by surprise: emerging bloodily huge on the horizon of an August evening, hanging unobserved in a midday June sky, scudding through oceans of fast-moving December cloud, or silently sovereign over wet March plough-lines. And that lunar face, blotchy and indistinct, still seems to peer down and invite a returning gaze. Plutarch, writing about 75 BC, described the moon's expression as 'seductive, smiling, placid'. *De facie quae in*

orbe lunae apparet brilliantly combines the poetics of lunar myth with scientific explanation of the moon's stains (*maculae*), not, as the Stoics believed, the smoke and charring of its dying fires but shadows cast by its gulfs and chasms.[1] Today we still hover between rational knowledge and description of the lunar surface, and romantic disinclination to abandon the metaphysics of moon.

No question about it, the moon is part of Earth's geography, both gravitationally and imaginatively. But why a man in the moon? Curious, when overwhelmingly lunar gendering has been female. In the mythic and symbolic language of most peoples on earth the moon has been figured as consort to a male-gendered sun. The moon's mensual changes – swelling and waning – and its soft and mutable coloration have suggested intimate associations between womanly bodies and things lunar. Diana, virgin mistress of the forest hunt, bathed in moonlight, her hair gathered within a diadem and shaped into the archer's symbol of the crescent moon. The Roman moon goddess metamorphosed into Mary, virgin and mother of the incarnate Christian God. Specifically, Mary is associated with the moon in her appearance as Queen of Heaven, her crown now twelve apostolic stars and the crescent moon under her feet, at once appropriating while rejecting Diana's pagan associations. Or she is Star of the Sea, light to sailors, casting a 'mile of moon' to soften the troubled waves. In Counter-Reformation Catholic Mariology (Mariolatry to Protestants) she is Mary Immaculate, conceived, like her son, unstained by sin. This doctrine rendered the stains on the moon's surface purity a very considerable theological embarrassment in precisely those years when the vague lunar visage was resolving into the complex geography of 'mountains' and 'seas' (craters and striations of debris), which science has spent four centuries mapping and naming.

As a feature of the earth's landscapes, the moon is tantalizingly located: at once too close to appear as an undifferentiated globe of light in the night sky, and too far for the unaided eye to distinguish clearly the marks on its surface. Plutarch himself, until 1600 the West's principal authority on the moon, recognized that 'the face which appears on the surface of the moon' (he did not give it a gender) was not an illusion created by poor vision: the more acute the eyesight, he remarked, the more distinct the marks on the lunar surface. *The* unaided eye does not of course exist; there are only individual pairs of human eyes. But even the most acute among them is not sharp enough to observe with accuracy the corrugations on the curving edge of the waxing or gibbous moon, or the lengthening shadows of the larger crater rims. It was the telescope that revealed these features. And we have specific records of the first observations, and of their cultural impacts.

The year was 1610. Galileo Galilei published in his 'Starry Messenger' (*Siderius Nuncius*) images showing the moon's surface, as it appeared magnified by the telescope. As the moon passes through its phases, the spots on its surface are shown to alter in length exactly as shadows cast across an irregular surface by an angular light. Galileo's drawings are the first 'maps' of the moon. They would be followed by ever more detailed studies, some denoting a lunar geography to reflect the world's own pattern of lands and seas (illus 62). More significantly for Galileo's contemporaries, they challenged the dominant assumption, inherited from Aristotle, that the moon, like all heavenly bodies, of which it is the nearest, was a perfect, smooth sphere. Lunar geography, along with the sun spots and Jovan moons

also revealed by the telescope, was a major contributor to the shift in spatial apprehension that we call the Copernican revolution.

Papal Rome's response to Galileo's science is a familiar story. Less frequently remarked is that part of the great dialogue between 'science' and doctrine that concerned lunar geography. Galileo's 'starry messenger' compares the surface of the moon to an opaque, spotted and cracked wineglass, a demeaning re-description of the spotless, smooth and transparent sphere of Aristotelian and Mariological orthodoxy. Bizarrely, insistence on the perfection of the lunar surface was most intense immediately *after* the invention of the telescope. Foremost among its supporters were members of the Jesuit Order, who included some of the finest scientists of seventeenth-century Europe. Their reason is clear. A stained or 'maculate' moon undermined the emerging doctrine of the Immaculate Conception, which was for many

62 Johannes Hevelius' map of the lunar surface, naming its patterns of 'lands and oceans' after those on earth and drawing on a long-standing belief that the moon's markings were the reflections of terrestrial geography on the mirrored lunar surface. From his *Selenographia, sive Lunae descriptio, atque accurata tam macularum ejus . . .* (Gdansk: Hünefeld, 1647).

63 Francisco Pacheco: *Immaculate Conception with Miguel del Cid c.* 1619; Seville Cathedral.

Nonhumans

Bruno Latour

If, from the start, sociology has been marked by the discovery that when we act many other aliens are acting as well, that action is always taken over, it has been defined to an even greater degree by the ethical, political and scientific realization that there exist hierarchies, asymmetries and inequalities in society; that the social world is just as differentiated a landscape as a rugged and mountainous terrain; that no amount of enthusiasm, free will or ingenuity can make those asymmetries go away; that some unequal distribution of forces seems to weigh as heavily as walls, buttresses, pyramids, fortresses – whatever architectural metaphor is chosen to describe the overarching social order; that such massive inertia counteracting individual action explains why society should be considered as a specific *sui generis* entity; that any thinker who denies those inequalities and differences is either naïve or somewhat reactionary; and, finally, that denying social gravity is as ridiculous as denying its Newtonian equivalent.

Catholics a key signifier of difference from Protestant belief. The course of this debate can be traced in painted images of Mary and the moon from the second decade of the seventeenth century (illus. 63).[2]

The maleness of the 'man' in the moon remains an unexplained oddity. Gender theory, informed by psychoanalysis, could no doubt use the stories sketched here to weave wonderful theories for it. But *he* is not the most important player in shaping a lunar human geography.

How could we be faithful to this intuition and still maintain that groups are 'constantly' being performed and that agencies are 'ceaselessly' debated? Is not the choice of these departure points inspired by a naïve and even reactionary attitude that transforms the highly unequal social domain into a flat playing field where everyone has, it seems, the same chance to generate their own metaphysics? And yet, to say that society is unequal, hierarchical, that it weighs disproportionately on some instead of others, that it has all the character of inertia is one thing: to conclude that hierarchy, dissymmetry, inertia are made *of* social stuff is another argument altogether. Not only does the second point have no logical continuity with the first, but it contradicts it.

In the same way as the overtaking of action by other agencies does not mean that society is taking over, the flagrant asymmetry of resources does not mean that they are generated by *social* asymmetries. It just leads to the opposite conclusion: if asymmetries have to be accounted for, it means that other actors than social ones are coming into play. The reason is that 'social' is not the name of a specific thing, but the name of a movement, a displacement, a translation, a connection, a mobilization, an enrolment, an association: the name of a sort of fluid. Left to its own devices, a social tie made only of social ties would be limited to very short-lived, local, face-to-face, unequipped interactions. But where has this situation ever been observed? Even baboon troops cannot provide such an extreme case. When power is exerted for good, it is because it is not made of social ties. When it has to rely on social ties only, it is never exerted for long. As Hobbes and Rousseau remarked long ago, no Cyclops is strong enough not to be easily overcome, in his slumber, by some insignificant human; no coalition is solid enough not to be run over by an even larger coalition. It is when power is exerted through things that don't sleep and associations that don't break down that it can last longer and expand further – and for this, of course, links made of another stuff than social contracts are required.

Thus, the accusation of forgetting 'power relations' and 'social inequalities' should be shifted to the sociologists of the social. By ignoring the practical means through which inertia, durability, asymmetry, extension, domination is produced, and by conflating all those different means with the powerless power of social ties, they are the ones who have disguised the causes of social inequalities. If there is one point where confusing cause and consequence makes a huge difference, it is at this juncture, when an explanation should be provided of the vertiginous effect of domination. If absolute power, as the saying goes, corrupts absolutely, then absolutely gratuitous use of the concept of power by so many social scientists has corrupted them absolutely – or at least rendered their discipline redundant. They have simply added to the studiable and modifiable skein of means to achieve powers, an un-studiable, invisible, immovable, homogeneous world of power in itself.

Social action is not only taken over by foreign agencies, it is also shifted or delegated to different genres of actors that transport the action further through other modes of action, other types of forces altogether. To say this, I am well aware, is like proposing a reversal of background and foreground, a radical paradigm shift: objects begin to appear visible only once you start to have doubts about the ability of social ties to expand durably. As long as you believe that society could hold its own weight, then objects vanish from view. (The ambiguous word 'object' is being kept here only as a convenient place holder.) So if a sociology is to exist, the social fluid has to be followed wherever it circulates, even through things made of non-social stuff. But in order to be able to travel with such a freedom of movement, traditional social ties have to be rendered comparable, compatible, commensurable with objects. This is possible only once the definition of what an actor is has been slightly modified.

At first blush, bringing objects back into the normal course of action would appear innocuous enough: after all, there is hardly any doubt that kettles 'boil' water, knives 'cut' meat, baskets 'hold' provisions, hammers 'hit' nails on the head, rails 'keep' kids from falling, locks 'close' rooms against uninvited visitors, soap 'takes' the dirt away, schedules 'list' class sessions . . . and so on *ad infinitum*. Are those verbs not designating actions? How could these humble, mundane and trivial activities be news to any social scientist? And yet they are. The main reason why objects have had no chance to play any role before is the very definition of actors and agencies chosen by the sociologists of the social. If action is defined a priori as what 'intentional' 'meaningful' humans do, it is hard to see how a hammer, a basket, a door closer, a cat, a rug, a mug can act: they might exist in the domain of 'material' 'causal' relations, but not in the 'reflexive', 'symbolic', domain of social relations. By contrast, if we stick to our decision to start from the controversies about actors and agencies, then anything that modifies a state of affairs by making a difference is an actor – or, if it has no figuration as yet, an actant. Thus, the question to ask about any agent is simply the following: does it make a difference in the course of some other agent's action or not?

The rather common-sense answer is a resounding 'yes'. If you can, with a straight face, maintain that hitting a nail with and without a hammer, boiling water with and without a kettle, fetching provisions with or without a basket, walking in the street with or without clothes, zapping a TV set with or without a command, slowing down a car with or without a speed-bump, are exactly the same activities, that the introduction of these mundane implements changes nothing in the realization of the tasks, then you are ready to transmigrate to the Holy Land of the social and disappear from this lowly world. But for all of the other members of society, it does make a difference, and so, according to our definition, these implements are actors, or more precisely, participants in the course of action, waiting to be given a figuration.

This does not mean that these participants 'determine' the action, that baskets 'cause' the fetching of provisions or that hammers

'impose' the hitting of the nail. Such a reversal of the direction of causality would be simply a way to transform objects to the main cause whose consequences would be simply transmitted through human actions. Rather, it means that there might exist many metaphysical shades between full causality and sheer non-existence: things might authorize, allow, afford, encourage, permit, suggest, influence, block, render possible, forbid and so on, in addition to 'determining' and serving as a 'backdrop for human action'. No science of the social can even begin if the question of who and what participates in the action is not first of all opened up, even though it might mean letting elements enter that, for lack of a better term, we can call *nonhumans*. This expression is meaningless in itself. It does not designate a domain of reality, but only what has to be added to any action by the analyst to make sense of it. To explain some human action by the addition of nonhumans is a perfectly legitimate way of practising our various social sciences: after all, structure, discourse, trajectory, unconscious, culture, episteme, interest, habitus, calculation, rationality, are nonhuman agencies too.

What is new is not, of course, the multiplicity of objects that any course of action mobilizes along its trail – no one ever denied that they were there by the thousands; what is new is that objects are suddenly highlighted not only as being full-blown actors, but also as allowing society to exist as a durable thing, to exert a dominating influence, to have power. This is the surprise from which I wish to start, instead of considering, as do most of my colleagues, that the question is obviously closed and that objects do nothing, nothing at least comparable or even connectable to human social action, and that, if they can sometimes 'express' power relations, 'symbolize' social hierarchies, 'reinforce' social inequalities, 'transport' social power, they are not at the origin of social inertia. Against this position, I simply want to reopen this question again, or at least make sure that, even in the unlikely case that the answer is negative, it has become a matter for empirical research and not the dictate of an a priori moral pronouncement.

It is true that, at first sight, the difficulty of registering the role of objects comes from the apparent incommensurability of their modes of action with traditionally conceived social ties. And indeed, they are incommensurable: that's the reason why they are there in the first place! The force exerted by a brick onto another brick, the spin of a wheel on its axis, the balance of a lever on a mass, the multiplication of a force through a pulley, the effect of fire on phosphorus, all of these relations seem to pertain to a general category so obviously different from the one exerted by a 'stop' sign on a cyclist or that of a crowd over an individual mind that it seems perfectly reasonable to separate material and social entities. Reasonable, but absurd if one realizes that, in any workplace, any course of action might weave together, for instance, a shouted order to lay a brick, the chemical connection of cement with water, the force of a pulley on a rope with a movement of the hand, the strike of a match to light a cigarette given by a colleague, etc. Here, the apparently reasonable division between material and social becomes just what obfuscates any enquiry into how a collective action is possible. Provided of course that, by collective, we do not mean an action carried over by homogeneous social forces, but, on the contrary, an action that collects different types of forces, because they are different.

Any course of action will thread a trajectory through completely foreign modes of existence that have been brought together in spite of their heterogeneity. Social inertia and physical gravity might seem unconnected, but not when a team of workers is building a wall of bricks: only when the wall is completed or has not yet started. If we want to be a bit more realistic about social ties then as 'reasonable' sociologists we have to accept that the continuity of any course of action will rarely be between human–human or object–object connections, but will constantly zigzag from one to the other. And this has nothing to do with a 'reconciliation' of the much too famous object / subject dichotomy. To distinguish a priori 'material' and 'social' ties before linking them together again makes about as much sense as to account for the dynamic of a battle by imagining, first, a group of soldiers and officers stark naked; second, a huge heap of paraphernalia – tanks, paperwork, uniforms – and then claim that 'of course there exists some (dialectical) relation between the two'. No! one should retort, there exists no relation whatsoever between the material and the social world, because it is the division that is first of all a complete artefact. To abandon the division is not to 'relate' the heap of naked soldiers with the heap of material stuff, it is to rethink the whole assemblage from top to bottom and from beginning to end. There is no empirical case where the existence of two coherent and homogeneous aggregates, for instance technology 'and' society, could make any sense. There are divisions that one should never try to pass over, go beyond, try to overcome dialectically: rather they should be ignored, left to their own devices, like a once formidable castle now a ruin in the midst of a deserted moor.

Viruses

Steve Hinchliffe

We evolve and die more from our polymorphous and rhizomatic flus than from hereditary diseases, or diseases that have their own lines of descent.[1]

Viral Patterns

Viral patterns are often tragic patterns. They are also sometimes revealing patterns. By 2000, the World Bank estimated that 95 per cent of Human Immune Deficiency (HIV) positive cases would occur in developing countries.[2] In this case, it is not difficult to read off a political economy of a viral disease. Indeed, it may be said that viruses thrive on tragedy as well as often being an attributed cause of suffering. The word virus once meant poison, and is usually used to refer to a small package of information that can unsettle and, given the right (or wrong) conditions, wreak havoc within an established order into which it inserts itself. Viruses use their hosts' internal workings as a means to replicate, and follow pre-established social pathways in order to disperse and find new hosts. In this sense, there may be little difference between biotic and computer viruses. Both are assigned causal agency in the poisoning of what otherwise could or even should be life-enhancing activities. The Love bug virus that infected computer systems across the world in 2000 traded on the promise of romance. HIV moves between hosts most commonly during sexual intercourse.

In other circumstances, viral patterns may be creatively destructive. In the Dutch Republic between 1634 and 1637 a futures market developed based on tulip bulbs. This was a market of signs, if ever there was one (to the extent that tulip weights or *azens*

64 From Crispyn de Passe's *Hortus Floridus* (1614). Broken tulips, like this one, commanded huge sums of money in the Netherlands in the seventeenth century. The patterning is viral, and not so much hereditary as 'rhizomatic'.

became a currency divorced from the exchange of tulip bulbs[3]). Part of the surge in interest and demand for tulips was the production of new 'breaks' – tulip flowers that were delicately patterned with fine lines of a second shade or colour. One such flower was the Semper Augustus (see illus. 64), a single bulb of which could command a price in excess of the cost of a canal-side house in the centre of Amsterdam.[4] The feathered or flamed patterning on each specimen of Semper Augustus was unique, a jewel valued for its individual intricacy.[5] Given the prices, it is no surprise that the cause of such a valuable characteristic was the subject of much debate and experimentation in the seventeenth-century Dutch Republic. While the bulbs of broken specimens could reproduce the precious flower, curiously, when seeds were collected from the same plants, very few, if any, of the offspring developed the valuable trait. There was no obvious genealogy that expert breeders could discern. Desperate to hit the big money, various 'catalysts' were sold to those who wanted to break plain tulips. Growers were sometimes duped into buying special rainwater, plaster from old walls and pigeon dung at great expense. It was another 300 years before the cause of breaking was attributed to a virus.

Narrative Patterns

Destructive and creative patterns. These patterns can be read in a variety of ways. One way is to divide the world up into the poisonous and the pure. Viruses, as the etymology suggests, are the poisons. Even when their effects are beneficial, they are construed as outsiders that break into nucleated cells and disrupt normal cell functions. In medical and veterinary practice, this purification may have certain advantages (although there are limits to dividing the world up in this way, even in the practical world of curing diseases). This is a Platonic world of pure objects, with any infected individual being defined as impure – and sent to slaughter if you happen to be a sheep with the potentially harmless foot-and-mouth virus, or into isolation if you are a human being with a socially undesirable infection. It is also a world for evolutionary supremacists. A narrative of progression, from simple to complex life forms, is asserted. A tree-like genealogy is drawn, from the primordial soup to the high branches of human achievement (and beyond). So viral infection of higher organisms is in this sense a deviation from the established order and is retrogressive. Interestingly, in the 1930s, at the height of European fascism and at the point at which viruses were linked to the production of broken tulips, multicoloured flowers went out of a fashion.

A second way of understanding viral patterns is to refuse these purifications, and run with the more symbiotic, rhizomatic imagery that can be found in another politics and another biogeography. A less species-ist diagramming of life emerges. For symbiosis teaches us a 'filthy lesson . . . : the human is an integrated colony of amoeboid beings, just as these amoeboid beings are integrated colonies of bacteria'.[6] Moreover, the genealogical trees that have interested the supremacists are scrambled.[7] As human genetic engineers have started to appreciate (the techniques if not the indeterminate range of consequences), 'viroid life is one of the key means by which the transferral of genetic information has taken place'.[8] Rather than being descended from lower organisms, we are more their co-productions. That is, we are a product of involutions rather than evolution. For the philosophers Deleuze and Guattari, 'we form a rhizome with our viruses, or rather our viruses cause us to form a rhizome with other animals'.[9]

Involvement

This is a different story. We / they are not simply patterned by time or evolution, but, as importantly, we / they are patterned and make patterns in time and space. As the broken tulips demonstrate, lives are involved and not simply evolved. Viruses connect. To be sure, these connections are sometimes far from welcome, and the technologies of keeping people, animals, plants and viral networks apart are often vital. But, at the same time, viral patterns remind us that we are not purely human, or purely tulip, and they are not purely viral. We exist in mixes. Striving for pure stock, during a foot-and-mouth outbreak, or pure, delineated and bounded human bodies, denies the inevitability of viroid lives and the geographies of living. As the scandal surrounding global drug pricing makes evident, viral patterns mix biology and political economy. Neither outsiders nor insiders, viruses are things, in the sense that they are assemblies made up of micro-organisms, immune systems, boardroom arguments, markets, debts, wars and so on.[10] It is as well to remember that solving some of the problems that viral patterns can generate requires a political imagination that links together, rather than holds apart, the various controversies that together make viruses into difficult things.

Lichens

Vanessa Winchester

Lichens are organisms that perfectly reflect the title of this book. Part algae, part fungi, not to be confused with moss, they pattern the landscape in multicoloured mosaics that grow almost unnoticed on any surface or crevice where there is light and moisture and not too much abrasion or pollution. I even had some on my old Morris Minor van, but their more usual habitats are rocks, trees and soil, which they cover with forms ranging from powdery effusions or crusts to minute stems, leafy patches or hairy tufts.

Apart from their uses for medicine, food, dyes, decorations and as perfume fixatives, lichens can tell us a great deal about what people do to the environment (indicative)

and what environments can do to people (predictive).

In the simplest sense, as environmental indicators, lichen-clad trees or stones have been widely used as landmarks and boundary markers since the earliest times. One particularly notable example was the hoar apple tree on Caldbec Hill where King Harold told his armies to meet before the Battle of Hastings in 1066. (The word hoar, Anglo-Saxon *har*, means a tree or stone that is grey or shaggy with lichen.[1])

The relevance of lichens as air pollution indicators was noticed in the nineteenth century as soot from industrialization increasingly darkened the landscape: Grindon in 1859 commented that 'the quality [of lichens near Manchester] has been much lessened of late years through the cutting down of old woods and the influx of factory smoke, which appears to be singularly prejudicial to these lovers of pure atmosphere.' However, almost a century was to elapse before the effect of air pollution on lichens began systematically to be mapped across Britain, following the establishment in the 1950s and '60s of a network of sulphur dioxide (SO_2) measuring stations.[2]

These maps show that lichen diversity declines as SO_2 levels increase. However, a complicating factor is that the presence or absence of species can also be minutely controlled by habitat. Moderately sensitive species may persist in quite polluted areas on surfaces having a high pH buffering the effects of acidity, or in places where vegetation or topography provides shelter or there is a high nitrogen input. Alternatively, species can be absent far from pollution sources due to acid rain or where high places catch the wind. Relict specimens clinging on from a former period when pollution levels were lower further complicate the pattern and reveal lichen tenacity despite sulphurous air that precludes the colonization of younger individuals. The good news is that, since the late 1960s, declining levels of SO_2 have led to reinvasion of some of the more sensitive species, even into the parks of London.

Lichens are also noted as monitors for a range of other pollutants, including radio-activity, metals, chemicals and gasses,[3] and rock-inhabiting lichens can be used as predictive tools for investigating land-forming processes and rates of environmental change. Estimates of how, when and at what rates changes are occurring in environments where they flourish are produced using lichenometry.

Lichenometry, in its original form,[4] relies on establishing lichen growth rates from size/age correlations. However, the technique is based on semi-assumptions that are difficult to verify: species growth rates vary both over time and space and sensitively depend on habitat and climate. In addition, although lichens could theoretically colonize almost any bare rock surface, this may not happen until the surface has become weathered. Consequently, both growth rates and colon-ization time lapses need to be investigated at each site. Due to these and other problems, the technique is best applied where some alternative independent dating framework can provide a measure of corroboration.

Despite these problems, useful results have been obtained in a large number of studies, with lichen dating often revealing far more than a simple date for rock surface exposure. For example, I have used lichen-ometry to investigate glacier retreat in Swedish Lappland, the French Alps, the Southern Andes and the Tien Shan Moun-tains where glaciers are fast retreating and where the big question concerns inter-hemisphere climatic synchronicity. Results from these studies show that glaciers in these regions are retreating fast and confirm that warming is likely to be a global phenomenon.

In another study, lichen dating suggests that human actions may be affecting exposed shorelines in the Bothnian Gulf in Sweden. Icebreakers, used to cut a shipping channel to the northern ports when the northern end of the Gulf freezes over, were re-routed in 1972 to bring the channel closer inshore. A lichen-ometric date of 1981 suggested a possible connection between icebreaker re-routing and changes in shoreline profile on a remarkable beach at Bådamalen (62°53′N 18°18′E), where, due to isostatic uplift, boulder ridges formed on the shoreline rise from the sea in a series of giant 'steps'. The three most recently formed ridges on the beach are approximately twice as high as any of the other ridges. The date of 1981 for the top of the third ridge suggested that this was formed by ice pressure during an especially stormy end to the winter of 1979, when ice floes, no longer separated from the land by 'fast' ice, were driven directly against the exposed lee shore.

A completely different use of the technique was an attempt to date ancient stone circles at Keswick in Cumbria and Great Rollright, Oxfordshire.[5] This attempt was doomed to failure, since stones weather and many lichen populations have doubtless come and gone in

65 The Rollright Stones as illustrated by Robert Plot (1677).

the 4,500 years since the circles were constructed. However, the studies showed that dating correlated with much more recent events in the circles, such as the re-erecting and cleaning of stones, and drew attention to persistent human interest in these monuments over the centuries.

Trees

Phil Macnaghten

My first taste of freedom was of climbing a tree, a tall elm at the end of the drive. At the time it appeared huge, awesome and deeply inviting. I remember those early experiences of climbing: hands on branch, reaching, stretching, pulling myself up into the heights, into that space of bliss at the top. I remember the feeling of being truly separate from the world of adults and parents for the first time. At the top of the tree my life had become literally my own, dependent on a mixture of skill, agility, judgement and above all risk taking. My experience of self and nature became embodied through such adventurous activity, in the immersed, participatory body of 'the climber'. Later, a childhood friendship became cemented through the mutual passion for climbing trees. And later still climbing trees became a refuge from the institutional cruelties and boredom of boarding school, where the act of climbing trees became a symbol of resistance against the sterile disciplinary regime.

These childhood memories were reawakened in a recent research project set up to explore why people like trees and what they mean in contemporary society. In the short essay that follows I provide a modest account of the intense and intimate personal signific-

ance that trees appear to have in Britain today and the ways in which this stems from the dynamic temporality of trees, their contribution to a sense of place, their life-enhancing qualities and their uniqueness.

Trees are alive, yet also fixed in the landscape. They live a long time, ranging from hundreds, even thousands of years. The life of a tree commonly exceeds that of humans. But trees, unlike, for example, mountains or rocks, are rarely static. Trees change both seasonally and annually, at a pace that unfolds often in symmetry with the unfolding relationships of people, families and communities. Trees mark history in 'lived' terms. As Ingold points out, 'people . . . are as much bound up in the life of the tree as is the tree in the life of the person'.[1] Trees thus exhibit a rhythmic pattern of persistence and change, from the swaying, bending and twisting of branches, to the growth of leaves and ripening of fruit, to eventual death and decay. Trees embody an intergenerational model of time.

Trees also embody time in a more evolutionary manner. Until comparatively recently, most human societies developed in the presence of trees. Trees pre-exist human societies yet have a contemporary form that reflects long and often bitterly contested historical patterns of custom, tradition and management. And until comparatively recently the relationship between people and trees was intimate and productive, reflected in customs of hunting, foraging, burning, beekeeping, building, grazing, and so on. The collective use and management of trees were thus central to the sustenance and ordering of social life. Only recently, and in what might be termed 'modernist' discourses, have trees tended to be conceived of in more abstract terms – as sources of biodiversity, or economic value, or even aesthetic appeal.

The above dynamics can help explain the complex and evolving ways in which trees are

66 Spring leaves.

commonly seen as symbols of the abstract notion of 'life'. Recent anthropological research shows that tree symbols often revolve around two essential qualities, vitality and self-generative power.[2] Hence the common use of tree materials in rituals used to mark the ongoing cycle of birth, menstruation, initiation into adulthood, marriage, parenthood and death; where the continuity and stability associated with trees comes to signify and 'naturalize' certain, fairly prescribed stages of life.

Trees are also signifiers in modern societies, playing a crucial role in structuring social relations. However, the role tends less to be one of sustaining 'life' at a local proximate level. Rather the values of life, continuity and stability – seen as embodied in trees – have often come to symbolize popular unease with elements of industrial modernity. The seasonality and longevity of trees become potent symbols of a nature under threat from modern, urban society. Road protesters place their bodies dangerously in the path of earth-moving machines to save trees, especially from roads and airports. Pressure groups fight illegal logging and deforestation, appealing to images of pristine rainforest and indigenous peoples whose 'traditional' forms of life are seen to coexist 'with' nature. Dying trees, victims of acid rain, become especially emotive icons for contemporary environmentalism.

Yet, people seem to be part of the unfolding temporality of the landscape in different ways. In a recent book entitled *Meetings with Remarkable Trees*, Thomas Packenham travels the length and breadth of Britain and Ireland to select 60 trees remarkable in age, size, shape and history.[3] Himself a member of the Anglo-Irish aristocracy, he describes the oak and beech trees, planted by his forebear seven generations ago, only now reaching their prime. On his travels he encounters barons and earls, viscounts and dukes, each of whom talk of particular trees as 'old friends' and 'companions', marking common reference points between themselves and their ancestors. Not all of us share such lineage. In our research young urban ethnic groups in particular felt disconnected from the intergenerational temporalities of trees and woodlands. The symbolism of 'English' trees and woods simply did not connect with everyday, multicultural realities. The resource of an 'intergenerational temporality' in which to oppose and resist an unwarranted modernity was simply unavailable.

Nevertheless, trees appear to have personal significance for most social groups in British society. In everyday life, the significance of trees is reflected in a wide variety of micro-practices, such as walking, rambling, picnicking, mushrooming, playing 'hide and seek', making dens and climbing. Woods and trees are seen as affording particular settings for tranquillity and bodily relaxation, where one can escape the perceived stresses of modern life. Trees remove the presence of modernity and provide a setting for intimate social relations, for therapy, for play, for fantasy, for revitalization. As one woman stated, 'as soon as our relationship gets under stress we need to go to the woods, and that really does us, it really sorts us out'. What many people desire are places that they see as free from signs of human interference and control, in which they experience a profound engagement with oneself or others through a 'raw' and unmediated nature.

Jungle

Hugh Raffles

Until recently, I did not know the collective noun to use for the Amazon. Both 'jungle' and 'rainforest' made me despair. Jungle was contaminated by its associates, corrupted by the bad company it had been hanging out with all these years. Rainforest might seem elevated and up to date: but scientized, managerial and trying to be spiritual, it had problems of its own.

To Amazonians, all those trees are the *mata*, a word that translates as 'woods' and suggests hunting and fishing, a familiarity, an accommodation. But God forbid you're lulled into letting your guard down, that you relax for a moment, lose your way, and end up walking, walking, walking, and it all looks familiar but not quite, and night comes down and the animals start calling and the monsters begin to stalk . . . Forget about woods and rainforests. That's when *mata* means jungle.

As a child, I loved the wildness of the tropical jungle. Like the other kids I knew, I crept into its mysteries through zoos and circuses and TV, finding a tangle of unpredictable excitements and pleasures. But even as that jungle spectacle inspired frantic games and lazy dreams, it was, we knew, only a confection. Somewhere out there lay something real. And we yearned for that sticky heat of authentic jungle-ness, the thrill of untamed surplus.

I remember an animal at Chessington Zoo in south-east England. I still feel its presence vividly. It was a once-wild animal, a lion – the absolute monarch in the jungle of our minds, no matter its yearnings for the open spaces of the savannah. And it was always there, cramped in its cage, with barely room to turn and nowhere to hide.

From time to time I'd meet up with my friends and we'd take the number 65 bus through the long brown stretches of suburban London. It was a full day out, with sandwiches and stories, endless jokes, and always new ways to skirt trouble. Some things – sensations mostly – catch in the memory with the tactility of the right-now. Without even closing my eyes I can feel myself leaning out and over the street from the window of the top deck, the hot breeze against the skin of my face, my smooth arm with its dark hairs bleached golden in the sunshine. And then – ducking back inside – scanning for movement and, quick, the giggling rush and grab of vacated seats, worming our way to the front for the panoramic view above the driver.

Oh, those days at the zoo! We dragged ourselves past the rodents, the penguins, the birds of prey, wolfing down our packed lunches as we went. It was always hot. We'd get tired, retreat to the cool darkness of the snake house. And then, before leaving: the lion. My dad had recited Stanley Holloway's 'Albert and the Lion' so many times that I knew exactly what happened if you got too close to the cage. Poor Albert had been swallowed whole; only his cap was left. But that was Blackpool. The Chessington beast was a mangy supplicant with a battered tin plate that he pushed under the bars with his paw, begging for food. We ignored the sign that warned us – for the animal's own good – not to feed him, and we dropped in whatever we had saved from lunch, our scraps poor penance weighted with a sense of loss.

Why is it so hard to see anything but our own creations in other creatures? We stared into that animal's defeated eyes and felt guilty for things we hardly understood but sensed were done in our name. The jungle was supposed to be our journey, and the zoo its point of departure. But what had happened? Jungle was a quest, a trial of endurance and self-knowledge; a voyage into histories of darkness and futures of light; into the horror, the horror, and the innocence of the primitive. Instead, the zoo gave us just that sense of loss, a nostalgia for something we had never really known.

And now I work in the Amazon, the greatest jungle of all. I won't deny the thrill of it. Recently – after so many years of trying to make the Amazon normal and everyday, trying to relativize its exoticism, coerce it into forests and woods – I've come once more to love it as a jungle, as a place of normal extremity, of real difference. I'm rediscovering the power of the jungle.

Find a way through the treachery, guilt and disappointments of the jungle and you find a way to come close to other beings without succumbing to the objectivism of science or a

67 'Albert's face and hands were quite clean' by John Hassall.

too-easy anthropomorphism. The power of the jungle is that it can never be tamed: once tamed, it's no longer jungle. But should you find it, should you meet its wildness, there'll be flashes of recognition, moments of transcendence and pulses of instability that will sweep you through the extremis of ecstasis and ground you in the depths of the intimate. Of course, if it really is the jungle, you'll only ever make it out of there insane. Isn't that the entire point of the jungle, after all?

Is there redemption in the wild? Even after feeding the lion we seemed to think so. For a few minutes we wandered around, a little flat, not really talking much. Then we found ourselves back on the top deck, chattering like monkeys, until one by one we dozed off in the failing sunshine as the bus took us home to the city.

Slums

Richard Dennis

In the beginning, a slum was just a single room – a place for slumber. For some it still is; who hasn't uttered, or ignored, those familiar words: 'your room is a slum'? But during the nineteenth century, State intervention and property speculation conspired to convert slums into areas, sufficiently large to warrant 'slum clearance'. Social commentators did

68 'Three kinds of metropolitan slum', 1934, by Catherine Bauer. The middle image depicts Farringdon Road Buildings.

discuss rural slums, but slums were overwhelmingly urban phenomena. Slums required density and an absence of fresh air. Slums seemed far from nature.

In her advocacy of 'modern housing' published in 1934, the American reformer Catherine Bauer illustrated 'three kinds of metropolitan slum' for which the only remedy was 'comprehensive planning'.[1] The first and third were slums of disorder: nature deformed in pollution and ill health, typified by Victorian back-to-backs, courts and cellar dwellings; or nature to excess, as in self-help Hoovervilles on city outskirts, where Depression-hit families turned to growing vegetables or keeping pigs, just as Irish immigrants had done in the mid-nineteenth century in shanty towns in Notting Dale in West London and the Upper West Side of New York, places still on the margins of their respective cities. But Bauer's second category were slums of excessive order, nature denied by the discipline of a misconceived modernity of purpose-built tenement blocks. Bauer's illustration of a 'built-in slum' depicted the Farringdon Road Buildings, erected in 1874 by the Metropolitan Association for Improving the Dwellings of the Industrious Classes and immortalized a decade later by George Gissing in his story of despair, demoralization and determinism among the London poor, *The Nether World* (1889). To Gissing, the buildings were 'barracks': 'housing for the army of industrialism. . . . Pass by in the night, and strain imagination to picture the weltering mass of human weariness, of bestiality, of unmerited dolour, of hopeless hope, of crushed surrender, tumbled together within those forbidding walls.' The only hint of nature lay in the 'mud-coloured surface' of the walls. More than 80 years after Gissing, when Farringdon Road Buildings were at last scheduled for demolition, they had evolved into more conventional slums, 'dark, damp, rotting', their human residents sharing space with black-beetles, cockroaches, mice and maggots.[2]

Were Gissing or Bauer writing today, their built-in slums would be the high-rise carbuncles of 1960s modernism, urinated, syringed, graffitied, permanently out of order. Meanwhile, the de-smogged intimacy of surviving inner-city terraces is cherished as evidence of 'community', and the spontaneous self-help of suburban shanties is commended for its organic improvisation.

High-rise slums would have challenged the Victorian imagination. You went *down* into slums, into the abyss. Slums were the bargain basement, home to society's remaindered stock, the 'residuum'. Slums were the source of the middle classes' deepest fears: of plague, disorder and revolution. Writing in 1902, Charles Masterman described the London poor as 'a cave bear emerging from his dark den', for the moment happy to 'gambol with heavy and grotesque antics in the sunshine'. But 'How long before, in a fit of ill-temper, it suddenly realizes its tremendous unconquerable might?'[3] And to B. S. Townroe in the late 1920s slums were responsible for 'disease, degenerate morals and communistic ideas'.[4]

To the Victorians, slums were *like* nature: an urban jungle. The East End of London was as impenetrable as the equatorial rain forest. Darkest England, like darkest Africa, was a place of savagery, brutality and gloom. Slums were damp places, malarial swamps, where morals were stained by the rising damp of idleness and misguided charity, and bodies were corrupted by miasmic vapours. Describing the inappropriately named Paradise Row, near King's Cross, George Godwin, editor of *The Builder*, noted the stench, animal faeces, vermin, cesspools and sheets of standing water in contrast to the lack of fresh, running water.[5]

For Masterman, the inner city resembled a forest where slum-dwellers constituted the undergrowth, 'driven under, forced to adapt themselves to unnatural surroundings, distorted into repulsive, twisted, grotesque forms of existence'.[6] Even Jack London, who lived in the East End for several months in the guise of an American seaman, and whose progressive socialist credentials were impeccable, depicted an East End 'slime', inhabited by 'gutter-wolves' and 'gorillas': 'The slum is their jungle, and they live and prey in the jungle.'[7]

Slums were also 'black spots', literally so on Charles Booth's Poverty Map of late nineteenth-century London. Booth coloured the streets of London from the gold of wealth to the blue of 'chronic want' and the black of the 'vicious, semi-criminal'.[8] But were they susceptible to 'improvement', like an agricultural estate or landscaped park, or good only for 'slum clearance': washable blue or permanent blue-black?

Victorian liberals blamed slum-dwellers for the slums: 'the pig made the sty'; if not pigs then rooks, migratory, precariously perched in garrets and cellars. 'Rookery' was a common epithet for slum. For Progressives, it was 'the sty that made the pig', but blame was seldom attributed – whether to builders, landlords or ground landlords – for making the sty in the first place. Somehow it was inevitable, a product of innumerable, separately rational decisions, that slums would emerge.

To Chicago ecologists (for whom ecology and economy were almost interchangeable), too, slums were part of the city's natural order, 'natural areas' defined by processes of invasion and succession. Yet, until Gerald Suttles's corrective analysis of 1968, *The Social Order of the Slum*, they were also considered *dis*ordered, socially disorganized, sites of 'deviant' subcultures.

On the assumption that there was no nature – no evidence of God's grand design – in slums, early Victorian missionaries encouraged an awareness of the natural world among slum-dwellers. At the very least there was plentiful scope for entomology! Yet slums were also part of a natural system adapted to socio-economic ends: the slime, sludge and slush, waste products all, diverted from their miasmatic destiny by night-soil collectors and sewage farms to boost agricultural productivity on the urban fringe.

For all their decay, slums were really very 'modern' places, classified and culturally constructed by outsiders as 'slums', although their residents rarely thought of themselves as 'slum-dwellers'. For all their unnaturalness, slums contained nature in abundance, most of all in the metaphors and imagination of reformers. But for slum residents, nature was some other place.

Buildings
Tim Ingold

When we speak of a building we generally have in mind some sort of artificial structure, made of relatively durable materials and fabricated by human hands. Its form is that of an enclosure, with foundations sunk in the ground, and of such a scale that one or more humans will fit inside, with room to spare to move about.

On closer inspection every one of these features of what we might call the 'prototypical building' turns out to be questionable in one way or another. In what follows I shall take up each in turn.

. . . some sort of artificial structure

A building, however ancient, has surely once been made. It has not grown over the generations like a tree, nor was it sculpted by geological forces like a cave. But how, exactly, are we to distinguish between making and growing, or between the forces of art and nature? Is it that in the making of artefacts we start with some sort of idea in mind, some design or representation, and end once that design has been realized in the form of a material structure? Is building an imposition of preconceived form upon raw material? Of course there may be a plan for the building,

but it is not from the plan that the form or structure of the building arises. Rather it arises from the more or less (often less) coordinated activity of builders, with their various skills, working over a period of time within a particular environmental setting. Nor is the building ever complete, for even to maintain its form it must be continually shored up against the effects of weather, or the invasions of animals, plants and fungi. Thus every building has a life history: of how it was raised and maintained, of how it, in turn, protected and nurtured the lives of those who grew up within its walls, and of how, perhaps, it eventually fell into ruin only for its remnants to be used in future projects.

. . . made of relatively durable materials

The kinds of materials that may be used in building are extraordinarily diverse, including stone, wood, mud, brick, dung, grass, turf, bones, snow, skins, corrugated iron, cardboard, glass, concrete, used drinks cans and old clothing. The durability of these materials varies greatly. Some – such as granite blocks – are virtually indestructible; others – such as straw – require periodic renewal. More importantly, however, their materiality is not an invariable that is given prior to, and independently of, the forms into which they are built. Rather, the properties of materials undergo significant changes partly related, partly unrelated, to their incorporation into the building process. Cut planks, for example, have very different properties from rough-hewn trunks, even though they may come from the same trees. The former gradually decay and have eventually to be replaced; the latter – though they may crack and twist with age – only gain in resilience as they do so.

. . . fabricated by human hands

Human builders work above all with their hands – they are manual labourers. Even in these days of prefabricated components and large-scale, mechanical equipment, skilled hands guide the work at every stage. Human beings, however, are apparently not the only builders. Termites build mounds, bees hives, birds nests and beavers dams. And in the process they use their mouths, teeth, beaks, claws and any other parts of the anatomy that come in handy. But are the constructions of nonhuman animals really buildings? Certainly they have life histories, just as human buildings do. Yet it is unlikely that the animal, embarking upon a building project, has any conception of the task before it – for if it did, it would be hard to explain why it should not experiment, as humans manifestly do, with alternative forms and procedures. If the essence of making lies in the prior conception of form, in advance of its realization in the material, then animals do not build. But if it lies in the skilled practical engagement of the animal with salient components of its environment, then they do.

. . . its form is that of an enclosure

A spatial division is thus set up between 'inside' and 'outside'. This does not mean, however, that the life of inhabitants is lived exclusively on the inside. Not every building is a prison, nor is dwelling the equivalent of occupation. Indeed the question of the relation between the building and its inhabitants is much like the old philosophical conundrum of the relation between body and mind. There is a school of thought that claims that the self is confined within the body, hidden behind the façade of its public persona expressed in dress and demeanour.

Likewise the individual, private lives of inhabitants are said to be hidden within the walls and exterior decorations of buildings that present their outward, social face to the world. But in our lived experience, the self is not locked in the body but open to its surroundings; thus the mind overflows into the environment. And so, too, the life of inhabitants overflows into gardens and streets, fields and forests. In the contrary direction, just as the world pours into the mind through the senses, so the environment pours into the building, giving rise to characteristic echoes of reverberation and patterns of light and shade. The significant division, then, is not so much between inside and outside, as between the movement 'from the inside going out', and 'from the outside going in'.

. . . with foundations sunk in the ground

Once erected, buildings are generally considered to be immovable. They are secured to foundations that are part of the bedrock, to piles that are driven deep into the ground or – occasionally – to the stumps or trunks of trees that are similarly rooted. In this sense, buildings are quite different from tents. They cannot readily be packed up and taken to another place. Tents, along with other such moveable dwellings as yurts and tipis, are tensile structures, comprising a frame of rigid poles and flexible cords, covered with soft material and fastened with knots and bindings. Buildings, by contrast, are adhesive structures, composed of solid blocks and plastic fillers, and held together by the sheer weight of blocks or beams placed atop one another. However, even buildings may be transportable. A timber house can be taken apart, piece by piece, and reassembled on another spot.

Some buildings can even be transported by truck and trailer. But once they are equipped with wheels themselves, they become caravans and mobile homes.

. . . of such a scale that one or more humans will fit inside, with room to spare to move about

We need the first criterion to distinguish buildings from chests, trunks and storage boxes, and the second to distinguish them from such structures as sentry boxes and telephone kiosks. Yet buildings can be of a very much larger or smaller scale. Paradoxically, the larger the building, the less people tend to move about in it. Many of these buildings are places of work, such as factories or office blocks, where everyone has their allotted station and where movement is mechanical, by lift or conveyor. At the other extreme are the buildings that humans make to house animals significantly smaller than themselves, such as kennels, hutches and dovecotes, or buildings inhabited by miniature humans, such as the ubiquitous doll's house.

Let us say, then, that a building is a condensation of skilled activity that undergoes continual formation even as it is inhabited, that it incorporates materials that have life histories of their own and that may have served time in previous structures, living and non-living, that it is simultaneously enclosed and open to the world, that it may be only semi-permanently fixed in place, and that it affords scope for movement in inverse proportion to its scale. Buildings, in short, are not so different from organisms. They are raised and nurtured in an environment that includes, most importantly, their human as well as nonhuman builders-cum-inhabitants; they embody – in the life that goes on within them – their rela-

tions with their surroundings; and they figure as an integral part of the environment in which the manifold beings to be found in and around them grow up and live their lives.

Archives

Miles Ogborn

Memory is chemical and biological. The storehouses of memory, the central cortices of social formations of print and the written world, are ecologies where the materials of remembrance are living, dying and being devoured. The continuation of written cultures depends upon managing the nature of old and stretched animals' skins, pulped and reshaped wood or rags, and chemical compounds on tapes or disks.

Memories fade, and archives are fighting the decay and deterioration that time's chemistry brings. The medium holds the message, and some media – nitrate film, thermofax and newsprint – lose their hold faster than others. In the 1940s US libraries – prompted by pioneers such as William Barrow and the Council on Library Resources – began laminating and de-acidifying their collections with alkaline salts to prevent the embrittlement of pages of acidic paper by hydrolytic degradation. Some books had to be sacrificed so that others could be saved. Specific notions of value meant that Richard Smith's PHD research at the University of Chicago in the late 1960s destroyed multiple remaindered copies of *Cooking the Greek Way* as he developed a solvent-based de-acidification process that could treat other books without their paper swelling and their ink bleeding. Much earlier, in 1855, the 'Fading Committee' of the Photographic Society of London set about trying to ensure the future of photography on paper as a reliable holder of memory by investigating the gradual disappearance of images. Their conclusion – that it was all in the processing – has been questioned by more recent research, which, drawing on the food industry's interest in knowing the nature of egg dehydration and the causes of discoloration in egg rolls, now suggests that for everything from albumen prints to microfilm it is the storage conditions that are crucial.

The ecology of archiving is a matter of heat, light and, most of all, water. If the paper on which words and images are stored is to be usable it must contain water. Under normal library conditions 7 per cent of these collections of knowledge should be water. Without it the cellulose molecules cannot be held apart and move as the fibres flex, and the paper begins to break. Books and manuscripts are hygroscopic. They are always trying to maintain their equilibrium with their environment. As the temperature and moisture content of the air changes so the books absorb or expel moisture, expanding and contracting as they do so. More importantly, the elements of the books – paper, covers of leather or cloth, the sizing that holds the pages in – expand or contract at different rates. Books can literally pull themselves apart as their volumes change. Librarians and archivists are recommended to keep the temperature at 16–21°C and the relative humidity at 40–50 per cent. The books would like it to be much colder, but the readers need some zone of comfort.

Other species are part of the ecology of the archive. At above 21°C and 70 per cent relative humidity certain fungi begin to thrive in the low latitudes of collections where things are warm and moist and the wind does not blow too hard. Moulds and mildews spin out their masses of branching filaments (*hyphae*) into dense cobwebs (*mycelium*) and release spores into the air. These fungi absorb nutrients from the dead or living organic matter on which they grow. For them books are good sources of cellulose and starches, albeit hard to digest. Their consumption softens up the books and may re-colour pages and images. Some are poisonous to humans, including the highly toxic strain found in the basement of the Museum of Contemporary Art in New York in 1990. Some are just a nuisance when they use the library. In 1997 the undergraduate library of the University of California at San Diego had to be quarantined after it was taken over by the mould *Aspergillus* and the book lice that feed on it. The only solution was to freeze and clean the entire collection. In other places and times archival fungi have been starved of oxygen, irradiated and vacuumed up. It has, however, become recognized that chemical fungicide is no longer acceptable, but more because of the friendly fire suffered by readers who got in the way or licked their fingers after turning treated pages.

Along the food chain, these organisms are fed on by creatures that also like dampness and high relative humidity. Book lice (*psocids*) are all-female parthenogenetic communes of minute, soft-bodied insects that are transparent when young and become opaque as they age. They move with a jerky, halting and hopping motion, graze on microscopic fungi and convert books and paper to their own non-literate uses during their short lives. So-called book worms are the larvae of some 160 species of beetle, including *Anobium domesticum, Anobium eruditus, Anobium punctatum, Acarus cheyletus, Acarus eruditus, Dermestes lardarius* (better known as the larder beetle), *Aecophora pseudospretella, Sitodrepa panaceum* (aka the drugstore beetle), *Attagenus pellio, Ptinus fur* (the spider beetle, first mentioned by Linnaeus in 1766), *Antharinus varius, Lyctus brunneus* (alias the

69 A 'Book Worm' (*Rhizopertha dominica*)

powder-post beetle), *Catorama mexicana* (or the Mexican book beetle) and *Rhizopertha dominica*.

All will drill their tunnels through books and bookshelves alike, reducing art to dust. They have, to more or less effect, been tackled in the past with alum and vitriol (sulphuric acid), beeswax, benzene, bitumen, borax, camphor, chilli, cinnamon, cloves, copper, creosote, formaldehyde, kerosene, khuskhus, lavender, mercuric chloride, nitro-benzene, musk, myrrh, naphthalene, nicotine, ozone, pennyroyal, pepper, petrol, sandal-wood, sassafras, snuff, thyme, turpentine, vermouth and wormwood. It is currently more customary to re-engineer the environ-ment, to make the archive a comparative desert or tundra, and, where that does not work, to slaughter them with hydrogen cyanide, carbon disulphide or methyl bromide. Finally, certain collections may be host to *Lepisma saccharina* (silverfish), which will feed on the glazed surfaces of photo-graphs, or even small rodents chewing the past into fragments. Organisms are living now off the images of moments passed and munching on memories.

So the nature of cultural memory matters and so does the political economy of that nature. The recommendations of the Euro-pean Meeting on Paper Preservation aim to 'enhance awareness of the risks threatening the memory of Europe'. Across the Atlantic, if the rights and freedoms of the American people are preserved by the Charters of Freedom – the Declaration of Independence, the Constitution and the Bill of Rights – then those parchments are in turn preserved by encasements designed by the National Institute of Standards and Technology, NASA, the National Archives and Records Adminis-tration Service and the Heery International construction corporation. Pure titanium cases; layers of cellulose-only paper; gold-plated ultra-smooth sealing surfaces; 74 steel bolts providing a sealing pressure of 50 newtons per millimetre; built-in pressure, temperature and relative humidity sensors; and ports for spectroscopic analysis of the interior keep the parchments free from oxidation and surrounded by argon gas at a constant 19.4°C and 40 per cent RH. It is only the rich and powerful that can afford to remake nature to defy time and decay.

Streets

Chris Otter

'Paving', declared J. E. Newton, President of the London Association of Foremen Engineers, in 1877, was 'the great question of the day'.[1] Falling horses, slipping pedestrians, endless maintenance and cacophonous rattle threatened the harmonious circulation of traffic and the urbane sociability upon which the vitality of the modern city relied. Materially reconstructing the pavements of London, Newton argued, would enable the equine and human populations of the capital to travel less hazardously, and the commodi-ties and capital from which London drew its strength to circulate more securely. In short, he suggested, the material, the animal and the human could be mutually adjusted for the good of all.

Granite and macadam surfaces, it was apparent, were noisy and slippery, as well as being hard on horses and wheels. Civil engineers had experimented with an assortment of materials to counteract such perils: along with asphalt, glass, rubber and even grass infused with resin and tar, wood aroused particular interest and excitement as a potentially civilizing, 'softening' technology. The road builder Henry Allnutt, who re-laid Kensington High Road with wood blocks in 1880, emphasized the gentleness of his surface, speaking of 'the silence of wood compared with the intolerable noise of the traffic over stones', and its 'infinite advantage to that noble, docile and invaluable creature – the horse', quoting statistics proving that the average horse slipped every 446 miles on wood compared to every 132 miles on granite. Wood, he continued, was apposite for all gradients, unlike asphalt, which could become treacherously slippery; 'it is like walking on ice.'[2]

Various hardwoods, including pine and eucalyptus, were being deployed at that time consciously to improve the speed and ease of metropolitan circulation. By 1892 it was possible to traverse the City of London entirely on wood pavements. In addition to its kindness to hooves, ligneous paving, by actively reducing noise, promised to reduce the distractions and neuroses associated with the increasing level of street vibration and clatter, which was being blamed for everything from overwork, poor concentration and stress to insomnia and alcoholism. Street surfaces, then, are intimately associated with social questions, and, in examining why these quixotic projects ultimately failed to encrust Britain's roads in mahogany or hemlock, the inability of engineers to cajole and force the material world to induce palpable social effects is apparent.

Like rivers and mountain passes as well as canals, tramlines and railways, streets are not

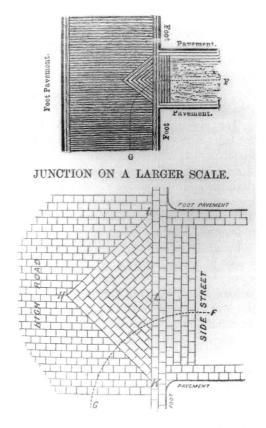

JUNCTION ON A LARGER SCALE.

70 Henry Allnutt's wood pavement on Kensington High Road, 1880.

everlasting routes etched into the face of the earth. In order to become relatively durable, they require the cooperation of humans (workmen, pedestrians, cleaning systems), matter (which must be resilient and cohesive) and atmosphere (by avoiding corrosive chemicals, dampness and climactic extremes). If these elements are harmonized, the street's fundamental impermanence can be masked. In the case of wood paving, the ineluctable tendency of organic matter to decay was the initial problem. Allnutt estimated the limit for a hardwood surface as seven years, before it needed to be removed, chopped up, sold as firewood and replaced. Coating with creosote gave the wood a tough shell against fickle English weather, but this gradually eroded beneath cantering hooves and speeding carriages. Once this process was underway, the surface itself was inexorably permeated by rain, dung, urine and smoke.

The subterranean world, then, was where the failings of wood pavements really became manifest. Ostensibly solid and resilient, the streets soon had 'little or nothing to prevent the fibres and pores of the wood from becoming saturated with rain water and other far more noxious liquids', which collected in hidden, putrid pools, the particles of which 'subsequently escape in the form of poisonous gases and miasma'. In summer, this desiccated matter was 'disseminated into the air we breathe, and it [was] not difficult to predict its effect upon delicate and sometimes unsound pulmonary organs'.[3] Designed explicitly to reduce wear on carthorse hooves and the ears of over-wrought clerks, these pavements provided a perfect haven for the clotted, toxic detritus of the Victorian street, and accordingly rotted from the bottom up. In New Orleans, in 1879, a terrible epidemic was principally blamed on emanations from wood pavements. Other material qualities of wood militated against its use on the street; during a fire in Chicago in 1871, newly laid blocks helped to spread the flames. Increasing use of underground electric cables added another variable to this perilous equation.

Maps suggest that streets are permanent (unbroken, virile lines of black or vermilion), two-dimensional (a surface, hard and strong) and non-social (devoid of people or animals). The example of wood paving demonstrates that streets have lifespans that are intimately related to the traffic, atmosphere and earth that envelop them. A street is a site where nature, society and matter meet and mingle, a permeable membrane on, through and under which bodies, pipes, dust and liquids ambulate, circulate, dribble, sink and collect. To succeed, it must secure the maximum circulation of traffic (without which no economy can flourish) while minimizing the dangers and nuisances to the public. Modifying human practices, as well as animal performances, required roadways less vulnerable to the unyielding siege of a modern, messy and complicated urban environment.

Experiments with wood paving continued beyond 1900, but gradually declined thereafter. Although designed as a material technology through which to promote bodily motion, health and concentration, traffic circulation, and ease the wear on horses, its organic frailties generated problems for human health and vehicles alike. Virulent disease, decomposing foundations and frequent maintenance were not conducive to the socio-economic harmony of London, Manchester or New York.

Streets have widely varying lifespans, from a few years to millennia. Compared to Roman roads, those seemingly timeless chords of stone that pattern the ground of Britain, wood paving might seem somewhat inglorious and pitifully ephemeral. Yet fragments of it obstinately endure, according to one historian, in at least one backstreet in Bloomsbury, demonstrating its powers of persistence.[4]

Subways

Maria Kaika

'I work where the Madeleine breathes', she had said the previous night, with a smile that conveyed a mixture of irony and genuine amusement. Marshall knew he should have been less of a coward and asked for her phone number. Now he wanted to find her. He had worked out that she lived and worked in London: her knowledge of the city revealed someone who wears her feet regularly on its streets. But where? Maybe if he figured out where the Madeleine breathed? Not an easy riddle. It sounds like an exotic flower. But where can a wild flower 'breathe' in the middle of bloody London?

He is a city lover himself. But when it comes to Madeleines – or any other flower for that matter – he is not just ignorant, he is a convicted foe. He profoundly detests those 'loonies', as he calls them, who spend their Sundays looking for different species of flowers, trees and other kinds of nature in the city. He believes that such activity is a perversion; if they love nature that much, why don't they go and live in the Cotswolds? Needless to say, Marshall has a genuine aversion for the rural. The mere thought of it – a place where he would have to suffer the caprices of nature and negotiate his time with the natural world – gives him the creeps. He is thankful to the big city and to its 'men of good will' who had carefully disposed of nature, just for him, the city dweller.

It is not exactly that you can't find nature in the city; what amazes him though is how controlled it is wherever it appears: although, admittedly, on occasion it does run wild. Water runs plentiful and clean through his tap, but only when he wants it to, and then at his preferred temperature; his waste disappears gratefully down the drain; air comes purified and at the right temperature out of his air-conditioning system. Mind, his city even caters for the 'loonies': if they want parks and wildlife, they can get them – safely controlled and managed, mostly.

Paradoxically, for Marshall such places also were part of the pleasure of the city. He

would occasionally walk through Hyde Park, enjoying the whispers of those around him. There's nothing Marshall loves more than being a *flâneur* in his city. But right now, no matter how hard he tried, he could not recall any place in London where Madeleines could be found.

On that Sunday afternoon, laziness invited him to conduct some further research on the flower (all right . . . and the woman!), just for fun, to pass the time. He looked for further clues: 'Madeleines could perhaps grow next to rivers . . . '. Rivers. Right. This was a good place to start. However, he could not immediately bring to mind any river flowing through London, other than the Thames. And, in his experience, the banks of the Thames were filled up with concert halls and film theatres and fancy restaurants and sleek office buildings, but he couldn't recall seeing even one wild flower, dead or alive. The matter really intrigued him now.

Marshall googled 'London' and 'Rivers': the search engine listed a large number of hits. He never imagined that there would be so many rivers running through London. He went on; clicked on a website about 'The Fleet'. He read about the river as it was in the seventeenth century; about how it was an open sewer that stank, as it carried Londoners' foul dirt – dead puppies, Jonathan Swift had said – to the Thames. The thought made him shiver. Does the river still run underneath his feet? If so, where does it go? Is there a danger of it ever flooding? Does it reach his tap? Would it be safe to have a house on that street? Then Marshall remembered having read about the multi-million pound basement flats in the centre of London being in danger of flooding because of the rising water table. Suddenly, he found an anger rising within him as he recalled the £75 million subsidy that the Government had paid just to pump water out from under London's – his! – feet. He couldn't bear to think of Madeleines down there.

Despite being unsettled by this subterranean London, Marshall was captivated and intrigued as to what lay beneath his feet, the erotic encounter with the 'Madeleine' woman now receding from his memory. His certainty that nature had been safely contained within, or expelled from, the city began to dissolve. In fact, as he now realized, a dangerous nature ran still beneath his feet: invisible, yet always there, present and hidden at the same time. A shuddering thought came to his mind: who controls these subways? who is responsible for the subterranean networks, the veins of his city? what if one day they failed to deliver his water, or electricity or e-mails?

His search changed direction once again. Marshall now wanted to investigate the city's subways, craving for more discoveries. So, what else lies down there, apart from the obvious passages for London Underground? For fun's sake, he types 'Subways and London' in the search engine's window. Scrolling down the results list, he is struck to see one of them featuring the word 'Madeleine' next to 'London Underground'. Marshall's memory sparks: Madeleine! He nervously clicks on the hyperlink, the memory of the woman flooding back unwittingly. 'Madeleine: the new French aroma that will perfume London's underground: on trial from tomorrow on Victoria line.'

Marshall laughs a nervous long laugh: the Underground stinks! He feels compelled to smell Madeleine's scent. He gets up and heads out towards the Underground station. That's it then, he thinks, she works for the London Underground! That explains the breadth of her knowledge of the city! He reaches the Victoria line. Gets into a carriage looking around in all directions, hoping it

will be she who checks his ticket, that she will be at the next station. A sweet, flowery smell mixed with sweat and grime welcomed him in subways of the Underground; so this is Madeleine's breath, he thought, wryly smiling to himself. All too soon, the smell of Madeleine subsided, giving way to that of urine, stale beer and unwashed bodies. And, as the sweet perfume disappeared, so did his hopes of ever finding his 'Madeleine' again.

Cities

Steve Pile

For many, the city represents the epitome of all that human hands and minds can achieve – it is civilization embodied. So it was for Robert Park, a leading member of the renowned Chicago School of Sociology. For him, people in cities had a civilized mentality characterized by a scientific mode of thought. Cities created a scientific mentality because they demanded of their citizens a capacity for detachment, for critical reflection, for rationalism, for logical thought, for calculation, for exchangeability between things and for an ability to understand the relationship between means and ends – all key features of science. Indeed, cities were a visible sign of the successful application of this way of thinking. You could see it in the concrete, glass and metal – and in the very machines that are found in, and indeed make, cities. Elsewhere, Park hypothesized, 'uncivilized' peoples were (still) in thrall to magic. Thus, the measure of civilization – of urbanity – was (the abandonment of) magic: 'magic may be regarded . . . as an index, in a rough way, not merely of the mentality, but of the general cultural level of races, peoples, and classes'.[1]

To show that city culture was a higher stage of cultural development, Park wished to apply his magical measure of civilization to a 'living laboratory'. For this, he chose the West Indies. Here, Park asserted, there existed relatively isolated social units. Untouched by 'modernity', island cultures were sites where the dichotomy between city culture and folk culture could truly be determined. By examining West Indian cultures, he argued, the inherent predispositions of relatively 'uncivilized' peoples / races / classes could be revealed (as if he were Darwin on the Galápagos Islands). This unquestionably racist – and perverse – logic propelled Park forward: the belief in obeah, he averred, demonstrated that West Indian folk cultures were distinct from, and beneath, American urban cultures. There are at least 101 ways to take this argument apart, but in this piece I will suggest two: (1) that America's city cultures are inextricably intertwined with magical mentalities; and (2) that cities themselves should be understood as magical sites.

While Park notes that West Indian magic is to be found in parts of American cities, he makes it seem as if the appearance of magic in cities is somehow both external to the city and also constantly being undermined by the civilizing, scientific influence of city life. If Park had been less anxious about distinguishing between the West Indies and urban America, he might have noticed a long and intimate history of influence and connection between the two. Of course, these connections were drawn from the earliest colonizations of the American continent and the Caribbean, particularly by the Spanish and French. In fact, the Spanish and French were transferring slaves between West Africa and the Caribbean and the American South in vast numbers throughout the eighteenth century. From the earliest moments of contact, various West African religious beliefs

71 New York scrying.

were mixed together, and mixed again with various Roman Catholic practices, to make syncretic varieties of 'obeah' – or voodoo. In fact, voodoo in America is a particularly urban set of practices and beliefs, whether in New York or New Orleans.[2]

In New Orleans, the particular circum-Atlantic mixing of West African and Catholic beliefs led to a set of magical practices based on herbal remedies, divination and casting spells. In these practices, rituals were (and are) used to formulate and express wishes, and various elements used to create spells. These elements were – and are – highly eclectic mixings of human and nonhuman elements, everything from snakes and skulls to Malibu rum and fags, all designed to appeal to the particular voodoo god (or saint) capable of delivering the wished-for outcome. In some ways, of course, this voodoo is urban simply because it is performed in the city. More than this, however, cities act as alchemical sites by bringing together different – even conflicting – peoples and beliefs and mixing them into new syncretic forms. And, part of this magic is the particular mix of the spiritual, the natural and the human in the creation of its practices.

But, maybe, the city is itself magical. A resident of New York, the urban shaman Chris Penczak, would certainly like to think so: 'Many of those in rural settings think they have a monopoly on what is natural, magical, and spiritual. They don't. Everything is natural.'[3] Everything – including the city, including the elements that go to make up cities, including the concrete, glass and metal. In a fine alchemy, cities connect and combine energies, elements of nature (earth, air, water, fire) and spirits. Magic is everywhere, according to this logic, in cities: in their machines, in their buildings, in their flora and fauna, in their territories. Skyscrapers, in particular, connect worlds, from deep in the earth, to high in the sky (see illus. 71). Instead of seeing the city, science and civilization in opposition to, or higher than, nature, magic and the wild, Penczak wishes urban dwellers to (re)connect the various worlds, using shamanic rituals and practices (including some drawn from voodoo). In this way, he argues, a new harmony and settlement can be achieved between the unseen and secret (super-, natural) forces creating life. Even if this outcome seems fanciful, perhaps there is something in this. Even if we cannot close our eyes and conjure up a better city, perhaps at least we might think that science and magic could help us formulate and express our heartfelt wishes for a better city – perhaps a networked city guided by the spider totem (think of New York's *Spider-Man*, or of World Wide Webs!) – or a magical city full of spirit and energy, wisdom and charm.

Organics
Andrew Barry

Juan had lived all his life in a remote area of Portugal, several hours from Lisbon. His dream was to retire from his job and work on his own farm with his wife and children. But for most of the year Juan was not at home. When I met him he had been visiting an organic farm in northern Italy. Generally he spent his time criss-crossing Europe. One week he would be visiting tomato growers in Spain, another week it would be potato farmers in Egypt and another, as it was today, a mixed organic producer near Ravenna. Most weekends he would return to his house in Portugal, but never for very long.

Michel Callon has written about what he calls the 'economy of qualities'.[1] In Callon's account the existence of markets depends on a vast number of experts of quality who mediate between the world of objects and the world of consumers. Juan was just such a specialist. He knew all about the relations between the attitude and skill of farmers, chemical fertilizers, regional weather conditions, the properties of potatoes, the interests of supermarkets and the habits of their customers. It was precisely because he understood so well the ways in which potatoes and other vegetables are entangled in relations with other natural and social things that he knew how to disentangle them from these relations. He was an expert in reification. He showed me pictures that he had taken on his digital camera of the potatoes he had just inspected. Each potato was photographed in isolation so that the viewer could see clearly any marks on the surface, which might be evidence of disease. Larger scale photographs showing lines of potato plants gave similar indications of the state of the soil and the quality of the crop as a whole. The following day these images would be mailed as attachments to a potential customer.

At that time, Juan worked for a company based near Canary Wharf in London that acted as an importer for several of the leading supermarket chains in Britain. I met his boss, Greg Johnson, at the company offices to discuss the organics business. Unlike Juan he did not tend to visit individual growers, but he had a PhD in agriculture, and he trusted Juan's judgement. For many consumers, organics represents purity in a world of contamination, pollution and risk. For Juan and Greg, the consumers of organic produce are not deluded. Although the company they worked for also deals with conventional produce, they ate organics whenever they could. Juan had warned me never to eat tomatoes from Spain out of season. Many Spanish growers simply did not follow the instructions given to them by the agrochemical companies about how much pesticide to use. Greg laughed at the way in which Londoners liked to put lemon in their mineral water. The skin of most citrus fruits, he noted, was saturated with chemicals.

For Greg and Juan, however, the difference between organics and conventional produce was not just a question of purity. Indeed, from one point of view, produce grown by conventional methods was more pure. Protected by chemicals, conventional crops were more resistant to the peculiarities of social and physical geography. The trouble with organic produce was that it was much more thoroughly entangled in locality. Its availability varied considerably, depending

72 A field of organic potatoes in northern Italy, June 2001.

on the time of year, the region, the weather condition and the local farming culture. In speaking of the timing of organic production, Greg mapped out a complex trajectory. From July to October, local (British) produce was available. However, British produce did not tend to store well, so that by November it was necessary to rely on foreign suppliers. For some reason (he couldn't fully explain why) German and Austrian organic potatoes lasted later into the season. By December, however, it was necessary to rely on produce from Israel. His opinion was that while Israeli organic farming methods were good, sensitive chemical tests would almost certainly reveal residual quantities of potent chemicals such as methyl bromide that had been used prior to the introduction of organics. In April, produce from southern Europe was available once again.

In thinking about politics, commentators have tended to focus their attention on conventional political institutions and actors. Juan and Greg clearly didn't see their role as a political one at all. They were doing a professional job. But, even for them, politics could not be kept entirely outside the frame. Much of the regulatory work in the organics business was, after all, delegated by governments to organizations such as the Soil Association that, from one perspective, could be seen as part of a social movement. A militant regulator! At the same time, as experts in the field, Juan and Greg were acutely aware of the importance of the politics of quality. Juan told me the story of a leading British supermarket that insisted that a particular chemical was not used on the farms of its producers in the UK after its effects had been publicized by the media, while ignoring its widespread use on a number of the farms of their suppliers in other countries.

For some, organics represents the possibility of a return to a more natural state that existed prior to the development of agrochemicals, supermarkets and government regulators. But to see it as a return to nature would be a mistake. Although organics does represent an alternative, the nature that is produced relies on a remarkable level of artifice. The designation 'organic' does not represent an absence of technology. Rather it depends on the use of forms of technology and expertise that are attuned to the peculiarities of geography.

73 A Paris café.

Food

Lisa Law

> If you are lucky enough to have lived in Paris as a young man, then wherever you go for the rest of your life, it stays with you, for Paris is a moveable feast.
> Ernest Hemingway (1950)[1]

The Lost Generation of American expatriates who inhabited the cafés of Paris in the 1920s could appear an odd starting point for thinking about food. Young men the likes of Ernest Hemingway and F. Scott Fitzgerald – as well as women such as Alice Toklas and Sylvia Beach – are far better known for the taste of their words than the food they may have mentioned in passing. Disillusioned by the First World War and life in the postwar American city, Hemingway and his compatriots found exilic comfort and creativity in the daily rhythms of Parisian cafés where they wrote, dined and drank with friends. Hemingway's memoir, *A Moveable Feast* (1964), recollects this literary landscape through colourful descriptions of struggles against hunger (both imposed and self-inflicted) and a myriad of tastes. That memories of food and place might fuse in Paris is, perhaps, unremarkable given its culinary repute. The bread, *eau-de-vie*, chestnuts and oysters that Hemingway describes were tasted and remembered, and in his memoirs he re-consumes these pleasures across time and space through memories and language. His narrative suggests a Paris that was embodied in memory and sense during the 1920s and passionately recalled in the writing of his book. Food plays a central role in these embodiments and recollections, and in mapping an enduring sensory route through the city.

In a world of mobility these interconnections between food, memory and sense of place seem relevant. The desire to share a meal with compatriot friends is a well-known yearning for dislocated people around the world – be they expatriates, exiles, refugees or migrants, or more sedentary communities whose local worlds have become less familiar through globalization. Yet for Hemingway, unlike many displaced people, fulfilling this desire was not achieved through consuming nostalgic cuisine. Hemingway's longings were not for home cooking but a cosmopolitan milieu; his hunger not for hotdogs or apple pie but *pâté de foie gras* and *café au lait*. French gastronomy propelled his re-embodiment in this different Parisian world, helping to mould an identity that was bound up with cosmopolitan longing and desire. Food and identity thus complexly entwine, weaving together the sociality and culture of Paris that Hemingway consumed. Perhaps it was not food per se that was eaten and digested, but a more enduring sense of place that pulled these diverse meanings together.

Food memories – particularly those of childhood but also those that attach to other significant events or places – are often memories of social relations. It is not individual menus that Hemingway recalls, for example, but a more encompassing sociality of Paris and his own placement within it. Eating food is one means through which identities and relations are constituted and gain meaning, and what is eaten with whom and the manner of preparation is also about the symbolic organization of culture. As anthropologists have long been aware, cooking and eating are part of the means by which 'nature' (raw food) becomes 'culture' (meals). There is obviously more to eating than the simple scenario of satiating biological hunger, but Hemingway's memoirs also imply a more complex relation at the interface of the nature / culture divide. It is not sitting down to a meal that gets his memories of Paris

flowing, as the more common-sense view would presume, it is memories of Paris that trigger the concurrent flow of his saliva and words. Perhaps nature is already cultured and culture already natured, and our yearnings culture our supposedly natural desire to eat. In other words the smell of bread baking or coffee brewing can set off memories that simultaneously invest our cravings and saliva with symbolic meaning. Perhaps memory too is a kind of hunger.

Hemingway's Parisian reminiscences intimate a sensuousness of both experience and thought, and therefore more embodied ways of knowing and remembering: a visceral state. These links between place, memory and the body insinuate the importance of the several senses – taste, touch, smell, sound and vision – in constituting meanings that shape individual sensibilities and different ways of being in the world. The multi-sensuous character of food helps to embody Hemingway in Paris. The taste of fried *goujon*, the smell of coffee and the feel of oysters on his tongue combine with the smoky colour of afternoon light and the cold feel of winter to produce a 'sense' of Paris that is his alone. This sense of the city is a different kind of map. Paris is known through the memories and sense that cohere in his body, and it is his body that remembers place.

Food is enmeshed with these dialectical processes of naturing culture and culturing nature. Eating food is how we satiate a biological need through complex social and symbolic systems that help to organize the meaningful rhythm of daily life. Yet the visceral state that this engenders, and the embodied memories that linger long after we have physically moved on, suggests that traces of what we eat somehow remain with us. We may even hunger for them. These foods help to embody a sense of place and, like Hemingway's Paris, become a movable feast.

Livestock

Mike Crang

Farms in geography seem at once a rather over-emphasized terrain, while at the same time being generally seen as a residual and declining category. Generations of children still learn about putative crop patterns on putative isolated, undifferentiated plains. The environmental synthesis so often spoken about frequently comes down to agriculture reshaping the landscape. Meanwhile, as an arena of study, farms have come to be seen as intellectually uninteresting as the economic significance of agriculture in industrialized nations declines. My aim here is not to make any claim for the centrality of agriculture, but rather to consider farms as an arena for thinking through the way that different spatialities collide and conflict – connected to some surprising spaces and separated from others. I want to do this principally in the context of British agriculture, largely since it is the example that I know best. I want to make these connections through two objects – a bucket and a fly screen.

Bucket

The British 'yeoman' farmer has been a conservative symbol (and voter), credited with prompting capital accumulation and efficient production enabling the rise of industry and compelling the migration of people to become an urban proletariat. The symbol of the family farm, of proud self-reliance, has been invoked repeatedly – as a model of citizenship, as national model in post-war attempts at national self-sufficiency – and in diverse (and contradictory) ways extolling property ownership, notions of generational stewardship and economic rationality. All of this was brought rather pointedly into relief in 2001, when an outbreak of foot-and-mouth disease swept through swathes of the country. Suddenly, farmers were seen behind thin and apparently futile lines of disinfectant-sodden straw at their gateways – isolated and beleaguered. I want to use foot-and-mouth to highlight how contradictory spaces collide on the farm.

After several food scares, governments across Europe had introduced tougher environmental policing. From contaminated offal in the BSE saga, to sewage in French cattle feed, governments had been given ample cause to act to increase hygiene requirements. The result was an escalation of overhead costs and a move to fewer larger capacity plants, and consequently the demise of local abattoirs that entailed animals being driven hundreds of miles to slaughter. The scale of movement meant that outbreaks of disease were no longer geographically localized but instead followed a web of corporate connections. Alongside this was a subsidy regime where estimates in 2000 put the average subsidy to a British hill farmer at £30,000, while their annual income was estimated at £9,000 – begging the question of who gets the difference. The subsidy is administered per sheep and has led to over-stocking to maximize earnings. Moreover, the value of any given sheep is slightly less than the cost of calling out a vet to examine it; and at sale the farmer will receive £1.50 per kilogram compared to the on the shelf price of £5.10 at the supermarket (on current monthly Meat and Livestock Commission figures). The sheep become just a means of getting subsidy. This produces a long-distance trade in animals – cattle and sheep – between markets effectively speculating, or adjusting herd numbers. These long, large-scale and rapid movements between holding centres were the main means that foot-and-mouth spread between the far corners of England and into Scotland and Wales.

Flyscreen

In terms of farms themselves, regulatory pressure has been growing. As the unsustainability of the subsidy regime becomes apparent, many have called for dropping support mechanisms. The coverage of recent food scares repeatedly implicates industrialized agriculture in declining standards of animal welfare and practices that have shocked a wilfully ignorant, but carnivorous, public. Except, it is also clear that sectors outside subsidy and controlled price regimes have seen the most intense industrialization. It is in the free market for pigs or chicken where the most 'unnatural' regimes pertain. It is in the subsidized dairy sector that animals are allowed to 'waste' energy (and thus money) wandering to and from their food, in fields that need maintenance, in herds that need fetching. Already Dutch and German designers are marketing the self-milking parlour, where cows are year round in nearby sheds, yards and fields and come by themselves to be milked, and are recognized by electronic tags that in turn provide individually calibrated quantities and types of food. Literally we are waiting until the cows come home.

Meanwhile, the pressure to account for subsidy and to prevent food scandals means that every cow and calf is now possessed of a passport – a full transcript of their life to be completed at the entirely logical interval of every sixteen days, logging any medicine given by batch number. Not only are the animals precisely traceable and identifiable but also the land is more intensively measured than ever before. Big agribusiness has moved to precision farming, where GPS allows the administering of quantities of fertilizer that vary over the course of a field – allowing closer control and quite possibly reducing excessive and polluting use. But even on smaller farms, cows graze in fields whose precise boundaries have been registered to an accuracy of around 5 metres. Each field in pasture or eligible to attract subsidy, or indeed those left uncultivated to attract subsidy, can thus be logged. This is a level of surveillance that makes complaints about a once-in-five-years quality audit ring rather hollow.

Thus, far from sturdy independence farms are deeply regulated spaces, as illustrated by the reclassification of milking parlours. Milking parlours are not farm spaces but 'food preparation areas'. Simply put, this means that the same environmental health regimes that apply to, say, college kitchens also apply to them. So, hats must be worn to prevent stray hairs passing from human head to furry quadruped. As well as obviously sterilizing the milking machines and tanks, it means that each cow's udders should be washed before milking. Moreover, on a recent inspection one parlour was issued with a remedial action notice since it had a window that was broken. It must be fitted with a fly screen to prevent the ingress of any insects and to keep unwanted nature out of the food preparation area. But, of course, it is still a farm – and although the fly screen is now in place, the flies can still appear, along with the 140 cows that enter and exit via the 3×2-metre doors at each end of the parlour.

Horses
Mike Pearson

At Pleugh Jag time there used ter be a gran percession – men in tall 'ats trimmed wi' belts an' jewellry, an' fine clothes on, used to go first; then there was the 'obby 'orses, made ov a wicker sieve wi' bottom out put round a man an' an 'orse-cloth right over

74 Burringham Plough Jags, January 1934.

'im so's just 'is eyes looked out, an' a pair o'
ears on. Rear an' kick, they would, these
'ere 'obby 'orses, an' run after folks an'
scare 'em nigh ter dead!

The last of its breed, from Burringham, is in
the museum in Scunthorpe, mounted in a
glass case, on a bed of straw. Red caddis, once
used to plait the manes of farm horses, edges
its ghostly white hide. A horsehair tail bound
with string protrudes from the rear. At the
front, its smaller, wooden head – hobnails for
nostrils and teeth and brass studs for eyes –
bears a snapping lower jaw hinged with
leather and operated by a single cord. On its
larger head, erect ears, empty eye sockets and
flapping snout hint at its potency to terrify.
In a photograph of 1934 it stands to the
right, slightly apart, labelled 'Hobby-Horse –
Anthony Lingo'.

These creatures were once a familiar sight
in the winter landscape of north Lincolnshire:
accompanying the Plough Jags as they sought
alms door-to-door or the closely related
performers – often horsemen drawn from a
single farm – of a rudimentary folk drama
known as the Wooing Play. Sometimes they
participated in the drama; at others they were
present as obscure functionaries. Always they
acted as a link to the land and to the plough.
On occasion they spoke: to protest their identity, 'In comes two four-year-old colts'; to
boast of their physical prowess and supernatural powers, 'We can hop-scotch, And carry a
butter pot nine miles high, Without it touching the clear blue sky'; to beg for their staple
diet, 'In comes I who's never been before, If
you give me some of your best ale I'll never
come no more. I am hungry as well as dry,
And would like a bit of your best pork pie.'
In their own words they could 'otch', 'bitch-
botch, trot or gallop'; their behaviour included
the imitation and parody of horse steps and
actions resulting from the operation and
animation of the frame and its cover –
swaying, dipping, crouching: 'accompanied
by a fiery and curveting horse'. In North
Kelsey the Farmer's Man struggles to control
a mute though clearly active beast: 'Gee!
Whoa back! Spanker'.

They were descended from the tourney
horse: a frame in the shape of a horse
fastened around the waist of a performer
who appears to ride the beast. In the Lincolnshire variant – the sieve horse – the outer
rim of a large farm sieve was suspended,
on two ropes, from the shoulders of the
performer. Sometimes he straddled a scythe
shaft attached to the rim facilitating lateral
and rotational movement. A covering draped
from his neck shrouded both his own body
and the sieve.

Towards the end of the nineteenth century,
they began to mutate into something altogether more disturbing. In ostensible affirmation of their horsiness, they were fashioned
from one-piece horse jackets. The jacket –
with fitted earpieces and large orbits – was
fastened over the head and neck of the performer, the muzzle often gathered into a
beak-like form. The rider disappears but the
horse retains its original wooden head. In
place of horse / rider, there is horse / horse:
deformed hybrid with two heads, or rather
ghostly apparition. It had become an 'it'.

Its demeanour changed from benign luck-
bringer to something darker, effective disguise
increasing opportunity for licence and licen-
tiousness. Horses chased and 'covered' girls

who in turn tried to steal lucky hairs from their tails, tails that had nails, pins and fish-hooks hidden in them to prick grasping fingers. They became more dangerous, drunken and violent. With no rider left to goad the horse, horses themselves lashed out at innocent passers-by. 'Sometimes they come with horse cloths over their heads and ride "hobby-horse" and this often leads to horse-play, and fights used to take place between rival parties of villages on the opposite sides of the Trent.' By tradition, plough boys regarded themselves as beyond the law, though decreasing public tolerance and increasingly attentive magistrates made their extinction inevitable. In 1898 the whole Barrow team was summoned for assaulting a local farmer.

Some say it was the breaking of agricul-tural estates, the dispersal of labourers with mechanization and the drift to the cities – or the First World War and the killing of so many carriers of tradition – that finished the boys and their beasts. But their diet surely programmed them for self-destruction. In 1887 one of the Alkborough team was found frozen to death in the snow, literally 'dead drunk'. And a horse from Winterton died of exposure after his collapse went unremarked by his equally inebriated companions.

Culture's imitation of nature is fraught with potential danger: Ernst Gombrich warns that if the hobby horse becomes too lifelike it might gallop away on its own. And so too its emulation: in a homily attributed to Severian we read: 'The new year is consecrated with old blasphemies. Whatever deformities are lacking in nature, which creation does not know, art labours to fashion. Besides, people are dressed as cattle, and men are turned into women.' But these hobby-horses result not from mimesis. 'There is a becoming-animal not content to proceed by resemblance and for which resemblance, on the contrary,

would represent an obstacle or stoppage.' After Deleuze and Guattari, we might regard them as anomalies, phenomena at the bor-derline, haunting the fringes of both culture and nature: the result not of evolution, of descent and filiation, but of *involution*, conta-gion, infection, between the terms in play and their assignable relations, between man and animal.

Wildlife

Gail Davies

> Their life in the garden revolved around three distinct occupations – hunting for food, sleeping and attending to their love and the language lessons. Imperceptibly the barrier between them was dissolved.[1]

The accepted definition of wildlife denotes the lives of animals and plants lived out in ways not substantially influenced by domest-ication or artificial selection. Illustrated through the classic structure of the life cycle, the wild animal passes through a series of stages, from birth, development, to the birth of the next generation; unconstrained by human actions, realizing its evolutionary potential within uncultivated landscapes. Such classifications separate the paths of human and animal existence, placing wildlife at the furthest distance from human animals, in both spatial and evolutionary terms. This deceptively simple geometry of evolu-tionary order and spatial differentiation is foundering, however, to be replaced by more complex patterns of coexistence as human and nonhuman animal spaces and species dislocate and fold into one another. The physical spaces reserved for wildlife diminish, while explorations into human and animal genomics create new understanding of species difference. Nowhere is this more apparent than in human relationships with nonhuman primates. Human primate relations carry historical meanings of gender, race and empire,[2] and remain sites where new discourses in sociobiology, biosciences and animal exchange are contested. Radically new cycles of life emerge, as the fabric and meaning of human and nonhuman lives are intricately woven together through sites of connection, which refashion the conditions and limits for the mutual coexistence of human life and wildlife.

Birth: The evolutionary path of humans separated from their nearest living primates relations more than 6 million years ago, but subsequent generations have been obsessed with tracing these patterns of divergence and convergence. Archaeology and genealogy are political projects, as humans search ancient primate DNA for understanding of their accidental origin and the source of variation in their species. Having erased the idea of creator in their own development, the human animal increasingly assumes this role in the breeding choices and habitat selections of primate evolution. With the destruction of many wild spaces the genetic diversity of endangered species now resides in the computerized studbooks of captive-breeding programmes. In the 1970s fewer than 200 wild golden lion tamarin remained in a fragment of Brazilian Atlantic forest outside Rio. Since then an international network of breeding programmes in 140 zoos has boosted the numbers to 1,000. With the success of this breeding programme in zoos, and problems expanding their viable habitat in the wild, many of the tiny primates remaining in cages have been placed on the contraceptive pill to prevent unwanted births.

Drinking: In February 2001 a six-year-old female chimpanzee bought a soft drink from the vending machine, which had been in her cage for six months at the Tama Zoological Park in Hino, Tokyo. Picking up a ten-yen coin between thumb and forefinger, inserting it into the slot, pressing the button, she received a canned drink, which was then promptly grabbed by another chimpanzee. This is just the latest, though perhaps the most trivial, experiment on primate language and tool use, which humans use to study the characteristics marking their difference from animals. Through pet keeping, research and experimentation we use apes as models for understanding what constitutes human development and identity. But although we invite them to learn our cultural attributes, we rarely celebrate their animal competencies in return. Compared to most species who share our homes, primates have little interest in the spatial separation of faeces or urine from their living space. Primates in human spaces thus remain infantilized or constrained, clothed in nappies or housed in cages. Development for primates involves many of the characteristics of human adolescence: inter-sibling aggression, sexual rivalry and straying from the home. These behaviours make adolescent primates good candidates for reintroduction to the wild, but means that domesticating adult primates is difficult. The family unit represented in the ritual of tea drinking chimpanzees, in the British *PG Tips* advertisements, can be achieved only by filming each animal on the set individually and editing the result together into simulacra of human civility.

Eating: Primate predations on crops are not spatially random; farms and gardens located on the forest margins are most at risk. In many parts of Central and West Africa baboons and chimps are considered vermin for the damage they cause to crops and the incidence of 'wildlife pest impacts' is growing.[3] As human populations expand, so does the rate of contact with nonhuman animals, especially for village communities lying immediately outside wildlife conservation areas. Crop raiding threatens symbolically important spatial boundaries between human and nonhuman animals, wild habitat and cultivated land. This fear is not only of the real threat to food supply, but also that contact with aggressive primate behaviour will encourage humans to revert to these strong, violent and sometimes cannibalistic beings – found in myths of 'were-chimps'. In other parts of the West African diaspora this association with the animality of apes is actively sought. The trade in bushmeat, including endangered species like gorilla and

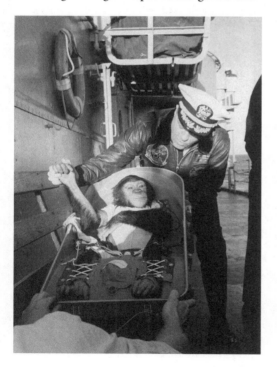

75 The famous 'handshake' welcome. Chimpanzee Ham is greeted by the recovery ship's commander after Ham's flight on the Mercury Redstone Rocket, 31 January 1961.

chimpanzee, is progressively commercialized as logging companies open up routes through the forests. Caught and consumed throughout equatorial Africa and illegally exported for sale as far afield as the Ridley Road market in London, demand for such meat is fuelled by the status and power of the wild animal it confers to the person eating it.

Sex: Primatology is unique within the biological sciences for the reversal of the usual gender imbalance. Women make up the majority of all primatologists, although the substantial periods of time they spend in the field generating empirical data mean that they often fail to make the theoretical contributions needed to progress through academic hierarchies. Women are attributed with the perception, patience and insight to study the constitution and behaviour of ape social groups. The first generation of so-called Leakey ladies – Jane Goodall, Dian Fossey and Biruté Galdikas – studied chimpanzees, mountain gorillas and orang-utans respectively, originally under the tutelage of Louis Leakey. This gender distinction is reinforced by sociobiological interpretations of their work, which places these women nearer to the objects of study and further away from academic rationality and status. Louis Leakey suggests that 'women as nurturers of children have evolved a special intuition that allows them to interpret, better than men, the emotions of apes from eye contact, facial expression and gesture'.[4]

Death: The mapping of the human genome has reversed the previously downward trend in animal experimentation in laboratories. For the foreseeable future non-human primates will play an ever-increasing role in biomedical research, in particular for research into infectious diseases and immune disorders and their treatments. In Europe an estimated 10,000 primates, genetically related to this affluent and ageing population, are required each year. The quality of animals needed for research means that wild-caught animals are increasingly replaced with captive-breed stock. Their similar physiology means the wild apes are often infected with pathogens harmful to humans. For this reason primates have been ruled out as source animals in the development of trans-species organ transplantation. The fear of spreading primate retroviruses means that transgenic pigs are most likely to be harvested for these organs. Great apes, however, retain their transitional role between human and nonhuman animals. Applications for human trials of xenotransplantation will be considered only when pig organs remain viable in primate recipients for periods over two months. Primate vivisection has emerged as a crucial arena for activists seeking to extend to nonhuman apes the same moral and legal protection as humans. In these spaces of the laboratory they claim that the human fear of death is driving us to sacrifice our sense of humanity.

Animals

William S. Lynn

Several years ago I was giving a talk on animals, ethics and social theory. In the middle of the talk, I asked my friend Beau to jump up on my desk and sit with me. He did so obligingly, gently meeting the gaze of my amused students. Referring to Beau, I asked: 'What is this?' My students provided a plethora of answers: *Canis familiaris*; fur-ball; moral being; community resident. Each answer held its own truth and encapsulated humanity's complicated relationship with animals.

76 'Jac' by Catherine McIntyre.

The concept of 'animal' is ancient, developing out of readily observable differences between living and non-living nature, as well as animal and plant biology. The word has its roots in Latin, where *animalis* means animate, a characteristic associated with the possession of *anima* or soul. For the Greeks, animals were living beings, or *zoon*. Thus Aristotle described humans as *zoon politikon* – political animals. Animals and plants were also the 'two kingdoms' by which medieval and modern taxonomists classified living nature. This schema has since been elaborated into five phyla, including *Animalia* (e.g., wolves) and *Plantae* (e.g., white pine), as well as other forms of life that are neither animal nor plant, that is *Monera* (e.g., bacteria), *Protictista* (e.g,. seaweed) and *Fungi* (e.g., moulds and mushrooms). As for human beings, we are simply another animal species, *Homo sapiens sapiens*, the 'wise earthly ones'. Like all other creatures, we share in the drama and heritage of life, having evolved through a lineage of hominids and primates.

Yet in everyday life and language, we draw a sharp line between people and animals. An animal is a nonhuman, such as a mammal, reptile, amphibian, fish or octopus, the rest of the living world being divided into insects, bugs, germs, plants, slime and stuff. If humans are but one species of animal, why do we stress our differences from other beings? There is no simple answer, but we can make a start by noting one indispensable element – our moral sensibilities about the animal world.

An animal is not simply a description of something in nature; it is a culture-laden concept that incorporates ethical sensibilities. These sensibilities are readily identified in classifications that separate the moral standing of humans from the rest of nature. Especially noteworthy are mythic stories that posit a special role or value for humankind. Sometimes these stories are religious, such as the supernatural acts related in Genesis. As the favoured creatures of God, Adam and Eve are born through a special act of creation and given dominion over the (other) animals of the earth. Sometimes these stories are secular, such as the 'social construction of nature' thesis so popular in social theory. Here, humans are mysteriously decoupled from the natural world, as if persons and societies were disembodied spirits governed by intentions and social forces alone. The natural world thereby becomes the 'external body' of humankind, 'resources' for economic activity, or a 'social nature' produced by political-economic processes. The belief that nature is made for or by one particularly clever species is breathtaking, if self-absorbed.

Despite clear differences in content and application, these myths share an anthropocentric prejudice against the natural world. This prejudice is rooted in the belief that only humans have moral standing and significance. Were the lines of anthropocentric privilege drawn strictly, we could simply refer to speciesism – the uncritical privileging of humans over all other animals. This

is not the case. Anthropocentrism creates a *scala naturea* ('chain of being'; natural hierarchy) that, in addition to species, invokes race, class, gender and ethnicity as criteria of discrimination. This makes the conceptual and practical resonance between anthropocentrism and other oppressions too blatant to ignore. Both racism and sexism (to name but two) involve an explicit process of bestialization – construing a person or group as less than fully human. To the anthropocentric eye, some people and all animals are *Other* – creatures different from one's individual or collective identity, creatures with whom we cannot identify or empathize, creatures we are excused from caring about. Examples of the process of bestialization abound. To justify the horrors of the Holocaust, the Nazis claimed that Jews, Gypsies and gays were sub-human. To justify the marginalization of women from public life, Aristotle claimed that women lacked the virtue of reason and were thereby imperfect men. The First Peoples of North America were likened to wolves, thence slaughtered like their fellow creatures to make way for more worthy Europeans. These insights should have profound implications for social theory in geography and beyond. Racism, classism, sexism and ethnocentrism are human-focused brands of anthropocentrism, part of a broader practice of *othering*. This destabilizes the ethical theories we routinely use to justify a concern for human well-being, while peripheralizing concerns for the well-being of animals. It also points toward new possibilities of solidarity between those struggling for a vision of justice that embraces the natural world.

What can be said, then, about the state of animals in the new millennium? Both human and nonhuman animals are co-residents in a diversity of landscapes. These landscapes were created through a combination of natural and social forces (e.g., evolutionary-ecology and human agency). This combination generates the selection pressures that privilege the existence or flourishing of some animals (including humans) over others. Environmentalists tend to be more comfortable with the pressures of natural selection. Devoid of human caprice, natural selection is presumed to be 'wise' in the sense that it promotes fitness and biodiversity. Yet over the last millennia, social forces became the prime source of selection pressure. Social constructionists are at ease with this shift. This is primarily because, in their own eyes, there is nothing in the world except humans that is worth caring about. To be fair, there are pressing issues of injustice and need within the human community. This well-meaning concern for the human world is perhaps the root source of the social construction's antipathy towards the 'rights' of animals and nature. Even so, the state of the world is such that unless animals serve an instrumental human purpose, their existence (much less well-being) ranges from uncertain to dire. This needs to change.

We cannot eliminate humanity's geographic agency – our ability to affect the living earth for good or ill. We can, however, take moral responsibility for our impact on the animal world. Across the globe, human activity generates animal suffering, species extinction, ecosystem dysfunction and social crisis. How then should we respond? Justice is one (of several) correct answers. As the dominant species on earth, humans have yet to find a way of life that secures a just world for people, animals and the rest of nature. One reason for this failure is a narrow sense of procedural justice that marginalizes the moral claims of disempowered beings, human and nonhuman. To counteract this marginalization, we need a richer understanding of justice, one that embraces the animal world. A *trans-species justice* should unmask the ideo-logical connections and material manifestations that oppress others based on their race, class, gender, ethnicity *or* species. It should envision a world where animals are valued as individuals as well as functional units in ecosystems. It should regard 'the environment' as habitat for human and nonhumans, and assess whether the *humanitat* (the built and social environment) empowers equal, free and diverse individuals and societies. A trans-species justice should seek nothing less than the creation of just landscapes – spaces where people and animals, domestic or wild, companion or carnivore, may flourish as respected co-residents on a shared planet.

Shadows

Stephen Cairns

The 'radiant city' is a dazzling image in rhetoric on urban form. So much so that the association of cities with light is often naturalized in the Western imagination. In fact, this association was explicitly made quite recently, in the late eighteenth and early nineteenth centuries, and even then in an unexpected way through an obsession about darkness. This association coincided with a broader societal confrontation with a perceived psychological and physical menace. This menace took the form of populations deemed to be aberrant – the mad, the diseased, the criminal – and was understood to be incubated by darkness, and so came to be represented by darkness. As Foucault put it, '[a] fear haunted the latter half of the eighteenth century: the fear of darkened spaces, of the pall of gloom which prevents the full visibility of things, men and truths'. This fear generated an obsession for 'the regulation of phenomena of population, controlling their fluctuations and compensating their irregularities'. As a consequence, an almost fetishistic concern for light emerged 'to break up the patches of darkness' and to 'eliminate the shadowy areas of society'.[1] Light became a crucial component in the management of this fluctuating menace, and it began to appear at the heart of new immobilizing technologies of power. The most famous of these was Jeremy Bentham's Panopticon.

But any exploration of more recent manifestations of this (not so) old story quickly shows that this tension between light and darkness has not remained so fixed in its relation to architecture and urbanism as the example of the Panopticon suggests. Indeed, what Foucault goes on to say is that the tendency to give importance to the gaze in Bentham's thought was already 'archaic' in his own time; the 'spatializing, observing, immobilizing' technologies of power were already 'being transcended by other and much more subtle mechanisms'. These relied less on materially demarcated space, and invested in another space altogether: head space. As the workings of power are interiorized so a psychical dimension is added to the city-light story. The trope of darkness follows along in this transposition, but now untethered from the material spaces of the city, it operates in an altogether more fluid and imagistic way.

One such update to the city-light story is found in Val Lewton's and Jacques Tourneur's extraordinary horror classic *The Cat People* (1942, RKO Radio Pictures). The film is set in Chicago and concerns the life and loves of a recent Serbian immigrant, Irena. What gives this film its horror cachet is that, along with the baggage of immigrant optimism and energy, Irena brings to the new world a particular personal burden: 'the spectre of a Satanic medieval curse' that dooms her 'to

exist as a murderous, shape-shifting creature of darkness' (as the video jacket has it). Irena's burden, as it transpires, is her belief that she transforms into a deadly panther whenever she is sexually aroused and jealous.

The key scene comes late in the film – the point where the protagonists, and we in the audience, first come to realize the deadly seriousness of what had seemed to be nothing more than a zoomorphic fantasy, an old-world superstition or an immigrant's delusions. Irena's husband, Oliver, works as a draughtsman with a firm of naval architects. The draughting room, high in a modern downtown office block, is a clean and nondescript universal space furnished with standard office furniture along with more specialized equipment such as tracing tables, drawing boards, T-squares, slide rules and draughting pens. Here, while working late one night, Oliver, with his workmate and burgeoning love interest, Alice, are stalked by a jealous Irena transmogrified as the deadly panther. Eventually they are cornered by the panther and appear doomed. In desperation Oliver reaches around for some instrument with which to defend himself and his lover, and the only thing that comes to hand is a T-square that happens to be hanging on the wall above him. Taking the drawing instrument by the shaft, Oliver brandishes it at the panther. The shadow cast of this momentary *tableau vivant* generates a strikingly gothic image: the T-square has generated an image of a cross on the wall behind two figures, who are now seen cowering beneath it. On seeing this image the panther retreats, and Oliver and Alice are saved.

The Cat People is no generic horror. The film's most obvious horror trigger, the panther, is jet black and rarely seen on screen, even then as a fleeting shadow. Additionally, the key scene of the film is set in the banal and anonymous space of a high-rise office furnished with the decidedly un-atmospheric accoutrements of technical drawing. So director and producer hinge a monster horror film in an unassuming office space around an insubstantial shadow rather than, as was more typical of the genre, a more fully present giant fanged creature – a decision that for the RKO studio bosses, their eye on the box office, was a more obvious source of horror. It is what I take to be Lewton's and Tourneur's attraction to the flip-side of form – the shadow and not the creature, the generic and not the distinctive space – and its possibilities for the generation of horror, which makes this film worthy of our attention. The resolution of the panther-in-the-draughting-room dilemma is a highlight of the film in these terms. In Lewton's and Tourneur's hands the technical drawing instruments, the tracing table and its light of reason, are transformed into something altogether strange. The uplights of the tracing table strike the underside of the protagonists' faces and deflect off the smooth surfaces of the draughting-room walls to generate a grotesque and barely definable space filled with warped and shadowy figures. It is as if the other side of the story is being exploited here. It is as if the tools of a rational trade are turned against themselves so that they become instruments of confusion, so that darkness is allowed to seep into the clean and clearly lit spaces of rationality.

Lewton and Tourneur offer a happy ending to the story where light and right (the glowing white T-square / cross) banish the forces of darkness and superstition (Irena's animal, shadowy, black-magic irrationality). But this happy ending barely assuages what Lewton called 'dark patches' into which 'the mind's eye will read anything'. The ominous 'dark patches' became a core structural device in many of Lewton's and Tourneur's horror films, what the film critic J. P. Telotte describes as 'black holes in the fabric of the commonplace'.[2] So *The Cat People* represents a provocative update of the city-light story: darkness moves into a psychical space and lodges there as a more fluid and formless shadow. In contrast to an Enlightenment obsession with 'breaking up the patches of darkness' (as Foucault put it), this film deliberately explores the dark patches of everyday urban fabric to generate a kind of aesthetic pleasure – or even a kind of comfort – within them.

Mammals

Steve Baker

'Animals don't need us, but we need them', insists the artist Britta Jaschinski. The visual form of the mammals in so many of her photographs over the past decade is a sustained interrogation of this neediness. Human desire, it seems, is for the look of these particular animals rather than for any useful knowledge of them. Shorn of background and context, there is no way of knowing whether the giraffe in her recent series *Wild Things*, for example, was photographed in the wild or in a zoo: an apt reminder of human disregard for the preservation of the natural habitats of other mammals.[1] And in the absence of the mimosa trees whose dappled shade would make particular sense of this creature's camouflage, its beautiful patterned skin can offer no more than a fleeting visual pleasure to the needy human viewer.

The strong desire for the continuing visibility of mammals reflects an attempt to make sense of the world at large. When, in May 2002, the Geo-3 report from the United Nations Environment Programme predicted the extent of environmental degradation

77 Britta Jaschinski's 'Giraffe', 2000.

over the next thirty years, and the unprecedented fall in biological diversity that is likely to accompany it, a British newspaper made the complexity of this intangible future immediately intelligible with the front-page headline 'Quarter of Mammals Faced with Extinction'.[2]

If we are reluctant to see mammals disappear, it is because we seldom get beyond their appearances in our understanding of the other-than-human world. As Kate Rawles has noted, the word 'animal' calls to mind mammals first and foremost, much as the treatment of mammals dominates ethical debates about animals. No matter that mammals are numerically insignificant in the animal world: the biologist whom Rawles quotes as saying 'as a rough approximation, every living thing on earth is an insect' fails to register the insistent visibility of mammals in human thought.[3]

This human demand is nevertheless subject to complex regulation. It is not only a matter of keeping mammals visible, but of keeping up appearances. When this is no longer possible, their visibility is far less welcome. It was *seeing* the pyres, seeing the falling-apart of cows and sheep that would otherwise have been destined for an unseen death in the slaughterhouse that so offended British sensibilities during the outbreak of foot-and-mouth disease in 2001.

Visibility is central to the idea that animals are increasingly lost to the modern world – a loss addressed by cultural analysts from John Berger to Akira Mizuta Lippit, as well as in stark media warnings of the imminent extinction of the great apes, for example. In the zoo and on safari, it is our looking (our presumption of the *right* to look) that is offended by the animal's disappearance. And it is usually only the disappearance of the 'charismatic megafauna' such as elephants, pandas and whales, of course, that is even noticed.

Visibility is intimately tied to matters of desire. What a mammal is will very much depend on what we want from it, and the mammal that does not exist can be invented – in the laboratory just as much as in the imagination. 'OncoMouse™ is my sibling', insists the postmodern theorist and historian of science Donna J. Haraway of the mammal whose sole logic is to bear mammary glands as a home for a transplanted human gene that 'reliably produces breast cancer'. Haraway's determined trans-species identification with such mammals resists the attempt to reduce them to a merely visual metaphor, as in the director of GenPharm's chilling assertion that 'We view them as the canvas upon which we do these genetic transplantations'.[4]

As such examples suggest, there is something both human and inhuman in this space of desire and of fable, which is perhaps the space in which the mammal most tellingly exists. The contemporary shape of that fable (which has nothing to do with the taxonomic classification of mammals as monotremes, marsupials, eutheria and multituberculata) is revealing. It is told in several tongues, all of which now address a kind of post-human unravelling and un-mammalling, and the uncertainties that follow from these.

Kate Rawles tells it from the ecological perspective, noting that animals are 'typically perceived as individuals; as creatures with fairly neat edges that act as demarcation boundaries', but that this perception is open to challenge: 'One familiar source of such challenge is the suggestion that animals – including humans – are inseparable parts of the ecosystems in which they live. . . . But if the neatly edged fox is dissolved into her environment so that all we see is an eco-system, our current ethical concepts do not really get a purchase'.[5] The individual mammal disappears, and with it human certainty.

Something similar is heard in Jo Shapcott's sequence of 'mad cow' poems (mammals falling apart, again), especially in lines from 'The Mad Cow Believes She is the Spirit of the Weather': 'I'm dangerous to the earth. / I spat and a blanket of algae four miles long / bloomed on the Cornish coast'.[6] There may be echoes here of Deleuze's and Guattari's philosophical concept of 'becoming-animal', a tale of creative escape from the bounds of individual identity into multiplicity and contagion, in which the nonhuman mammal is no more secure than the human: the wolf is only ever 'a wolfing', and 'every animal is fundamentally a band, a pack'. This is a condition utterly beyond familiar identifications: 'Human tenderness is as foreign to it as human classifications'.[7]

Even the philosopher Alphonso Lingis's more explicitly humane expression of the fable cannot contain or confine the mammal's form. His observation on marine mammals – 'When we watch the seals glide up and down the rocks and into the sea, we feel the tedium of the bodies we had to evolve when we left the ocean' – reflects his broader conviction that humans 'move and feel in symbiosis' not only with other mammals, but also with 'birds, reptiles and fish'.[8]

It is unclear whether this fable of reconsidered appearances amounts to anything more than wishful thinking about the future of human and nonhuman mammals, but a common ground of welcome unfamiliarity can be glimpsed through the new patterns it seems to create.

Fish
Nigel Clark

Today the idea that human cultures are always already dispersed and composite is displacing any notion of pure identities sprung from a substrate of native soil. But precisely where this leaves other species, or soil itself, remains less clear. On the one hand, there is growing appreciation of the human cosmopolitan impulse, a recognition that leaving 'home' can be a positive and creative experience. On the other, however, there is a deepening sense of the ecological danger of displacing biological life from its normal surroundings. In this context, leaving home is known as 'bioinvasion'.

Like islands, lakes are particularly vulnerable to bioinvasion. When the Nile perch was introduced to Lake Victoria in East Africa in the 1950s, the intention was to add a large edible component to a food web dominated by a huge variety of cichlids, a family of fish

78 The picture was taken in Lambu, a small village near Masaka, Uganda, on the western shores of Lake Victoria. It shows relatively large specimens (around 80 cm) of Nile perch, *Lates niloticus*, an introduced predatory fish. The fish were caught by beach seine by artisanal fishermen in the morning of 26 July 1993.

mostly too small to interest commercial fishers. The predatory perch turned out to be an aggressive acclimatizer. The intervening decades witnessed the extinction of some 200 species of cichlid, the greatest single erasure of biodiversity ever recorded. As the biologist Tijs Goldschmidt put it, 'for the total disruption of the largest tropical lake in the world, nothing more had been needed than a man with a bucket'.[1]

The obvious lesson of Lake Victoria and similar bioinvasive disasters is that we shift species from their natural environments at our peril. But there is more to lacustrine life and its distributions than this. Indeed, the whole question of the dispersal of freshwater species poses some of the thorniest issues of evolutionary biology. Darwinian theory rests on the notion of a single centre of origin for each species from which a chancy dispersion works its wonders. This dispersion is contingent on whatever mode of locomotion is available: be it legs, fins, wind or currents. Subsequent speciation occurs if barriers arise that isolate part of the population for some significant period from its relatives. Accordingly, the various means of mobility are expected to play a major role: a set of legs or wings effecting a rather different pattern of distribution from a slimy underbelly or a seed pod. Until the idea of mobile plate

tectonics or 'continental drift' took hold, biologists were obliged to think up ways for species to have found their way to landmasses over the sea from their supposed 'point of origin'. The positing of lost intercontinental land bridges was a favoured explanation, as was rafting on driftwood and other debris. Clearly, neither of these hypotheses held much promise for explaining how freshwater fish got around.

When a few biogeographers in the mid-twentieth century actually got down to the task of mapping out life's consanguinities on a global scale, what they discovered raised some profound questions for the Darwinian 'point of origin and subsequent migration' argument. Not only did the disjunct location of most species bear little relationship to the current arrangement of landmasses, but entirely unrelated species turned out to have remarkably similar patterns of distribution. Irrespective of whether they had wings, legs or roots, organisms were turning out to share common ranges, even when these territories were scattered across lands that were oceans apart. Freshwater life, not surprisingly, offered particularly telling evidence.

The family of mostly freshwater fishes *Galaxiidae*, for example, are found in New Caledonia and New Zealand, and in parts of South America and Eastern Australia, with a single representative in Southern Africa. Although there is a marine stage in the life cycle of some galaxiids, migration across whole oceans seems an unlikely feat. But what is most intriguing is that the disjunctures of galaxiid distribution are echoed by earthworms, crustaceans, molluscs, midges, birds, and a whole range of plants.[2] Indeed, when presenting us with the parallel distributions of the marine crab *Leptograpsus variegatus*, the *Galaxiidae* fishes, beech trees of the genus *Nothofagus*, and the midge flies of the family *Chironomidae*, the zoologist

Roderic Page defies us to guess which species range is which.[3]

Several decades before geologists settled on the notion of mobile plate tectonics, some biogeographers had worked out from the patterns of life's placement that shifting landmasses had played a crucial role. For the maverick biogeographer Leon Croizat, writing half a century ago, evidence that the major tracks or baselines of life's distribution crossed ocean basins suggested not only that species came into being across broad fronts rather than at 'points of origin', but that space itself played a much more active role in biological diversification than previously thought. It was not simply that living creatures had rafted around the planet as continents drifted. Croizat surmised that many landmasses as they now appear are composed of heterogeneous fragments; chunks and shards that may have come apart and together in many previous combinations – each journeying with their own contingent of life.

But Croizat went further, suggesting that life itself was a significant geological agent, and not simply a passenger in these manoeuvrings. As he saw it, it is 'the interplay of rocks and flesh that accounts for evolution' – with biology playing the role of a geological layer, a participant in the building up and wearing down of landforms.[4] In this way, Croizat and subsequent 'panbiogeographers' came to view the existing distribution of species as an expression of earth and life evolving together over broad fronts. While different forms of mobility and chance migrations are seen to have played some part, far more important are the zones of tectonic convergence, which operate as hinges or gateways between different biogeographic regions.

'Biodiversity', the panbiogeographers Craw, Grehan and Heads argue, 'is made up not of genes, species, and habitats, but of the tracks and nodes of life'.[5] This may seem small comfort to Lake Victoria's vanishing cichlid population, but it does have important implications for the way that we go about global biodiversity management – which remains largely based on the identification of species with the discrete regions they now inhabit. It is not just that the environmentalist decree that species should be confined to the places to which they belong that is brought into question, however, but also its flip-side, the 'cosmopolitan' vision that accredits human cultures with an exceptional restlessness and mobility.

What the evidence assembled by panbiogeographers hints at is an ancient but ongoing 'cosmopolitanism' that humans share with all forms of life. In this light, the tracks and channels that *Homo sapiens* are engraving on the planet's surface do not ultimately divorce us from other living things, nor even from the soil. But this is no licence for indiscriminate movement or translocation. Rather, the recognition that our own routes, nodes and gateways overwrite more ancient paths and junctions seems to suggest a new set of responsibilities. For only through an appreciation of the full history of mobilities might we begin to distinguish generative displacements from trails of destruction: a judgement that needs to be inclusive of every sort of life and all matter in motion.

Waves
Robert Low

We are all familiar with waves, particularly waves on the surface of water, and less obviously waves of compression in air, which we perceive as sound, or in the electromagnetic field, which we perceive as light. These different types of wave are modelled by certain mathematical expressions, which allow us to form an abstraction of the idea of 'wave' in terms of the mathematics used to describe them. In this article we will see that the distinction between the phenomena of waves and those of particles is rather less clear than one might expect, and that in fact phenomena most naturally associated with waves seem to have a deep connection with the properties of particles.

Now, one of the basic properties of wave propagation is interference. This property is well demonstrated by a shallow tank of water containing a barrier with two gaps in it separated by a distance a, and a mechanism that sets waves in motion as shown in the illustration below.

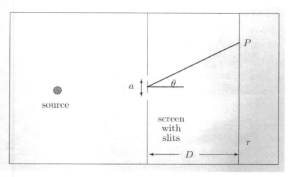

79 Interference apparatus.

The gaps in the barrier have the effect of producing circular wavefronts, and these then meet. Where both waves have a peak or a trough, the resulting wave has a higher peak or deeper trough; where one has a peak and the other has a trough the result is no disturbance. These phenomena are called constructive and destructive interference respectively.

On a reference line, labelled r in our diagram, we can consider the amplitude of

the resulting wave at each point on that line. We get constructive interference at a location when the distances from this location to the slits differ by a multiple of λ, the wavelength of the waves. Near the point labelled P, the distance between successive such locations is $\lambda/\sin\theta$.

Now, let us keep this same diagram, but change its meaning. We now have a light source instead of a machine to disturb the water, an opaque sheet with two nearby slits in it, and a photo-sensitive sheet in the place of the reference line. Knowing that light is a form of electromagnetic radiation, we are not too surprised to see again a resulting pattern of exposure to the photo-sensitive sheet build up; high exposure where the interference is constructive, low where it is destructive, and the degree of exposure of the photo-sensitive sheet is determined by the amplitude of the electromagnetic wave hitting it.

This is as we would expect. The first surprise occurs when we turn the intensity of the light source down very low. Now we find that instead of the whole photo-sensitive screen gradually darkening at a rate determined by the amplitude of the incident wave, what happens is that small spots are darkened; but the distribution of these spots is determined by the amplitude of the incident wave. As we wait, we see that the exposure pattern that appeared before is gradually built up: but in a discrete local manner, rather than the more continuous, spread-out manner that was suggested by the previous experience.

From this, we observe that light appears to have a kind of dual nature. It behaves like a wave (spread out, exhibiting interference) in its propagation through the apparatus, but like a particle (local and discrete) in its interaction with the screen.

We can change the meaning of the diagram again, and rather more drastically this time. The source now emits electrons, and the screen records their arrival. Since electrons are particles, and we know how particles behave, we know what to expect: two spots of high intensity in a direct line of sight from the source through each slit to the screen. But this is not what is experimentally observed. Again we find a pattern of high and low intensity arrivals. This pattern is given by the same relationship as before, if we replace the wavelength by h / p, where h is Planck's constant and p is the momentum of each electron.

So we see that electrons, which we already know to be particles, can behave like waves in their propagation, even although they still behave like particles in their interaction with the screen: and this wave-like propagation, together with interference, survives even when the rate at which electrons are emitted is low enough that there is only ever one electron at a time in the apparatus.

This suggests that perhaps both the particle and the wave pictures of electrons and light are unsatisfactory, and must be replaced by something more comprehensive. This something is, of course, quantum mechanics.

In quantum mechanics, the motion of a particle of mass m and energy E is now described by the Schrödinger wave equation,

$$-\frac{\hbar^2}{2m}\left\{\frac{\partial^2 \psi}{\partial x^2} + \frac{\partial^2 \psi}{\partial y^2} + \frac{\partial^2 \psi}{\partial z^2}\right\} + V\psi = E\psi$$

where $\hbar$ is Planck's constant divided by 2π, and V is a function that described the environment in which the particle is travelling.

The relationship between the function ψ and the position of the particle is that the probability of the particle being detected in a small box of volume A around the point (x, y, z) at time t is given by $A|\psi(x, y, z, t)|^2$. The consequences of this mathematical model are that a single particle's propagation through our apparatus can undergo inter-

ference; that it can be detected only in one place; and that many repetitions of the experiment will result in a pattern of detections at the detector screen, which looks just like the intensity of classical waves impinging on it.

There are many debates on just what all this means. One answer (sometimes called the Copenhagen interpretation) is that the Schrödinger equation gives us a way of predicting what will happen when microscopic objects (which behave according to the laws of quantum mechanics) interact with macroscopic ones (which behave according to the laws of classical physics). Exactly how the classical behaviour arises in a system composed of microscopic objects is also the subject of lively debate.

Nonetheless, we can take away at least one basic lesson from all this. The question 'is an electron a wave or a particle?' is not one with a simple answer. If we try to find behaviour characteristic of a wave, such as interference, we find that. If we try instead to find behaviour characteristic of a particle, such as its position at a particular time, then we find that.

The moral of all this is that the universe is in fact constructed in such a way that the sorts of answers it will provide depend to some extent on the types of question that we ask. This is a fundamental property of physics at the microscopic level; but it serves also as a reminder that the sort of information we obtain in other settings may be severely constrained by the type of questions we ask. In particular, objects that we naturally think of as particles have behaviours that (on close investigation) are most easily explained in terms of waves. Consequent to this is the mystery that somehow the classical behaviour of macroscopic objects – which is what forms our intuition of particulate behaviour – arises from this underlying wave nature.

Radio

Nigel Thrift

Some things stick. I must have been ten or eleven, I suppose. I was walking down to my grandmother's house from my parents' house further up the hill. It was a wild, wild night with the wind coming straight off the sea. In my memory, I can still retrace each one of my steps. I remember that my path was lit only by periodic streetlamps (which, at the time, must have been single bulbs, not the ubiquitous orange glow of the contemporary night sky). I remember the warning crackle of the beech hedge, its leaves desiccated by winter, that I brushed past – and nearly fell into headlong. But, most of all, I remember the continuous banshee wail of the wind forcing its way past the tensioned cables of Portishead radio station, rising and falling, rising and falling. A pure intensity; wild, scary but also exhilarating.

At the time, had I but known it, that radio station on the Somerset coast was one of the most important nodes in the world long-range maritime radio communications network. Opened in 1927 and operated by the Post Office, from its four 300-foot-high masts radio signals pulsed out to all corners of the world, for the station provided a long-range ship-to-shore message transmission service by media such as morse and later radiotelex and radiotelephone. By the 1960s, when I took my walk, 86 radio officers were handling more than 11 million words of traffic per year. By the mid-1970s that figure had increased still further with 154 radio officers handling more than 20 million words a year. Here was a geography of the sea that had fetched up on land.

The Portishead transmitting site closed in July 1978, with the work transferred to other sites. But, by then, the name of Portishead

Radio had become so well known that it was maintained in order to provide the maritime community with its own radio landmark. It was finally given up as a call sign only when the 'Portishead' radio station was closed in April 2000. (Amazingly, communication by morse code was finally phased out only in 1999.)

All there is to remember the Portishead radio station by now are serried rows of housing estates with road names like 'Marconi Road'. And those four impressive masts have been replaced by a plethora of different kinds of radio transmitting devices, of which the most visible now are the much smaller masts that can be found scattered about on tops of hills, attached to church towers or marking out the progress of roads. These masts signify that we live in an environment in which the radio spectrum has become a taken-for-granted resource, a mine of frequencies that can be exploited at will.

When people talk about natural resources, they tend to mean things you can have and hold and husband: tangibles like water and air or various kinds of mineral or vegetation. They usually forget to mention one of the most precious of these resources: that part of the electromagnetic spectrum that encompasses radio waves. Yet 'radio waves' are now one of the main means through which humanity communicates, transmitting all manner of conversations, music, pictures and data through the air every day, sometimes over millions of miles. We are surrounded by technologies that depend on radio waves – from mobile phones to radio and television broadcasts and from microwave ovens to baby monitors – and the number of these technologies has been steadily increasing, especially as a result of the increasing use of digital technologies. And now, wireless systems are making another leap forward: all around us radio frequency identifier tags (RFIDs) are beginning to populate every nook and cranny of every-day life: it will not be long before many people and nearly all other things are permanently 'on air'. We are living in the age of radio-active environments.

You might think, then, that ownership of such a precious resource would be a pressing political issue: after all, around the world there are fierce struggles over the rights to land and water, and increasingly protests about the right to 'own' many parts of nature at all. But you would be wrong. In most countries there is almost no comment on the fact that the rights to the electromagnetic spectrum are owned lock, stock and barrel, nearly always by Government (which decides, through bodies like the Federal Communic-ations Commission in the United States, which frequencies are used for which purposes and allocates licences accordingly). Increas-ingly, however, private concerns have become more and more prominent owners, since governments have auctioned off some of their rights.

But that is now changing. As the electro-magnetic spectrum becomes more and more crowded and as the uses of radio multiply, so it is becoming increasingly clear that this usage is a live political issue. For example, some writers argue for making large parts of the spectrum open, for treating the spectrum as a commons.[1] Indeed, in some parts of the world, as in Tonga and a number of Native American tribal lands, this is already happen-ing, allowing their inhabitants to gain super-fast access to the Internet, while some new wireless protocols like Bluetooth rely on there being at least some unallocated spectrum. Other writers suggest that the best way forward are new technologies that can vacuum up parts of the spectrum that are temporarily unused and momentarily reallocate them for free use. Whatever the solution, what seems obvious is that the radio spectrum has now become one of the key resources of the modern world, one whose patterns of use and abuse should concern us all as more and more of the world becomes radio-active. It might seem a long way from Portishead but it is really only a short step.

Island Nations
Aihwa Ong

No society is an island, delimited by the sea. Older images of islands are of isolation, safe from attack or unwelcome influence. Shakespeare celebrated 'this scepter'd isle, this England' in *King Richard the Second*. Such splendid isolation, however ,did not prevent British islanders from embarking on an adventure that in time spawned an empire linking far-flung continents, islands and all. In the struggle to build modern nations, there is a more ambivalent Asian image of the limits of islands. The Japanese have long bemoaned their archipelago's lack of suitable resources, and, imitating European powers, set about conquering near-by countries in the early twentieth century. The two images of islands have persisted: the self-enclosed entities – tourist escape, refugee camp, wildlife refuge, tax haven and even 'homogenous' genome pool – but also the stony citadel that must draw its wealth from across the sea. Island nations play off their intertwined roles as citadel and as nodes in transnational networks. Just as Hong Kong's future depends on maintaining distinctiveness yet thickening relations with mainland China, Singapore too must care-fully balance its economic fortress against the need to weave connections with the Malay archipelago.

In island nations, human welfare as a political problem takes on rather specific geographical challenges of concentrating and dispersing infrastructure systems. There is perhaps no other island nation more obsessed by its material limitations than Singapore. The island has a total area of 647.5 square kilometres, an area constantly enlarged by land reclamation. Singapore has placed itself on the world map by promoting a pleasant and highly efficient environment friendly to global business, achieving the distinction of being the favourite site for multinational companies in Asia. In addition, Singaporeans consider themselves world-class subjects, enjoying living standards comparable to those in Switzerland, their favourite alter-ego. This status of affluent society and business paradise pivots on the mastery of two kinds of environmental limitations: the limits of comfort and the limits of territory. The Government has resolutely grounded its legitimacy in 'the politics of comfort and control', whereby autocratic rule is legitimized by its design to secure the creature comforts of the inhabitants.[1] Questions of human welfare are at the forefront of island-landscaping – public housing estates substantiating the political rhetoric of 'a home-owning democracy'; and in the materiality of a self-styled 'intelligent island' – green oasis, climate control and plentiful, clean water. In this 'air-conditioned' nation, citizens can work efficiently in conditions that approximate temperate zones. Bio-politics and geo-politics collide and collude to make Singaporeans materially contented in a poverty-stricken Malay archipelago. But while temperature can be locally managed – plans are afoot to build a centralized cooling system downtown – water supply has become a transnational issue at the mercy of geography and other governments. Singapore has assessed itself the sixth most water-short

country in the world. The synchronization of welfare needs and geo-political coordination is perhaps nowhere else more slippery than the island's search for 'water drinkable straight from the tap'.

The island has built a multi-segmented infrastructure to harness water for its citizens. The Public Utilities Board draws upon local resources, and purchases half of its water supply from the Malaysian mainland to which Singapore is linked by a causeway. On the island, a system of drains and canals catches clean rainwater run-off from roofs, gardens and open spaces. The water supply system consists of nineteen raw water reservoirs, fourteen service reservoirs and nine water treatment plants. Water purchased cheaply from neighbouring Malaysia is treated locally and sold at a high price to consumers. Despite a water-conservation tax, per capital consumption continues to rise.[2] Thus a turn to other rain-rich jungled islands. A project funded by a World Bank loan will build an offshore catchment area 80 times the size of Singapore island in neighbouring Indonesia. Plans include a 250-kilometre line from the Sungai Kampar basin in Riau (Northern Sumatra) to the Indonesian island of Bintan, and a 200-kilometre line from Bintan to Singapore. The agreement for Singapore to develop water resources in Indonesia allows up to 1,000 million gallons of water a day to flow into the island nation for 100 years.[3] The offshore strategies of the intelligent island reassembles an older archipelago, re-linking Singapore to the Riau islands and Sumatra (all parts of the pre-colonial Malay kingdom of Riau), in order to access natural resources under other sovereignty.[4]

Singapore is known to poor but resource-rich neighbours as a sanitized, Chinese-dominated island that absorbs the wealth of surrounding Malay lands while exporting its wastes and political dangers. Its offshore industrial zone permits Singapore not only to take advantage of cheap Indonesian natural resources and labour, but also to displace the dangers of labour discontent onto the Riau islands. In the aftermath of the financial crisis, Indonesia charged Singapore – 'a tiny red dot' in the teeming Indonesian archipelago – with providing refuge for 'economic criminals', that is, well-off Indonesian-Chinese refugees escaping communal violence. The former President Wahid threatened to punish Singapore's perceived arrogance and racial prejudice by withholding water, while encouraging Malaysia to raise charges for its water.[5] Singapore has tried to increase the domestic water supply by building a desalination plant and exploring other ways to purify used water. But the threats to cut off or otherwise interrupt foreign water show the limits of island power that comes from controlling flows while filtering out impurities. Trans-island infrastructures create contested watery landscapes that are precariously balanced between sovereignty and nature.

The water works that link poor neighbouring countries to an island citadel suggest a new kind of hydraulic society. In the Wittfogelian hydraulic society, state power was based on state control of water works that sustained food production.[6] Our Singaporean hydraulic society is a kind of humming, benign power that conditions post-tropical comfort and pampered citizens. But the control of offshore water supply is more daunting than the control of local temperature. Island governance based on hydrotherapy is highly vulnerable to foreign resentment, which threatens to liquefy Singapore's hyper-modern bedrock.

Regions

Orvar Löfgren

Towards the end of the twentieth century a regional panic swept over the world. In order to position themselves as dynamic places, hot-spots for investors or attractive tourist destinations in a global economy, local actors were busy constructing regional networks that would preferably cross national borders. A transnational region was the thing to be with a fancy name like Cascadia, eBay, Pomerania or Euro-Arctic. Some got nicknames like The Blue Banana.

But stop: weren't regions supposed to be primordial entities, rather than the results of energetic imagineering and place-marketing? Wasn't region the name given to territories that had evolved 'naturally' over the centuries and whose ecological, economic and cultural boundaries geographers and ethnologists had been busy mapping for centuries?

The classic story of regions is often told as a slow process in which sedimented layers of natural growth slowly make a cultural superstructure possible. In the beginning natural regions were slumbering everywhere all over the world, delineated by a distinct geography, a local geology and climate: valleys, plateaus, peninsulas, archipelagos. Such solid platforms developed a specific combination of flora, fauna and other natural resources that created the basis for a distinct human settlement and a regional economy. Transport possibilities like rivers and plains and physical barriers like mountains, deserts and forests channelled social and economic integration and helped to turn the region into a *Gemeinschaft*. Social interaction then created a regional culture and a distinct language.[1] In this sense regions were seen as naturally grown territories, unlike the nation states and empires that had taken control over them.

But the idea of the region as a distinct entity uniting 'nature' and 'culture' and positioned between the local and the national has a long and varied history. In earlier periods of European nation building, regions were seen as the spaces that should be united into not only a state formation but also a national culture. Regionalism was defined as an obstacle to this process of integration and homogenization. Countries such as France, Italy and Spain are good examples of highly varied relations between the state and region. Here regional movements have changed not only focus and intensity but also their political profile during the last two centuries.

Many forms of regionalism may function, not as a potential threat to national cohesion but rather as a kind of tension that may keep the national project alive and vital. In the Scandinavian countries regionalism has often functioned as a stable (and more integrating than threatening) element in the national landscape. In some ways the province or region here had the role of providing a micro-level model for patriotism. By learning to love your home region – one part of the national whole – you prepared yourself for national feelings on another level, this was the general idea of school education at the beginning of the twentieth century.

But regions were also the product of nation building. As scholars and administrators took up the task of mapping and describing the nation, its people and cultures, the region or province turned out to be a handy organizational principle. The question of symmetry became important. There should preferably be distinct regions all over the nation and they should be systematized according to the kind of cultural grammar developed for nation building. Thus emerged the model of the generic region, which should have its own local geography and economy, distinct dialect, cuisine, flora and folklore.

This was a process of domesticating local differences within a national framework, creating regional administrations, building regional museums.

With the return of the region as a political force towards the end of the twentieth century, the paradox is that it is this well-established national narrative of the regional that has been set to work against the nation.

The late twentieth century scramble for region-hood has been most marked in the European Union.[2] Here local actors saw the region as a possibility to bypass the national capital and deal directly with Brussels and the larger world. Already in 1958 *The Euroregio* was constructed between the borders of Germany and the Netherlands, and others would follow later.

There are two main tendencies in this process. One has to do with the wish to do away with antiquated national borders in creating new flows of people, goods and ideas: creating viable and innovative economic units for a global economy. Another tendency is to rekindle traditional and 'natural' regions, but placing them within a transnational argument against the provincial centralist policies of the nation state. An example of the first is the attempts to develop an Öresund region with the help of the new bridge between Denmark and southern Sweden.[3] Here is the idea of the transnational region as an Euro-experiment for greater cultural integration and innovative pooling of national resources. The second case can be illustrated by the revitalization of Istria, as a cosmopolitan and open territory, playing down national allegiances.[4]

In using the regional card wannabee-regions look to the success stories, such as Catalonia, which unlike the Basque countries has carried out a non-aggressive campaign for greater regional independence. Other actors, inside and outside Spain, have copied the Catalonian case and imitated the ways in which language policy has been handled as well as the Catalonian style of branding and marketing the region.

But again the old idea of national symmetry has created a kind of Pandora's box situation. If some parts of nation states, like Catalonia, can argue that they for historical or economic reasons deserve greater independence, other corners of the same state may claim the same status and thus start digging for their own roots.

But the paradoxes remains. Are regions 'natural' or intensely constructed spaces, are they a local or global phenomenon? Are they examples of grass-root politics or elite projects, in which an economic base or administrative unit is given a cultural superstructure, by busy entrepreneurs, local bureaucrats or intellectuals? Most regions live a difficult life between the identity space of the local and the national. Some people find it hard to 'be regional'; in other cases this regional revitalization has a stronger popular following. The region is thus a chameleonic concept, which may cover a lot of very different kinds of spaces and places. Modern regionalism is Janus-faced. It can be used as an argument for bringing power closer to local people but also as a xenophobic defence: a *Blut und Boden* type of a 'nature-given' territory that should keep out not only centralist bureaucrats but also immigrants, all those who do not belong to 'our own region'.

The history of regions illustrates the constant tension between 'natural' and 'cultural' geographies, the ways in which boundaries and territories are seen as nature-given or human constructs. In the beginning there was only a mosaic of regions, the old story runs. The new regional landscapes often return to this narrative, as territorial units busy turning themselves into old regions, not invented but rediscovered – digging both for their cultural and natural roots.

The arguments for their cultural uniqueness and antiquity is often loaded with metaphors from a natural geography: dialects, customs, mentalities and identities have grown naturally out of this local eco-system. In this complex history we can see how concepts of nature and culture become hopelessly entangled.

Territory

Anssi Paasi

In the late autumn of 1941, soon after Finnish troops had occupied a part of the territory of Soviet Karelia, Professor Väinö Auer, a Finnish physical geographer and geologist, published a provocative article on 'The Future Finland as an Economic Geographical Entity'. The article appeared in an issue of *Terra*, the journal of the Geographical Society of Finland, which also included a number of other articles written by zoologists, botanists and geologists on the territorial shape of the Finnish state. Auer's main message, which was echoed by other writers, was that Finland, like all states, had a natural territory and natural boundaries in terms of both nature and culture. The occupation of the Karelian area was seen to have improved the situation but did not yet mean that the country had achieved its full 'natural territory'. It was assumed in most of the articles that scientists could decide the correct location of the boundaries – and indeed that it was their duty to do so – by analysing existing natural and cultural patterns: topography, soil, flora, fauna, landscape and language. These patterns, so they believed, would provide a real basis for a harmonic daily life for the country and its citizens.

These efforts were not unique; in fact they conformed with geopolitical ideologies that political geographers operating in various states had been developing for decades. In a word, Finnish scholars were mapping what they regarded as the crucial constitutive elements of the territory. Their efforts show how the idea of 'territory' usually refers to classifying and controlling things and ideas in material and metaphorical spaces, and how it is located in the fuzzy area that brings patterns of nature and culture together to form specific landscapes.[1]

Ideas of 'naturally' expansive territories have been abandoned in political geography. Basically, the dividing line between natural and cultural patterns is clear in the case of territories, for much of the research carried out in animal ethology and sociobiology suggests that the construction and maintenance of territories is based on innate characters of animals and on their supposedly 'natural' links with certain places. Human territories, for their part, are social constructs, combining elements of power, space and knowledge. They are based on meanings associated with territories, on boundaries that distinguish one territory from all others, and on institutions that are significant for the maintenance of both boundaries and meanings. Human territoriality is based on abstract symbolism and its use in legislation and social control. A further implication is that narratives concerned with the identity of territories – especially national territories – often draw on history and memory to make sense of the present form of the territory in question, and even of its utopian future. In a way, these narratives try to create a vision of a *natural* link between a group of people and a territory, and, as we saw in the case of the Finnish geographers, they try to define what the territory is and where its limits lie.

Physical and human patterns come together in many ways in territories. The topography and shape of a territory can have a crucial influence on the forms and success of its governance. Rivers, lakes and mountains can be important as territorial boundaries, but they may also be major identity symbols. In Finland, for instance, the numerous lakes were a crucial element in the construction of national landscapes during the nineteenth century, just as other natural elements such as rivers or seashores were regarded as marking 'natural boundaries' of the state. One more illustration of the fusion of natural and cultural patterns is that human territories are often symbolized in national iconographies by wild animals, such as a lion, eagle or bear. The lion has been used in European coats of arms for at least 1,000 years and has been the unquestionable symbol for the Finnish state and its territory since the nineteenth century, being adopted on postage stamps in 1856 and later on coins. Even the new Finnish euro coins include a lion as the national symbol.

While a territory is denoted in a number of spheres, its power is based on *territoriality*, a strategy that is used to control human, natural and other resources by controlling the area.[2] This area can be any unit where human actors exercise control over other actors, ideas or resources. Once they are internationally recognized, bounded states become crucial for global territorial patterns, although the territories of local gangs, the 'academic spaces' of various disciplines, or the homes of individual persons or families are parallel examples of territories that have their rules, symbols and rituals. Territories thus exist through agency, in the form of overlapping human and physical patterns, and not just as backdrops that provide a framework for social action.

Although the current world harbours some 200 states, these bounded spaces are increasingly being challenged by immigration, refugees, economic patterns, information flows and environmental risks. These tendencies will lead in time to the de-territorialization of the fixed, bounded system of territories, and the consequent re-territorialization will produce a less rigid, 'porous' territorial structure in which several forms of territoriality may exist simultaneously. This means that the supposedly self-evident connection between such principles as sovereignty or democracy and territorial state power will be challenged. The result of these processes will not be homogenization but a spatial fragmentation in which economic, cultural and environmental interests may be in serious conflict.

While many of the challenges to the existing territorial order are based on the globalization of the economy and the increase in information flows, these elements may also prove able in part to motivate new forms of territoriality. All around the world people are constructing new geographies of exclusion, often on ethnic and economic grounds. Numerous 'nations' are struggling to create their own autonomous or independent (state) territories. The 'first nation' movements are also examples of new challenges to territorial thinking. Often supporting traditional identities, environmental values and people's rights over land, these movements challenge the territorial governance that has been established by the existing hegemonic groups. This is not a totally new tendency. Nomadic territories have always been more open and more clearly linked with the rhythms of nature than the territories that are monopolized by existing nation states. We also have to understand that new territories are not always symmetric, bounded units, for they can equally well be asymmetric trackways or networks – territorialities based on nodes. All these examples imply

that one major challenge for democratic societies lies in creating and tolerating increasingly open forms of territoriality.

Mountains
Stephan Harrison

From the Indus Valley Nanga Parbat, the ninth highest mountain in the World, rises 7 kilometres into the Himalayan air to 8,126 metres, the greatest vertical rise on Earth. The name Nanga Parbat means 'Naked Mountain' and refers to its sheer glacial flanks and, in the twentieth century, was used in an anthropomorphic sense to describe its aggression in killing the cream of German mountaineering in their attempts to climb it. The term 'naked' also has other connotations. It implies simplicity, openness and one-dimensionality; yet as complex an object as a mountain resists easy explanation and exploration, and we can therefore use the idea of mountains and the ways in which humans have attempted to climb them as a metaphor to bring out some of the ideas surrounding human scientific responses to complex systems in the natural environment.

During the 1930s German mountaineers had made several attempts on the mountain without success, ending with the deaths of 31 climbers. Their urge to be the first to climb a 8,000-metre peak was driven by the need at this time for Nazi propaganda successes and involved the use of siege tactics; large numbers of climbers, supporting porters and well-stocked camps. Such a view reflects the belief that the best way to attack a problem such as climbing a huge peak is to throw resources at it. Had they climbed Nanga Parbat (or successfully 'assaulted' it as some persist in writing), they would have been able to claim that they had 'conquered' it. Note the military, technological use of language. Eventually, after one of the most astounding climbs in Himalayan history, Nanga Parbat was finally climbed by Hermann Buhl in 1953. While Buhl was also involved in a large expedition, his skill as a renowned solo climber and his extraordinary fitness enabled him to make a 41-hour successful solo climb from his highest camp to the summit and back.

How do we put these different styles of climbing in context? From the 1950s to the 1980s the dominant approach to climbing huge Himalayan mountains was by sending vast organized expeditions to them, which could take months to reach the summit. For instance, the unsuccessful American expedition of 1975 to K2 employed 10 climbers and took 600 porters to carry 14 tons of gear to the bottom of the mountain. However, starting in 1975, a handful of brilliant climbers led by Reinhold Messner and Peter Habeler, and spurred on by the memory of Buhl's exploits, sought to climb these peaks by lightweight 'Alpine style'; no fixed camps or ropes, fast and without oxygen. This was a risky game, for you could be trapped high on the mountain by bad weather or accident with no prospect of rescue. But for the few good enough to attempt it, such ascents seemed cleaner and more 'ethical'. No longer would such mountains be climbed only by being subjugated under the weight of cumbersome expeditions.

So with science. One approach to understanding complexity in natural systems such as mountains and glaciers has been to throw resources at it; to conquer and to assault. Present-day reductionist computer modelling, which forms the ruling paradigm of systems theory and (in geomorphology) process-form studies, involves hugely sophisticated measurement and data analyses. For instance, in fluvial geomorphology, complicated Digital Terrain Models are integrated with three-dimensional hydraulic models in order to probe the behaviour of rivers at small spatial and temporal scales. Such endeavours make the explicit claim that better understanding of the landscape at large scales will result and that each attempt reaches further towards some sort of statement of 'truth'. Implicit in this is the suggestion that given enough time we will obtain the answers to our questions once we have the technological and mathematical tools. This seems to me to be the scientific equivalent of siege tactics.

However, complexity beats us. Nanga Parbat, like all mountains, is made up of a myriad of interacting systems, including climatic, geological, glacial, periglacial, fluvial and biological. In addition, the mountain interacts with its environment, and is changed by it, and the environment interacts with, and is changed by, the mountain. As a result, isolation of any of these systems or their specification into a chain of cause and effect relationships is practically (and perhaps logically) impossible. This negates the linear modelling approaches by which systems theory attempts to understand complexity and also means that the reductionist approach to the in-depth study of any complex system comes up against insuperable difficulties that are inherent in that system. These include intractability, algorithmic complexity and non-computability. An example of this is the problems posed by intractable behaviour. Certain problems may be very easy to pose but practically impossible to answer; that is, their solution would take a prohibitively long time to solve even with the fastest computer program that could be written. Such problems are called Non-deterministic Polynomial (NP) problems. The algorithm required for their solution increases faster 'than any mathematical power of N . . . as N, the number of ingredients to be dealt with, increases'.[1] There are many examples of such problems in mathematics and in biology (the protein-folding problem may be an example of the latter), but it remains to be seen whether our understanding of geomorphological landscapes are constrained by such barriers.

Our emerging views of science downplay the reductionist approaches to complex systems and stress the need for a simpler engagement with nature. We can see this paradigmatic shift as the scientific equivalent of Messner's and Habeler's 'clean' and efficient ascents in the 1970s and '80s. The identification and study of emergence and the recognition that explanation is scale-dependent may be the new route to follow.

One story relates how, on one dark night, a person walking down a street comes across an old man crawling on his hands and knees beneath a streetlamp as he looks for something. 'What have you lost?' 'A pound note' replies the man, 'I think I lost it over there.' He points into the shadows. 'So why are you looking over here?' the pedestrian asks. 'The light's better' replies the man. As humans we may make the same decisions. What we really want to know about complex systems may not be found where we are looking. But we look where we are able to obtain the easier answers.

Moraines

Nick Spedding

Moraines memorialize glaciers. Tombstones mark the graves of people. Moraines mark the point at which the ice made its last (still) stand. Both tombstones and moraines shape large tracts of the land surface, and designate a symbolic architecture that fills this space with meaning. Freshly erected, these monuments stand stark and sharp, but, as time passes, crisp edges crumble, polish turns dull, inscriptions disappear beneath a crust of lichens – and memory fades.

Unlike most people, glaciers act as their own monumental masons, shaping their own headstones (although the more ambitious designs might perhaps be better described as sepulchres) and writing their own epitaphs. Unlike all people, glaciers erect their own memorial at the time and place of their passing. The cloak of debris that clothed the ice in life is transformed into a shroud, on which is found the shadowy imprint of the body it once contained.

As with tombstones, the arrangement of moraines varies. Sometimes we stumble across an isolated mound of earth and rock that takes us by surprise, much as might the discovery of an overgrown grave in the corner of a field. Why this seemingly random act of deposition? Sometimes the moraines are laid out in a series of neat rows: a rubble cemetery charting the geography of an orderly and progressive demise. Sometimes the dignity of an individual plot is denied, and we find multiple remains stacked higgledy-piggledy, one upon another: a mass grave, testament to a chaotic, lingering death.

How, then, do we locate ourselves in this landscape of glacial extinction? As with the evidence of human death, moraines elicit a mixture of sympathy and curiosity. School geography lessons teach us the necessary spatial niceties: if we encounter the debris of a funeral recession, we act the role of respectful bystander, pausing to bow our heads and remember: 'Here lies a glacier!' A small number of necro-cryophiles choose to make their living in the field. The identification of moraines as the product of refrigeration, not faulty plumbing, created several new vocations. One profession acts as geological coroners, attempting to ascertain the where, when and why of glacier death – all details for entry in a burgeoning register of mortality. Their search for ever greater accuracy and completeness defines a geo-forensic science that affirms death, not life.

As we wander around a graveyard, it is difficult to escape the sense of death. The profusion of tombstones and their dates projects a powerful logic of closure. However, we also let our thoughts wander into territories less rigidly constrained by the quantitative evidence. What can we read into the size and shape of the memorial? What is the significance of the quality of the stone, or the flamboyance of the ornamentation? What was this person like? What did he or she do? Monuments fuse historical fact and imagination to inspire memories of past personalities and events. Similarly, a suitably inclined observer can take the inanimate stones of a moraine, and resurrect the matter, motion and work of the glacier for which it stands. How big was it? How fast was it? How did it move? Where did this rock come from? Why are some stones polished or scratched, rounded or angular? Why this delicate fluting, or that massive block? As we strive to answer questions such as these, land systems are transformed into life systems.

Anyone who looks at rock rubble, but sees ice, can indulge in speculation of this kind, but there are some of us who support our resuscitations with claims of special skills and knowledge. What do we call ourselves? Glacial geomorphologists? Yes. Scientists? Perhaps, perhaps not. We labour painstakingly to construct a coherent plot and rich, full characters about the moraines that we represent, but does this not make us biographers rather than scientists? If so, do we speak of the glacier, or for the glacier? Do we write of frozen ghosts, or are we chosen to ghost-write?

Ice

Francis Spufford

Freezing is no mystery. At zero degrees centigrade the molecules of water interlock. They brace, then they expand, pushing a little further apart from each other than they do in the sliding tangle of the liquid state. Each kinked trio of two hydrogen atoms, one oxygen, slots into place in a structure like a flanged, puckered hexagon. Water gains about 9 per cent extra volume, goes rigid, turns to glassy crystal: you've got ice. In the chilled base of a cloud, ice grows in grains. The hexagons multiply on every rung of the ladder of size that leads up from the molecular to the visible world, until wafers of ice arranged in every possible permutation of the basic shape are mimicking, on a scale large enough to see, the molecule that first seeded the process. And snow begins the long tumble to earth – 'like feathered rain', said a Renaissance poet.[1]

Mystery re-enters the science of ice in explanations of its bulk behaviour. The hard mathematics of complexity come in when you ask how the genesis of a billion individual flakes becomes the thrust of a blizzard, how the forces working on icebergs in Antarctica produce a particular candy-twisted specimen. Water's solid state can arrange itself in many forms, many textures, many colours even. Ice glossaries and catalogues have been published by learned bodies to try and build, at least, an anecdotal vocabulary for the things you can observe ice doing at the macroscopic level. They'll tell you about *pancake ice* and *sastrugi, growlers* and *bergy bits*. These are only the counterparts in the wild landscapes that ice dominates – the Arctic, the Antarctic – to the cold plethora of freezings that visits a winter garden. The fur of frost on a clothes-line; the hard white rim of leaves; puddles like windows or stirred to a cloudy porridge; snow (of course) crusted or sludgy or powdery. Or waxy and audibly squeaking beneath the first shoe to compress it. But the intent look at the differences of the ice (as hard to resist as the gaze upward into the numberless white-on-grey whirl of falling snow) involves you in a long history of fascination. You've been seduced by qualities of ice not reckoned by physics or chemistry. What happens to the billion molecules of ice is one thing: what happens in the onlooker is less calculable still.

In countries where snow defines the landscape half the year, or all of it, snow may be disenchanted. Where it is temporary, as in Britain, it is never wholly reduced to ordinariness, never quite aligned alongside mud and stubble as a constituent of the material economy of the real, from which no more can be expected than that it does what it does. It still promises transformation, a vague and magical erasure in accord with the dusting and muffling of familiar lines in whiteness. 'A miracle', said an Anglo-Saxon riddle for ice: 'water become bone'. When it snows, the ground is prepared. For strange departures: it's snowing outside the window just before Alice steps through the looking-glass. 'I wonder if the snow *loves* the trees and fields, that it kisses them so gently?' she asks her cat. Snow confounds ears, as well as eyes. Sound dwindles as snow wraps the surfaces of the world, abolishes echoes, takes the bounce out of the air. Yet the muting imposed by the snow registers as a positive hush rather than a simple absence of sound: a null signal broadcast by the cold, an

unmistakable white noise in the air that can be recognized on first waking without opening the curtains. The hush roared so loud it actually interrupted Coleridge's train of thought while he was writing *Frost at Midnight* (1798, lines 8–10).

'Tis calm indeed! so calm that it disturbs
And vexes meditation with its strange
And extreme silentness.

Meanwhile the 'secret ministry of frost' was hanging up icicles, 'quietly shining to the quiet moon'.

If ice seems unearthly, part of the reason must be that water is so intimate a substance for us. We drink, we spit, we cry. Blood is a solution of chemicals in water; human cells are a honeycomb largely filled with warm water. Below zero, the solvent of life has hardened into an altogether different material. And left out naked in the cold, we would too. Even when it's artfully sheathed in clothing, the difference between the temperature of freezing air and human operating temperature imposes an exact sense of the body's boundaries. It makes the body a bubble of warmth rolling on a cold surface, life surrounded by something that would slow, immobilize, halt life if let in. The extra degree of conscious awareness of life that cold brings can be exhilarating. Existence fizzes in you while the faint retreat of your blood makes your fingers tingle. You're sole, sovereign, indivisible in a hostile world. A Victorian mountaineer said that climbers above the snowline have 'the sensation that they do not actually press the ground, but that the blade of a knife could be inserted between the sole of the feet and the mountain-top'.[2]

But this casts ice, in imagination, as deathly, almost as a kind of anti-flesh. The ramifications go down into the unconscious, deep and knotted. Dreams of ice signal –

sometimes – wishes for a fixity, a hard calm, incompatible with the warm scurrying of being alive. St Francis of Assisi plumbed ice's possibilities one winter night in Italy when carnal thoughts were bothering him. He built a mound of snow, took off his robe and (the story goes) leapt onto it, crying 'This is my wife! This is my wife!'. He came back indoors, though, when he had achieved a state of indifference. To become ice would be a monstrous reversal, a metamorphosis of body into statue. The recoil is instinctive to the story of the seaman on a polar expedition in the 1820s who got his hand supercooled. Put into a bucket of cold water, it froze the water. It had ceased to behave like a part of a human.

Yet along with ice horrors go wonders, icy metamorphoses that enlarge human senses instead of curtailing them. The ice and snow of the Alps, wrote another Victorian, are substances so malleable to imagination 'that every human soul can fashion them according to its own needs'.[3] Into the delicate and extraordinary shapes of ice, the mind projects meaning; moulds; plays. In *Mont Blanc* (1816, lines 103–4) Shelley looked up at the mountain's glaciers, where to his vision

Frost and Sun in scorn of mortal power
Have piled; dome, pyramid and pinnacle

People have seen cities in ice for centuries. The curious thing is that the style of the architecture changes faithfully with changing tastes. Towers and spires were perennial, while seventeenth-century sailors in the Arctic started glimpsing Baroque fretwork, and Victorians added in Egyptian obelisks and Stone Age dolmens. Captain Scott's men saw a complete model of St Paul's Cathedral float by in the Antarctic – just like a 'Visit London' poster on the Edwardian Tube. But the impression of

shape is always temporary, always fleeting. The illusion visits, forms, slips back into disorder. 'Yet not a city but a flood of ruin', Shelley's poem continues. Ice is a magic mirror to the imagination, but a mirror shattered, giving back fragments of reflection, to be enjoyed for the moment only.

There's a warning against lingering too long in Hans Christian Andersen's perfect winter's tale *The Snow Queen*, where the nuances of ice all meet. Little Kay has been seduced away from warmth: he thinks that the 'flowers' of snowflakes are far more beautiful than living flowers. He sits on the floor of the queen's great ballroom where the polar bears dance, trying to make ice-fragments into legible words. If he can spell ETERNITY she has promised him the world, and a pair of silver skates. Every child who encounters the story knows he mustn't succeed. Complete the puzzle, and he'll be choosing eternity in the sense of rejecting time; choosing autonomy in the sense of forever losing connection; choosing the apparent permanence of words over the messy, generative processes of culture that give them meaning.

References

STEPHAN HARRISON, STEVE PILE, NIGEL THRIFT:
'Introduction: *Grounding Patterns*: Deciphering (Dis)Order in the Entanglements of Nature and Culture'

1 M. Foucault, *The Order of Things: An Archaeology Of The Human Sciences* (1966) (London, 1970), p. xv.
2 J. Borges, 'John Wilkins' Analytical Language', in his *The Total Library: Non-Fiction, 1922–1986* (1942) (Harmondsworth, 1999), both quotes p. 231.
3 Foucault, *The Order of Things*, p. xvii.
4 Borges, 'John Wilkins', both quotes p. 229.
5 *Ibid.*, both quotes p. 230.
6 D. Harkness, *John Dee's Conversations with Angels: Cabala, Alchemy and the End of Nature* (Cambridge, 1999), especially chapter 5.
7 B. Woolley, *The Queen's Conjuror: The Life and Magic of Dr Dee* (London, 2002), pp. 69–70.
8 Borges, 'John Wilkins', both quotes p. 231.
9 See Woolley, *The Queen's Conjuror*; see also N. Clulee, *John Dee's Natural Philosophy: Between Science and Religion* (London, 1988), and P. French, *John Dee: The World of an Elizabethan Magus* (London, 1972).
10 These numbers also lay at the basis both of harmonics and of cosmic proportions.
11 French, *John Dee*, chapter 2.
12 See also N. Crane, *Mercator: The Man Who Mapped the Planet* (London, 2002), chapter 5.
13 *Ibid.*, especially chapter 16. From Mercator and others, Dr Dee would learn the basic principles of global navigation – skills that he would pass on to English seafarers, who were yet to dominate the oceans: see E.G.R. Taylor, *Tudor Geography, 1485–1583* (London, 1930), pp. 76–139.
14 On this, see D. Wood, *The Power of Maps* (London, 1992), and D. Cosgrove, ed., *Mappings* (London, 1998).
15 Clulee, *John Dee's Natural Philosophy*, and Harkness, *John Dee's Conversations with Angels*.
16 On the history of geography, see D. Livingstone, *The Geographical Tradition: Episodes in the History of a Contested Enterprise* (Oxford, 1992), especially chapter 4.
17 A. von Humboldt, *Cosmos: A Sketch of a Physical Description of the Universe, Volume 1* (1845) (Baltimore, 1997), p. 76.
18 *Ibid.*, p. 63.
19 *Ibid.*, p. 73.
20 *Ibid.*
21 As Donna Haraway would put it: see D. Haraway, *Modest_Witness@Second_Millenium.FemaleMan©_ Meets_OncoMouse™: Feminism And Technoscience* (London, 1997).
22 Perhaps this is a better description of the modern scientist.
23 Von Humboldt, *Cosmos*, p. 7.
24 *Ibid.*
25 *Ibid.*, p. 50.
26 *Ibid.*, p. 25.
27 *Ibid.*, p. 40.
28 See A. Buttimer, 'Beyond Humboldtian Science and Goethe's Way of Science: Challenges of Alexander Von Humboldt's Geography', *Erdkunde*, LV/2 (2001), pp. 105–20; and A. Buttimer, 'Landscape and Life: Humboldt and the Heart of Geography', Keynote address at the Institute of British Geographers annual conference, Belfast, 2002.
29 For a discussion of the aesthetics of wonder and its relation to thought, see P. Fisher, *Wonder, the Rainbow and the Aesthetics of Rare Experiences* (Cambridge, MA, 1998).
30 Buttimer, 'Beyond Humboldtian Science', pp. 105–20; M. L. Pratt, *Imperial Eyes: Travel Writing and Transculturation* (London, 1992); and F. Driver, *Geography Militant: Cultures of Exploration and Empire* (Oxford, 2001).
31 This point has strong resonances with A. Buttimer, 'Renaissance and Re-membering Geography: Pioneering Ideas of Alexander von Humboldt,

1769–1859', Keynote address at the International Geographical Union regional conference, Durban, 2002. Copies available from the author.

32 R. Omnes, *Quantum Philosophy: Understanding and Interpreting Contemporary Science* (Princeton, 1999).

33 G. H. Mead, *The Philosophy of the Act* (Chicago, 1938), p. 31.

34 E. Squires, *Conscious Mind in the Physical World* (New York, 1990).

35 Such a view has misled some researchers into thinking that the way to crack the problems of understanding landscapes is merely to throw more resources at it. The only winners here are those who sell computers and software to universities.

36 D. R. Hofstadter, *Gödel, Escher, Bach: An Eternal Golden Braid* (Harmondsworth, 1980).

37 J. M. Jauch, *Are Quanta Real?* (Bloomington, IN, 1973), pp. 63–5. Salviati and Sagredo are two characters from Galileo's *Four Dialogues Concerning Two New Sciences*.

38 Hofstadter, *Gödel, Escher, Bach*.

39 Navier-Stokes equations are the differential equations governing fluid mechanics and consist of equations covering conservation of mass, linear momentum and general fluid motion.

40 G. Nicolis and I. Prigogine, *Exploring Complexity* (New York, 1989).

41 G. Nicolis and I. Prigogine, *Self-Organization in Nonequilibrium Systems* (New York, 1977).

42 S. Harrison, 'On Reductionism and Emergence in Geomorphology', *Transactions of the Institute of British Geographers*, XXVI/3 (2001), pp. 327–39.

43 J. Myhill, 'Some Philosophical Implications of Mathematical Logic', *Review of Metaphysics*, VI (1952), p. 165.

44 J. D. Barrow, *Impossibility* (Oxford, 1999), p. 215.

45 *Ibid.*, p. 216.

46 Myhill 'Some Philosophical Implications', p. 165.

47 J. Dupré, *The Disorder of Things: Metaphysical Foundations of the Disunity of Science* (Cambridge, MA, 1993), p. 7.

48 For example, see most recently, F. Capra, *The Hidden Connections: A Science for Sustainable Living* (London, 2002); J. Urry, *Global Complexity* (Cambridge, 2002).

49 E. F. Keller, *Making Sense of Life: Explaining Biological Development with Models, Metaphors and Machines* (Cambridge, MA, 2002).

50 J. S. Turner, *The Extended Organism: The Physiology of Animal-Built Structures* (Cambridge, MA, 2000), p. 6.

51 See T. Lenoir, *The Strategy of Life: Teleology and Mechanics in Nineteenth-Century Biology* (Chicago, 1982); A. Harrington, *Re-enchanted Science: Holism in German Culture from Wilhelm II to Hitler* (Princeton, 1996); A. Zimmerman, *Anthropology and Antihumanism in Imperial Germany* (Chicago, 2001).

52 He even went to Paris to learn the techniques of serial cinematography pioneered by Etienne-Jules Marey.

53 N. J. Thrift, 'Bare life', in *Cultural Bodies*, ed. J. Ahmed and H. Thomas (Oxford, 2003).

54 J. von Uexküll, 'A Stroll through the Worlds of Animals and Men: A Picture Book of Invisible Worlds', in *Instinctive Behavior: The Development of a Modern Concept*, ed. C. H. Schiller (New York, 1957).

55 Which, of course, still exists in reductionist genetic accounts that strive to make the world computable.

56 Harrington, *Re-enchanted Science*, p. 48.

57 Cited in *ibid.*, pp. 42–3.

58 Turner, *The Extended Organism*. Heidegger looked favourably on von Uexküll's work and it may well have contributed to his notion of 'being-in-the-world': see Harrington, *Re-enchanted Science*.

59 Thus, at times, it is clear that von Uexküll was a romantic holist (C. Kwa, 'Romantic and Baroque Conceptions of Complex Wholes in the Sciences', in *Complexities: Social Studies of Knowledge Practices*, ed. J. Law and A. Mol, Durham, NC, 2002), pp. 22–52) who believed that heterogeneous individuals came together as a single entity at a higher 'superorganic' level of organization. In contrast, Deleuze, whom we meet below, takes his cue from Leibniz and is a baroque holist. He is much less severe on this point and sees higher levels of organization as a political matter, formed from fleeting alliances. This kind of view, it might be added, works in well with certain forms of neurology, with their emphasis on the brain as a sort of society formed out of and working through all kinds of unlikely alliances (Goldstein 1995).

60 N. Cartwright, *The Dappled World: A Study of the Boundaries of Science* (Cambridge, 1999), p. 1.

61 This middle voice is, of course, the predecessor of the resurgence in theories of practices. In a certain sense, theories of practices are attempting to restore this missing middle register.

62 R. Kudielka, *Paul Klee: The Nature of Creation* (London, 2002), p. 54.

63 J. May and N. J. Thrift, *Timespace: Cultural Geographies of Temporality* (London, 2001).

64 Kudielka, *Paul Klee*, p. 137.

65 M. Merleau-Ponty, *The Eye* (Paris, 1964), p. 93; see also M. Merleau-Ponty, *La Nature: notes cours du College de France* (Paris, 1994).

66 Merleau-Ponty, *The Eye*, p. 93.

67 H. Duchting, *Paul Klee: Painting Music* (Munich, 1999).

68 Indeed, Klee often used this analogy.

69 K. V. Maur, *The Sound of Painting: Music in Modern Art* (Munich, 1999).

70 C. J. Stivale, 'Summary of *L'Abecedaire de Gilles*

Deleuze, avec Claire Parnet' (2000), http://www.lang
lab.wayne.edu/Romance/FreD_G/ABC1.html.
71 Kwa, 'Romantic and Baroque Conceptions', pp. 22–52.
72 C. J. Stivale, 'Summary', p. 2.
73 D. W. Smith, 'Deleuze's Theory of Sensation:
Overcoming the Kantian Duality', in *Deleuze: A Critical
Reader*, ed. P. Patton (Oxford, 1996), pp 29–56. Quote
from p. 40.
74 Smith, 'Deleuze's Theory', quote from p. 43.
75 B. Massumi, 'The Autonomy of Affect', in *Observing
Complexity: Systems Theory and Postmodernity*,
ed. W. Rasch and C. Wolfe (Minneapolis, 2000),
pp. 273–97. Quote from p. 288.
76 And they seem to do this in some profusion. So, for
example, ecosystems exhibit 'the baroque of nature'
(Margalef, cited in R. Solé, R. Goodwin and
B. Goodwin, *Signs of Life: How Complexity Pervades
Biology*, New York, 2000, p. 179) in that they contain
many more species than would ever be necessary
if biological efficiency were the only criterion for their
organization.
77 Here, we are registering our pleasure and indeed surprise at the 'pre-disciplinary' (rather than 'post-disci-
plinary') feel to this project, despite the 'disciplinary'
divides that would normally keep the pieces that this
book contains well apart!
78 G. Deleuze, *Spinoza: Practical Philosophy* (1970) (San
Francisco, 1988), p. 124.
79 R. E. Kohler, *Labscapes and Landscapes: Exploring The
Lab-Field Border in Biology* (Chicago, 2002).

section one: *'Flow*

STEPHEN J. COLLIER: 'Pipes'
1 See Stephen Graham and Simon Marvin, *Splintering
Urbanism: Networked Infrastructures, Technological
Mobilities and the Urban Condition* (London, 2001).
2 See, for example, The World Bank, *Russia: Toward
Medium-Term Viability* (Washington, DC, 1996).
3 Anna Raff, 'Gazprom Follows Path Laid by the West',
Moscow Times, 26 July 2001.

ERIC SHEPPARD AND WILLIAM S. LYNN: 'Cities'
1 S. J. Gould, *Life's Grandeur* (London, 1997).

Further Reading
Cronon, W., *Nature's Metropolis: Chicago and the Great
West* (New York, 1991)
Harvey, D., *Spaces of Hope* (Berkeley, CA, 2000)
Lynn, W. S., '*Canis Lupus Cosmopolis*: Wolves in a Cosmo-
politan Worldview', *Worldviews* VI/3 (2003), pp. 300–27.
Sandercock, L., *Towards Cosmopolis* (London, 1998)

Wolch, J., 'Living in Harmony: A City for People and
Animals', *Sustainable Cities Program Newsletter*, no. 3
(April 2001), p. 6

LAURA CAMERON: 'Ecosystems'
1 A. G. Tansley, 'The Temporal Genetic Series as a Means
of Approach to Philosophy', 5 May 1932, Tansley
Archive, Department of Plant Sciences, Cambridge;
L. Cameron, *Anthropogenic Natures: Wicken Fen and
Histories of Disturbance, 1923–43*, PHD dissertation,
University of Cambridge, 2001, pp. 156–60. For a fuller
discussion of Tansley's talk at the Magdalen Philosophy
Club, see Peder Anker, *Imperial Ecology: Environmental
Order in the British Empire, 1895–1945* (Cambridge, MA,
2001), pp. 136–43; Anker's book also contains interest-
ing analyses of ecology–psychology connections in
Tansley's work.
2 A. G. Tansley, *The British Islands and their Vegetation*
(Cambridge, 1939), p. vi.
3 A. G. Tansley, 'The Use and Abuse of Vegetational
Concepts and Terms', *Ecology*, XVI (16 July 1935), p. 303.

Further Reading
Cameron, L., 'Histories of Disturbance', *Radical History
Review*, LXXIV (1999), pp. 4–24
—, and Forrester, J., 'A Nice Type of the English Scientist:
Tansley and Freud', *History Workshop Journal*, XLVIII
(Autumn 1999), pp. 64–100
—, 'Tansley's Psychoanalytic Network: An Episode out of
the Early History of Psychoanalysis in England',
Psychoanalysis and History, II/2 (2000), pp. 189–256

KEITH RICHARDS: 'Rivers'
1 S. E. Nicholson, 'Environmental Change within the
Historical Period', in *The Physical Geography of Africa*,
ed. W. M. Adams, A. S. Goudie and A. R. Orme
(Oxford 1966), pp. 60–87. Quote is from p. 70.
2 *Ibid.* Quote is from p. 71.
3 P. A. Shaw, 'Late Quaternary Landforms and
Environmental Change in Northwest Botswana: The
Evidence of Lake Ngami and the Mababe Depression',
Transactions of the Institute of British Geographers,
X (1985), pp. 333–46.
4 International Court of Justice, *Kasikili-Sedudu Island*
(Botswana / Namibia, 1996–9). http://www.icjcij.org/
icjwww/idocket/ibona/ibonaframe.htm

MARTIN KIRKBRIDE: 'Scree'
1 B. J. Skinner and S. C. Porter, *Physical Geology*
(New York, 1987), p. 227.
2 C. K. Ballantyne and C. Harris, *The Periglaciation of
Great Britain* (Cambridge, 1994), p. 220.
3 *Ibid.*, p. 219.

DEBORAH PARSONS: 'Drifts'

1 Le Corbusier, *The City of Tomorrow and its Planning* (London, 1929).
2 Roland Barthes, *The Pleasure of the Text*, trans. Richard Miller (London, 1976).
3 Mike Davis, *City of Quartz: Excavating the Future in Los Angeles* (New York, 1992).
4 Michel de Certeau, 'Walking in the City', in *The Practice of Everyday Life*, trans. Steven Rendall (Berkeley, CA, 1984).

KEN HILLIS: 'Virtual Space'

1 Rob Shields, 'Virtual Spaces?', *Space and Culture*, IX (2000), pp. 1–13.
2 Pierre Lévy, *Becoming Virtual: Reality in the Digital Age*, trans. Robert Bononno (New York, 1998).
3 See http://www.kbyu.org/membership/card/zions.html For the Zion Canyon Theatre, see also http://www.zioncanyontheatre.com/randbody1.htm (last accessed 6 October 2001).

DAVID MATLESS: 'Post Offices'

1 Bernhard Siegert, *Relays*, (Stanford, CA, 1999).
2 Karal Ann Marling, *Wall-to-Wall America: A Cultural History of Post-Office Murals in the Great Depression*, (Minneapolis, MN, 1982).
3 'My Early Life, by Allan, the Singing Postman', *East Anglia Magazine*, January 1976, pp. 106–7.

JOHN MENZIES: 'Drumlins'
Further Reading
Menzies, J., and J. Rose, eds, *Drumlin Symposium* (Rotterdam, 1987)
Menzies, J., and W. W. Shilts, 'Subglacial Environments', in *Modern and Past Glacial Environments*, ed. J. Menzies (Oxford, 2002), pp. 183–278

NICK SPEDDING: 'Glaciers'

1 F. Fleming, *Killing Dragons: The Conquest of the Alps* (London, 2000).
2 F. Spufford, *I May Be Some Time: Ice and the English Imagination* (London, 1996).
3 See G.K.C. Clarke, 'A Short History of Scientific Investigations on Glaciers', *Journal of Glaciology* (Special Issue, 1987), pp. 4–24.
4 P. G. Knight, 'Progress Review: Glaciers', *Progress in Physical Geography*, XXII/3 (1998), pp. 407–11.

DAVID N. LIVINGSTONE: 'Climate'

1 Samuel Haughton, *Six Lectures On Physical Geography* (Dublin and London, 1880), p. 74.
2 A. Austin Miller, *Climatology* (London, 1931), p. 2.

3 Immanuel Kant, 'On Countries that Are Known and Unknown to Europeans', from *Physical Geography*, trans. K. M. Faull and E. C. Eze, in Emmanuel Chukwudi Eze, ed., *Race and the Enlightenment: A Reader* (Oxford, 1997), pp. 58–64, on pp. 63, 64.
4 William Diller Matthew, *Climate and Evolution* (London, 1939), p. 43.
5 Ralph Abercromby, *Seas and Skies in Many Latitudes; or, Wanderings in Search of Weather* (London, 1888), pp. 365, 366.
6 Robert DeCourcy Ward, *Climate, Considered Especially in Relation to Man* (London, 1908), p. 227.

Further Reading
Frisinger, H. H., *The History of Meteorology to 1800* (New York, 1977)
Jankovic, V., *Reading the Skies: A Cultural History of English Weather, 1650–1820* (Manchester, 2000)
Livingstone, D. N., 'Race, Space and Moral Climatology: Notes toward a Genealogy', *Journal of Historical Geography*, XXVIII (2002), pp. 159–80
Middleton, W.E.K., *A History of the Theories of Rain and other Forms of Precipitation* (New York, 1966)
Naraindas, H., 'Poisons, Putresence and the Weather: A Genealogy of the Advent of Tropical Medicine', *Contributions to Indian Sociology*, XXX (1996), pp. 1–35

JOHN WESTERN: 'Rivers'

1 There is some anachronism here, because apparently the use in common parlance of the term 'The Hexagon' really took root only in the mid-1960s. See E. Weber, 'In Search of the Hexagon', *Stanford French Review* (Fall–Winter 1988), pp. 367–85.

DAVID PINDER: 'Meanders'

1 Le Corbusier, *Precisions on the Present State of Architecture and City Planning*, trans. Edith Schreiber Aujame (1930) (Cambridge, MA, 1991), p. 4.
2 *Ibid.*, p. 60.
3 *Ibid.*, pp. 29–30.
4 Le Corbusier, *The Radiant City*, trans. Pamela Knight, Eleanor Levieux and Derek Coltman (1935) (London, 1967), p. 82.
5 Le Corbusier, *Precisions*, p. 5.
6 Le Corbusier, *The Radiant City*, p. 80.
7 Le Corbusier, *Precisions*, p. 154.
8 *Ibid.*, p. 239.
9 *Ibid.*, p. 143.
10 Louis Aragon, *Paris Peasant*, trans. S. W. Taylor (1924–5) (London, 1980).
11 Roger Cardinal, 'Soluble City: The Surrealist Perception of Paris', *Architectural Design*, II–III (1978), pp. 143–9. Quote from pp. 146–7.

GEORGE REVILL: 'Railways'
1 D. Nye, *American Technological Sublime* (Cambridge, MA, 1994), pp. 75–6.
2 W. Schivelbusch, *The Railway Journey: The Industrialisation of Time and Space in the 19th Century* (Leamington Spa, 1986), pp. 52–65.
3 S. Kern, *The Culture of Time and Space, 1880–1918* (Cambridge, MA, 1983), pp. 217–18.
4 Nye, *American Technological Sublime*, p. 58; see also L. Marx, *The Machine in the Garden: Technology and the Pastoral Ideal in America* (Oxford, 1964), pp. 191–5.

PETER MERRIMAN: 'Freeways'
1 Lawrence Halprin, *Freeways* (New York, 1966), p. 37.
2 *Ibid.*
3 J. Pearsall and B. Trumble, eds, *The Oxford English Reference Dictionary* (Oxford, 1996), p. 1601.
4 Peter Nichols, *The Freeway* (London, 1975).
5 J. G. Ballard, *Concrete Island* (1974) (London, 1994), p. 131; J. G. Ballard, *Crash* (London, 1973).

TIM UNWIN: 'Trade'
1 F. Braudel, *Civilization and Capitalism 15th–18th Centuries. Volume II: The Wheels of Commerce*, trans. S. Reynolds (London, 1982), pp. 400–01.
2 T. Unwin, *Wine and the Vine* (London, 1996).
3 Herodotus, *The Histories*, trans. A. de Sélincourt (Harmondsworth, 1954), p. 92.
4 Diodorus Siculus, *Bibliotheca Historica III*, trans. C. H. Oldfather (London, 1939).
5 M. K. James, *Studies in the Medieval Wine Trade*, ed. E. M. Veale (Oxford, 1971).
6 G. F. Steckley, 'The Wine Economy of Tenerife in the 17th Century: Anglo-Spanish Partnerships in a Luxury Trade', *Economic History Review*, XXXIII (1980), pp. 335–50.

LUCIANA MARTINS: 'Continents'
1 Greg Dening, *Performances* (Chicago, 1996), p. 210.
2 Alexander Dalrymple, *An Account of the Discoveries made in the South Pacifick Ocean Previous to 1765* (London, 1767), p. 92.
3 Jonathan Lamb, Vanessa Smith and Nicholas Thomas, eds, *Exploration & Exchange: A South Seas Anthology, 1680–1900* (Chicago, 2000), p. xv.
4 See Horacio Capel, *La física sagrada* (Barcelona, 1985), pp. 51–5.
5 Quoted in Jean-Paul Duviols, 'The Patagonian "Giants"', in *Patagonia: Natural History, Prehistory and Ethnography at the Uttermost End of the Earth*, ed. C. McEwan, L. A. Borrero and A. Prieto (London, 1997), p. 134.
6 Nicholas Thomas, Harriet Guest and Michael

Dettelbach, eds, *Observations Made during a Voyage round the World, by Johann Reinhold Forster* (Honolulu, 1996), p. 192.
7 Richard D. Keynes, *Charles Darwin's Beagle Diary* (Cambridge, 1988), pp. 222–3.

DAVID G. PASSMORE: 'Battlefields'
1 J. Keegan, *The Face of Battle* (London, 1976).
2 *Ibid.*
3 D. D. Scott, R. A. Fox jr, M. A. Connor and D. Harmon, *Archaeological Perspectives on the Battle of the Little Big Horn* (Norman, OK, 1989).
4 J. Carman 'Bloody Meadows: The Places of Battle', in *The Familiar Past? Archaeologies of Later Historical Britain*, ed. S. Tarlow and S. West (London, 1999).

PHIL DUNHAM: 'Dust'
1 That endless, irksome chore, 'dusting'.
2 The title of an article by Thomas, written in 1914 and published in the *English Review*.
3 Edward Thomas, from 'After You Speak' (1916).

Further Reading
K. Pye, 'Dust', in *The Oxford Companion to the Earth*, ed. P. Hancock and B. Skinner (Oxford, 2000), p. 267.
D. Wright, ed., *Edward Thomas: Selected Poems And Prose* (Harmondsworth, 1981).

ISMO KANTOLA: 'Pollution'
1 Ismo Kantola 'Towards a Sociology of Energy Issues', in *Green Moves, Political Stalemates: Sociological Perspectives on the Environment*, ed. Annamari Konttinen (Turku, 1996).
2 Terry Shinn, 'Formes de division du travail scientifique et convergence intellectuelle: la recherche technico-instrumentale', *Revue Française du Sociologie*, XLI–XLIII (2000), pp. 447–73.

ALASTAIR DAWSON: 'Climate'
1 'Greenland Summit Ice Cores: Greenland Ice Sheet Project 2 / Greenland Ice Core Project', *Journal of Geophysical Research*, CII/C12 (1997), pp. 26, 317–26, 885.
2 K. J. Kreutz and P. A. Mayewski, 'Bipolar Changes in Atmospheric Circulation during the Little Ice Age', *Science*, 277 (1997), pp. 1294–6; L. D. Meeker and P. A. Mayewski, 'A 1,400-Year High-Resolution Record of Atmospheric Circulation over the North Atlantic and Asia', *The Holocene*, XII (2002), pp. 257–66.
3 B. A. Haggart, 'Little Ice Age', in *The Oxford Companion to The Earth*, ed. P. L. Hancock and B. J. Skinner (Oxford, 2000), p. 1174.

LAURA CAMERON: 'LAKES'
1 The phrase 'topographies of forgetting' is the title of a paper given by Paul Connerton at the 'Forgetting' conference, co-organized by Connerton and held at the Institute of Romance Studies, School of Advanced Study, University of London, Senate House, 4–5 July 2002; the paper is part of his forthcoming book, *How Modernity Forgets.*

Further Reading
Cameron, Laura, *Openings: A Meditation on History, Method and Sumas Lake* (Montreal, 1997)
Carlson, Keith Thor, ed., *A Stó:lō Coast Salish Historical Atlas* (Vancouver, 2001), pp. 104–7
Spielman, Andrew, and Michael D'Antonio, *Mosquito: A Natural History of our Most Persistent and Deadly Foe* (London, 2001)

JULIAN A. DOWDESWELL: 'Oceans'
1 H. W. Menard and S. M. Smith, 'Hypsometry of Ocean Basin Provinces', *Journal of Geophysical Research*, LXXI (1966), pp. 4305–25.

DAVID SUGDEN: 'Ice Sheets'
1 R. F. Scott, *Voyage of the 'Discovery'* (London, 1905), vol. II, p. 415.
2 H. T. Ferrar, 'Summary of the Geological Observations made during the Cruise of the ss "Discovery", 1901–1904', in Scott, *ibid.*, vol. II, p. 460.
3 F. Nansen, *The First Crossing of Greenland* (London, 1890).
4 *Ibid.*
5 E. H. Shackleton, *The Heart of the Antarctic* (London, 1909), vol. I, pp. 328–47.
6 S. Solomon, *The Coldest March* (New Haven and London, 2001).
7 D. Mawson, *The Home of the Blizzard* (London, 1915).
8 V.L.A. Campbell, 'Narrative of the Northern Party', in R. F. Scott, *Scott's Last Expedition* (London, 1913), vol. II, pp. 60–140.

ERIK SWYNGEDOUW: 'Water'
1 S. Postel, *The Last Oasis* (London, 1992); C. Ward, *Reflected in Water* (London and Washington, DC, 1997).
2 D. Rothenberg and M. Ulvaeus, eds, *Writing on Water* (Cambridge, MA, 2001).
3 E. Swyngedouw, *Flows of Power* (Oxford, 2004).

ANNA R. DAVIES: 'Pollutants'
1 Mary Douglas *Purity and Danger: An Analysis of Concepts of Pollution and Taboo* (London, 1966).
2 *Ibid.*

IAN COOK: 'Trade'
1 Donna Haraway, 'Modest_Witness@Second_Millennium', in *The Social Shaping of Technology*, ed. Donald MacKenzie and Judy Wajcman (2nd edn, Buckingham, 1999), pp. 41–9. Quote from p. 47.

Further Reading
Anon., *Codex Alimentarius Volume 5B: Tropical Fresh Fruits & Vegetables* (Rome, 1993)
Harrison, Michelle, *King Sugar: Jamaica, the Caribbean and the World Sugar Economy* (London, 2001)
Heal, Carolyn, and Allsop, Michael, *Queer Gear: How To Buy and Cook Exotic Fruits & Vegetables* (London, 1986)
Lee, Roger, 'Trade', in *The Dictionary of Human Geography*, ed. Ron Johnston, Derek Gregory, Geraldine Pratt and Michael Watts (4th edn, Oxford, 2000), pp. 844–6
Medlicott, Andrew, *Product Specifications and Post-Harvest Handling for Fruits, Vegetables and Root Crops Exported from the Caribbean* (Barbados, 1990)

MARK GOTTDIENER: 'Airports'
1 M. Gottdiener, *Life in the Air: Surviving the New Culture of Air Travel* (Boulder, CO, 2001).
2 Joe Palco, 'Morning Edition', *National Public Radio*, 9 August 2002.

section two: *Site*

DAVID MATLESS: 'Fields'
1 T. J. Barrett, *Harnessing the Earthworm* (London, 1949).
2 For a comprehensive account of the field customs of the region, see Peter Fenn, *Folklore of the Eastern Counties* (Lavenham, 1974), pp. 79–97.

CHARLES WARREN: 'Wilderness'
1 W. Cronon, 'The Trouble with Wilderness; or, Getting Back to the Wrong Nature', in *Uncommon Ground: Rethinking the Human in Nature*, ed. W. Cronon (New York, 1995), pp. 69–90.
2 J. Lister-Kaye, 'The Enjoyment and Understanding of Nature and Wildness', in *Enjoyment and Understanding of the Natural Heritage*, ed. M. B. Usher (Edinburgh, 2001), pp. 3–10. Quote from p. 10.
3 S. Budiansky, *Nature's Keepers: The New Science of Nature Management* (London, 1995), p. 16.
4 Cronon, 'Trouble with Wilderness', quote from p. 79 and p. 80.
5 Aldo Leopold, *A Sand County Almanac, and Sketches Here and There* (New York, 1949), p. vii.

6 J. Vidal, 'A Great White Lie', *The Guardian*, 1 December 2001.

7 Leopold, *Sand County Almanac*, p. 201.

8 Henry David Thoreau, cited in M. Oelschlaeger, *The Idea of Wilderness: From Prehistory to the Age of Ecology* (New Haven, 1991), p. 2.

TARIQ JAZEEL: 'Parks'

1 William Cronon, 'Introduction: In Search of Nature', in his *Uncommon Ground: Rethinking the Human Place in Nature* (New York, 1995), pp. 23–68. Quote from p. 36.

2 *Ibid*. Quote from p. 32.

3 Denis Cosgrove, 'Ideas and Culture: A Response to Don Mitchell. Exchange: There's No Such Thing as Culture?', *Transactions of the Institute of British Geographers*, XXI (1996), pp. 572–82. Quote from p. 575.

4 'Papers Relating to the Working of the Game Ordinance, No. 6 of 1872', by the Assistant Government Agent of Tangalle, Ceylon, Mr F. C. Fisher, *circa* 1873–4 (Public Record Office Library, London, CO57/84).

MICHAEL MAYERFELD BELL: 'Farms'

1 Horace, *The Essential Horace*, trans. Burton Raffel (San Francisco, 1983).

2 Horace, *Satires and Epistles of Horace* (*c.* 20 BC), trans. Bovie Palmer Smith (Chicago, 1959).

3 *Ibid.*

4 C. T. Onions, *The Oxford Universal Dictionary on Historical Principles* (1933) (3rd edn, Oxford, 1955).

CALVIN HEUSSER: 'Bogs'

1 P. V. Glob, *The Bog People* (New York, 1971).

2 J. Iversen, 'Land Occupation in Denmark's Stone Age', *Danmarks Geologiske Undersøgelse*, II/66 (1941).

3 T. E. Maenza-Gmeltch, 'Holocene Vegetation, Climate and Fire History of the Hudson Highlands, Southeastern New York', *The Holocene*, VII (1977), pp. 25–37; C. J. Heusser, 'Paleoindians and Fire during the Late Quaternary in Southern South America', *Rev. Chilena Hist. Nat.*, LXVII (1994), pp. 435–43.

4 A. M. Solomon and M. F. Buell, 'Effects of Suburbanization upon Airborne Pollen', *Bull. Torrey Bot. Club*, XCVI (1969), pp. 435–45.

ROBYN LONGHURST: 'Humans'

1 Roger Ebert, 'Review of *Planet of the Apes*', *Chicago Sun-Times*, 27 July 2001 (http://www.suntimes.com/ebert/ebert_reviews/2001/07/072701.html).

2 *Ibid.*

3 Tim Ingold, 'From Trust to Domination: An Alternative History of Human–Animal Relations', in

Animals and Human Society, ed. A. Manning and J. Serpell (London, 1994).

4 Kay Anderson, 'Animals, Science and Spectacle in the City', in *Animal Geographies: Place, Politics and Identity in the Nature–Culture Borderlands*, ed. J. Wolch and J. Emel (London and New York, 1998), pp. 27–50. Quote from p. 30.

5 See Chris Philo and Chris Wilbert, eds, *Animal Spaces, Beastly Places: New Geographies of Human–Animal Relations* (London and New York, 2000).

BETH GREENHOUGH: 'Islands'

1 Bill Bryson, *Notes from a Small Island* (London, 1995), pp. 32–3, emphasis added.

2 Alfred Russel Wallace, *Island Life* (London, 1880), p. 207.

3 Bryson, *Notes*, p. 32.

4 *Ibid.*

YVONNE RYDIN: 'Beaches'

1 Roland Barthes, *Mythologies* (Paris, 1957).

DAVID J. NASH: 'Deserts'

1 T. Pringle, *African Sketches* (London, 1834).

2 B. Watterson, *The Gods of Ancient Egypt* (London, 1984).

3 P. Coelho, *The Alchemist* (London, 1988), p. 117.

4 M. Leach and R. Mearns, 'Challenging Received Wisdom in Africa', in *The Lie of the Land*, ed. M. Leach and R. Mearns (Oxford, 1996), pp. 1–33.

5 M. Ondaatje, *The English Patient* (London, 1992), p.150.

6 D.S.G. Thomas, 'Arid Environments: Their Nature and Extent', in *Arid Zone Geomorphology: Process, Form and Change in Drylands*, ed. D.S.G. Thomas (Chichester, 1977), pp. 3–12.

JULIAN A. DOWDESWELL: 'Floods'

1 R. B. Waitt, 'Case for Periodic, Colossal Jökulhlaups from Pleistocene Glacial Lake Missoula', *Bulletin, Geological Society of America*, XCVI (1985), pp. 1271–86.

2 V. R. Baker, 'Erosional Processes in Channelized Water Flows on Mars', *Journal of Geophysical Research*, LXXXIV (1979), pp. 7985–993.

3 M. G. Wolman and R. Gerson, 'Relative Scales of Time and Effectiveness of Climate in Watershed Geomorphology', *Earth Surface Processes*, III (1978), pp. 189–208.

NINA LAURIE: 'Dams'

1 Roy, Arundhati, 'The Greater Common Good', *World Watch*, XIV (2001), pp. 33–6. p. 33.

2 World Commission for Dams, *Dams and Development: A New Framework for Decision Making*

(World Bank, 17 November 2000). www.dams.org.
3 'A River Damed Tamed to Power Stripped of Salmon: What Next for the Columbia Power?', *National Geographic* (April 2001).
4 N. Laurie and S. Marvin, 'Globalisation, Neo-Liberalism and Negotiated Development in the Andes: Bolivian Water and the Misicuni Dream', *Environment and Planning A*, XXXI (1999), pp. 1401–15.
5 N. Laurie, S. Radcliffe and R. Andolina, 'The New Excluded "Indigenous"?: The Implications of Multi-Ethnic Policies for Water Reform in Bolivia', in *'Pluri-Cultural and Multi-Ethnic': Implications for State and Society in Mesoamerica and the Andes*, ed. R. Sneider (London, 2001), pp. 252–76.

ROBBIE B. H. GOH: 'Churches'
1 C. Cunningham, *Stones of Witness: Church Architecture and Function* (Phoenix Mill, 1999), p. 1.
2 J. Wesley, *The Journal of John Wesley*, ed. Christopher Idle (Tring, Hertfordshire, 1986), p. 56.
3 J. McAndrew, *The Open-Air Churches of Sixteenth-Century Mexico* (Cambridge, MA, 1965), p. 344.
4 W. Wordsworth and S. T. Coleridge, *Lyrical Ballads*, ed. W.J.B. Owen (London, 1969), pp. 16, 117.

DAVID MATLESS: 'Villages'
1 Skipper Ronnie Balls MBE, from *Fish Capture* (1961).

CHRISTOPHER TILLEY: 'Tors'
1 J. Folliot-Stokes, *The Cornish Coast and Moors* (London, 1928), pp. 341–4.
2 T. Bound, *The A to Z of Dartmoor Tors* (Torquay, 1995).
3 C. Tilley and W. Bennett, 'An Archaeology of Super-natural Places: The Case of West Penwith', *Journal of the Royal Anthropological Institute*, VII (2001), pp. 335–62.
4 N. Johnson and P. Rose, *Bodmin Moor: An Archaeological Survey*, English Heritage Archaeological Report 24 (London, 1994).
5 C. Tilley, 'Rocks as Resources: Landscapes and Power', *Cornish Archaeology*, XXXIV (1995), pp. 5–57; C. Tilley, 'The Powers of Rocks: Topography and Monument Construction on Bodmin Moor', *World Archaeology*, XXVIII (1996), pp. 161–76; B. Bender, S. Hamilton and C. Tilley, 'Leskernick: Stone Worlds; Alternative Narratives; Nested Landscapes', *Proceedings of the Prehistoric Society*, LXIII (1997), pp. 147–78.
6 C. Tilley, S. Hamilton, S. Harrison and E. Andersen, 'Nature, Culture, Clitter: Distinguishing between Cultural and Geomorphological Landscapes: The Case of Tors in South-West England', *Journal of Material Culture*, V (2000), pp. 197–224.

SARAH G. CANT: 'Caves'
1 A. Gemmell and J. O. Myers, *Underground Adventure* (Clapham, Yorkshire, and London, 1952), p. 5.
2 C.H.D. Cullingford, ed., *British Caving: An Introduction to Speleology* (London, 1962), p. 560.
3 D. Robinson and A. Greenbank, *Caving and Potholing* (London, 1964), p. 9.

NICK FYFE: 'Police Stations'
1 J. Foster, 'Two Stations: An Ethnographic Study of Policing in the Inner City', in *Crime and the City*, ed. D. Downes (London, 1989), p. 131.
2 S. Choongh, *Policing as Social Discipline* (Oxford, 1997), p. 87.
3 S. Herbert, *Policing Space: Territoriality and the Los Angles Police Department* (Minnesota, 1997).
4 Choongh, *Policing*, p. 88.
5 *Ibid.*, p. 97.
6 M. Young, *An Inside Job: Policing and Police Culture in Britain* (Oxford, 1991), p. 154.

ANSSI PAASI: 'Boundaries'
1 M. Anderson, *Frontiers: Territory and State formation in the Modern World* (London, 1996).
2 G. Perec, *Espèces d´espaces* (Paris, 1974).

MICHAEL WATTS: 'Natural Resources'
1 R. Kapucinski, *Shah of Shahs* (New York, 1982), p. 45.
2 F. Coronil, *The Magical State* (Chicago, 1997).
3 Kapucinski, *Shah of Shahs*, p. 34.
4 D. Harvey, *Justice, Nature and the Geography of Difference* (Oxford, 1996), p. 147.

TREVOR BARNES: 'Central Places'
1 W. Christaller, *Central Places in Southern Germany*, trans. C. W. Baskin (1933; Englewood Cliffs, NJ, 1967).
2 A. Lösch, *The Economics of Location*, trans W. H. Woglom and W. F. Stolper (1940) (2nd edn, New Haven, CT, 1954), p. 4.
3 *Ibid.*, p. 364.

MICHAEL J. SHAPIRO: 'States'
1 S. Alexie, 'Indian Country', *New Yorker* (13 March 2000), p. 82.
2 *Ibid.*, p. 77.
3 W. Boelhower, 'Stories of Foundation, Scenes of Origin', *American Literary History*, V/3 (Fall 1993), p. 391.
4 *Ibid.*, p. 392.
5 J. Fenimore Cooper, 'American and European Scenery Compared,' in M. F. Deakin's facsimile reproduction of *The Home Book of the Picturesque; or, American Scenery, Art and Literature: Comprising a Series of Essays by Washington Irving, W. G. Bryant, Fenimore*

Cooper and Others (1952) (Gainesville, FL, 1967), p. 52.
6 Ibid., p. 68.
7 Ibid., p. 52.
8 K. H. Basso, *Wisdom Sits in Places: Landscape and Language among the Western Apache* (Albuquerque, NM, 1996), p. 34.
9 Ibid., p. 32.
10 Ibid., p. 7.
11 A. Trachtenberg, 'Naming the View', in *Reading American Photographs* (New York, 1989), p. 12.

SOPHIE WATSON: 'Refuges'
1 G. Mason, 'Violence', in *Oxford Companion to Australian Feminism*, ed. B. Caine et al. (Oxford, 1997), p. 343.

HENRY WAI-CHUNG YEUNG: 'Enterprise Zones'
1 Jonathan Potter and Barry Moore, 'UK Enterprise Zones and the Attraction of Inward Investment', *Urban Studies*, XXXVII/8 (2000), pp. 1279–312. See p. 1280.
2 See http://www.cssd.com.cn/index_e.htm
3 Carolyn Cartier, *Globalizing South China* (Oxford, 2001).
4 Richard Walker, 'California's Golden Road to Riches: Natural Resources and Regional Capitalism, 1848–1940', *Annals of the Association of American Geographers*, XCI/1 (2001), pp. 167–99.

GARETH A. JONES: 'Slums'
1 Olavo Bilac, cited in Jeffrey D. Needell, 'Rio de Janeiro and Buenos Aires: Public Space and Public Consciousness in Fin-de-Siècle Latin America', *Comparative Studies in Society and History*, XXXVII (1995), pp. 519–40. Quote from p. 533.
2 Aldous Huxley, *Beyond the Mexique Bay* (London, 1934), p. 18.
3 Robert D. Kaplan, 'The Coming Anarchy', *Atlantic Monthly*, CCLXXIII/273 (1994), pp. 44–76. Quote from p. 54.
4 Samuel Schulman, 'Latin American Shantytown', *New York Times Magazine*, 16 January 1966, pp. 30–33.

JOE KERR: 'Garden Cities'
1 Ebenezer Howard, *To-morrow, a Peaceful Path to Real Reform* (London, 1898); revised in the same year as *Garden Cities of To-morrow*.

MATTHEW GANDY: 'Towns'
1 Frederick R. Hiorns, *Town-Building in History* (London, 1956), p. 5.
2 Fox Butterfield, 'Why America's Murder Rate is so High', *New York Times*, 26 July 1998.
3 Henri Lefebvre, 'Notes on the New Town', in *Introduction to Modernity: Twelve Preludes, September 1959–May 1961*, trans. John Moore (1962) (London and New York, 1995), pp. 116–26. Quote from p. 116.
4 Ibid., quote from p. 117.

DYDIA DELYSER: 'Ghost Towns'
1 Mark Twain (Samuel L. Clemens), *Roughing It* (Hartford, CT, 1872; facsimile of first edition, New York, n.d.), p. 435.
2 Dydia DeLyser, 'Authenticity on the Ground: Engaging the Past in a California Ghost Town', *Annals of the Association of American Geographers*, LXXXIX/4 (1999), pp. 602–32.
3 Richard White, *It's Your Misfortune and None of My Own: A New History of the American West* (Norman, OK, 1991).
4 DeLyser, 'Authenticity on the Ground'.
5 Anon., 'Here and There on the Desert', *Desert Magazine*, I/11 (September 1938), p. 28.
6 'Throngs Visit Ghost Town and Knott's', *Long Beach Press Telegram*, 16 October 1941.

MARK GOTTDIENER: 'Cities'
1 See M. Gottdiener, *The Social Production of Urban Space* (2nd edn, Austin, TX, 1994); M. Gottdiener and R. Hutchison, *The New Urban Sociology* (2nd edn, New York, 2000).
2 M. Dear, *From Chicago to LA* (Oxford, 2001).
3 Gottdiener, *The Social Production of Urban Space*.
4 R. Venturi, S. Brown and S. Izenour, *Learning from Las Vegas* (Cambridge, MA, 1972).
5 See M. Gottdiener et al., *Las Vegas: The Social Production of an All American City* (Oxford, 1999).

NANCY DUNCAN: 'Suburbs'
1 A. Barbour and D. Fish, 'The Biological and Social Phenomenon of Lyme Disease', *Science*, 260 (11 June 1993).
2 M. Purdy, 'Don't Go in the Water, or the Sun or the Shade', *New York Times*, 8 July 2001, p. 21.
3 A. Karlen, *The Biography of a Germ* (Guernsey, 2001), p. 19.

LEWIS HOLLOWAY: 'Farms'
1 A. O'Hagan, 'The Killing Fields', *The Guardian*, G2, 10 May 2001, pp. 3–4.
2 Suffolk farmer, quoted in A. O'Hagan, 'Bitter Harvest', *The Guardian*, G2, 26 March 2001, pp. 4–5
3 O'Hagan, 'The Killing Fields'.

SUE HAMILTON: 'Hills'
1 R. Bradley, *An Archaeology of Natural Places* (London and New York, 2000), p. 6.
2 D. Cosgrove, 'Landscapes and Myths, Gods and

Humans', in *Landscape Politics and Perspective*, ed. B. Bender (Oxford, 1995), pp. 283 and 289.
3 C. Tilley, *A Phenomenology of Landscape* (Oxford, 1994), pp. 124 and 159.
4 B. Bender, S. Hamilton, and C. Tilley, 'Leskernick: Stone Worlds; Alternative Narratives; Nested Landscapes', *Proceedings of the Prehistoric Society*, LXIII (1997), pp. 147–78.
5 J. Thomas, 'The Politics of Vision and the Archaeologies of Landscape', in *Landscape Politics and Perspective*, p. 38.
6 J. Barrett, *Fragments from Antiquity* (Oxford, 1994), pp. 136–8.

section three: *Matter*

INTRODUCTION
1 J. A. Amato, *Dust: A History of the Small and Invisible* (Berkeley, CA, 2000).
2 A. Mackenzie, *Transductions: Bodies and Machines at Speed* (London, 2002).
3 D. Tiffany, *Toy Medium: Materialism and Modern Lyric* (Berkeley, CA, 2000).
4 L. Marks, *Touch: Sensuous Theory and Multisensory Media* (Minneapolis, MN, 2002).
5 P. Rabinow, *French DNA: Trouble in Purgatory* (Chicago, 1999).

TED BENTON: 'Bees'
1 P. R. Harvey, 'A Remarkable Example of Biodiversity: Aculeate Hymenoptera in the East Thames Corridor', *BWARS Newsletter* (1999), pp. 11–12.
2 W.F.L. Sladen, *The Humble-bee and How to Domesticate It* (London, 1912; reprinted Woonton, Herefordshire, 1989).
3 N. M. Saville, W. E. Dramstad, G.L.A. Fry and S. A. Corbet, 'Bumblebee Movement in a Fragmented Agricultural Landscape', *Agriculture, Ecosystems and Environment*, LXI (1997), pp. 145–54.
4 Ted Benton, *The Bumblebees of Essex* (Wimbish, 2000).

DIANE WATSON AND TONY WATSON: 'Pubs'
Further Reading
Dunkling, L. and G. Wright, *A Dictionary of Pub Names* (London, 1987)
Honeybone, M., *The Book of Grantham* (Buckingham, 1980)

NIGEL CLARK: 'Pigs'
1 Captain J. Cook, *Captain Cook in New Zealand* (1770) (Wellington, 1961 [1769–77]), p. 137.
2 Cited in N. Thomas, *Entangled Objects: Exchange, Material Culture and Colonialism in the Pacific*

(Cambridge, MA, 1991), p. 147.
3 Cook, *Captain Cook in New Zealand* (1769), p. 50.
4 *Ibid.* (1774), p. 216.
5 G. Park, *Nga Uruora: The Groves of Life: Ecology and History in a New Zealand Landscape* (Wellington, 1995), pp. 95–6.
6 Cook, *Captain Cook in New Zealand* (1770), p. 139.
7 *Ibid.* (1773), p. 200.

MYRA J. HIRD: 'Humans'
1 Asserting that mankind can speak for all humankind is not equivalent to denying the existence of womankind.
2 M. Rothblatt, *The Apartheid of Sex* (New York, 1995).
3 Sherri Groveman, 'The Hanukkah Bush: Ethical Implications in the Clinical Management of Intersex', in *Intersex in the Age of Ethics*, ed. Alice Domurat Dreger (Hagerstown, MA, 1999), pp. 23–8.
4 P. Califia, *Sex Changes: The Politics of Transgendering* (San Francisco, 1997).
5 Manuel DeLanda, *A Thousand Years of Nonlinear History* (New York, 1997), p. 103.
6 Lynn Margulis and Dorion Sagan, *What is Sex?* (New York, 1997).
7 *Ibid.*
8 For a fuller discussion, see M. Hird 'Re(pro)ducing Sexual Difference', *Parallax*, VIII/4 (2002), pp. 94–107.

DENIS COSGROVE: 'Moon'
1 Paul Coones, 'The Geographical Significance of Plutarch's Dialogue "Concerning the Face which Appears in the Orb of the Moon"', *Transactions, Institute of British Geographers*, VIII/3 (1983), pp. 361–72.
2 Eileen Reeves, *Painting the Heavens: Art and Science in the Age of Galileo* (Princeton, NJ, 1997).

STEVE HINCHLIFFE: 'Viruses'
1 G. Deleuze and F. Guattari, *A Thousand Plateaus: Capitalism and Schizophrenia* (London, 1988), p. 11.
2 World Bank, *World Development Report 1993: Investing in Health* (Oxford, 1993).
3 See A. Pavord, *The Tulip* (London, 1999).
4 *Ibid.*, p. 133.
5 *Ibid.*, p. 12.
6 K. Ansell-Pearson, *Viroid Life: Perspectives on Nietzsche and the Transhuman Condition* (London, 1997), p. 124.
7 Deleuze and Guattari, *A Thousand Plateaus*, p. 11.
8 Ansell-Pearson, *Viroid Life*, p. 133.
9 Deleuze and Guattari, *A Thousand Plateaus*, p. 10; see also Ansell-Pearson, *Viroid Life*, p. 134.
10 See B. Latour, 'When Things Strike Back: A Possible Contribution of Science Studies to the Social Sciences',

British Journal of Sociology, LI/1 (2000), pp. 107–23.

VANESSA WINCHESTER: 'Lichens'
1 Oliver Gilbert, 'Lichens', *The New Naturalist* (London, 2000), pp. 1–66, 167–87.
2 David L. Hawksworth and F. Rose, 'Lichens as Pollution Monitors', *Studies in Biology*, LXVI (1976), pp. 1–59.
3 David H. S. Richardson, 'Pollution Monitoring with Lichens', *Naturalists' Handbooks*, XIX (1992), pp. 1–76.
4 John L. Innes, 'Lichenometry', *Progress in Physical Geography*, IX (1985), pp. 187–254.
5 Vanessa Winchester, 'An Assessment of Lichenometry as a Method for Dating Recent Stone Movements in Two Stone Circles in Cumbria and Oxfordshire', *Botanical Journal of the Linnean Society*, XCVI (1988), pp. 57–68.

PHIL MACNAGHTEN: 'Trees'
1 T. Ingold, *Perceptions of the Environment: Essays in Livelihood, Dwelling and Skill* (London, 2000), p. 204.
2 L. Rival, *The Social Life of Trees: Anthropological Perspectives on Tree Symbolism* (Oxford, 1998).
3 T. Packenham, *Meetings with Remarkable Trees* (London, 1996).

RICHARD DENNIS: 'Slums'
1 Catherine Bauer, *Modern Housing* (Boston, MA, 1934).
2 *The Daily Telegraph*, 26–8 August 1970.
3 C.F.G. Masterman, *From the Abyss* (London, 1902), p. 8.
4 B. S. Townroe, *The Slum Problem* (London, 1930), p. 19.
5 George Godwin, *London Shadows* (London, 1854), pp. 7, 39 and 65.
6 Masterman, *From the Abyss*, p. 16.
7 Jack London, *The People of the Abyss* (1903) (London, 1978), p. 114.
8 David Reeder, *Charles Booth's Descriptive Map of London Poverty, 1889* (London, 1987).

Further Reading
Gaskell, S. M., ed., *Slums* (Leicester, 1990)
Mayne, A., *The Imagined Slum* (Leicester, 1993)

CHRIS OTTER: 'Streets'
1 Reported in *The Architect* (14 April 1877), p. 245.
2 Henry Allnutt, *Wood Pavements as Carried Out on Kensington High Road, Chelsea &c.* (London, 1880), pp. 3 and 16.
3 'Street Paving and Hygiene', *The Engineer* (28 December 1894), p. 573.
4 James Winter, *London's Teeming Streets* (London, 1993), p. 39. Unfortunately, I have been unable to locate any surviving portions myself.

STEVE PILE: 'Cities'
1 R. Park, 'Magic, Mentality and City Life', in *The City: Suggestions for Investigation of Human Behavior in the Urban Environment*, by R. E. Park, E. W. Burgess, R. D. McKenzie and L. Wirth (1925; reprinted Chicago, 1984), pp. 123–41. Quote from p. 131.
2 K. McCarthy Brown, *Mama Lola: A Vodou Priestess in Brooklyn* (revised edn, Berkeley, CA, 2001).
3 C. Penczak, *City Magick: Urban Rituals, Spells and Shamanism* (York Beach, ME, 2001), p. xiv.

ANDREW BARRY: 'Organics'
1 Michel Callon with Cécile Méadel and Vololona Rabeharisoa, 'The Economy of Qualities', *Economy and Society*, XXXI/2 (2002), pp. 194–217.

LISA LAW: 'Food'
1 From *A Moveable Feast* by Ernest Hemingway. Copyright © 1964 by Mary Hemingway. Copyright renewed © 1992 by John H. Hemingway, Patrick Hemingway and Gregory Hemingway. Text excerpt used by permission of Scribner, an imprint of Simon & Schuster Adult Publishing Group.

MIKE PEARSON: 'Horses'
This text draws upon E. C. Cawte, *Ritual Animal Disguise* (Cambridge, 1978); G. Deleuze and F. Guattari, *A Thousand Plateaus: Capitalism and Schizophrenia*, trans. B. Massumi (London, 1988); E. H. Gombrich, *Meditations on a Hobby Horse, and other Essays on the Theory of Art* (London, 1963); Alex Helm, *The English Mummer's Play* (Woodbridge, 1981); Ethel Rudkin, *Lincolnshire Folklore* (Gainsborough, 1936).

GAIL DAVIES: 'Wildlife'
1 P. Høeg, *The Woman and the Ape* (London, 1996).
2 D. Haraway, *Primate Visions* (London, 1989).
3 J. Knight, ed., *Natural Enemies: People–Wildlife Conflicts in Anthropological Perspective* (London, 2000).
4 Louis Leakey, cited in C. Jahme, *Beauty and the Beasts* (London, 2001).

WILLIAM S. LYNN: 'Animals'
Further Reading
Midgley, Mary, *Animals and Why They Matter* (Athens, GA, 1984)
Noske, Barbara, *Beyond Boundaries: Humans and Animals* (Montreal, 1997)
Philo, Chris, and Chris Wilbert, eds, *Animal Spaces, Beastly Places: New Geographies of Human–Animal Relations* (London, 2000)
Wolch, Jennifer, and Jody Emel, eds, *Animal Geographies:*

Place, Politics and Identity in the Nature–Culture Borderlands (London, 1998)

STEPHEN CAIRNS: 'Shadows'
1 M. Foucault, *Power / Knowledge: Selected Interviews and other Writings, 1972–1977* (Brighton, 1980), pp. 147 and 159–60.
2 J. P. Telotte, *Dreams of Darkness: Fantasy and the Films of Val Lewton* (Urbana, IL, 1985), p. 23.

STEVE BAKER: 'Mammals'
1 Britta Jaschinski, *Wild Things* (London, 2003).
2 Steve Connor, 'Quarter of Mammals Faced with Extinction', *The Independent*, 21 May 2002, p. 1.
3 Kate Rawles, 'Animals', *Environmental Values*, VI/4 (1997), p. 375.
4 Donna J. Haraway, *Modest_Witness@Second_Millenium.FemaleMan©_Meets_OncoMouse™: feminism and technoscience* (New York and London, 1997), pp. 79 and 98.
5 Rawles, 'Animals', p. 376.
6 Jo Shapcott, *Her Book: Poems, 1988–1998* (London and New York, 2000), p. 79.
7 G. Deleuze and F. Guattari, *A Thousand Plateaus: Capitalism and Schizophrenia* (London, 1988), pp. 239 and 244–5.
8 Alphonso Lingis, *Dangerous Emotions* (Berkeley, CA, 2000), pp. 32 and 27.

NIGEL CLARK: 'Fish'
1 Chris Bright, *Life out of Bounds* (London, 1999), p. 87.
2 Leon Croizat, Gareth Nelson and Donn Eric Rosen, 'Centres of Origin and Related Concepts', *Systematic Zoology*, XXIII/3 (1974), pp. 265–87. Quote from pp. 266–8.
3 Roderic D. M. Page, 'New Zealand and the New Biogeography', *New Zealand Journal of Zoology*, XVI/4 (1989), pp. 471–83. Quote from p. 474.
4 Cited in Russell Gray, 'Oppositions in Panbiogeography: Can the Conflicts between Selection, Constraint, Ecology and History be Resolved?', *New Zealand Journal of Zoology*, XVI/4 (1989), pp. 787–806. Quote from p. 797.
5 Robin Craw, John Grehan and Michael Heads, *Panbiogeography: Tracking the History of Life* (New York, 1999), p. 179.

NIGEL THRIFT: 'Radio'
1 L. Lessig, *The Future of Ideas. The Fate of the Commons in a Connected World* (New York, 2001).

AIHWA ONG: 'Island Nations'
1 George Cherian, *Singapore, the Air-Conditioned Nation: Essays on the Politics of Comfort and Control* (Singapore, 2000).
2 With a population of just under four million, in 1999 the per capita annual consumption was 113 cubic metres, and the average daily water consumption was 1.2 million cubic metres. There are no lakes or rivers to tap, and there is fear that the island is running out of water. 'Housing and Urban Redevelopment', Singapore Government, 2000. *http://www/sg/flavour/profile/Housing/Putili.htm*
3 'Singapore Floats Massive US$1.5b Water Project with Indonesia', *Straits Times*, 2 July 2000.
4 Aihwa Ong, 'Zones of New Sovereignty' in her *Flexible Citizenship* (Durham, NC, 1999).
5 'Singapore vs. Indonesian Relationship: Is Racism the Problem?', *Surat Kharbar*, 12 November 2000. See *http://www.suratkabar.com*
6 Karl Wittfogel, *Oriental Despotism* (New York, 1948).

ORVAR LÖFGREN: 'Regions'
1 See Anssi Paasi, *The Institutionalization of Regions: Theory and Comparative Cases* (Joensuu, 1986).
2 Christer Jönsson, Sven Tägil and Gunnar Törnqvist, *Organizing European Space* (London, 2000).
3 Per Olof Berg, Anders Linde-Laursen and Orvar Löfgren, *Invoking a Transnational Metropolis: The Making of the Oresound Region* (Lund, 2000).
4 See Jonas Frykman, 'Belonging in Europe: Modern Identities in Minds and Places', *Ethnologia Europea*, XXIX/2 (1999), pp. 13–23.

ANSSI PAASI: 'Territory'
1 A. Paasi, *Territories, Boundaries and Consciousness* (Chichester, 1996).
2 R. D. Sack, *Human Territoriality* (Cambridge, 1986).

STEPHAN HARRISON: 'Mountains'
1 J. D. Barrow, *Impossibility* (Oxford, 1999), p. 103.

FRANCIS SPUFFORD: 'Ice'
1 Thomas Carew (?1595–?1639), 'Chloris in the Snow'.
2 James Forbes, 'Pedestrianism in Switzerland', *Quarterly Review* (April 1857).
3 John Tyndall, *The Glaciers of the Alps* (London, 1860).

Contributors

KAY ANDERSON is Professor of Geography at Durham University, where she teaches courses on race, colonialism, culture and nature. She is the author of books, articles and chapters on these subjects, and co-editor of the *Handbook of Cultural Geography* (2002) and the journal *Progress in Human Geography*.

STEVE BAKER is Reader in Contemporary Visual Culture at the University of Central Lancashire. He is the author of *The Postmodern Animal* (2000) and of *Picturing the Beast: Animals, Identity and Representation* (2nd edn, 2001), and is on the Board of Editors of *Society and Animals*.

VIC BAKER is Regents' Professor and Head of the Department of Hydrology and Water Resources, Professor of Geosciences and Professor of Planetary Sciences at the University of Arizona. His varied research interests include fluvial geomorphology, palaeohydrology and planetary geomorphology. His particular research focus is on flood processes.

TREVOR BARNES is a Professor at the Department of Geography, University of British Columbia. His research interests are in economic geography, and, most recently, in the history of that discipline. He is the co-editor of *A Companion to Economic Geography* (2000), with Eric Sheppard.

ANDREW BARRY is Senior Lecturer in Sociology, Goldsmiths' College, University of London, and author of *Political Machines: Governing a Technological Society* (2001). He comes from a family of Somerset farmers, but now lives near an agrochemical research laboratory on the outskirts of Cambridge.

MICHAEL MAYERFELD BELL is Associate Professor of Rural Sociology at the University of Wisconsin-Madison and a part-time composer of songs, fiddle tunes and classical music. He is particularly interested in dialogue, democracy and un-finalizability in social, ecological and musical life. His most recent book is *Farming for Us All* (2004).

TED BENTON is Professor of Sociology at the University of Essex, where he teaches social theory, philosophy of social science and environmental sociology. Recent books include *The Greening of Marxism* (1996) and, with Ian Craib, *Philosophy of Social Science* (2001). He is an active field naturalist and wildlife photographer.

STEPHEN CAIRNS writes on architecture, urbanism and post-colonial theory, and has particular interests in Southeast Asia. He teaches in the Department of Architecture at the University of Edinburgh.

LAURA CAMERON is Canada Research Chair in Historical Geographies of Nature at Queen's University, Kingston, Ontario. She is the author of *Openings: A Meditation on History, Method and Sumas Lake* (1997). Much of her work explores local and disciplinary studies of natures / cultures, particularly in the context of British and Canadian ecology and conservation.

SARAH G. CANT is a Lecturer in Human Geography at the University of Wales, Aberystwyth. She was a graduate student in the Department of Geography at Royal Holloway, University of London. Her doctoral thesis examines cultural geographies of cave exploration and speleology in Britain during the twentieth century.

NIGEL CLARK lectures in Social Science at the Open University, Milton Keynes. His recent publications, 'The Demon-Seed' (*Theory, Culture and Society*, 2002) and 'Turbulent Prospects' (in *Shaping the City*, ed. Tim Hall and Malcolm Miles, 2003), explore the implications of the dynamic and unpredictable aspects of the natural world for both environmentalism and social thought.

STEPHEN J. COLLIER is Core Faculty at the Graduate Program for International Affairs at the New School University. He is co-editor, with Aikwa Ong, of *Global Assemblages: Technology, Politics and Ethics as Anthropological Problems* (forthcoming), and author of a book on post-Soviet Russia, *Post-Soviet Social: City Building in Neoclassical Times* (forthcoming).

IAN COOK is a Lecturer in Human Geography at the University of Birmingham. He traced papayas from UK supermarkets to Jamaican farms. But he promised not to name the fruit. Farmers feared consumer boycotts. That was ten years ago. Now, you can't find Jamaican papayas in UK supermarkets. So, he can write.

DENIS COSGROVE is Alexander von Humboldt Professor of Geography at UCLA. He has written and edited books and scholarly papers in cultural geography, notably on landscape, historically and, today, in Italy, Britain and America. His most recent book, *Apollo's Eye* (2001), explores the history of visualizing the globe.

MIKE CRANG grew up on a farm but wanted a job with holidays and a pension, so he left Devon and became a Lecturer in Geography at the University of Durham. He now produces papers and talks about things (including *Thinking Space*, co-edited with Nigel Thrift, 2000).

ANNA R. DAVIES is a Lecturer in Environmental Geography at Trinity College, University of Dublin, Ireland. She has research interests in the broad field of environmental policy and politics and is currently examining the role of transnational environmental networks in relation to environmental governance.

GAIL DAVIES is a cultural geographer interested in the hybrid spaces of science, nature and the media. She is currently working on a public consultation on options for organ transplantation, including xenotransplantation. Previous research has looked at the contested wildlife value of brownfield sites, and the development of natural history film-making.

ALASTAIR DAWSON is Professor of Quaternary Science in the Division of Geography at Coventry University. His research interests lie in palaeoclimatology and in the geomorphology of sea level change. He is the author of *Ice Age Earth* (1991).

JOHN DEARING is Professor of Physical Geography at the University of Liverpool. His main research interests lie in the use of environmental magnetism on lake sediments to reconstruct Holocene environmental change. He is

leader of the IGBP-PAGES Focus 5 programme: Past ecosystem processes and human-environment interactions.

DYDIA DELYSER is an Assistant Professor of Geography at Louisiana State University. A former of resident of Bodie, California, she has published on ghost towns in journals such as the *Annals of the Association of American Geographers* and the *Geographical Review*. She is currently at work on a book about ghost towns.

RICHARD DENNIS teaches historical geography at University College London. He has published extensively on housing in nineteenth- and early twentieth-century cities, and is currently working on a book on cities and modernity, incorporating material on London, New York and Toronto.

JULIAN A. DOWDESWELL is Director of the Scott Polar Research Institute and Professor of Physical Geography in the University of Cambridge. Julian is a glaciologist, whose research interests include investigating the form and flow of glaciers and ice caps and their response to climate change, and the links between former ice sheets and the marine geological record.

FELIX DRIVER is Professor of Human Geography at Royal Holloway, University of London, and the author of *Geography Militant: Cultures of Exploration and Empire* (2001) His current research is concerned with British visions of the tropical world. He recently worked on a collaborative art project at Royal Holloway entitled *Visualising Geography*.

NANCY DUNCAN, an affiliated Lecturer in the Department of Geography, University of Cambridge, is a cultural geographer with interests in social and political theory. She is a co-author of a monograph on the politics of a suburban landscape and editor of a collection of articles on gender and sexuality in the production of space.

PHIL DUNHAM is a Senior Lecturer in Geography at Coventry University. His principal research interests are in the fields of rural economic change and local economic development, but he has also published articles on the philosophy of geography using ideas derived from quantum theory.

NICK FYFE is Reader in Human Geography at the University of Dundee. His research interests include the geographies of crime and criminal justice and the voluntary sector and volunteering. He is author of *Protecting Intimidated Witnesses* (2001), editor of *Images of the Street* (1998) and co-editor of *The Urban Geography Reader* (2003).

MATTHEW GANDY teaches geography at University College London. His has published widely on cultural, urban and environmental themes. He is the author of *Concrete and Clay: Reworking Nature in New York City* (2002). His current research interests range from cultural histories of urban infrastructure to cinematic representations of industrial landscapes.

BRENDAN GLEESON is Deputy Director of the Urban Frontiers Program, University of Western Sydney, Australia. Dr Gleeson's research interests include the political economy of planning, urban social policy, environmental theory and policy. He is currently working with Nicholas Low on a new book, *The Green City*.

ROBBIE B. H. GOH works in the Department of English Language and Literature, National University of Singapore. He has also held visiting appointments at the Universities of Washington, Sydney and Birmingham. His research interests include the culture of religion, gothic literature, science fiction and fantasy, and urbanism.

CHARLES GORDON is Chair of Sociology and Anthropology at Carleton University, Ottawa, where he holds a joint appointment in Sociology and Architecture as well as teaching in the School of Industrial Design. His research pursuits include studies of the design professions, education in the professions, and social relations in and with the designed environment.

MARK GOTTDIENER is Professor of Sociology and Adjunct Professor of Urban Planning and Architecture at SUNY Buffalo. Author of fourteen books and more than sixty published papers, his path-breaking work has involved fashioning both the *New Urban Sociology* and the *Socio-Semiotics* cultural analysis as approaches to urbanism, tourism, postmodern culture and contemporary political economy.

BETH GREENHOUGH is a Post-Doctoral Research Fellow at the Open University, UK. Her research interests include the relationships between science, nature and society. She has recently completed fieldwork in Iceland, looking at its use as an island-laboratory for genetic research.

SUE HAMILTON is Lecturer in Later European Prehistory at the Institute of Archaeology, University College London. Her research has focused on the landscape contexts of later prehistoric settlement in southern

Britain, France and southern Italy. She has recently worked at the Iron Age hillfort of the Caburn (East Sussex) and on the Bronze Age settlement and ritual site on Leskernick Hill, Bodmin Moor.

STEPHAN HARRISON teaches in the School of Geography and the Environment at the University of Oxford. He has worked extensively on mountain geomorphology and geomorphic responses to climate change in Patagonia and Kazakhstan. He also has research interests in the philosophy of geomorphology, and spends much of his time thinking on mountains.

CALVIN HEUSSER is a palaeoecologist and Emeritus Professor in Biology at New York University. His research is mainly concerned with the use of palynology in environmental reconstructions, and he has worked widely in both South and North America.

KEN HILLIS is Associate Professor of Communication Studies and Adjunct Professor of Geography at the University of North Carolina at Chapel Hill. His work focuses on visual cultures and the history, theory and criticism of new technologies and digital media. He is the author of *Digital Sensations: Space, Identity and Embodiment in Virtual Reality* (1999).

STEVE HINCHLIFFE works at the Open University, where he teaches Geography. He has co-edited and written a number of books and articles that have a nature and society theme. He is currently working on city natures with colleagues at the OU.

MYRA J. HIRD is a sociologist at Queen's University, Belfast. She is the author of several articles on materiality, sexual difference, intersex and transgender, including 'Intersex: A Test-Case for Psycho-Analytic Theory?' in *Signs*; 'Gender's Nature: Intersexuality, Transsexualism and the 'Sex' / 'Gender' Binary' in *Feminist Theory*; and 'For a Sociology of Transsexualism' in *Sociology*.

LEWIS HOLLOWAY is Senior Lecturer in Human Geography at Coventry University. His research interests involve farmed spaces and places, and those people, non-human animals, technologies, knowledges and moralities implicated in farming assemblages, discourses and practices. He is also interested in 'alternative' modes of food production-consumption.

KEVIN HOWETT is the National Officer for the Mountaineering Council of Scotland. He has climbed very widely in the British Isles and abroad. He is the author of *Rock Climbing in Scotland* (2001) and *Highland*

Outcrops (1995) his writings appear regularly in mountaineering journals.

TIM INGOLD is Professor of Social Anthropology in the Department of Anthropology at the University of Aberdeen. His principal research interests, at present, are in the anthropology of technology and in aspects of environmental perception. Recent books include *Companion Encyclopaedia of Anthropology: Humanity, Culture and Social Life* (2002) and *The Perception of the Environment* (2000).

TARIQ JAZEEL is a Post-Doctoral Research Fellow in Human Geography at the Open University. His interests include post-colonial geographies, expressions and experiences of identity in Sri Lanka and in the global Sri Lankan diaspora, and music, performance and identity in British Asian communities.

GARETH A. JONES is Senior Lecturer in Development Geography at the London School of Economics. Whenever possible he conducts research into squatter settlements and the lives of street children. He is a trustee of the Consortium for Street Children and chair of the International Children's Trust.

MARIA KAIKA is Lecturer in Urban Geography, at the School of Geography, University of Oxford, and Fellow of St Edmund Hall. Her research interests lie with the theoretical investigation of the relationship between nature and the city; political ecology; governance and environmental policy.

ISMO KANTOLA has been active as a research and teaching associate at the Department of Sociology, University of Turku, since 1986. Research and teaching experience include environmental sociology, sociology of science and technology, and study of social movements and cultural change. He is currently doing doctoral research on the sociology of energy politics.

JOE KERR is an architectural historian and writer. He is Head of the Department of Critical and Historical Studies at the Royal College of Art, London, and a commissioning editor at Reaktion Books. Co-editor of *Strangely Familiar* (1996), *The Unknown City* (2000) and *Autopia: Cars and Culture* (2002), he is currently writing a book on Detroit.

MARTIN KIRKBRIDE lectures in geomorphology, glaciology and environmental change at the University of Dundee. He has an abiding passion for the mountainous and frozen regions of the world, and has spent research time in New Zealand, Antarctica and Italy. His current fascination is with the interactions between the glaciers, volcanoes and people of Iceland.

BRUNO LATOUR is Professor at the Centre de Sociologie de l'Innovation at the Ecole Nationale Supérieure des Mines in Paris. After field studies in Africa and California he specialized in the analysis of scientists and engineers at work. In addition to work in philosophy, history, sociology and anthropology of science, he has collaborated with many studies in science policy and research management. Among his most recent books are *La Fabrique du droit* (2002) and *Politiques de la nature* (1999).

NINA LAURIE is a Senior Lecturer at Newcastle University, UK. Working on social development for more than fifteen years, she is passionate about water and all things Latin American. She works with San Simón University, Bolivia, San Marcos University, Peru, and Latin America Studies at the University of Illinois, USA.

LISA LAW teaches social and cultural geographies at the National University of Singapore. She is author of *Sex Work in Southeast Asia: The Place of Desire in a Time of AIDS* (2000). Her current research focuses on migration and senses of home and belonging, and on the cultural politics of food in Asia.

ALPHONSO LINGIS is Professor of Philosophy at Pennsylvania State University. He has published a number of books, among which are *Abuses* (1994), *The Community of Those Who Have Nothing in Common* (1994) and *Dangerous Emotions* (2000).

DAVID N. LIVINGSTONE is Professor of Geography in the School of Geography at Queen's University, Belfast. He has research interests in the history and theory of geography, cartography and scientific culture. His most recent books include *Putting Science in its Place: Geographies of Scientific Knowledge* (2003) and *Science, Space and Hermeneutics* (2002).

ORVAR LÖFGREN is Professor of European Ethnology at the University of Lund, Sweden. His research has centred on the study of national identities and transnational movements in an everyday perspective, as well as on tourism, travel and the cultural analysis of consumption. His latest book is *On Holiday: A History of Vacationing* (2002).

ROBYN LONGHURST is Senior Lecturer in the Department of Geography, University of Waikato, New Zealand. She has published essays in a number of edited collections and geographical journals and is author of *Bodies: Exploring Fluid Boundaries* (2001) and a co-author of *Pleasure Zones: Bodies, Cities, Spaces* (2001).

NICHOLAS LOW is Associate Professor in Environmental Planning at the Faculty of Architecture, Building and Planning, University of Melbourne, Australia. He is the author or editor of seven books, Fellow of the Royal Australian Planning Institute, a member of the editorial team of the journal *Urban Policy and Research* and a consultant to the Volvo Foundation.

ROBERT LOW studied mathematics and natural philosophy at Aberdeen University, then went on to take his DPhil in mathematical physics at Oxford under the supervision of Roger Penrose. Since then, he has been with the Mathematics Department of Coventry University, teaching and carrying out research in mathematical physics.

WILLIAM S. LYNN is a Research Scholar and Executive Director at the Center for Humans and Nature in New York. With research foci in animal ethics and global ethics, he is the principle investigator for the People, Animals and Nature Initiative, Editor for the *Americas, Ethics, Place and Environment* and Research Associate at Vassar College.

PHIL MACNAGHTEN is Lecturer and Director of Research at IEPPP, Lancaster University. He has published widely on the sociology of the environment and is author, with John Urry, of *Contested Natures* (1998) and *Bodies of Nature* (guest editor of special issue of *Body and Society*).

LUCIANA MARTINS is Lecturer in Luso-Brazilian Studies at Birkbeck, University of London. She is the author of *O Rio de Janeiro dos Viajantes: O Olhar Britânico, 1800–1850* (2001) and co-editor, with Felix Driver, of *Tropical Views and Visions* (forthcoming). She has published on the visual culture of tropicality, geographical thought, world cities and modernity.

DAVID MATLESS is Reader in Cultural Geography at the University of Nottingham, and author of *Landscape and Englishness* (1998). He is currently researching cultures of nature in twentieth-century England, and the life and work of the ecologist and artist Marietta Pallis. He has also published widely on the history and philosophy of geography.

JOHN MENZIES is Professor of Earth Sciences and Geography at Brock University in St Catharines, Ontario, Canada. He obtained his PHD at the University of

Edinburgh in 1976, studying the drumlins of Glasgow in Scotland. As a 'drumlinophile' he continues to study and be fascinated by drumlins worldwide.

PETER MERRIMAN is a Lecturer in Human Geography at the University of Reading. His research focuses on mobility, space and social theory, historical geographies of transport, and cultures of landscape in twentieth-century Britain. He is currently writing a cultural geography of England's M1 motorway.

DAVID J. NASH is Reader in Physical Geography at the University of Brighton. His research interests lie in environmental change and geomorphology in drylands. He has worked extensively in southern Africa.

MILES OGBORN is Reader in Geography at Queen Mary, University of London. He is the author of *Spaces of Modernity: London's Geographies, 1680–1780* (1998) and has spent time in various archives around the world.

AIHWA ONG is Professor of Anthropology and of Southeast Asian Studies at the University of California, Berkeley. Her recent books include *Buddha is Hiding: Refugees, Citizenship and the New America* (2003), *Flexible Citizenship* (1999) and *Ungrounded Empires* (1997). She is co-editor, with Stephen Collier, of *Global Assemblages: Technology, Politics and Ethics as Anthropological Problems* (forthcoming).

CHRIS OTTER is a visiting scholar at the Institute of Urban and Regional Development at the University of California, Berkeley. He recently completed a PHD on the history of modern light technology, and is currently working on a study of meat, milk and vitality in the nineteenth century.

ANSSI PAASI is Professor of Geography at the University of Oulu, Finland. His research fields are the history of geographical thought, political and regional geography and the problems of territoriality, boundaries and identity at various spatial scales. His publications include theoretical and empirical studies on the meanings of boundaries and territories, such as the book *Territories, Boundaries and Consciousness* (1996).

DEBORAH PARSONS is Lecturer in English Literature at the University of Birmingham. Her research interests focus on the relationship of cities and their representation. She is the author of *Streetwalking the Metropolis* (2000) and has recently completed a book on the cultural history of Madrid.

DAVID G. PASSMORE is Head of the School of Geography, Sociology and Politics at the University of Newcastle upon Tyne. His research interests lie in fluvial geomorphology over Holocene timescales. He works in Ireland, Kazakhstan, northern England and the Mediterranean.

MIKE PEARSON has pioneered innovative approaches in the practice, theory, pedagogy and documentation of performance. From 1981 to 1997 he was an artistic director of the Welsh theatre company Brith Gof. He is currently Professor of Performance Studies in the Department of Theatre, Film and Television Studies at the University of Wales, Aberystwyth. He is the co-author of *Theatre/Archaeology* (2001).

STEVE PILE is Reader in Cultural Geography in the Faculty of Social Sciences at the Open University. He is author of *The Body and the City* (1996) and co-editor, with Nigel Thrift, of *City A–Z* (2000). He is currently preparing a book on the more phantasmagoric aspects of city life.

DAVID PINDER is Lecturer in Human Geography at Queen Mary, University of London. His research focuses on the cultural politics of urban space and on connections between modernism, avant-garde movements and the city. He is the author of *Visions of the City: Utopianism, Power and Politics in Twentieth-Century Urbanism* (forthcoming).

JOHN POLKINGHORNE is an Anglican priest, a KBE, a Fellow of the Royal Society and former Professor of Mathematical Physics at the University of Cambridge. He has written widely on the compatibility of religion and science. He is the winner of the 2002 Templeton Prize.

STEPHEN J. PYNE is a Professor in the Biology and Society Program, School of Life Sciences, Arizona State University; Tempe. He has written fifteen books, and is a former member of the North Rim Longshots, a forest fire crew at Grand Canyon National Park.

HUGH RAFFLES teaches anthropology at the University of California, Santa Cruz. He is the author of *In Amazonia: A Natural History* (2002) and is currently at work on a short history of insects.

GRETA RANA was born in Yorkshire. After university she worked for the Government of Ontario. Nepal, her husband's home, put mountains into her life. Currently she works at the International Centre for Integrated Mountain Development. She has also written a novel,

Im Schatten des Heiligen Baumes, set in the Himalayas of Nepal.

GEORGE REVILL is Principal Lecturer in Geography at Oxford Brookes University. His research interests include cultural histories of travel and transport and the study of music, landscape and national identity. Current research includes work on industrial action in the nineteenth-century railway industry and the cultural history of noise pollution.

KEITH RICHARDS is Professor of Geography at the University of Cambridge. While his interests lie in the general field of fluvial geomorphology, he has concentrated on the study of channel form, the modelling of fluvial systems and the nature of ecological and geomorphological interactions in rivers.

YVONNE RYDIN is Professor of Environmental Planning in the Department of Geography and Environment at the London School of Economics. She has written widely on planning and sustainability, including the role of discourse. Her most recent book is *Conflict, Consensus and Rationality: An Institutional Discourse Approach* (2003).

MICHAEL J. SHAPIRO is Professor of Political Science at the University of Hawaii. Among his recent publications are *Cinematic Political Thought: Narrating Race, Nation and Gender* (1999), *For Moral Ambiguity: National Culture and the Politics of the Family* (2001) and *Reading 'Adam Smith': Desire, History and Value* (new edn, 2002).

ERIC SHEPPARD teaches Geography, and is a member of the Institute for Social, Ecological and Economic Sustainability, at the University of Minnesota. His current research interests include environmental justice, urban sustainability, inter-urban networks, critical GIS and the spatio-temporality of globalization. Recent books include *A World of Difference* (1998) and *A Companion to Economic Geography* (2000).

ROB SHIELDS is Professor of Sociology and Anthropology at Carleton University, Ottawa. He is editor of *Space and Culture* and the author of a number of books including *Places on the Margin* (1992), *Lefebvre: Love and Struggle* (1998) and *The Virtual* (2002) (further information: www.carleton.ca/~rshields).

NICK SPEDDING is a glacial geomorphologist at the University of Aberdeen. Most of his field research has been based in Iceland, where he has worked on fluvio-glacial landforms and processes and the nature of moraine formation. He also has research interests in the philosophy and practice of geomorphology.

FRANCIS SPUFFORD is the author of *I May be Some Time* (1996), a cultural history of British polar exploration, and of *The Child That Books Built* (2002), a memoir of a childhood as a compulsive reader. With Jenny Uglow, he edited *Cultural Babbage* (1996), a collection of essays on the history of technology.

DAVID SUGDEN has been Professor of Geography at the University of Edinburgh since 1987. An expedition to Norwegian glaciers inspired him to do geography. Subsequently he has been privileged to work in Antarctica on twelve occasions.

ERIK SWYNGEDOUW is University Reader in Economic Geography at Oxford University and Fellow of St Peter's College. He is also Associate Fellow of the Environmental Change Institute. His main research interests are political-economy and political-ecology, globalization, the political ecology of water and the urban condition.

NIGEL THRIFT is Head of Division of Life and Environmental Sciences at Oxford University. Among his wide-ranging research interests are new forms of capitalism (especially the engineering of new forms of management body) and cities as foci of spatial and temporal experiment. Recent books include *The Handbook of Cultural Geography* (co-edited with Kay Anderson, Mona Domosh, and Steve Pile, 2002) and *Cities* (co-authored with Ash Amin, 2002)

CHRISTOPHER TILLEY is Professor of Anthropology and Archaeology in the Department of Anthropology at University College London. His research interests focus on archaeological theory, material culture and phenomenological perspectives on landscapes. Recent books include *Metaphor and Material Culture* (1999) and *The Materiality of Stone* (2004)

RICHARD TIPPING is a Senior Lecturer in the School of Environmental Science at the University of Stirling. Much of his research is on Holocene environmental and land-use history of riverine environments in upland Britain.

YI-FU TUAN is an Emeritus Professor in Human Geography at the University of Wisconsin. He started his academic career as a geomorphologist but he is best known for his work in phenomenology. He has published widely; his books include *Topophilia* (1990) and *Space and Place* (1990).

TIM UNWIN is Professor of Geography at Royal Holloway, University of London. He is on secondment from 2001 to 2004 to the UK's Department for International Development, where he is leading *Imfundo: Partnership for IT in Education*. His research interests include rural development and the historical geography of the wine trade.

CHARLES WARREN holds degrees in geography, resource management and glaciology from Oxford and Edinburgh universities. Since 1995 he has been lecturing in the School of Geography and Geosciences at the University of St Andrews. He has published widely in glaciology and environmental management, including his recent monograph *Managing Scotland's Environment* (2002).

DIANE WATSON is a Staff Tutor and Senior Lecturer in Sociology in the Open University. Previous research has covered careers in industrial relations (*Managers of Discontent*, 1988) and current research looks at the working lives and personal identities of people involved in the public house business.

SOPHIE WATSON is Professor of Sociology at the Open University. Her most recent publications include *The Blackwell City Reader* (2002) and *The Blackwell Companion to the City* (2001), both edited with Gary Bridge. She is currently working on a book on reconsidering public space and the multicultural practices of everyday life.

TONY WATSON is Professor of Organisational and Managerial Behaviour in the Nottingham Trent University. He researches and writes about processes of organizing and managing work (most recently *Organising and Managing Work*, 2002) and the sociology of work (*Sociology, Work and Industry*, 4th edn, 2003).

MICHAEL WATTS has taught at the University of California, Berkeley, for 25 years and is currently Director of the Institute of International Studies and Chancellor's Professor of Geography. He is currently working on a book on petroleum and modernity.

JOHN WESTERN is Chair of Geography at Syracuse University, New York. He is an urban-social-cultural-political geographer, his two books addressing apartheid South Africa (*Outcast Cape Town*, 1996/1981) and Barbadian migrants to London (*A Passage to England*, 1992). He hopes to write a third about Strasbourg, where he had just lived for three years.

VANESSA WINCHESTER works in the School of Geography and the Environment, Oxford University. Her doctorate on lichenometry focused on lichen growth rates and glacial retreat in Lappland and the western Alps and an investigation of two stone circles in Britain. Her subsequent research on glaciers and on slope dynamics has involved trees as well as lichens in western Patagonia, Kazakhstan and Colorado.

HENRY WAI-CHUNG YEUNG is Associate Professor at the Department of Geography, National University of Singapore. His research interests cover broadly theories and the geography of transnational corporations, Asian firms and their overseas operations. He is the co-editor of *Environment and Planning A*, Associate Editor of *Economic Geography* and Asia-Pacific Editor of *Global Networks*.

Photo Acknowledgements

The editors and publishers wish to express their thanks to the below sources of illustrative material and/or permission to reproduce it:

Photo Lucien Aigner, reproduced with permission of CORBIS: 73; photo W.J.R. Alexander, reproduced with kind permission: 7; courtesy of Armagh Productions: 67; photo Nick Bagguley, reproduced with permission of The Freud Museum, London: 5; from Catherine Bauer, *Modern Housing* (Boston, 1934), reproduced courtesy of Sarah W. Super: 68; photo William Bell: 51; photo Ted Benton: 59; reproduced with permission of The British Library, London: 22, 70; courtesy of the Centre for the Study of Cartoons and Caricature, University of Kent: 40; photo Nick Cobbing: 32; reproduced with kind permission of Sue Coe: 4; collection of the Corcoran Gallery of Art, Washington, DC, reproduced with permission: 17; photo Dydia DeLyser: 57; photo Julian Dowdeswell: 28; © FLC/ADAGP, Paris and DACS, London: 16; photo Matthew Gandy: 56; from *Geographical Magazine* (January 1938): 18; from the Handbook of the Institute of British Geographers annual conference (1968): 19; by kind permission of the Hans Knoll Institute, Jena: 21; photo Lorenz Hauser: 78; Chris Howes Collection, reproduced with kind permission of Chris Howes/Wild Places Photography: 47; photo Kevin Howett: 10; photo *Hull Daily Mail*, reproduced with permission: 74; courtesy of the Huntington Library, San Marino, CA: 30, 62; reproduced with permission of Britta Jaschinski: 48, 49, 77; photo Tariq Jazeel: 38; photo Gareth Jones: 54; graphics by Ismo Kantola: 24 [from numeric survey data provided by courtesy of Dr Pentti Kiljunen and the companies Teollisuuden Voima Oy and Fortum Corporation], 25 [based on P. M. Grootes, M. Stuiver, J.W.C. White, S. J. Johnsen and J. Jouzel, 'Comparison of Oxygen Isotope Records from the GISP2 and Grip Greenland Ice Cores', *Nature*, 366 (1993)], 26 [from original data from K. J. Kreutz and P. A. Mayewski, 'Bipolar Changes in Atmospheric Circulation during the Little Ice Age', *Science*, 277 (1997)]; from E. Katson, *The American Midland Naturalist*, Monograph no. 3 (1946), reproduced with permission: 27; photo Martin Kirkbride: 11; photos Nina Laurie: 42, 43; photo Nicholas Low: 52; reproduced with kind permission of Catherine McIntyre: 76; photo Phil Macnaghten: 66; photos David Matless: 36, 45; montage by John Menzies: 14; photo Jim Miller, reproduced with kind permission: 44; photo NASA: 75; photo José Nazaré, reprinted with kind permission: 72; courtesy of the National Maritime Museum, London: 29; photos Steve Pile: 1, 2, 71; photo Mark Pink: 53; redrawn based on maps by Bruce Quarrie, *The Ardennes Offensive: V Panzer Armee, Central Sector* (Oxford, 2000): 23; photos Greta Rana, © International Centre for Integrated Mountain Development: 34, 35; map by Keith Richards: 6; photos Timothy Roscoe, reproduced with permission: 13; courtesy Yvonne Rydin: 8, 9, 41; photo Erik Swyngedouw: 31; photo Dmitryi Ternovoy: 3; photo Richard Tipping: 58; photo David Gasca Tucker: 12; © 2001 Twentieth Century Fox, all rights reserved, reproduced with permission: 39; reproduced with the author's permission from Tim Unwin, *Wine and the Vine* (London, 1991): 20; photo courtesy of the US Department of the Interior/National Archives: 37; photos Diane and Tony Watson: 60, 61; sketch by John Western, July 1999: 15.

Index

Note: Page numbers in italics refer to
illustrations: e.g. drumlins 72–5, 74; those
followed by (map) refer to maps, e.g.
Ardennes (Belgium) 96–7, 97 (map).
Titles, other than book titles, are followed
by a suffix denoting the type of work:
e.g. Brooke, Rupert, *The Soldier* (poem)
   98, 99
   Coe, Sue, 'Puppy' (illus.) 53
   Nichols, Peter, *The Freeway* (play)
   87–8

Abercromby, Ralph 78
Aboriginal people 141, 189
accessibility:
   of enterprise zones 186, 187
   of water 119–21
action, and object 225–7
actuality 68–9, 70
Adams, Ansel, 'Grand Teton National Park,
   Wyoming' (photo) 140
advertisements 124, 125
Aedes vexans (Meigen), female 106
aesthetic experiences, and responses to:
   fell walking 60–62
   food 251
   God 110
   landscape 88, 187
   London Underground 246
   the moon 223
   patterns 22–5
   rock climbing 62–4
   scientific observation 24–5, 32, 41
   the seaside 152
   snow and ice 280–81
   the sublime 75, 76
   tors 168, 169
   virtual space 69–70
   zoos 173–4
Africa 57–9, 57 (map), 264–5
agriculture *see* farming/farms
aid (economic) 158
air:

pollution 230–31
   temperature chronology 103–5, 103
airports 49, 126–7
Akasachetiya (Sri Lanka) 143, 143
Alexie, Sherman 181–2
Allnutt, Henry 243
Alsace 80–82
Amazon jungle 234, 235
America *see* Latin America; North
   America; United States
An Stac screes (Isle of Skye, Scotland) 65
analytical:
   knowledge 101
   thought 18
Andersen, Hans Christian, *The Snow
   Queen* 281
Anderson, Kay 149, 172–4, 282
angels 21
animals:
   behaviour of 34–6, 38, 256–7, 257
   and boundaries 175, 176–7
   as builders 239
   concepts of 258–60, 258
   exotic 218–19
   farm livestock 252–3
   in films 148–9, 148, 261–2
   fire as an animal 108–9
   and humans 148
   mammals 262–4, 263
   and motorways 87, 87
   in pub names/signs 216–17
   in slums 191, 192
   in urban landscapes 53, 54, 199–200,
      201–3
   in zoos 172–4, 234–5
   see also nonhumans; wildlife
Antarctic Ice Sheet 115–16
anthropocentrism 54, 78, 259
anti-GM groups 122, 122, 123
Aotearoa (New Zealand) 218–19
Apaches 182–3
apes 148–9, 148, 255–8, 257
aquarians 112, 113

Aragon, Louis, *Le Paysan de Paris* 84
arcades 67, 84
archaeology, of:
   battlefields 98
   bogs 146
   deserted villages 162
   hills 209–10
   see also archives; history
architectural projects 82–3
   see also buildings
archives 240–42
   see also archaeology; history
Ardennes (Belgium) 96–7, 97 (map)
Aristotle 258, 259
art:
   climbing as 62–4
   and nature 238
   public 70–71
   and representation 36–9
   the sun in 117–19
   three determinants of 38
   see also literature; painting
assemblages 204–5
asymmetries 224–5
Auer, Väinö 274
Australia 187–8, 189, 189

B. burgdorferi (*Bp*) 201, 202
bacteria 93, 201, 202
Bådamalen (Sweden) 231
Baker, Steve 262–4
Baker, Vic 111–13, 136–7
Ballard, J. G., *Concrete Island* and *Crash* 88
Balls, Ronnie 163
Barnes, Trevor 179–81
Barrett, Dr Thomas 135
barriers *see* boundaries
Barrow, J. D. 31, 332
Barry, Andrew 248–50
Basso, Keith 182, 183
battered women 184–5
'Battle of the Bulge' 96–7, 97 (map)
battlefields 96–8, 97 (map)

Bauer, Catherine 236
Bb (Borrelia burgdorferi) 201, 202
The Beach (film) 152
beaches 151–3, 152
The Beehive pub (Grantham, Lincolnshire) 216, 216
bees 214–16
beetles 241–2, 242
    see also insects
beliefs 146, 247–8
    see also myths
Bell, Michael Mayerfeld 144–6
Bell, William 183
Bentham, Jeremy 261
Benton, Ted 214–16
Berlioz, Hector, The Damnation of Faust (cantata) 146
Bible 18–19, 160
    people in 138–9, 166
Bierstadt, Albert, Last of the Buffalo (painting) 85
biodiversity 214–16, 266
biogeographers/biogeography 94, 264–6
bioinvasion 264–6
biology 35, 56
birds 126, 134
birth 256
'black boxing' 100–01
Black Elk 183
Black Mountains (Wales) 209
Blade Runner (film) 157
'block of sensations' 39
Blue Pig pub (Grantham, Lincolnshire) 216, 217, 217
Blythe, Ronald 162
Bodie (California) 197, 198, 198
Bodmin Moor (Cornwall) 169, 209
the body 100
bogs 146–8
book louse (psocid) 241
book worm (Rhizopertha dominica) 241–2, 242
Booth, Charles 237
borders see boundaries
Borges, Jorge Luis 17–18
Borrelia burgdorferi (Bp) 201, 202
Botswana 57, 57 (map), 59
boundaries 80–82, 175–7
    at the beach 153
    between humans and animals 149, 200–3
    and buildings 239
    of dust 99–100
    and islands 150–1, 150
    of mountains 133
    and organism as a process 34
    rivers as 57–9, 57 (map), 80–2
    territorial 274–6
    trade 91

brand names 70
Braudel, Fernand 91
Bretz, J. Harlen 136
Britain:
    air pollution 230–1
    anti-GM groups 122, 122, 123
    beaches 151–3, 152
    enterprise zones 186, 187
    farming 88–90, 146–7, 214, 252–3
    national identity 149–50, 151
    post offices 70, 71–2
    prehistoric 206, 208–10, 231, 231
    town planning 192–4, 195
    trees 232–4
    urban ecology 214–16
    see also England; London
Bronze Age 209
Brooke, Rupert, The Soldier (poem) 98, 99
brownfield sites 215–16
Bruegel, Pieter, The Battle between Carnival and Lent (painting) 161
Bryson, Bill 149–50, 151
Buddhism 143–4
buffalo 85
Buhl, Hermann 277
buildings 166–7, 238–40
    archaeological remains 205–6, 209
    churches 160–1, 160, 216
    in cities 247, 248
    pubs 216–17, 216, 217
    shelters 205–6
    slums 236–7, 236
    visions of 281
bumblebees 214–16
burial mounds 208–9
Burringham Plough Jags 254
Burton, Tim, Planet of the Apes (film) 148–9, 148
bus shelters 166, 167

Cairns, Stephen 260–2
California 196–8
Callon, Michael 248
Cameron, Laura 55–7, 105–7
Cant, Sarah G. 170–2, 282
capitalism 193, 194
Cardinal, Roger 84
The Cat People (film) 261–2
Catalonia 273–4
cattle 253, 264
cave metaphor (Plato) 27
caves 170–72, 171
central place theory 179–81, 181
Channeled Scablands (Washington state, USA) 136, 156
chemicals 242, 249
children 190, 191
    childhood memories 232, 234, 269
chimpanzee 257

China:
    ancient China 111
    enterprise zones 187
Chobe River (Africa) 57, 57 (map), 59, 59
Christaller, Walter, Central Places in Southern Germany 180–1, 181 (map)
Christianity 99, 223–4
    see also beliefs; Bible; Buddhism; God
churches 118–19, 160–61, 160, 216
cichlids 264–5
circulation 82–3
cities 52–5, 199–200, 246–8, 247
    colonization in 93
    different from towns 195–6
    on drumlin fields 73
    garden cities 192–4
    light and darkness in 160–62
    nature controlled in 245–6
    prehistoric 205–6
    as product of nature 190
    Russian heating infrastructure 50–52
    spatial experiences of 66–8
    urban planning 66–7, 82–3
    water supplies 119–20, 121, 199
    see also ghost towns; London; slums; suburbs; towns
civilization see culture
Clark, Nigel 218–19, 264–6
class (social) 185
classification 16–20, 258–9
clasts 64–5
cliffs 62–4, 63
climate 76–8, 103–5
    change, and
        floodplains 207
        lichen dating 231
        ocean circulation 113, 114–15
        peat bog growth 146, 147
    conditions of, and deserts 154, 155–6
    and heating infrastructure in Russia 51, 52
    and river boundaries 57, 58, 59
    scree affected by 65–6
climbing 62–4, 63, 65, 232
    mountains 276–8, 280
    glaciers 75, 76
clitter 169
Coe, Sue, 'Puppy' (illus.) 53
Coke, Sir Edward 184
Coleridge, Samuel Taylor, Frost at Midnight (poem) 280
Collier, Stephen J. 50–52
colonialism 57, 143, 147, 218–19
colonies 93–4
Colorado River 156, 183
colour symbolism 217, 237
commodification 68–70
    of oil 177, 178, 179
    of water 120–21

see also economics; trade
communication, radio 269–70
  see also language
communities *see* colonies; ethologies;
  society; towns; villages
commuters 162
complexity 32, 36, 41, 277–8
computability 31
computer:
  modelling 277
  searching 245, 246
conservation 200
consumers 125–6, 163
continents 94–6
contrails 127
control *see* power
convection cells 30–31
Cook, Captain James 94, 95, 96, 218
Cook, Ian 124–6
Cornwall 179–80
Cosgrove, Denis 117–19, 222–4
cosmology 20–21, 110–11
  see also pattern
cosmopolitanism 53–4
Cotman, John Sell, *Croyland Abbey*
  (painting) 161
countryside:
  ecology of 56
  walking in 60–62, *61*
coyote 199
Crang, Mike 88–90, 252–3
Craw, Robin 266
creative thinking 82–3
Croizat, Leon 266
Cronon, William 142
crops:
  animal pests in 256–7
  genetically modified 122–3, 124
Cuando River (Africa) 58, 59
culling 201, 205
culture and nature/natural order, and
  39–41, 43–4, 53–4, 77–8, 85–6
  animals 216–17, 258–60
  beaches 152–3
  Buddhist discourse 143–4
  church buildings 160, 161
  in cities 90, 245–8
  enterprise zones 187
  food experiences 251
  God 110
  hills 208–10
  islands 150–51
  multiculturalism 233
  patterns in 9–10
  prehistoric civilizations 169, 205–9, *206*
  railways 86
  regionalism 273, 274
  shelter 166–7
  suburbs 200–03

territorial boundaries 275
tors 168–9, 209
town halls 188, 189
water accessibility 120
wilderness 141–2
the wine trade 90, 91
zoos 172–4
  see also nature/natural order

Dalrymple, Alexander 94–5
dams 157–9
darkness 170
Darwin, Charles 96, 150, 151
Davies, Anna R. 122–3
Davies, Gail 255–8
Dawson, Alastair 103–5
de Certeau, Michel 67
De Saussure, Horace Benedict 75
Dearing, John 78–9
death 121, 257–8
DeCourcy Ward, Robert, *Climate* 77, 78
Dee, Dr John 19, 20–21, 23, 24, 25
deep-ocean basins 114–15
deer 201–2
definitions:
  and meanings 100
  of pollution 122–3
degradation, of land 154–5
Deleuze, Gilles 38–9, 229, 255, 264
DeLyser, Dydia 196–8
Dennis, Richard 235–8
deserted villages 162
deserts 153–6, 199
Diodorus Siculus 92
diseases:
  bacterial 201, 202–3
  epidemics 244
  foot-and-mouth 204–5, 229, 252
  research into 257–8
  viral 228–9
DNA 221
Dolphin (ship) 95
domestic violence 184–5
Donne, John 150
Dowdeswell, Julian A. 113–15, 156–7
drainage schemes 105–6, 107
Drake, E. L. 178
drama 87–8, 137–9, 253–5, *254*
dreams 55
drifts 66–8
Driver, Felix 93–4
drivers 86–8
drumlins 72–5, *74*
  see also moraines
Dudh Koshi Valley (Nepal Himalayas) *133*
Duncan, Nancy 200–3
Dunham, Phil 98–100
dust 98–100
Dutch Republic 228–9

earthworms 135
Ebers, Edith 73
ecology 55, 56, 94, 264
  of archiving 241–2
economics:
  aid and development funds 158
  capitalism 193, 194
  enterprise zones 186–7
  of farming 145, 252–3
  of food production 89–90, 124–6,
    248–50, 252, 253
  of GM crops 123
  of nuclear power 102
  and Russian heating infrastructure 51,
    52
  see also commodification; trade
ecosystems 55–7
Egypt 207
electrons 268
Eliot, George *see* George Eliot
emotional responses *see* aesthetic
  experiences and responses
empirical science 23
Encyclopaedia Britannica 17
endangered species 256, 257, 263
energy supplies *see* infrastructure; nuclear
  power
England:
  fields 134–5, 210
  floodplains 207
  folk customs 135, 232, 233, 253–5
  villages 161–3
  see also Britain
The English Patient (film) 155
Enlightenment:
  and climatology 77
  and travel 95, 218–19
enterprise zones 185–7
environment *see* environmental data;
  environmentalism; landscape;
  nature/natural order
environmental data:
  from deep-ocean basins 114–15
  from peat bogs 146–7
  lichens as indicators 230–32
  sampling 130
environmentalism 101–2, 262–3
  anti-GM groups 122, *122*, 123
  bioinvasion and biodiversity 264–6
  see also endangered species; pollution
estate villages 162
ethics:
  of GM testing 123
  of green issues 140
ethnic groups 233
ethologies of nature 33–6, 64–5
Euphrates, River *206*
Europe:
  boundaries in 80–82

colonial values of 143
explorers from 94–6, 116, 218–19
floodplains of 207
regionalism in 273, 274
evolutionary processes 151, 256, 265–6
experiences *see* aesthetic experiences and
responses
experimentation *see* research
experts 100, 101, 248–50
exploration 94–6, 113–14, 116, 218–19
export trade 124–6

familiarity 164
farming/farms 144–6, 203–5
in Britain 88–90, 89 (map), 146–7, 214,
252–3
papaya farming 124–6
prehistoric 206–7
Farringdon Road Buildings (London) 236,
236
Farrow, E. P. 55
Favela of the Rats (Recife, Brazil) 192
feminism 184
see also gender; women
Cooper, James Fenimore 182–3
Ferrar, H. T. 115
fields 88–90, 134–5, 135, 210, 249
fieldwork 136–7, 214–15
films:
beaches in 152
deserts in 155
floods in 157
horror 261–2
humans and apes 148–9, 148
IMAX 69–70
shelter and survival 167
Finland 100, 102–3, 274, 275
Finnish–Russian border 276–7
fire 107–9
'First Nation' peoples *see* native peoples
fish 107, 264–6, 265
Fisher, James 134
fishing villages 162–3
flâneurs 66, 245
floodplains 106, 205–7, 206
floods 112–13, 156–7
Bretz's flood theory 136
seasonal 59, 207
'Florentine' Residential District (painting)
(Klee) 8–9
flow 48–9
folk:
customs 135, 232, 233, 253–5
songs 71–2, 163
food:
crops 122–3, 124, 256–7
and the home 164
memories of 249, 250–51
production economics 89–90, 124–6,

248–50, 252, 253
supplies 199, 200, 218–19
foot-and-mouth disease 204–5, 229, 252
Forbes, James David 75–6
forests 147, 201
formalism 31
Forrabury Common (Boscastle, Cornwall)
135
Forster, George 218
Forster, Johann Reinhold 96
forts (Bronze Age) 209
Fossey, Dian 257
fossils, plant 147
Foucault, Michel 16–17, 18, 19, 260–61
frame message 28–9
France 80, 81, 150–51, 196, 250
Francis of Assisi, St 281
freeways 86–8, 87
Freud, Sigmund 55, 56
Freud's couch 55
Frisius, Gemma 21
Frost, Robert, *Mending Wall* (poem) 166
fruit 124–6
fungi 241
Fyfe, Nick 174–5

Galápagos islands 151
Galaxiidae 265
Galdikas, Biruté 257
Galileo Galilei 119, 223
images of sunspots 118
Gandy, Matthew 194–6
garden cities 192–4
gardens 201–2, 215
gas pipes 50–52
gated villages 162
gender 185, 220–21, 257
see also men; women
genetic modification (GM) crops 122–3, 124
genetics, human 229–30
GenetiX Snowball 122, 122, 123
geography/geographers 179–81
lunar (selenography) 222–4
geology:
of caves 170
of cliffs 62–3
of drumlins 73–4
fieldwork 136–7
floods and landscape change 156–7
of ocean basins 114
of tors 168–9
George Eliot, *The Mill on the Floss* 157
Germany 80, 81, 180–81, 276–7
ghost towns 196–8, 198
giants 95–6, 95
Gilbert, Grove Karl 137
Gilliam, Terry, *12 Monkeys* (film) 126
giraffe 262, 263
Girtin, Thomas, *Kirkstall Abbey* (painting)

161
Gissing, George, *The Nether World* 236
glaciers/glaciation 72, 73–4, 75–6, 231,
278–9
glacial meltwater 156
and sea level 114, 116
glaciologists 75–6, 279
Gleeson, Brendan 187–90
globalization 188–9
of food trade 90
and territoriality 276
GM crops 122–3, 124
God 19, 21–2, 99, 110–11
and churches 160
Yaweh 138, 139
see also beliefs; religion
goddesses 222
Godwin, George 237
Godwin, Harry 55, 56
Goh, Robbie B. H. 160–61, 284
Golding, William, *The Inheritors* 78–9
Goldschmidt, Tijs 265
Gombrich, Ernst 255
The Good, the Bad and the Ugly (film) 155
Goodall, Jane 257
Gordon, Charles 166–7
Gottdiener, Mark 126–7, 199–200
governance:
environmental 190
territorial 276
government:
control 271
local 188–91
ownership 270
Grand Canyon of the Colorado River,
Mouth of Kanab Wash (USA) 183
Grand Teton National Park (Wyoming)
140
granite 62, 168
Grantham (Lincolnshire) 216–17, 216
The Great Escape (film) 167
Great Southern Continent 94–5, 95–6
green spaces 200
Greenhough, Beth 149–51
Greenland 103, 104–5
Greenland Ice Sheet 115, 116
Grehan, John 266
Guattari, F. 229, 255, 264
Guayaquil (Ecuador) 190

Habeler, Peter 277
Halprin, Lawrence 86
Hamilton, Sue 208–9
Haraway, Donna J. 263
Harmony (Florida) 53, 54
Harrison, Stephan 276–8
Haseldon, W. K. (cartoon) 150
Hassall, John:
'Albert's face and hands were quite

clean' (illus.) 235
    in Wookey Hole 171
Haughton, Samuel 77
Hawaii 125
Heads, Michael 266
heat 50–52
heliography 117–19
Hemingway, Ernest, *Moveable Feast* 250–51
heritage industry 97
Herodotus 91–2, 207
Heusser, Calvin 146–8
Hevelius, Johannes, lunar map 223
Hill, Thomas 77
Hillis, Ken 68–70, 284
hills 72–5, 208–10
Himalayas 132, 133, 276–7
Hinchliffe, Steve 228–30
Hiorns, Frederick 194
Hird, Myra J. 220–21
history:
    of buildings 238
    of climate change 103–5
    of environmental change 79, 114–15,
        156–7
    historical continuity 192, 194, 195, 196
    mythologies of 196–8
    of Native Americans 181–3
    of oil industry 178
    prehistoric civilizations 169, 205–10,
        206
    and territoriality 275
    of trade 91–2
    and trees 232–3
    see also archaeology; archives; time;
        Victorian period
Hitler, Adolf 180, 181
HIV (Human Immune Deficiency) 228
hobby horses 253–5
Hofstadter, D. R. 28, 30
holidays 152, 163
Holloway, Lewis 203–5
Holloway, Stanley, 'Albert and the Lion'
    (poem) 235, 235
home 164–5, 184–5
Hopkins, Gerard Manley, *Inversnaid*
    (poem) 139
horses 253–5
hospital, dramatic performance in 137–9
Howard, Ebenezer, 'The Three Magnets'
    193, 193, 194
Howett, Kevin 62–4
Hughes, Shirley 151
Human Immune Deficiency (HIV) 228
humans 220–21
    battlefield experiences 97–8
    bodies 99–100
    brains, and message decoding 30
    as cavers 171–2
    and dam building 158–9

desert dwellers 155
    and ecology of countryside 56
    and fields 134, 135
    and floods 157
    individual survival of 167
    living standards 271
    and the natural order 140, 142–4,
        232–5, 237–8, 248
    and nonhumans
        as builders 239
        in cities 53, 54
        hobby horses 254–5
        mammals 262–4
        in police stations 174–5
        primates (apes) 148–9, 148, 255–8,
            257
    and scientific knowledge 101
    origins of life 112, 113
    relationship with mountains 132, 133,
        134, 276–7
    sub-humans 259
    viral networks in 229–30
    see also nature; non–humans
Humboldt, Alexander von *see* von
    Humboldt, Alexander
hunting 201
Huxley, Aldous 191
hydroelectricity 158
hygiene standards 252, 253

ice 279–81
ice sheets 49, 113, 115–17
ice-core records 103, 104–5
ICLEI (International Council for Local
    Environmental Initiatives) 189
identity:
    cultural 174
    national 149–50, 151
    social 160, 161, 232–4, 251
ideology:
    of American West 196–8
    of towns 192–6
illustrations/images 45
    of animals 85, 262, 263
    of deserts 155
    the mapping of North America 140,
        141, 183
    photographic archives 241
    of the sun 117–18, 118, 119
    US public art 71, 85, 85
IMAX 69–70
imperialism 93, 94
Indians *see* native peoples
individuals *see* humans
Indonesia 271–2
industry *see* enterprise zones;
    farming/farms; heritage industry
infrastructure:
    urban heating 50–52

water supplies 119–21, 199, 245–6, 271,
    272
Ingold, Tim 232, 238–40
inner message 28
insects 63–4, 94, 241, 242
    mosquitoes 106, 106, 107
interference (wave propagation) 267, 267
Intergovernmental Panel on Climate
    Change (IPCC) 157
International Council for Local
    Environmental Initiatives (ICLEI) 189
intersex conditions 220–22
IPCC (Intergovernmental Panel on
    Climate Change) 157
irrigation 159, 207
islands 149–51, 150
    island nations 270–72
    metaphorical 88
Ixodes scapularis 202, 210

Jakarta (Indonesia) 119–20
Jamaica 124–5
Jaschinski, Britta 262
    photographs by 173, 263
Jauch, J. M. 29
Jazeel, Tariq 142–4, 285
Job (biblical character) 138–9
Jones, Gareth A. 190–91
journeys *see* travel
jungle 234–5
justice 260

Kabbalists 18–19
Kaika, Maria 244–6
Kant, Immanuel 77
Kantola, Ismo 100–03
Kaplan, Robert 191
Kapucinski, Ryzsard 177, 179
Karelia 274
katabatic winds 105, 116
Keegan, John 97
Kensington High Street (London) 243, 243
Kerr, Joe 192–4
Kirkbride, Martin 64–6
Klee, Paul 36–9
    'Florentine' Residential District
        (painting) 8–9
Knott, Walter 196, 198
knowledge:
    systems of 19–20, 101–2
    and unknowability 28
Kuhn, Franz 16

Lake District (England) 60–62, 60 (map),
    61
Lake Victoria (East Africa) 264–5
lakes 78–9, 105–7, 264–5
land:
    colonization of 93, 94

degradation and reclamation 154–5
land-use patterns 105–7, 147–8
landforms 10
landscape:
     of battlefields 96–8
     ecology of 56
     of enterprise zones 186, 187
     of farms 203–5
     and floods as agent of change 156–7
     in garden cities 194
     and motorways 86–8
     in painting 8–9, 161
     and railway travel 85–6
     and scenery 88
     see also countryside; nature; wilderness
language:
     and analytical thought 18
     boundaries of 100, 150
     and creation of 'home' 165
     Hebrew 19
     human/non human communication
          148
     linguistic borders 80–81
     militaristic 276–7
     of oral histories 106–7
     Sinhalese 143
     see also meanings; words
Las Vegas (Nevada) 199, 200
Lates niloticus (Nile perch) 264–5, 265
Latin America 190, 190, 191, 192, 192
Latour, Bruno 224–7
Laurie, Nina 157–9
Law, Lisa 150–51
Lawrence of Arabia (film) 155
Lawrence, D. H., The Rainbow 157
Le Corbusier 66, 82–3
     The Law of the Meander 83
Leakey, Louis 257
Lefebvre, Henri 196
legends see beliefs; myths
Leopold, Aldo 141
Letchworth Garden City (Hertfordshire)
     192–3, 194
Lévy, Pierre 68
Lewisian gneiss 63
Lewton, Val, and Jacques Tourneur, The
     Cat People (film) 261–2
libraries 241, 242
lichens 63, 230–32
light:
     and shadows 260–61
     sunlight 117
     and wave propagation 267
limestone 170
Lingis, Alphonso 137–9, 264
lions 234–5, 235
listability 31
literature (subjects in):
     floods 157

islands 150, 150, 151
memoirs 250–51
Native Americans 181–3
seaside visits 151–2
snow and ice 280–81
travel 87–8, 95, 96, 116
Little Ice Age 103–5
livestock 252–3
living standards 271
Livingstone, David N. 76–8
local:
     government 188–91
     regions 274
Löfgren, Orvar 272–4
London, Jack 237
London 236, 237, 242–6
Longhurst, Robyn 148–9
Lösch, August 180, 181
Louis XIV, of France 118
Low, Nicholas 187–90
Low, Robert 266–8
Lucifer 138
Lyell, Charles, Principles of Geology 136
Lyme disease 201, 202–3
Lynn, William S. 52–5, 258–60

MacColl, Ewan 163
Machhepuchhare mountain (Pokhara,
     Nepal) 132
Macnaghten, Phil 232–4
Madeleine 244–6
magic 20–21, 246, 247–8
Malay archipelago 270–72
mammals 262–4, 263
man see humans; men; women
Maori 219
mapping:
     of Antarctic Ice Sheet 116
     of deep-ocean basins 115
     field mapping 137
     the moon 222–4, 223
     of North America 85, 85, 140, 141, 182–3
     physical features 60–61, 60 (map)
     regions and territories 273–6
     sixteenth century 21
     the sun 119
market see commodification; economics;
     trade
Martins, Luciana 94–6
Mary, Virgin 222, 224, 224
masculine see gender; men
Masterman, Charles 237
material/materiality 39, 212–13, 227, 238
mathematical models 18–19, 20–21, 27, 268
     and nature 82, 83, 277–8
Mather, Cotton, 'Exact Mapp of New
     England' (illus.) 182
Matless, David 70–02, 134–5, 161–4
matter 39, 212–13

Matthew, William Diller, Climate and
     Evolution 77–8
Mead, G. H. 27
meanders 57, 59, 59, 82–4, 83
meanings:
     and definitions 100
     attached to farms 203–5
     of 'home' 164–5
     of 'human' 149
     and messages 28–30
     of 'natural resource' 178
     and pattern 181
     of 'pollution' 122–3
     of pub names/signs 216–17
     see also language; symbolism; words
measurement:
     of flooding 156, 157, 207
     of space 21
medicine 78
medieval period:
     trade 92
     villages 162, 163
Melbourne Town Hall (Australia) 187–8,
     189
memory 106–7, 240, 250–51
     childhood memories 232, 234, 269
men:
     man in the moon 222, 224
     masculine subjectivities 159, 174
     social roles 165
     see also gender; women
Menzies, John 72–5
Mercator 21
merchants 91
Merriman, Peter 86–8
messages, and meanings 28–30
Messner, Reinhold 277
meteorology 77–8
Mexico 161, 191–2
micro-organisms 126, 127
Microsoft 68
Miller, Austin, Climatology 77
mining:
     towns (deserted) 197
     villages 163
model villages 163, 163
models:
     limitations of 27–8
     mathematical 18–19, 20–21, 27
Modernism 192, 194, 195, 196
monuments 206, 208–9, 231, 231, 278–9
moon 222–4, 223, 224
moraines 278–9
     see also drumlins
moral issues:
     of GM testing 123
     and God 110
     of nature and culture 54, 78, 260
     of pattern and meaning 181

Morris, William, *News from Nowhere* 193
mortality rates 121
mosquitoes 106, *106*, 107
mosses 63
motion:
    artistic representations of 36–8
    in the landscape 86–8
    time and space 48–9
    see also travel
motorways 86–8, *87*
mounds 206, 208–9
    see also drumlins; moraines
mountains 132–4, *132*, *133*
    climbing 75, 76, 276–8, 280
    scree 64–6
    walking in 60–62, *61*
Mourenx (France) 196
movement *see* motion
multi-centred metropolitan regions 199, 200
murals 71
music 8, 38
    pop/folk songs 71–2, 163
Myhill, J. 31
myths 170, 171, 206, 208, 259
    see also beliefs

names *see* language; meanings; words
Namibia 57, *57* (map), 59
Nanga Parbat ('Naked Mountain', Himalayas) 276–7
Nansen, F. 115, 116
Nash, David J. 153–6
nations:
    and boundaries 80–82, 176–7
    as homes 165
    island nations 270–2
    Native Americans 181–3
    and regionalism 273–4
native peoples:
    Aboriginal 141, 189
    Maori 219
    Native Americans 106–7, 141, 181–3
    Patagonians 95–6, *95*
natural resources:
    gas 51, 52
    and national boundaries 177
    oil 177–9
    the radio spectrum 269, 270
natural selection 151, 260
nature/natural order
    and art 238
    of boundaries 175, 176, 275
    city as product of 190
    and culture *see* culture
    ethologies of 33–6
    and God 110
    and humans 140, 142–4, 232–5, 237–8, 248

interface with urban space 200
and pollution 123
scientific theory and fieldwork 136–7, 277–8
slums as expression of 237–8
and space 69–70
    see also culture; natural resources
Nazi Germany 180–81, 276
Near East 205–7
Neolithic civilization 208–9
networks, regional 272–4
New Orleans 244, 247–8
New York 247
New Zealand (Aotearoa) 218–19
Newton, J. E. 242
Nichols, Peter, *The Freeway* (play) 87–8
Nicholson, S. E. 57–8
Nile perch (*Lates niloticus*) 264–5, *265*
Nile, river (Egypt) 207
nomads 276
Non-deterministic Polynomial (NP) problems 277–8
nonhumans 224–7
    as builders 239, 240
    and humans *see under* humans
    sexual characteristics of 220
    and wilderness 141
    see also animals; culture; humans; wildlife
North America:
    floods in 156
    fossil pollen data 147
    ghost towns of 196–8
    mapping of 85, *85*, *140*, 141, 182–3
    Native Americans 181–3
    Sumas Lake drainage 105–7
    urban planning 195
    see also United States
nostalgia 71, 196–8
    see also memory
NP (Non-deterministic Polynomial) problems 277–8
nuclear power 100, 102–3

'obeah' (voodoo) 247–8
object, and action 225–7
'occult' life forces 24
oceans 94–5, 96, 113–15, *113*
Ogborn, Miles 240–42
    'Book Worm' (illus.) *242*
oil industry 177–9
Okavango River (Africa) 58, 59
Ong, Aihwa 270–72, 286
oral traditions 106–7, 183
organ transplantation 258
organics 248–50
Other:
    otherness of nature 152–3, 259
    and Self 99

Otter, Chris 242–4
outer message 28

Paasi, Anssi 175–7, 274–6
Pacheco, Francisco, *Immaculate Conception with Miguel Cid* (painting) 224
Packenham, Thomas, *Meetings with Remarkable Trees* 233
painting:
    church buildings in 161
    landscape 8–9, 161
    for post offices 70–71
    representation of non-visible 39
    'rhythmic' 8–9, 36–8
    the sun 117
Pannini, Giovanni Paolo, *Cardinal Polignac Visiting St Peter's* (painting) 161
papaya 124–6, *124*
Paris 250–51, *250*
Park, Robert 246–7
Parker, Charles 163
parks:
    country/urban 214–15
    national 140, 142–4, *143*
    see also enterprise zones; green spaces
Parsons, Deborah 66–8
particles (wave propagation) 267, 268
Passe, Crispyn de, tulip 'Semper Augustus' from *Hortus Floridus* (illus.) *228*
Passmore, David G. 96–8
Patagonians 95–6, *95*
Paterson, W.S.B., *The Physics of Glaciers* 76
pattern(s) 26–45
    and central place theory 179–81
    classification of 16–20
    cultural and natural 9–10
    deciphering 28–30
    explaining 30–32
    of gendered space 185
    of ground 33–8, 45
    hidden relationships in 20–22
    of land use 105–7, 147–8
    scientific knowledge of 26–32
    sensory impressions of 22–5
    viral 229–30
    and the visual 45, 281
Pearson, Mike 253–5
peat bogs 146
Penczak, Chris 248
Perec, Georges 176
petroleum 177, 178
pets 53, 54, 199–200
philosophy ('biological') 35–6
photographs, archive preservation 241
    see also illustrations/images
physics 75–6
Piccadilly Arcade (New Street, Birmingham, England) 67
pigs 218–19

Pile, Steve 246–8
Pinder, David 82–4
Pinelo, Antonio de Léon, *El Paraiso en el Nuevo Mundo* 95
pipes 48–9, 50–2
pisceans 112–13
place:
    names of 183
    sense of 164–5, 250–51
place worlds 183
places of worship *see* churches
Planet of the Apes (film) 148–9, *148*
planning:
    motorway design 86–7
    national 271
    urban 66–7, 82–3, 192–6
plants:
    classification of 258
    as peat bog fossils 147–8
    in urban spaces 200, 214, 215
    viruses of 228–9
plate tectonics 266
Plato 27
pleasure, and transgression 66–7
Plough Jags 253–4, *254*
Plutarch 222, 223
poets/poetry 98–9, 161, 235, 264, 281
Poland 180–81
police stations 174–5
politics, of:
    boundaries 175–7
    colonialism 93
    organic food production 249–50
    pub names/signs 217
    race 78, 185
    shelter 166–7
    water 158–9, *158*
Polkinghorne, John 110–11
pollution/pollutants 100–03, 122–3, 126–7, 230–32, 249
    see also environmentalism
Portishead radio station 269
post offices 70–72
potatoes 90, 248–9, *249*
poverty 190–92, 237–8
Powell, John Wesley, *Canyons of the Colorado* 156
power relations, and:
    access to water 120–21
    boundaries 176–7, 275–6
    oil production 179
    the police 174–5
    pollution and environment 123
    social inequalities 224–5
prehistoric civilizations 169, 205–10, *206*
Pringle, Thomas 153–4
prisoners 175
private ownership 270
prospective characteristics 32

Psalm 104 184
psocid (book louse) 241
psychoanalysis 55, 56
psychology 56
public art 70–71
pubs (public houses) 216–17, *216*, *217*
Pyne, Stephen J. 107–9

quantum mechanics 268

rabbits 126
racial politics 78, 185
radio 163, 269–70
Raffles, Hugh 234–5
railways 84–6, 246
Rana, Greta 132–4
rats 191, 192, 199–200
Rawles, Kate 263, 264
reality:
    and God 110–11
    messages and meanings 28–30
    scientific knowledge of 26–7, 35
    virtuality and actuality 68–70
reason 181
reclamation, of land 154–5
Red Bartsia 214
refuges (women's) 184–5
regions 200, 272–4
religion 99, 143–4, 223–4
    see also beliefs; Buddhism; God
representation:
    of motion 36–8
    as object 38–9
research, animal 256, 257–8
resources *see* food; natural resources; water
Revill, George 84–6
Rhine, River 80–82, *80*
Rhizopertha dominica (book worm) 241–42, *242*
rhythm 8–9, 37–8, 48
Richards, Keith 57–9
ridges 60–2, *60* (map), *61*
rituals 146, 247–8
    see also traditions
The River (film) 156
rivers 57–9, 80–82, *80*, 183
    in flood 156
    and floodplains 205–7
    in London 245–6
    meanders 82–4, *83*
roads *see* freeways
rock 62–4, 168–9
    cave formation 170
    rockfalls 64–5
Rollright Stones (Oxfordshire) *231*
Rooker, Michael Angelo, *Interior of Ruins, Buildwas Abbey, Shropshire* (painting) 161
royal insignia 71

Rubens, Peter Paul, *The Triumph of Christ over Sin and Death* (painting) 161
Russia 50–52
    Finnish–Russian border 276–7
Rydin, Yvonne 60–62, 151–3

Saami 208
Saint Vith (Belgium) 96, *97* (map)
sampling 130
sandstone 63
Saville, N. M. *et al.* 215
Scandinavia 273
Scheiner, Christopher 119
    map of the sun *118*
schist 62–3
Schrödinger wave equation 268
Schulman, Sam 191
scientific knowledge:
    definitions of pollution 122–3
    of dust 99
    of ice 116, 117, 279–80
    and 'magic' in cities 246–7
    of pattern 26–32
    of the sun 117, 119
    and technology 101, 102–3
    of water 111–13
    see also biology; mathematical models; physics; psychology
scientific theory 136
Scott, R. F. 115, 116
scree 64–6, *65*
sea level:
    and glaciation 114, 116
    see also oceans
seaside 152, *152*, 153
Second World War 96–7
    post-war town planning 195
security 164–5
seeds 124, 125, 229
Self:
    and Other 99
    search for 145–6
    sense of 232
'Semper Augustus' (tulip) 228
senses *see* aesthetic experiences and responses
settlements *see* cities; suburbs; towns; villages
Severian 255
sexual:
    difference 220–21, 257
    relationships 148
Shackleton, E. H. 116
shadows 260–2
Shakespeare, William:
    King Richard the Second (play) 270
    A Midsummer Night's Dream (play) 167
shale 63
shamanism 248

Shapcott, Jo 264
Shapiro, Michael J. 181–3
sheep 252
Shelley, Percy Bysshe, *Mont Blanc* (poem)
281
shelter 166–7
of police stations 174–5
women's refuges as 184–5
Sheppard, Eric 52–5
Shields, Rob 68, 166–7
Shinn, Terry 101
shopping villages 163
shoreline profile 231
Showery Tor (Bodmin Moor, Cornwall)
169
Shrill Carder Bee (*Bombus sylvarum*)
214–16
sight 119
see also vision/visuality
Silbury Hill (Avebury, Wiltshire) 208
Silicon Valley (California) 187
silverfish (*Lepisma saccarina*) 242
Singapore 271–2
site 130–31
Situlpahuwa temple (Yala Park, Sri Lanka)
143
Skegness Model Village (Lincolnshire) 163
skyscrapers 247, 248
Sladen, W.F.L. 215
slums 190–92, 190, 192, 235–8, 236
Smethurst, Allan 71–2
snow 280–81
so$_2$ (sulphur dioxide) 230–31
society:
and animal rights 260
changes in, and railway travel 84–6
of colonies 93–4
community/social relations 160–61,
165, 166–7, 251
and industrialisation 193–4
nonhumans and social order 224–7
power and access to water 119–21
prehistoric 205–6, 208–10
role of the town hall 188–9
social imaginary of oil 178–9
and territoriality 275
town and city differences 195–6
see also human; power relations
soil quality 88–9
Somerset Levels 146–7
song 71–2, 163
space:
of battle 98
of caves 170–72
of confinement 167, 172, 175, 184
gendered 185
of humans and animals 149
inside/outside 239
of islands 150, 151

measurement of 21
in paintings 8–9
psychological 262
and regionalism 274
representations of 36–8
social 161
territorial 274–6
time and motion 48, 85
urban 53–4, 66–8, 83–4, 199–200
virtual space 68–70
Spain 273–4
spatiality *see* space
Spedding, Nick 75–6, 278–9
Spufford, Francis 75, 279–81
Sri Lanka 142–4
standards:
of hygiene 252, 253
of living 271
states 177, 181–3
Stó:lō people 106–7
stone circles 231, 231
Strasbourg 81, 82
streets 67, 82–3, 242–4, 243
the sublime 75, 76, 86
suburbs 190, 195, 200–3, 215
see also cities; towns; urbanization
subways 244–6
suffering:
and belief in God 110–11
the story of Job 138–9
Sugden, David 115–17
sulphur dioxide (so$_2$) 230–31
Sumas Lake (British Columbia) 105–7
sun 117–19, 118
supermarkets 89–90, 250
Surrealists 84
Surville, Jean François-Marie de 218
survival 167
Suttle, Gerald, *The Social Order of the Slum*
237
Swyngedouw, Erik 119–21
symbolism, of, 72–3, 99
churches 160–61
colour 217, 237
the cross 261
the moon 222, 223–4
the sun 117–18
territoriality 275
trees 233
see also meanings
systems theory 36, 277–8

T'ai-chi (or Tao) 111
Tansley, George 55–6
The New Psychology and its Relation to Life
55
taxonomy 16–17, 258
technico-instrumental knowledge 101,
102–3

technology:
of archive preservation 240–41, 242
fire as 108, 109
and organic food production 250
radio dependant 269–70
of the railway 84–6
and virtual space 68–70
wood street paving 243–4, 243
tectonics 266
telescope 23, 223
television programmes 15, 150
tells 206, 209
Telotte, J. P. 262
temperatures:
air temperature chronology 103–5, 103
and the ecology of archiving 241
effect of contrails 127
termites 94
territory 38, 274–6
Thales of Miletus 11
Thater, Diane, *Red Sun* (art installation)
119
theology *see* God; religion
theory:
central place theory 179–81, 181
scientific 35–6, 136–7, 277–8
thermohaline circulation 114
Thomas, Edward 98–9, 100
Thoreau, Henry 141
Thrift, Nigel 269–70
ticks 35–6, 201, 202
Tilley, Christopher 167–9
time:
and lake-bed detritus 79
space and motion 48, 85
and virtual space 69
see also history
Tipping, Richard 205–7
Tombstone (California) 197–8
tombstones 278–9
tool, fire as 108, 109
tors 167–9, 169, 209
tourists 133, 168, 172, 173–4, 196–8, 199
Tourneur, Jacques, and Val Lewton, *The
Cat People* (film) 261–2
town halls 187–90, 189
Townroe, B. S. 237
towns 194–6, 195
see also cities; ghost towns; suburbs
traces 49
Trachtenberg, Alan 183
tractors 88–9
trade 91–4, 124–6
global food trade 90
organic food trade 248–50
role of town halls 188–9
see also commodification; economics
traditions:
customs 135, 232, 233, 253–5

oral 106–7, 183
  see also rituals
transgression, and pleasure 66–7
transportation systems 84–6, 91–2, 200,
  246
  see also vehicles
travel:
  by air 126–7
  and exploration 94–5, 96, 113–14
  guidebooks 85
  literature 87–8, 95, 96, 116
  and mobility 87
  and social change 84–6
  through caves 171
trees 147, 230, 232–4, *233*
triangulation 21
tropics 78
Tuan, Yi-Fu 164–5, 288
tulips 228–9, *228*
Turner, J.M.W. 117
Twain, Mark:
  Roughing It 197
  A Tramp Abroad 75
12 Monkeys (film) 126
Tyndall, John 75, 76

Uexküll, Jacob von *see* von Uexküll, Jacob
UK (United Kingdom) *see* Britain
Umwelt theory 35–6
Underground (London) 246
United Kingdom (UK) *see* Britain
United States:
  cities 199–200, 246–8
  enterprise zones 186, 187
  mapping of 85, *85*, *140*, *141*, 182–3
  post offices 70–71
  suburbs 200–3
  wood street paving 244
  see also North America
Unwin, Tim 91–4
urban:
  cultures 246–8
  planning 66–7, 82–3, 192–6
  space 53–4, 66–8, 83–4, 199–200
water supplies 119–21, 199, 245–6
wildlife 53, 54, 199–200, 201–3, 214–16
  see also cities; slums; suburbs; towns
urbanization 121, 153, 163–4
  see also cities; slums; suburbs; towns
US *see* United States

values *see* culture and nature/natural order
vegetables (organic) 248–9
vegetational succession 55–6
vehicles 86–7, 88–9, 142
Victorian period:
  housing 193–4, 235–8
  street paving 242–4, *243*
villages 161–4, *163*

prehistoric 169, 205, *206*, 210
violence 184–5, 195–6
virtual space 68–70
viruses 228–30
vision/visuality 45, 262, 263, 281
visitors (tourists) 133, 168, 172, 173–4,
  196–8, 199
von Humboldt, Alexander, *Cosmos* 22,
  22–5
von Uexküll, Jacob 35–6
voodoo ('obeah') 247–8

Wainwright, Alfred 60
walking 60–62, *61*
  drifting 66–8
Wallace, Alfred Russel 150–51
war:
  for oil 179
  Second World War 96–7
Warren, Charles 139–41
warrior experience 97–8
Wat Tyler Country Park (London) 214–15
water 111–13
  at the beach 153
  and cave formation 170
  and the ecology of archiving 241
  as ice 280
  irrigation 159, 207
  politics of, and dams 158–9, *158*
  supply of 119–21, 199, 245–6, 271, 272
  see also floods; lakes; natural resources;
    oceans; rivers
Watson, Diane 216–17
Watson, Sophie 184–5
Watson, Tony 216–17
Watts, Michael 177–9
waves 266–8
  radio 269
wealth *see* commodification; economics;
  trade
weather:
  Antarctic 116
  records of, and climate change 103–5
  see also climate
Wesley, John 161
West Indies 124–6, 247–8
Western, John 80–82
wetlands 106
Weymouth Seven 122, 123
white-tailed deer 201–2
Wicken Fen (Cambridgeshire) 55–6
wilderness 139–41, *140*
wildlife 255–8
  at airports 126
  of cliffs 63–4
  of lakes 107
  and motorways 87, *87*
  in urban landscapes 53, 54, 199–200,
    201–3, 214–16

in Yala National Park 142
  see also animals
Wilkins, John 17, 18
Williamsburg (Brooklyn, New York) *195*
Winchester, Vanessa 230–32
wine trade routes 91–2, *92* (map)
women:
  battered women 184–5
  femaleness 220
  primatologists 257
  social roles 165
  women's movements 158, *158*
wood street paving 243–4, *243*
Wookey Hole (Somerset) *171*
words and names, for:
  Apache places 183
  bog 146
  church 160
  desert 154
  drumlins 72, 73
  farm 144, 145
  hoar 230
  ice 280
  jungle (*mata*) 234
  living species 258
  nature and landscape 144
  used by and about police 174–5
  regions 272
  slums 190, 191, 192, 235, 237
  used in Stó:lō oral histories 106–7
  see also language; meanings
Wordsworth, William, *Lines Written a Few
  Miles Above Tintern Abbey* (poem) 161
worms:
  book worm 241–2, *242*
  earthworms 135

Yala National Park (Sri Lanka) 142–4, *143*
Yaweh 138, 139
Yeung, Henry Wai-chung 185–7

Zambesi River (Africa) 57, *57* (map), 58–9
Zion Canyon (Utah) 69–70, 69
zoos 172–4, *173*, 234–5, *235*, 256